NO SLACK

NO SLACK

The Financial Lives of
Low-Income Americans

MICHAEL S. BARR

BROOKINGS INSTITUTION PRESS
Washington, D.C.

Copyright © 2012
Michael S. Barr

THE BROOKINGS INSTITUTION
1775 Massachusetts Avenue, N.W., Washington, D.C. 20036
www.brookings.edu

Library of Congress Cataloging-in-Publication data

Barr, Michael S.
No slack : the financial lives of low-income Americans / Michael S. Barr.
    p. cm.
  Includes bibliographical references and index.
  ISBN 978-0-8157-2233-5 (hbk. : alk. paper)
  1. Financial services industry—United States. 2. Banks and banking—Social aspects—United
States. 3. Poor—Finance, Personal—United States. 4. Low-income consumers—Finance,
Personal—United States. I. Title.
  HG181.B33 2012
  330.9730086'942—dc23   2012005711

9 8 7 6 5 4 3 2 1

Printed on acid-free paper

Typeset in Adobe Garamond

Composition by Circle Graphics
Columbia, Maryland

Printed by R. R. Donnelley
Harrisonburg, Virginia

Contents

Acknowledgments

The data presented and analyzed in this book are from the 2005–06 Detroit Area Household Financial Services (DAHFS) study, for which I served as principal investigator. The interviews were conducted by the Survey Research Center of the University of Michigan. Jane Dokko was a true partner in designing the survey. Jane and I were joined in analyzing the data by Benjamin Keys, and most of the chapters in this volume reflect our joint work. I could not have undertaken this project without them. In several chapters, other researchers joined in our analysis: Eleanor Feit coauthored chapter 4; Ron Borzekowski and Elizabeth Kiser coauthored chapter 5; and Sendhil Mullainathan and Eldar Shafir coauthored chapter 11. They are wonderful colleagues, and I have learned a great deal from working with them. When the book refers to "we" in the text, it is referring to me and the coauthors of that chapter. With respect to my coauthors from the Federal Reserve, I point out that the material in this volume does not reflect the views of the Federal Reserve Board or the Federal Reserve System. Similarly, my co-authors who are affiliated with the Consumer Financial Protection Bureau or with the President's Advisory Council on Financial Capability wish to make clear that the views expressed here are their own and not those of the bureau or of the council.

The DAHFS was generously supported by the Ford Foundation; the MacArthur Foundation; the Annie E. Casey Foundation; the Fannie Mae Foundation; the Mott Foundation; the Community Foundation of Southeast Michigan; the National Poverty Center; the Center on Local, State, and Urban Policy (CLOSUP); the Provost and Vice President for Research of the University of Michigan; and the Law School of the University of Michigan. Many individuals at these organizations helped me along the way, but I want in particular to thank Rebecca Blank, Evan Caminker, Paul Courant, Sheldon Danziger, Frank DeGiovanni, Elisabeth Gerber, Bob Groves, Ellen Lazar, Benita Melton, Mariam Noland, Marvin Parnes, Gwendolyn Robinson, Irene Skricki, Julia Stasch, Stacey Stewart, and Eric Wanner. I am grateful for their support and advice. The views presented here are mine alone, not those of the supporting organizations or these individuals.

The Survey Research Center is a phenomenal institution, and one of the wonderful aspects of the University of Michigan is its strong tradition of inter-disciplinary research, which made working across departments such a pleasure. I would like to thank our project manager, Esther Ullman; our production manager, Sara Freeland; our sampling and design expert, Terry Adams; the leadership, staff, and faculty of the Survey Research Center; the members of our advisory board—Phoebe Ellsworth, Robert Schoeni, and Rebecca Blank—who gave so generously of their time and expertise; Kirsten Alcser, Judith Clemens, and Fred Conrad for conducting cognitive interviews during pretesting of the survey; Ed Bachelder, for technical assistance in developing the discrete-choice portion of the survey and earlier analysis of the results; and my wife, Hannah Smotrich, for the graphic design of the discrete-choice survey cards presented to the respondents.

Many of these chapters received valuable comments from Ian Ayres, Bob Shiller, John Caskey, Reuven Aviyonah, Rick Lempert, Jeff Kling, Jeff Liebman, Nada Eissa, Karen Dynan, Fred Feinberg, Neil Bhutta, Glenn Canner, and Andreas Lehnert; participants in seminars or presentations at American Economic Association meetings, the American Law and Economics Annual Conference, the Conference on Empirical Legal Studies, the Federal Deposit Insurance Corporation, the Federal Reserve Board, Harvard University's Seminar on Inequality and Social Policy, the Internal Revenue Service Research Conference, the National Tax Association, New York University School of Law, Princeton University, University of Illinois–Chicago, University of Michigan Law School, University of Pennsylvania Law School, and Yale Law School; and a number of anonymous referees. I am also grateful to Neal Bajema, Dario Borghesan, Erika Brandner, Chester Choi, Maria Dooner, Evan Enarson-Hering, Andrew Hartlage, Robyn Konkel, and Christopher Reynolds for invaluable research assistance. I am thankful for the invaluable advice and editorial oversight of Robert Faherty, Janet Walker, Larry Converse, Eileen Hughes, and their team at the Brookings Institution Press. I want to thank my assistant, Linda Wielfaert, for her ongoing support of all of my research.

A number of these chapters have appeared in earlier form elsewhere. Chapter 1 draws from Michael S. Barr and Rebecca M. Blank, "Savings, Assets, Credit, and Banking: Introduction and Overview," in *Insufficient Funds: Savings, Assets, Credit, and Banking among Low-Income Households*, edited by Rebecca M. Blank and Michael S. Barr (New York: Russell Sage Foundation, 2009), pp. 1–24 Chapter 2 is an updated version of my chapter, "Financial Services, Saving, and

Borrowing among Low- and Moderate-Income Households: Evidence from the Detroit Area Household Financial Services Survey," in the same volume. Chapter 7 appeared in a similar form as Michael S. Barr, Jane K. Dokko, and Benjamin J. Keys, "Exploring the Determinants of High-Cost Mortgages in Low- and Moderate-Income Neighborhoods," in *The American Mortgage System: Crisis and Reform*, edited by Susan M. Wachter and Marvin W. Smith (University of Pennsylvania Press, 2011), pp. 60–86. Chapter 9 is adapted from Michael S. Barr and Jane K. Dokko, "Third-Party Tax Administration: The Case of Low- and Moderate-Income Households," *Journal of Empirical Legal Studies* 5 (2008), pp. 963–81. The material in chapter 11 has appeared in various forms for different audiences, starting as working papers—Michael S. Barr, Sendhil Mullainathan, and Eldar Shafir, "Behaviorally Informed Financial Services Regulation," New America Foundation, October 2008; and "An Opt-Out Home Mortgage System," Hamilton Project Discussion Paper 2008-14, Brookings, September 2008 (same authors)—and published as "The Case for Behaviorally Informed Regulation," in *New Perspectives on Regulation*, edited by David Moss and John Cisternino (Cambridge, Mass.: Tobin Project, 2009), pp. 27–63 (same authors); and as "Behaviorally Informed Home Mortgage Regulation," in *Borrowing to Live: Consumer and Mortgage Credit Revisited*, edited by N. Retsinas and E. Belsky (Brookings, 2008), pp. 170–202 (same authors). The chapter has been updated in light of the Dodd-Frank Act of 2010, the CARD Act of 2009, and other developments as well as comments received on earlier versions. I am grateful to my coauthors and to my publishers for permitting me to bring this body of research together in this volume.

The policy implications of this research were honed in two stints in the U.S. Department of the Treasury. I am grateful to Timothy F. Geithner, Robert E. Rubin, and Lawrence H. Summers for giving me the opportunity to serve and to try out some of these ideas in practice.

I want to thank my wife, Hannah Smotrich, and my children, Avital, Dani, and Etai, for all of their support and love, and my parents, Deborah J. Barr and the late David S. Barr, for inspiring me to get started down this path in ways too numerous to explain.

1

Introduction

MICHAEL S. BARR

L ow-income individuals often lack access to the type of financial services that middle-income families can take for granted, such as checking accounts, direct deposit, bank loans, or saving opportunities. High-cost or low-function financial services, barriers to saving, lack of insurance, and credit constraints increase the economic challenges faced by low-income families. Using a unique data set from a survey I designed and that was administered in 2005–06 by the Survey Research Center at the University of Michigan to more than a thousand households in the Detroit area, this book analyzes the financial constraints and choices of low-income families and describes the ways low-income families use financial services, through both formal ("mainstream") and informal ("alternative") financial institutions. It discusses policies that would help low-income families achieve more stable economic lives.

Access to affordable financial services is important to the lives of low-income families, who must deal with sometimes abrupt fluctuations in income that occur because of job changes, instability in hours worked, medical illnesses and emergencies, divorce or other changes in family composition, and many other factors. If these families have limited access to savings, credit, or insurance, even small income or expense fluctuations may create serious problems in their ability to pay rent, utilities, and other bills. That is because many low-income families often lack the financial "slack" that can permit other households to ride out tough times (see Mullainathan and Shafir 2009). Financial slack can be thought of as breathing room provided to households by the ability to make relatively costless adjustments to align resources with needs. The costlier or more difficult these adjustments are, the less slack these households can be said to have. Some amount of slack can be generated internally (as by increasing work, reducing nonessential expenditures, or selling assets), but generally speaking, households use the financial system to facilitate slack (as by holding savings, accessing credit, or buying insurance). No slack too often means that small problems can escalate rapidly and undermine the fragile financial stability of these households.

Unfortunately, families often have only limited access to the sound financial products that could help them generate financial slack. In fact, higher-cost financial services can reduce the slack available to households. For example, many low-wage individuals see their take-home pay reduced by the high transaction costs they face when using check-cashing services to obtain their income. Moreover, inadequate access to financial services—such as direct deposit to a bank account or its functional equivalent—can contribute to taxpayers' using refund anticipation loans and expensive check-cashing services that diminish the value of the earned-income tax credit.

Limited access to mainstream financial services can also hinder the ability of low-income families to save. Savings are important because they help to smooth short-term income and expense fluctuations. Small savings can be used to provide a buffer against unforeseen events, such as illness. Savings can also provide capital for important long-term investment opportunities. Middle- and upper-income families regularly use their savings to invest in educational opportunities, in the health of family members, in home ownership, and in pension funds for retirement; lower-income households face similar types of needs, including job training, higher education, or other strategies to improve their income prospects. Having a measure of financial stability through savings may also improve other outcomes, such as job training or education, both for heads of household and their children.

Constraints on access to mainstream financial services can also increase borrowing costs. The ability to borrow on reasonable terms can be important to low-income households for several reasons. Low-income households facing fluctuations in income and expenses may need to resort to high-cost borrowing because they lack lower-cost ways of generating financial slack. It is not easy for them to reduce expenditures; because of low asset holdings, low income, low credit scores, or thin credit files, it is often difficult for them to get access to lower cost debt; they may lack insurance; and they are less likely to have precautionary savings. They may be able to fall back on friends and family for help, but such borrowing can often put strains on those who lend, who are likely to be lower-income themselves. Access to credit can also be important beyond meeting short-term needs, for achieving educational goals, including vocational or job training. Access to reasonable terms for mortgages also facilitates more sustainable home ownership.

Generating Slack: Financial Services, Savings, and Credit

Transactional services, savings, and credit are critical for low-income households' financial stability. Because these households have no slack in their lives, small decreases in income or increases in expenses can cause major problems. Yet well-designed and appropriately regulated financial services could help these households build greater financial stability. Better access to transactional services, savings vehicles, and reasonable credit will not, in and of itself, transform the lives of low-income individuals, but better access would give households useful tools to manage their finances in order to generate financial slack. If households are able to set up a regular means to receive income and pay bills, to build savings, and to access reasonably priced credit, they would be less vulnerable to serious disruptions stemming from income and expense shocks, and perhaps better able to take advantage of new opportunities, such as job training, improved child care, or a better job.

Transactional Services

A quarter of low-income households, and 13 percent of moderate-income households, are "unbanked," that is, they have neither a checking nor a savings account (Bucks and others 2009; FDIC 2009). In lieu of bank-based transactions, savings, and credit products, these households often rely on more costly alternative financial services. Providers offer a wide range of services, including short-term loans, check cashing, bill payment, tax preparation, and rent-to-own products, most often in low-income urban neighborhoods.

Alternative financial services providers are the only source of basic financial services for many low-income persons, but those services come at a high price. For example, while check-cashing outlets offer essential services, the fees involved in converting paper checks into cash are high, relative both to income and to analogous services available to middle- and upper-income families, such as check deposit into a bank account or electronic direct deposit. Check-cashing fees vary widely across the country and between types of checks, but they typically range from 1.5 to 3.5 percent of face value. The Federal Reserve reports that financial institutions processed checks totaling nearly $31.6 billion in 2009 (FRS 2010). Almost all of these checks are low-risk payroll (80 percent) or government-benefit (16 percent) checks (Bachelder and Ditzion 2000). While even payroll checks are not without some credit and fraud risk, average losses from "bad" checks at check-cashing firms are low and compare favorably with interbank rates (Barr 2004).

Surprisingly, it is not just the unbanked who use alternative financial services. Many low- and moderate-income families with bank accounts regularly rely on high-cost nonbank providers to conduct much of their financial business—such as cashing checks, buying money orders, or taking out payday loans (Barr 2009; Rhine and others 2001). Recent literature sometimes refers to these households as "underbanked," although that of course assumes the outcome of the empirical analysis is that these households need more banking.

The high costs of alternative financial services raise several concerns. First, the costs of these basic financial transactions reduce take-home pay (Bachelder and Ditzion 2000; Kennickell, Starr-McCluer, and Surette 2000). As discussed below, our research shows that many low-income households can often avoid those high fees in practice, but they incur other costs as a result. High fees for tax preparation and filing, check cashing, and refund anticipation loans can reduce the value of earned-income tax credits by over 10 percent (Barr 2004; Berube and others 2002). Bringing low- and moderate-income families into the banking system, if key changes were made to financial products, could help reduce these high transaction costs, substantially increasing the purchasing power of these families. Second, without a bank account, low-income households face key barriers to saving. Promoting low-income household savings is critical to reducing reliance on high-cost, short-term credit; lowering the risk of financial dislocation resulting from job loss or injury; and improving prospects for longer-term asset building through home ownership, skills development, and education. Third, without a bank account, it is more difficult and more costly to establish credit or qualify for a loan. Holding a bank account is a significant predictor of whether an individual also holds mortgage loans, automobile loans, or certificates of deposit (Hogarth and O'Donnell 1999).

Although there are many reasons why some low- and moderate-income households lack a bank account, the financial and nonpecuniary costs of account ownership are important in their decision to become and remain unbanked. Despite the need to understand how the decisionmaking process of low- and moderate-income households interacts with external constraints, there has been little research to inform us about how these households make decisions about bank-account ownership or about the kinds of financial products that they would find attractive.

This study explores how the structure of accounts may influence household decisions. Checking accounts may be ill suited to the needs of many low- and moderate-income households. In particular, bank accounts are not structured to be low cost and low risk for low-income households. Financial institutions find low-balance accounts expensive and frequently require high minimum balances, credit checks to open accounts, high bounced-check and overdraft fees, and long check-holding periods (Barr 2004). The minimum-balance requirement on many checking accounts is a significant barrier for low-income households. In addition, households with little slack may overdraw frequently. Moreover, banks, unlike check-cashing outlets, sometimes hold checks for several days before crediting the deposit of funds; for low-income customers, this wait may not be practical. Such accounts are not designed for the lives and finances of low- and moderate-income households that live paycheck to paycheck.

Some low- and moderate-income households have had a bank account in the past but were unable to manage their finances, for example, engaging in repeated overdrafts that went unpaid. Households that have had past problems with their accounts are listed in the ChexSystems, a private clearinghouse that most banks use to decide whether to open accounts for potential customers. Thus not only does their own experience with high and unexpected fees as bank customers in the past keep some low-income households from opening an account, but they may also be formally barred from doing so by banks' use of ChexSystems.

These features of traditional bank accounts, and past problems households have had with managing their accounts, partially explain why many low- and moderate-income households are unbanked. In addition, as some researchers have pointed out, formal financial institutions are often less prevalent in low-income neighborhoods than alternative financial services providers (Temkin and Sawyer 2004). Still, for some households, noneconomic factors, such as mistrust of financial institutions, or inertia, may matter; and immigrant households often face documentation barriers to account ownership. Lack of financial education may also play a role in these choices. Our survey evidence helps to untangle these factors, as discussed further below.

Savings

Low-income families are less likely than higher-income households to hold significant savings or assets (Scholz and Seshadri 2009). These families often find it difficult to save and plan financially for the future. Living paycheck to paycheck leaves them vulnerable to medical or job emergencies that may endanger their financial stability, and their lack of savings undermines their ability to invest in improving their skills, purchasing a home, or sending their children to college. Yet low-income households often lack access to even basic institutional saving vehicles. High-income households receive a disproportionately large share of the tax benefits for retirement savings and home ownership (Gale and others 2009). Most low-income workers either work for firms that have no savings plans or are not covered by such plans (Orszag and Greenstein 2005). Twenty-five percent of low-income households lack a bank account, a critical entry point for saving (Bucks and others 2009). Given the low levels of assets among low-income households, most banks have historically not wanted to serve these customers. Thus saving by low-income households is depressed by the lack of sufficient income to afford saving, the low rates of return offered to the poor because of their low levels of wealth, and the lack of supply in savings products for the poor. Government tax incentives and employer-based savings plans tend to help better-off households the most, while leaving many low-income households to fend for themselves.

Yet evidence suggests that some low- and moderate-income households can and do save. For example, a high portion of low- and moderate-income workers participate in 401(k) plans if offered the chance to do so (Orszag and Greenstein 2005). From 2005 to 2006, nearly 78 percent of federal employees earning less than $40,000 participated in the Thrift Savings Plan (FRTIB 2007). Just under 34 percent of families in the bottom income quintile saved in 2007 (Bucks and others 2009). Automatic enrollment in employer-sponsored pension plans boosts participation and asset accumulation among low-income employees, as well as among African American and Hispanic employees (Choi and others 2002; Madrian and Shea 2001). If welfare-benefit asset limits were raised, low-income households might respond by saving more, although the empirical evidence to date is mixed (Hurst and Ziliak 2006; Nam 2008; Sullivan 2006). Low-income households can save, and savings are shaped in part by the institutional mechanisms that encourage saving.

Low-income households may have different uses for their savings compared with middle- and upper-income households. For example, Social Security covers a substantial share of low-income households' retirement needs, and it may be impractical to expect poor households to set aside more out of their current income for retirement. Yet there are many purposes for which low- and moderate-income households need savings, including housing, education, childbirth, divorce, emergencies, or simply managing cash flow. These households need easily accessible mechanisms through which to save and may need help in building up their savings. Many low-income households have been able to build up savings, for example, through home ownership. For some households, home ownership provides a means to build equity over time, as well as residential stability and economic security; for other households, the home ownership choice and the debt undertaken to purchase a home may be less beneficial (Bostic and Lee 2009).

Low- and moderate-income households have lower savings and fewer assets to fall back on in an emergency. At the same time, they have difficulty obtaining insurance for important life risks, including medical needs, divorce, and job loss. Insurance helps smooth consumption and protect asset accumulation while also preventing or minimizing cascading shocks. For example, an auto accident without insurance can lead to a job loss, which can have devastating consequences for family finances. Given insurance constraints, saving for precautionary reasons may be important for low-income households. At the same time, given income constraints, regular saving may put a heavy burden on consumption or contribute to high-cost borrowing for the poorest families. Government insurance programs might help provide some slack by making it unnecessary for families to rely solely on self-insurance through savings.

Credit

Many low- and moderate-income households use an array of short- and long-term credit products provided by a range of institutions both formal and informal. Alternative credit products include payday loans, tax-refund anticipation loans, pawnshop loans, rent-to-own products, and secured credit cards. Some households use bank overdrafts regularly, at high cost, while others use credit cards, which often charge high interest rates and high fees. Some households have access to home mortgage and home equity loans, including loans from both prime and subprime lenders, as well as automobile loans and consumer loans backed by car titles. Again, for many low-income households these sources of credit are often costly. In addition, short-term credit products, such as payday loans, are structured in a way that makes it easy for households repeatedly to overborrow, and many subprime home mortgages are structured to disguise their true costs (Barr 2004, 2005, 2007). At the same time, credit access may provide an important insurance mechanism for low-income households facing emergencies and may provide an important means for smoothing consumption in the face of income volatility. Abstract debates about whether credit access enhances or reduces welfare miss the point. Research on human failings in decisionmaking suggests that credit access through misleading products and inducements to overborrow can reduce the welfare of the household (Barr, Mullainathan, and Shafir 2008, and chapter 11, this volume), just as credit access through straightforward products can in principle be welfare enhancing. Policy needs to focus on how to move the market toward provision of welfare-enhancing products and services.

In sum, low- and moderate-income households are financially underserved. They often lack savings, rely on expensive, short-term credit (formal or informal), and have limited access to formal financial services of the sort that many middle-class families take for granted. Only recently, and on a small scale, have some financial institutions begun to offer banking accounts and other services tailored to the needs of low-income households. Moreover, regulatory gaps often leave families unprotected in credit transactions, and national saving policies focus heavily on middle- and upper-income Americans. As a result of these financial service failures in both public and private sectors, low- and moderate-income households face barriers that can make it difficult for them to advance economically by effectively managing their financial lives.

Overview of the Book

This book is based on information from a unique data set collected in a 2005–06 survey (that is, before the global financial crisis) of more than a thousand low- and moderate-income families in the Detroit area. I designed the Detroit Area Household Financial Services study to obtain detailed information on the financial services used by these families. As described more fully in chapter 2, the survey was conducted with the University of Michigan's Survey Research Center. We attained a 65 percent response rate and completed 1,003 household interviews. Data reported in this book are from the 938 respondents living in low- and moderate-income census tracts.

The Detroit area provides a useful context for studying the use of financial services by low- and moderate-income (LMI) households. Like many cities in the industrial Midwest and Northeast, Detroit has an eroding manufacturing base, high levels of unemployment and poverty, and strong patterns of residential segregation (see Farley, Danziger, and Holzer 2000). An in-depth look at the use of financial services in the local area permits us to understand household attitudes and behaviors within the context of local financial services offerings and market structures. Thus, this survey can provide a more nuanced and textured understanding of LMI households than can be gained solely with aggregated national data (see, for example, FDIC 2009).

The results presented in chapter 2 suggest that existing financial services, credit, and payment systems impose high transaction costs on lower-income households, increase their costs of credit, and reduce their opportunities to save. Like their higher-income counterparts, lower-income households regularly conduct financial transactions, but the financial services system is not designed to serve them well. About 30 percent of the adults surveyed were unbanked. A substantial share indicated that lower fees, less confusing fees, or more convenient bank hours and locations would make them more likely to open a bank account. The study shows that households use a range of formal and informal mechanisms to meet their financial service needs. A surprisingly large share (65 percent) of those with bank accounts had also used money orders in the recent past, as had 77 percent of the unbanked. Money orders, pawnshops, and payday lenders appear to complement formal financial services for many of these households, who commented on their convenience and ease of use.

There was significant variation in saving patterns. About one-third of these families contributed to savings each month, while 42 percent said that they never saved. Savers were more likely to be employed and to have more education. Many of those who did not save reported that they found it difficult to live on their current income. They were also more likely to have health expenses. When households faced a large expenditure need, they got help from family and friends, borrowed money, or spent down assets. Slightly less than 20 percent reported that they were in deep financial trouble.

Chapters 3, 4, and 5 explore financial services usage patterns in greater detail. Chapter 3 explores the full portfolio of low-income households, including transactional, credit, and saving behavior. For the vast majority of these households, annual outlays on financial services for transactional and credit products are relatively small, around 1 percent of annual income. This estimate suggests that many of these households are able to avoid regular use of the most expensive financial services options. As in other studies of consumer use of financial services, however, the top spenders take up a disproportionate share of spending. Moreover, although annual outlays are low, the study finds that LMI households face substantial nonpecuniary costs of using alternative financial services, such as waiting in line to pay bills in person, lacking ready mechanisms to save, and burdening friends and family with borrowing needs. Low-income households with bank accounts are more likely to be employed and have access to more forms of credit than unbanked households, resulting in greater use of financial services and higher total outlays; contrary to expectations, most outlays by the median banked household are for alternative financial services rather than banking services. Having a bank account is also related to the steps households take to maintain financial stability when income cannot cover their expenses. Finally, even when controls for income, education, and employment are implemented, large, unexplained racial differences in bank-account ownership are found: African American respondents are 12 percentage points less likely to have a bank account than their nonblack counterparts in the survey. These results suggest that policies designed to expand access to traditional bank accounts are unlikely to improve financial outcomes unless accompanied by improvements in the functionality of banking products for low-income households.

Chapter 4 characterizes the features of an account-based payment card—including bank debit cards, prepaid debit cards, and payroll cards—that elicit a high take-up rate among low- and moderate-income households, particularly those without bank accounts. The chapter applies marketing research techniques, specifically, choice modeling, to identify the design of specific financial services products for low- and moderate-income households, who often face difficulties acquiring or maintaining standard bank accounts but need banking services. After monthly cost, the nonmonetary features of a payment card, such as the availability of federal protection and the type of card, are the factors LMI consumers weigh most heavily when choosing among differently designed payment cards. The study estimates a high take-up rate for a well-designed payment card. The sensitivity of the take-up rate with respect to cost varies by income and bank-account ownership. These results can guide private and public sector initiatives to expand the range of financial services available to LMI households, particularly as the federal government embarks on a wide-ranging effort to move federal benefits and tax refunds to electronic transmission and as federal regulators weigh new consumer protections for payment cards in the wake of the passage of the Dodd-Frank Wall Street Reform and Consumer Protection (Dodd-Frank) Act of 2010.

Chapter 5 combines the household survey data with information collected on the location of banks and alternative financial services providers in the Detroit area. The chapter reports the results of testing whether proximity to a bank is associated with a greater probability of having a bank account. In fact, all else being equal, the probability of having a bank account is predicted not by bank proximity but rather by proximity to alternative financial service providers. To disentangle the simultaneity between household and business location decisions, the chapter implements an instrumental variables strategy using historical

bank-branch locations and municipal zoning laws as exogenous determinants of
the current location of banks and alternative financial services providers. The
results suggest that public policy efforts to attract low-income households to
the mainstream banking sector would be better focused on expanding the range
of products offered by depository institutions rather than solely focusing on
expanding geographic access to bank branches, although the presence of bank
branches in low-income neighborhoods is likely to have other benefits not fully
captured by this analysis.

Chapter 6 explores the use of alternative credit products. Households use
various sources for alternative credit, depending in part on their available collateral and borrowing needs. Rather than treating each source as a substitute,
LMI borrowers appear to use payday loans, pawnshops, refund anticipation
loans, and other services as complementary products. Unlike loans from mainstream providers (banks and credit unions), which, when used by LMI households, are mostly applied to home improvement or repairs and mortgage or car
payments, loans from alternative financial services sources are reportedly used
to pay off bills, to cover recurring expenses, or to consolidate debts. Individuals
who use these credit sources are more likely to be in financial trouble and have
experienced hardships in the past year. They are also more likely to believe that
borrowing is an acceptable way to make up for short-term reductions in income.

These results have important implications for the effective regulation of and
policy toward short-term credit markets. Understanding households' preferences
and behavior related to borrowing and saving is essential to analyzing how firms
and households would respond to government regulation designed to address
problems in this sector. The use of short-term credit, particularly for living
expenses and emergencies, suggests caution about overregulating. Moreover,
regulation of singular parts of the alternative financial services sector may be
counterproductive when borrowers' portfolios include multiple short-term credit
products.

Chapter 7 explores home mortgage credit. In spite of the recent impetus to
reform home mortgage markets and to hold lenders accountable for abuses, little
systematic evidence is available about the manner in which fair-lending violations and abusive practices in mortgage lending manifest in the mortgages held
by those households. While studies of racial discrimination in mortgage markets
have been conducted for decades, the role of mortgage brokers in lending has
only recently increased and been studied.[1] This chapter uncovers the mechanisms
through which differential mortgage pricing disadvantages two groups of LMI

1. Until the financial crisis, some 60 to 70 percent of loans were originated through the broker
channel. Some economists have argued that mortgage brokers contributed to the subprime boom
and bust by aggressively marketing high-cost and potentially confusing mortgages to low-income
borrowers (Quigley 2008).

home owners: black borrowers and borrowers who use mortgage brokers. These borrowers pay more for mortgage loans than other borrowers, after controlling for a wide variety of factors.

This robust, random, stratified household-level survey reports data on different dimensions of high-cost mortgage pricing, such as balloon payments, up-front points and fees, "teaser" rates, and prepayment penalties, along with whether a household uses a mortgage broker.[2] The data set links household and mortgage characteristics to describe mortgage pricing among low- and moderate-income households, their creditworthiness and attitudes about borrowing, and their use of mortgage brokers. Especially noteworthy is that the survey was conducted at the height of the subprime lending boom in 2005 and 2006 and in a state—Michigan—where antipredatory lending statutes were relatively weak.

The chapter estimates differences in mortgage pricing among home mortgage borrowers, focusing on price differences (the intensive margin), rather than on loan denial differences (the extensive margin). We attempt to control for the fact that the price and other features of mortgages may differ across borrowers because of their incomes, the size of their down payments, their risk appetite, their creditworthiness, and how much they shop around for the best terms. While the approach cannot completely rule out these demand-driven explanations, the empirical results are most consistent with lender and broker, that is, supply-driven, origins for differences in loan terms.

Within similar low-income neighborhoods, black home owners pay higher interest rates—110 basis points higher, on average—than similar nonblack home owners and are more than twice as likely to have prepayment penalties or balloon payments attached to their mortgages than nonblack home owners, even after controlling for age, income, gender, creditworthiness, and a proxy for default risk. In addition, borrowers who used a mortgage broker are over 60 percent more likely to pay more in points or fees than those who did not use a broker.

The heterogeneity in pricing across racial groups and across transaction types (broker versus nonbroker) is unexplained after accounting for many demand-driven explanations. However, there may be other potentially important sources of heterogeneity that are unobservable in the study but may be observed by the lender, such as more precise measures of income volatility or documentation of income and assets (see Edelberg 2007 for a discussion of these issues). Our approach cannot distinguish between racial differences in pricing and the presence of omitted financial characteristics that are correlated with race but are not included in our data. Nonetheless, a well-functioning mortgage market should

---

2. Susan Woodward and Robert Hall (2010) use loan-level data with mortgage-pricing variables but not many household-level characteristics, while Andrew Haughwout, Christopher Mayer, and Joseph Tracy (2009) merge data from LoanPerformance (LP) and Home Mortgage Disclosure Act compliance reporting to examine racial differences in subprime mortgage pricing.

eliminate the disparate treatment of minority borrowers and of borrowers who use mortgage brokers, and our results indicate that the mortgage markets were not functioning well during the subprime lending boom.

The differences in loan terms by race, particularly in the up-front costs, which are not fully captured by the Home Mortgage Disclosure Act, suggest that collecting a broader set of loan terms might be important for fair-lending enforcement.[3] The prevalence of brokers in this market and the finding that so many borrowers are presented with just a single mortgage option (and therefore know little about alternatives) potentially provide empirical support for models of predatory lending in which lenders use an informational advantage to their benefit (for example, Bond, Musto, and Yilmaz 2009). These results provide new insights into the ways in which brokers operate in low- and moderate-income communities and help researchers to understand the full costs of home ownership to low- and moderate-income borrowers.

Chapter 8 discusses personal bankruptcy, which affects nearly one in ten families over the course of their lives. The debate over bankruptcy reform in 2005 reflects policymakers' beliefs on the causes of bankruptcy. Those favoring bankruptcy laws that intend to make it more difficult to file or get relief argue that lenient bankruptcy laws increase the incentive to file and that a decline in bankruptcy's stigma has eroded moral restraints on filing. In their view, households engage in profligate borrowing knowing that they can evade paying debts by filing for bankruptcy. Others argue that bankrupt debtors face crushing financial burdens and that many people who could file for bankruptcy do not file, indicating that stigma may be an important deterrent. In the view of many, the credit-card industry's marketing and pricing strategies have increased the likelihood that households will become overly indebted and resort to bankruptcy.

The debate over bankruptcy reform has inspired a spirited dialogue among academics about households' decisions to file for bankruptcy (Keys 2010; Sullivan, Warren, and Westbrook 1989, 2000, 2003; Warren and Tyagi 2003; White 1998; Fay, Hurst, and White 2002; Jacoby, Sullivan and Warren 2001; Gross and Souleles 2002; Gan and Sabarwal 2005; Mann 2007). Four core explanations for the decision to file are the role of adverse events as triggers for bankruptcy, the financial benefits of bankruptcy as an incentive to file, decreases in stigma from filing, and market structure explanations (see Gan and Sabarwal 2005 for a partial literature review). Evaluating these explanations empirically is a challenging task, both because of the theoretical indeterminacy of the claims and because of the limitations of existing data sets in addressing the relevant questions. There are not sufficient data to permit an extensive comparison of the financial services behaviors, attitudes, and economic outcomes among low-, moderate-, and middle-income households who file for bankruptcy and those who do not. As explained further in chapter 8, the survey research design does not allow analysis that would untangle causation. At the same time, the survey

3. Specifically, the reported annual percentage rate in the Home Mortgage Disclosure Act includes up-front costs such as points and fees, but lenders are not required to disclose these separately. In addition, the annual percentage rate is disclosed only for high-cost originations.

results suggest that the decision to file is a complex one for households and that this decision is part of myriad economic decisions made by households experiencing other financial difficulties.

Low- and moderate-income households have few assets, human capital, or steady flows of income to cope with the financial difficulties that come their way. Many of them experience concurrent serious adverse events and a range of financial hardships. They often deploy a range of methods to cope, including filing for bankruptcy. The data would not tend to support theories of filing driven mostly by strategic factors. Bankruptcy is but one of the outcomes associated with financial instability. We see some meaningful differences among households who would benefit from filing and those who would not. These differences are muted when one looks at who actually files, suggesting that the decision to file may be based in part on unobservable factors.

Chapter 9 investigates the tax-filing experiences and refund behavior of low- and moderate-income households. The chapter documents households' tax-filing behavior, their attitudes about the withholding system, their use of tax refunds to consume and save, and the mechanisms by which they would like to receive their income. It also documents the prevalence of the use of tax preparation services and the receipt of tax refunds and refund anticipation loans. Finally, the chapter argues that there may be a role for tax administration to enable low- and moderate-income households to make welfare-improving financial decisions.

Chapter 10 extends the analysis of tax-filing behavior from the previous chapter to explore how and why LMI households use the tax system to save. This chapter analyzes the phenomenon that low- and moderate-income tax filers exhibit a "preference for overwithholding" their taxes. The chapter argues that the relationship between their withholding preference and portfolio allocation across liquid and illiquid assets is consistent with models with present-biased preferences and that individuals exhibit self-control problems when making their consumption and saving decisions. The results support a model in which individuals use commitment devices to constrain their consumption. Mental accounting and loss-aversion explanations for tax filers' preference for overwithholding are less likely to explain the patterns in the data. Dynamic inconsistency among LMI tax filers has important implications for saving policies and for tax administration generally.

Chapter 11 explains how insights from behavioral economics can improve our understanding of consumers' financial services behavior, market responses to that behavior, and different approaches to regulation. Policymakers typically approach human behavior through the perspective of the "rational-agent" model, which relies on normative, a priori analyses. The model assumes that people make insightful, well-planned, highly controlled, and perfectly calculating decisions guided by considerations of personal utility. This perspective is promoted in the social sciences and in professional schools and has come to dominate much of the formulation and conduct of policy. An alternative view, developed mostly through empirical behavioral research, and the one articulated here, provides a substantially different perspective on individual behavior and its policy implications. According to this highly empirical perspective, behavior is the amalgam of perceptions, impulses, judgments, and decision processes that emerge mentally. Actual human behavior is often unforeseen and misunderstood by classical policy thinking. A more nuanced behavioral perspective can yield deeper understanding and improved regulatory insight.

Consider the recent mortgage crisis in the United States. While the potential causes are myriad, a central problem was that many borrowers were offered and took out loans that they did not understand and could not afford, with disastrous results for borrowers, financial firms, and the national economy. Borrowers, and all of us generally, are not explained in important ways by the rational-agent model. At the same time, the chapter argues that a behavioral policy perspective that focuses only on the individual is incomplete. In some contexts, firms have strong incentives to exploit—or to overcome—consumer biases. Thus policy also needs to account for market context and the incentive and behaviors of firms. And, of course, firms will shape their conduct in response not only to the behavior of individuals but also to the actions of regulators. The chapter outlines some of the main research underpinning the behavioral perspective. It explores how firms interact with consumers in different market contexts and proposes a model for understanding this interaction. The chapter then develops an analytic framework for behaviorally informed regulation and concludes with examples of relevant policy applications.

Chapter 12 provides an epilogue to the study. The financial crisis from which the United States is only now emerging caused widespread harm to our economy, and low- and moderate-income households were least able to weather the crisis. In response to the crisis, a number of key reforms have been put in place, including the creation of a new consumer financial protection bureau, mortgage-market and credit-card reforms, and initiatives to reach out to the "unbanked." The chapter concludes the discussion by suggesting strategies to transform the financial services system to better serve low- and moderate-income households. In particular, it highlights how behavioral perspectives can shape better financial education, improve access, and enhance consumer protection. This "three-legged stool" holds promise for improving the financial stability of low- and moderate-income households.

Key Findings

Several key findings emerge from our research. First, low-income families are financial decisionmakers who need a range of financial services. Basic transactional services—receiving income, storing it, and paying bills—are less available and more expensive for low-income households. In addition, low-income households may have more acute needs for certain forms of finance. For example, less-skilled adults are more likely to face unemployment or involuntary part-time employment, and their incomes are more cyclical or volatile (Keys 2008; Bania and Leete 2007; Hoynes 2000). Their need to smooth consumption may therefore be higher than it is among high-income households. This means that flexible credit or moderate levels of short-term savings may be quite important to the economic well-being of these families.

Second, lower-income families use both formal and informal means to manage their financial lives. Although low- and moderate-income U.S. households are less likely to hold checking or savings accounts than middle- and upper-income households, many such households do have bank accounts, and many low-income households, both banked and unbanked, also use a range of alternative financial services (Barr 2009; Berube and others 2002). This suggests that formal financial institutions are not fully meeting their needs. For instance, changes in banking have made low-fee, low-balance bank accounts far less available in the past fifteen years—and many payday loan customers believe their loan is cheaper than the cost of returned check fees (Elliehausen and Lawrence 2001).

Third, lower-income families have substantially less wealth than high-income families. In itself, this is not surprising, since these families have less capacity to save and invest (Scholz and Seshadri 2009). But for some groups, particularly African Americans and immigrants, income differences alone do not explain these wealth differences; wealth holdings are lower even after accounting for income and demographic differences.

Fourth, the lower wealth holdings of low-income families have substantial implications for many aspects of their lives. Lower home ownership rates can mean more frequent residential relocation, which can in turn lead to poorer access to schools, doctors, or family support. The lack of short-term savings can lead to greater use of payday lenders for short-term loans and greater use of credit-card debt. Lack of checking accounts can result in fees paid to check-cashing outlets or increased use of tax-refund loans (Barr 2004). Use of these services increases the costs of financial services to lower-income families and makes saving even harder.

Fifth, when thinking of savings and the financial needs of lower-income households, policymakers should consider their need for short-run economic flexibility, which savings and access to formal financial institutions could provide. By contrast, much of the recent policy discussion about saving among the poor has focused on long-term investment gains such as home ownership or future educational needs. While saving as a vehicle for long-term asset accumulation and investment is important, this is only half the story. The value of low levels of savings and low-cost credit to short-term economic flexibility and consumption smoothing is equally important. Indeed, for many low-income families the substantial dollars needed to ensure access to college or to stable economic retirement may be unattainable and can only happen if individual savings are supplemented by government assistance programs, such as Pell grants and Social Security.

In sum, low- and moderate-income households have no financial slack. And the financial system as it is currently organized makes it harder for these families to cope. While many low- and moderate-income households engage in a range of strategies to manage their finances, these strategies can impose heavy economic and noneconomic costs on these households. Restructuring the financial system to better serve them could improve outcomes and social welfare.

Policy Directions

Policies that incorporate behavioral insights to improve the institutional context for financial decisionmaking may be especially useful in improving social welfare. Such insights can enhance financial education, access, and consumer protection—three essential areas for improving the financial lives of low-income households.

Far too often, financial education is pursued without a clear idea of the goals to be achieved or the ways in which financial decisionmaking actually occurs in particular contexts. There are three promising approaches in this regard. First, providers of financial education can come together to determine core financial competencies and to rigorously evaluate different approaches to embedding these competencies in educational offerings. The Treasury Department recently took the first steps in assessing these approaches.[4] Second, rather than attempting to "teach" these competencies divorced from institutional context, financial education providers, financial institutions, and the public sector can seek ways to improve customer understanding in the context of particular financial choices the individual is faced with at particular moments in time—the choice to save for retirement at the moment of hiring, for example. Third, policymakers could view disclosures as a useful moment to increase financial understanding rather than as a moment to increase the amount of financial information provided. For example, under the Credit Card Accountability, Responsibility, and Disclosure Act, credit-card monthly disclosures must now inform consumers of the financial consequences of making only the minimum payment and to indicate the amounts needed to pay off the balance in a shorter time.[5]

In addition to improving financial education, policymakers should focus on improving access to financial products and services that might better enable low-

4. Financial Education Core Competencies; Comment Request, 75 *Federal Register* 52596 (August 26, 2010).

5. Credit Card Accountability Responsibility and Disclosure (CARD) Act of 2009, Pub. L. No. 111-24, 123 Stat. 1734.

income households to manage their finances. For example, banks can be given incentives to expand their offerings of low-cost, electronically based accounts. These can be structured as individually owned, debit card–accessed deposit accounts without check-writing privileges or the ability to overdraw or can be offered as prepaid debit cards on a pooled basis with pass-through federal deposit insurance. Bank accounts and prepaid cards tailored to the needs of lower-income families are likely to expand their use of formal financial services.

Employers of low-wage workers also shape the financial choices these workers make. Employers can encourage the use of direct deposit, and they can work with local banks and other providers to ensure that their workers have access to accounts and other products structured to their needs. Employer-based savings plans, with automatic savings provisions, can encourage saving, not simply for retirement but also for shorter-term or emergency needs. Employers might have incentives to offer their workers debit-card accounts with "financial stability" features—such as direct deposit, automatic bill payment, and automatic savings plans. Such products might improve employee stability, reduce lost productive time, and improve retention. These theoretical outcomes need to be empirically tested.

Policymakers can advance these efforts in a number of ways. For example, the Internal Revenue Service could be authorized to establish an automatic way for unbanked households to receive their tax refunds. These accounts would decrease the use of refund loans, increase opportunities for saving, and lower administrative costs in the tax system (Barr 2007). States could use their electronic benefit transfer programs for cash welfare, unemployment, and other state-administered benefits to improve the types of financial offerings for these households, consistent with their goals of enhancing the economic welfare of low-income or unemployed households (Barr 2004).

Policies should also be pursued to encourage saving among low-income households. Making the IRS's saver's credit for retirement savings contributions refundable would expand the opportunity for tax-advantaged retirement savings to low-income families (Gale, Iwry, and Orszag 2004); Congress could enact a new automatic individual retirement account for a broad range of workers who have no access to pension plans at work (Iwry and John 2007); and new tax credits could be provided to banks and thrifts for setting up automatic savings plans for low-income households to meet their shorter-term savings needs (Barr 2007).

Moreover, government currently assists low-income families in crucial ways in meeting their financial retirement needs, investing in education, covering major health expenditures, and, in some instances, meeting other needs. These programs need to be preserved and strengthened. Long-term financial stability for Social Security is probably more important than improved access to individual retirement savings plans for low-wage workers, since 65 percent of retirees rely on

Social Security for more than half of their current income (Mishel, Bernstein, and Allegretto 2005). Broadly available health insurance could help workers avoid incurring long-term debt or filing for bankruptcy when faced with a health crisis. Pell grants and other forms of educational subsidies can help low-income families educate their children beyond high school and give their children greater economic opportunities. Moreover, the government plays a central role in enhancing the take-home pay of low-wage workers through the earned-income tax credit, which helps lift millions of families out of poverty every year. The tax credit has been effective and should be expanded and simplified.

While education and access are critical, so too is consumer protection. Improved disclosures might help consumers make better decisions about borrowing. There may be a need to require greater and more standardized disclosure of the financial implications of credit across both the mainstream and alternative financial sectors, including credit-card fees, overdraft policies, and payday loans. Such cross-sector disclosures could improve the ability of consumers to comparison-shop across functionally similar credit products. Tailored disclosures regarding the consequences of certain borrower behaviors, such as making only the minimum payment on credit cards, might also help consumers make better choices (Barr 2007).

Moreover, policymakers ought to consider how advances in behavioral economics, which have improved retirement savings outcomes, could be applied in the credit arena (Barr, Mullainathan, and Shafir 2008). While market forces in these two financial areas are quite different, the fundamental mistake that individuals make in not understanding the power of compound interest is strikingly similar. In the one case it leads to undersaving, and in the other to overborrowing. Congress could pursue opt-out strategies in the credit arena that would make it more difficult for households to make bad decisions with severe consequences. For example, credit-card companies could be required to establish opt-out credit-card repayment plans with the standard pay-down occurring over a reasonably short period of time (Barr 2007). As another example, Congress could require lenders to offer a standard set of home mortgages with straightforward terms; borrowers could opt out, but the opt-out rules would be "sticky," making it harder for lenders to encourage borrowers to take out loans not in their interest (Barr, Mullainathan, and Shafir 2008).

The Credit Card Act and the Dodd-Frank Act made a series of critical changes that are likely to significantly enhance consumer protection in the years ahead. Most important, the Dodd-Frank Act created the Consumer Financial Protection Bureau, which is authorized to supervise and enforce consumer protections across much of the bank and nonbank financial sector. For example, the bureau is authorized to improve and simplify mortgage disclosures; to police mortgage brokers and originators; and to ban unfair, deceptive, and abusive acts and practices. Behavioral insights and empirical testing can help the bureau improve disclosures and to be sensitive to the ways in which different contexts can lead to dramatically different outcomes based on sales practices and other factors.

In sum, a better understanding of the financial behaviors of low-income households can significantly help policymakers and private institutions to advance financial education, improve access to quality financial products and services, and create new consumer protections. Policies to improve education, access, and protection may enhance the financial stability of low-income households by providing them with better ways to generate financial slack. Improving financial stability, in turn, may hold out the prospect for significantly enhancing their well-being. It is to that task of better understanding household behaviors that the remainder of the book is dedicated.

References

Bachelder, Ed, and Sam Ditzion. 2000. "Survey of Non-Bank Financial Institutions for the Department of the Treasury." Boston, Mass.: Dove Consulting.

Bania, Neil, and Laura Leete. 2007. "Income Volatility and Food Insufficiency in U.S. Low-Income Households, 1992–2003." Discussion Paper 1325-07. Madison: University of Wisconsin, Institute for Research on Poverty.

Barr, Michael S. 2004. "Banking the Poor." *Yale Journal on Regulation* 21:21–237.

———. 2005. "Credit Where It Counts: The Community Reinvestment Act and Its Critics." *New York University Law Review* 80:513–652.

———. 2007. "An Inclusive, Progressive National Savings and Financial Services Policy." *Harvard Law and Policy Review* 1:161–84.

———. 2009. "Financial Services, Saving, and Borrowing among Low- and Moderate-Income Households: Evidence from the Detroit Area Household Financial Services Survey." In *Insufficient Funds: Savings, Assets, Credit, and Banking among Low-Income Households,* edited by Rebecca M. Blank and Michael S. Barr, 66–96. New York: Russell Sage Foundation.

Barr, Michael S., Sendhil Mullainathan, and Eldar Shafir. 2008. "Behaviorally Informed Home Mortgage Credit Regulation." Working Paper UCC08-12. Harvard University, Joint Center for Housing Studies.

Berube, Alan, Anne Kim, Benjamin Forman, and Megan Burns. 2002. "The Price of Paying Taxes: How Tax Preparation and Refund Loan Fees Erode the Benefits of the EITC." Brookings (www.brookings.edu/es/urban/publications/berubekimeitc.pdf).

Bond, Philip, David K. Musto, and Bilge Yilmaz. 2009. "Predatory Mortgage Lending." *Journal of Financial Economics* 94:412–27.

Bostic, Raphael W., and Kwan Ok Lee. 2009. "Homeownership: America's Dream?" In *Insufficient Funds: Savings, Assets, Credit, and Banking among Low-Income Households,* edited by Rebecca M. Blank and Michael S. Barr, 218–56. New York: Russell Sage Foundation.

Bucks, Brian K., and others. 2009. "Changes in U.S. Family Finances from 2004 to 2007: Evidence from the Survey of Consumer Finances." *Federal Reserve Bulletin* 95 (February): A1–A56.

Choi, James, and others. 2002. "Defined Contribution Pensions: Plan Rules, Participant Decisions, and the Path of Least Resistance." In *Tax Policy and the Economy,* edited by James M. Poterba, 16:67–114. MIT Press.

Edelberg, Wendy. 2007. "Racial Dispersion in Consumer Credit Interest Rates." FEDS Working Paper 2007-28. Federal Reserve Board (www.federalreserve.gov/pubs/feds/2007/200728/200728pap.pdf).

Elliehausen, Gregory, and Edward C. Lawrence. 2001. "Payday Advance Credit in America: An Analysis of Customer Demand." Monograph 35. Washington: Georgetown University, McDonough School of Business (www.fdic.gov/bank/analytical/cfr/2005/jan/CFRSS_2005_elliehausen.pdf).

Farley, Reynolds, Sheldon Danziger, and Harry J. Holzer. 2000. *Detroit Divided.* New York: Russell Sage Foundation.

Fay, Scott, Erik Hurst, and Michelle J. White. 2002. "The Household Bankruptcy Decision." *American Economic Review* 92:706–18.

FDIC (Federal Deposit Insurance Corporation). 2009. *FDIC National Survey of Unbanked and Underbanked Households* (www.fdic.gov/householdsurvey/full_report.pdf).

FRS (Federal Reserve System). 2010. *The 2010 Federal Reserve Payments Study* (www.frbservices.org/files/communications/pdf/press/2010_payments_study.pdf).

FRTIB (Federal Retirement Thrift Investment Board). 2007. *Thrift Savings Plan Participant Survey Results, 2006–07* (www.frtib.gov/pdf/FOIA/2006-TSP-Survey-Results.pdf).

Gale, William G., J. Mark Iwry, and Peter R. Orszag. 2004. "The Saver's Credit: Issues and Options." *Tax Notes* 103:597–612.

Gale, William G., and others. 2009. Introduction to *Automatic: Changing the Way America Saves,* edited by William G. Gale and others, 1–8. Brookings.

Gan, Li, and Tarun Sabarwal. 2005. "A Simple Test of Adverse Events and Strategic Timing Theories of Consumer Bankruptcy." Working Paper 11763. Cambridge, Mass.: National Bureau of Economic Research (www.nber.org/papers/w11763).

Gross, David B., and Nicolas S. Souleles. 2002. "An Empirical Analysis of Personal Bankruptcy and Delinquency." *Review of Financial Studies* 15:319–47.

Haughwout, Andrew, Christopher Mayer, and Joseph Tracy. 2009. "Subprime Mortgage Pricing: The Impact of Race, Ethnicity, and Gender on the Cost of Borrowing." In *Brookings-Wharton Papers on Urban Affairs: 2009,* edited by Gary Burtless and Janet Rothenberg Pack, 33–63. Brookings.

Hogarth, Jeanne M., and Kevin A. O'Donnell. 1999. "Banking Relationships of Lower-Income Families and the Government Trend toward Electronic Payment." *Federal Reserve Bulletin* 85 (July): 459–73.

Hoynes, Hilary W. 2000. "The Employment, Earnings, and Income of Less-Skilled Workers over the Business Cycle." In *Finding Jobs: Work and Welfare Reform,* edited by David E. Card and Rebecca M. Blank, 23–71. New York: Russell Sage Foundation.

Hurst, Erik, and James P. Ziliak. 2006. "Do Welfare Asset Limits Affect Household Savings? Evidence from Welfare Reform." *Journal of Human Resources* 40:46–71.

Iwry, Mark, and David John. 2007. "Pursuing Universal Retirement Security through Automatic IRAs." Working Paper 2007-2. Washington: Retirement Security Project.

Jacoby, Melissa B., Teresa A. Sullivan, and Elizabeth Warren. 2001. "Rethinking the Debates over Health Care Financing: Evidence from the Bankruptcy Courts." *New York University Law Review* 76:375–418.

Kennickell, Arthur B., Martha Starr-McCluer, and Brian J. Surette. 2000. "Recent Changes in U.S. Family Finances: Results from the 1998 Survey of Consumer Finances." *Federal Reserve Bulletin* 86 (January): 1–29.

Keys, Benjamin J. 2008. "Trends in Income and Consumption Volatility, 1970–2000." In *Income Volatility and Food Assistance in the United States,* edited by Dean Jolliffe and James P. Ziliak. Upjohn Institute Press.

————. 2010. "The Credit Market Consequences of Job Displacement." FEDS Working Paper 2010-24.

Madrian, Brigitte, and Dennis F. Shea. 2001. "The Power of Suggestion: Inertia in 401(k) Participation and Savings Behavior." *Quarterly Journal of Economics* 116:1149–87.

Mann, Ronald J. 2007. "Bankruptcy Reform and the 'Sweat Box' of Credit Card Debt." *University of Illinois Law Review* 2007:375–404.

Mishel, Lawrence, Jared Bernstein, and Sylvia Allegretto. 2005. *The State of Working America: 2004–2005.* Cornell University Press.

Mullainathan, Sendhil, and Eldar Shafir. 2009. "Savings Policy and Decisionmaking in Low-Income Households." In *Insufficient Funds: Savings, Assets, Credit, and Banking among Low-Income Households,* edited by Rebecca M. Blank and Michael S. Barr, 121–45. New York: Russell Sage Foundation.

Nam, Yunju. 2008. "Welfare Reform and Asset Accumulation: Asset Limit Changes, Financial Assets, and Vehicle Ownership." *Social Science Quarterly* 89, no. 1: 133–54.

Orszag, Peter, and Robert Greenstein. 2005. "Toward Progressive Pensions: A Summary of the U.S. Pension System and Proposals for Reform." In *Inclusion in the American Dream: Assets, Poverty, and Public Policy,* edited by Michael Sherraden, 262–80. Oxford University Press.

Quigley, John. 2008. "Compensation and Incentives in the Mortgage Business." *Economists' Voice* 5, no. 6: Article 2 (doi:10.2202/1553-3832.1431).

Rhine, Sherrie L. W., and others. 2001. "The Role of Alternative Financial Service Providers in Serving LMI Neighborhoods." Paper prepared for the Community Affairs Research Conference, "Changing Financial Markets and Community Development." Federal Reserve System, Washington, April 5–6.

Scholz, John Karl, and Ananth Seshadri. 2009. "The Assets and Liabilities Held by Low-Income Families." In *Insufficient Funds: Savings, Assets, Credit, and Banking among Low-Income Households,* edited by Rebecca M. Blank and Michael S. Barr, 25–65. New York: Russell Sage Foundation.

Sullivan, James X. 2006. "Welfare Reform, Savings, and Vehicle Ownership: Do Asset Limits and Vehicle Exemptions Matter?" *Journal of Human Resources* 41:72–105.

Sullivan, Theresa A., Elizabeth Warren, and Jay Lawrence Westbrook. 1989. *As We Forgive Our Debtors.* Oxford University Press.

————. 2000. *The Fragile Middle Class: Americans in Debt.* Yale University Press.

————. 2003. "Who Uses Chapter 13?" In *Consumer Bankruptcy in Global Perspective,* edited by Johanna Niemi-Kiesiläinen, Iain Ramsay, and William C. Whitford, 269–82. Oxford, U.K.: Hart Publishing.

Temkin, Kenneth, and Noah Sawyer. 2004. "Analysis of Alternative Financial Service Providers." Paper prepared for the Fannie Mae Foundation. Washington: Urban Institute, Metropolitan Housing and Communities Policy Center.

Warren, Elizabeth, and Amelia Warren Tyagi. 2003. *The Two-Income Trap.* New York: Basic Books.

White, Michelle J. 1998. "Why It Pays to File for Bankruptcy: A Critical Look at the Incentives under U.S. Personal Bankruptcy Law and a Proposal for Change." *University of Chicago Law Review* 65:685–732.

Woodward, Susan E., and Robert E. Hall. 2010. "Diagnosing Consumer Confusion and Sub-Optimal Shopping Effort: Theory and Mortgage-Market Evidence." Working Paper 16007. Cambridge, Mass.: National Bureau of Economic Research (www.nber.org/papers/w16007).

2

Managing Money

MICHAEL S. BARR

This chapter presents an overview of the empirical evidence documenting the financial services behavior and attitudes of low- and moderate-income (LMI) households. The Detroit Area Household Financial Services (DAHFS) survey uses a random, stratified sample to explore the full range of financial services used by LMI households, together with systematic measures of household preference parameters, demographic characteristics, and households' balance sheets.[1] Results from the study suggest that the structure of formal and informal financial services makes it more difficult for low- and moderate-income households to manage their money. Given the lack of financial slack these households have, managing their finances is a key task. Yet the financial services system, rather than facilitating this endeavor, often makes it harder.

Within the severe income constraints they face, LMI households seek to use both formal and informal mechanisms available to them to manage their financial lives. Like their higher-income counterparts, LMI households regularly conduct financial transactions: they convert income to a fungible medium, make payments, save, borrow, seek insurance, and engage in financial and economic decisionmaking. Yet the formal and informal financial services systems are not designed to serve them well. Often, the financial services available to these households are too high cost, or high risk, or confusing to them and make it more difficult to build a measure of financial stability.

---

1. I was the principal investigator for the DAHFS study.

The line between the formal and informal financial services systems used by LMI households is not impermeable. Contrary to popular belief, being unbanked is not necessarily a fixed state. Approximately 70 percent of the unbanked previously had a bank account, and more than 10 percent of banked households were recently unbanked. While the unbanked are much more likely than banked households to turn to alternative financial services (AFS) providers, such as check cashers, even banked individuals often use some such provider. In fact, one type of alternative credit provider, the payday lender, exclusively serves banked individuals.

The financial services choices facing households are complicated; these choices not only involve trade-offs among functionality, convenience, and cost but also require cost comparisons across highly differentiated products in both the AFS and formal sectors. Alternative financial transactions are often described as convenient but high cost; at the same time, bank accounts are also perceived as high cost and not usually well structured to serve LMI households. For example, over half of banked LMI households reported paying minimum balance, overdraft, or insufficient funds fees in the previous year. The financial services mismatch—between the needs of LMI households and the products and services offered to them—forces these households to choose among the high-fee, ill-structured products offered by both banking and AFS institutions. These constrained choices reduce take-home pay and make it harder to save and more expensive to borrow.

The Financial Services Marketplace for Low- and Moderate-Income Households

Although the overwhelming majority of low- and moderate-income households have and use bank accounts, both these households and their unbanked counterparts often face high costs for using basic financial services, significant barriers to saving, and more expensive forms of credit (Barr 2004; Barr and Blank 2009). High-cost and inadequate financial services reduce take-home pay and increase the costs of administration and compliance for essential governmental programs, including Social Security, the earned-income tax credit, and income transfer and welfare-to-work programs administered by states. In addition, high-cost and inadequate financial services diminish the opportunities for LMI households to readily save. Saving is critical for LMI households, in part because they are vulnerable to income shocks, medical emergencies, and other expenses such as car repairs that can upset their fragile financial stability. Moreover, the lack of a bank account and savings increases the cost of credit for these households, reduces their opportunities for stable home ownership through sound credit choices, and diminishes their ability to save or borrow to invest in their own human capital and that of their children.

According to national figures, about 25 percent of low-income American households (defined as the bottom 20 percent, who earn under $20,600 a year) are "unbanked," that is, they have neither a checking nor a savings account (Bucks and others 2009). Even among moderate-income households (those earning up to $30,000 a year), 13 percent lack any bank account (FDIC 2009). These households lack the basic mechanisms provided by the formal financial system for the receipt of income, the store of its value, and the payment of bills. They also lack ready opportunities for saving in interest-bearing accounts as well as the ease of direct deposit and automatic savings plans that can significantly increase the level and rate of savings over time.

These unbanked households do not, however, escape the need to use financial services. Rather, they piece together strategies to use formal and informal mechanisms to achieve their financial needs. In doing so, they often seek to optimize their financial behavior within external constraints that impose serious financial costs, but they often lack the time or resources to take a step back and determine whether it would be possible to expand their choice sets. For example, while check cashers offer essential services, the fees involved in converting paper checks into cash are high relative both to income and to analogous services that middle- and upper-income families use, such as depositing a check into a bank account or using electronic direct deposit (Barr 2004). Pawnshops, check cashers, rent-to-own stores, tax-refund lenders, and other AFS providers are often the dominant means for LMI households to access financial services in their neighborhoods, but such services come at a high cost and leave these households with little opportunity to save.

Many more low- and moderate-income families who have bank accounts also rely on high-cost AFS providers to conduct much of their financial business—such as cashing checks, buying money orders, paying bills, or taking out payday loans. One might think of these families as "underbanked," in the sense that formal financial institutions are not offering them the products and services they need in their daily lives, even though they have bank accounts. Such families use a mix of mainstream and alternative providers. Far too little attention has been paid to the ways in which even banked LMI households are ill served by the financial system.

Despite the importance of financial services to the lives of LMI households, little scholarly attention was paid to the topic until the pathbreaking work of John Caskey (1994). Caskey shows that careful attention to financial behaviors and attitudes can yield a more nuanced understanding of the choices LMI households face. Existing national data sources that focus on wealth holdings, such as the Survey of Consumer Finances, are geared toward questions most relevant to middle- and upper-income households and oversample wealthy households; the survey collects limited data on financial services or transactions, particularly those services geared toward low- and moderate-income households. Surveys that include large numbers of low-income households, such as the Survey of Income and Program Participation, are not focused on financial services (Scholz and Seshadri 2009). Constance Dunham and her colleagues (Dunham 2001; Dunham, Scheuren, and Willson 1998) broke new ground when they implemented the first random, stratified survey geared toward understanding the financial behaviors of LMI households in two communities. Shorebank, a leading community development bank, implemented a second such study (Seidman, Hababou, and Kramer 2005). Both studies, however, were constrained in the data that they collected regarding income, asset, and debt levels; employment; the broad range of financial services usage patterns across transactional services, credit, insurance, and savings; and the attitudes and preferences of LMI households.

To explore the range of financial services needs, behaviors, and attitudes of LMI households, as well as the constraints they face, collecting additional field data was imperative. Low- and moderate-income households operate in the context of severe constraints on income and wealth and a limited supply of financial services. Understanding the costs of different financial services choices, the nature of the products and services offered to LMI households, the framework within which these households make their financial decisions, and their preferences and attitudes can help shed light on both why households are unbanked and whether and how to alter that status. Although there are many reasons why LMI households lack bank accounts, their preferences interact with the financial and nonpecuniary costs of account ownership in their decisions to become and remain unbanked. Uncovering the trade-offs households are willing to make between the costs and benefits of bank-account ownership is paramount to ascertaining how to integrate the unbanked into the financial mainstream. In addition, households' preferences determine whether varying account features will induce more of them to own bank accounts. Despite the need to understand the role of preferences, there is little research on households' preferences for bank-account ownership, as well as the kinds of products they would find attractive enough to induce them to open some type of bank account, if banks were willing to offer such accounts.

As currently structured, the financial services system does not work for LMI households. Many of these households find that checking accounts are ill suited to their needs, and many financial institutions find low-balance checking accounts unprofitable (Barr 2004). Living paycheck to paycheck, LMI households face a significant risk of overdrawing their checking accounts and paying high fees as a consequence. Many of them have had a bank account in the past but were unable to manage their finances to avoid overdrafts or insufficient funds fees, or they were unwilling to pay high fees. Minimum balance requirements may also be a significant barrier for low-income households. By contrast, if banks could be encouraged to offer low-cost, electronically based bank accounts and payment cards, without the costly attributes of the checking system, these types of accounts in principle might provide a more efficient and effective means of serving the financial services needs of LMI households, if such households would use them. No previous empirical study, however, has asked LMI households about their preferences for these types of products and services.

Description of Survey, Sampling, and Data

The DAHFS study, conducted with the University of Michigan's Survey Research Center, was designed to advance understanding of the attitudes and behaviors of LMI households toward financial services. The survey focuses on LMI individuals' experiences with formal and informal financial institutions, in addition to their socioeconomic characteristics. Because there is no such comprehensive survey about the financial services experiences and attitudes of low- and moderate-income households, the questionnaire required extensive development, pretesting, and validation. There were numerous challenges in tailoring a survey to LMI households. The study built on the work of the Office of the Comptroller of the Currency and Shorebank, whose surveys, described earlier, are more limited regarding low-income households' banking status. Although the Survey of Consumer Finance, the Panel Study on Income Dynamics, and the Health and Retirement Study are not focused on low-income households and are not tailored to their experiences, the DAHFS study adapted questions from these sources for LMI households. The survey also required development of a wide range of new questions to cover the broad range of financial services of interest. The research team vetted the survey instrument with an advisory board and a wide range of outside experts in financial services, low-income communities, survey methodology, psychology, sociology, economics, and related disciplines, as well as with practitioners.

The Survey Research Center's Survey Methods Group provided invaluable assistance in working on question wording and ordering. The research team also conducted extensive pretesting on a representative subsample of LMI households to validate the methodology and instrument. Given concerns about the overall literacy level and the ability of LMI households to provide reliable responses to seemingly difficult questions about financial behavior and individual preference parameters, the team conducted cognitive interviews with low-income individuals regarding the most difficult questions and modified the instrument based on how these subjects processed the questions. To improve the accuracy of self-reported information, participants were encouraged to locate any documents—such as tax returns, pay stubs, receipts, or mortgage paperwork—that might validate their responses. The final survey was programmed for computer-assisted, in-person interviewing, and the programmed survey was then tested again multiple times.

In addition to standard survey methodology, the survey included a discrete choice study of preferences for a payment card. This part of the survey asked respondents to choose from among sets of hypothetical purchase cards with varying features and prices. The research team analyzed these data using a hierarchical discrete-choice model and investigated consumers' preferences for alternative payment-card designs. The conjoint analysis focused on a payment card intended to facilitate the receipt of income, storage of value, and payment of bills. The study focused on this type of account because electronically based bank accounts and payment cards can be offered by financial institutions, payment-card providers, employers, and government agencies at lower cost and lower risk to LMI households than checking accounts. But little is known about whether such products provide sufficient utility to LMI households to generate scale.

After a year's work on sample design and survey development, the Survey Research Center was in the field interviewing households from July 2005 through March 2006. In addition to the center's regular oversight of field staff, its Survey Design Group aided in monitoring and, as necessary, adjusting field strategy. The final survey instrument was seventy-six minutes in length on average and required nearly nine hours of interviewer effort for each completed interview. All interviews were conducted in person, usually in the home of the respondent. Occasionally, interviews were conducted at the respondent's place of work, in the respondent's automobile, or at another location.

The sample consists of 1,003 completed interviews, representing a response rate of 65 percent. The sample members were selected to form a stratified random sample of the Detroit area (Wayne, Oakland, and Macomb Counties). The Survey Research Center drew sample members from census tracts with median incomes of 0 to 60 percent (low), 61 to 80 percent (moderate), and 81 to 120 percent (middle) of the Detroit area's median income of $49,057. The sample frame includes more census tracts from the LMI strata than the middle one. Hence, sample members are more likely to be drawn from the low- and moderate-income strata. Stratum definitions do not, however, require that the income levels of the sample members fall within these ranges. Once a household had been selected, the Survey Research Center randomly selected an adult from that household to be interviewed (Kish 1949). The data set thus generalizes to both the adult individuals and the households living in census tracts with median incomes less than 120 percent of the Detroit area's median. For purposes of this chapter, data are restricted to households living in LMI census tracts and are weighted to represent these communities.[2]

Overall, the demographic characteristics of the sample reflect the average characteristics of low- and moderate-income households in the Detroit metropolitan

---

2. Household income largely mirrors tractwide medians, but data reported here are not restricted with respect to the income of households in LMI tracts.

area as reported by the census, although a significantly higher percentage of the sample is female compared with census data for the Detroit area (see table 2-1). The sample is socioeconomically disadvantaged relative to the average American household.[3] The sample is more than two-thirds African American and nearly two-thirds female. Only 20 percent of respondents are currently married, and 46 percent have never been married. Nearly 30 percent have less than a high school diploma, but 47 percent have some education beyond high school. Although most of the respondents are of working age, only 54 percent were employed at the time of interview. The median household income of the sample is $20,000, much lower than the Detroit metropolitan area's median income of $49,057 and the national median of $44,684. Thirty-three percent of these households live below the poverty line. The modal respondent to the survey is an African American working-age woman, without children, who has lived in the Detroit area for a long time. Her income from work is low and close to the federal poverty line, and she is likely to receive some public assistance.

The DAHFS sample, while it is not designed to be representative of LMI households nationwide, gives valuable insights into common financial hardships and LMI households' behavior. Detroit has many of the same problems facing cities in the industrial Midwest and Northeast. An in-depth look at the use of financial services in the local area illustrates usage patterns within the context of local financial-services offerings and market structures. Surveys such as this provide a more nuanced and textured understanding of LMI households than can be gained solely with aggregated national data (see, for example, FDIC 2009). Broadly speaking, however, the DAHFS sample does match the LMI census tracts in Detroit, and those are similar to the average LMI census tract in the United States, with caveats for differences in racial composition.[4] Moreover, aggregate results in the survey are broadly consistent with results from both national samples (for example, FDIC 2009) and other local studies (for example, Dunham 2001; Seidman, Hababou, and Kramer 2005).

Unbanked Household Financial Behaviors and Preferences in Banking Services

Although most LMI individuals in the sample have bank accounts, a significant portion—29 percent—do not. However, nearly one-fifth of unbanked respondents live with another adult who has a bank account, leaving 23 percent

---

3. Although immigrant households are a disproportionate share of LMI households nationwide and disproportionately likely to be unbanked (see, for example, Osili and Paulson 2009), the Detroit metropolitan area, and therefore the Detroit-area study sample, does not have enough immigrants to make meaningful comparisons between immigrants and the native born.

4. Table 3-1 in the next chapter illustrates those similarities.

Table 2-1. *Characteristics of Sample Members by Banked Status*[a]
Percent unless otherwise noted

	Census	All	Banked	Unbanked
Black	70.5	69.1	65.3	78.3
White	21.8	20.4	23.1	13.6
Arab	n.a.	1.9	2.0	1.5
Other	7.7	8.6	9.5	6.5
Female	52.3	66.3	66.5	65.6
		(1.6)	(2.3)	(3.4)
Less than high school diploma	35.8	29.6	26.6	37.1
High school diploma or GED	31.0	23.0	19.1	32.7
Greater than high school diploma	33.2	47.4	54.3	30.2
Employed at interview	44.5[b]	54.3	59.3	41.9
Unemployed at interview	8.2	5.8	3.9	10.7
Not in labor force at interview	47.0	39.9	36.8	47.5
Age (years)	n.a.	43.5	44.9	40.0
		(1.0)	(1.1)	(1.2)
Born in the United States	92.7	92.1	90.5	95.9
		(1.9)	(2.4)	(1.4)
Single or never married	44.1	45.6	37.7	65.1
Married and living with spouse	24.5	19.7	24.0	9.1
Living with partner	n.a.	4.1	3.7	5.0
Separated, widowed, or divorced	31.3	30.6	34.6	20.9
Percentage households with no children	n.a.	67.2	70.6	58.9
		(2.2)	(2.5)	(4.3)
Mean household monthly income (dollars)	n.a.	2,248	2,703	1,156
		(334)	(439)	(399)
Mean household annual income in 2004 (dollars)	n.a.	28,435	33,224	17,078
		(2,118)	(2,573)	(1,467)
Median household annual income in 2004 (dollars)	24,146	20,000	25,000	10,000
Percentage below the poverty line	31.5	33.2	26.2	50.5
		(2.4)	(2.5)	(3.9)
Sample size	626[c]	938	668	270

Source: Detroit Area Household Financial Services study.

a. Standard errors are in parentheses. "Not in labor force" includes respondents who said they were retired, homemakers, students, those who did not have the required documentation, or those who chose not to work. "Unemployed" is the percentage of people currently unemployed who are in the labor market. Poverty guidelines come from the U.S. Department of Health and Human Services (2004).

b. Based on the civilian employment rate.

c. The sample in the "Census" column consists of census tracts in the Detroit area (Wayne, Oakland, and Macomb counties) with median income under $36,073 (80 percent of the Detroit area's median $49,051).

of all households in the DAHFS sample unbanked. This sample proportion is consistent with the estimates of previous surveys that 20 to 30 percent of low- and moderate-income households and 28 to 37 percent of such individuals are unbanked (Aizcorbe, Kennickell, and Moore 2003; Dunham, Scheuren, and Willson 1998; Seidman, Hababou, and Kramer 2005; Bucks and others 2009; FDIC 2009).

The unbanked subpopulation of the sample differs from the banked population in several observable ways (see table 2-1). The unbanked group is younger, is predominantly African American, and has relatively less education than the banked. The unbanked are much more likely to be unemployed and much more likely to live below the poverty line. Only 42 percent of the unbanked are employed, and 50 percent of the unbanked live in poverty. The unbanked are economically more isolated and have worse job prospects than those with bank accounts.

Being unbanked is not a permanent state (see table 2-2). Of the subsample of unbanked respondents, 70 percent previously had a bank account, and 66 percent of these individuals had an account within the past five years. Among those who formerly had a bank account, 70 percent chose to close the account themselves, citing moving, worrying about bouncing checks, or excessive fees as their reasons for closing the account. The remaining formerly banked, 30 percent, report that their bank closed their account. In the majority of cases in which the bank closed an account, the primary reason was bounced checks and overdrafts.

Not only are the bulk of the unbanked formerly bank-account holders, but the reverse is sometimes true as well: many banked households were previously involuntarily unbanked. Despite currently being banked, 12 percent of bank-account holders previously had a bank account closed by their bank. For nearly two-thirds of previous account holders, their account was closed because they had a low balance or an inactive account (63 percent) or bounced checks or overdrafts (51 percent). Despite having previously been unbanked because a bank closed their account, these households were able to transition back into the banking system. In addition to those whose accounts were involuntarily closed, a large portion of the banked previously closed a different account. Nearly 55 percent of the banked subpopulation closed a previous bank account, most commonly because of the convenience of another bank (27 percent) or a desire to reduce excessive fees (21 percent). Unbanked status does not appear to be a permanent state or tightly linked to demographics or attitudes; rather, some unbanked LMI individuals make transitions into and out of being banked.

Moreover, the unbanked report that they would prefer to be banked. There is significant interest among the unbanked population in entering the mainstream financial services sector. Of the unbanked respondents, 75 percent say that they would like to open a bank account in the next year, and 33 percent that they recently looked into getting a bank account. However, 17 percent report that

Table 2-2. *Transitions into and out of Banking*
Percent

	All	Banked	Unbanked
Respondent has bank account	71	100	0
Household has bank account	77	100	20
Previously had bank account	91.5	100	70.3
Chose to close account	n.a.	54.6	70.3
Reason for closing account			
Worried about bouncing checks	n.a.	4.2	14.2
Moved	n.a.	n.a.	13.0
Minimum fees too high	n.a.	21.0	11.5
Convenience of a different bank	n.a.	27.4	n.a.
Bank closed account	n.a.	12.3	29.9
Reasons bank closed account			
Bounced checks	n.a.	51.3	55.2
Low balance or inactive	n.a.	63.4	29.2
Fraud	n.a.	7.2	9.5
Grew up with banked adults in home	72.2	72.9	70.7
Has shopped around for bank accounts[a]	36.1	37.3	33.2
Wants to open bank account in next year	. . .	. . .	75.1
Denied when tried to open account	. . .	. . .	16.9
Income volatility previous twelve months			
Gone up	24.0	27.5	15.3
Gone down	17.0	15.1	21.4
Up and down a little	23.0	22.3	25.0
Up and down a lot	7.0	5.1	11.6
Stayed the same	29.1	30.0	26.7
Lost job in past twelve months	22.9	18.9	32.8
Sample size	938	668	270

Source: Detroit Area Household Financial Services study.

a. Banked respondents are asked if they shopped around before getting their current account; unbanked respondents are asked if they have shopped around to look into getting an account.

a bank had denied their application to open an account, reflecting continued constraints on account opening.

Unbanked individuals report a variety of reasons for being unbanked (see figure 2-1). About two-thirds cite primarily financial reasons for their current status. These financial reasons are described in different ways, but they can be analyzed as relating to the low income and asset levels of the household in relation to high bank fees or other bank requirements. For example, 15 percent report that they do not have enough money to open a bank account, 10 percent that they are unemployed, 16 percent that they do not need a bank account, and

Figure 2-1. *The Top Reasons Given by the Underbanked for Why They Were Unbanked*

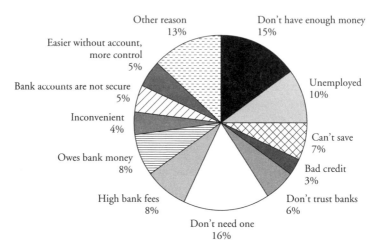

Source: Detroit Area Household Financial Services study.

8 percent cite high bank fees. Nonfinancial reasons include not trusting banks (6 percent), inconvenience (4 percent), the belief that bank accounts are not secure (5 percent), and the belief that one can have more control over one's finances or conduct transactions more easily without an account (5 percent).

To assess which barriers to account opening are most important to the unbanked, interviewers asked them what improved feature of a bank account would make them most likely to open an account (see the distribution of responses in figure 2-2). For 29 percent of the sample, lower fees are perceived as the primary facilitator to opening an account, while 20 percent consider more convenient bank hours and locations the most important reason to open an account with a particular bank. Respondents cite less confusing fees (16 percent), lower minimum balances (14 percent), and the ability to get money faster (10 percent) as the other main obstacles that they would like to see removed. More than 10 percent state that none of these changes in bank-account features would persuade them to open an account.

Household Preferences for Electronic Banking and Payment Cards

To further examine these preferences, the study included a discrete-choice method to predict consumer interest in payment cards as a function of the features that the card offers the consumer. The study explores the potential use of debit cards, prepaid debit cards, and payroll cards by low-income households, including individuals without bank accounts. Such payment cards may be a means of providing financial services to low- and moderate-income households that is less expensive and not as risky as traditional checking accounts and that may thus be attractive

Figure 2-2. *Unbanked Desired Account Changes to Induce Bank Account Opening*

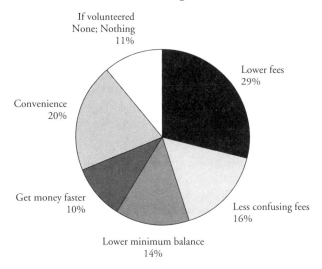

Source: Detroit Area Household Financial Services study.

to both banks and LMI households. In particular, debit cards can be designed to avoid overdrafts, lowering the risks and costs of the checking account. Debit cards also have lower cost structures than checking accounts and so can be offered at lower prices.

Discrete-choice analysis is a statistical method of identifying the structure of consumer preferences for a product with many attributes (Green and Srinivasan 1978; Luce and Tukey 1964). Based on individuals' responses to a series of questions about the characteristics of a payment card they would like, it is possible to uncover several aspects of their decisionmaking process. The analysis decomposes products and services into discrete components and then methodically varies the product configurations while measuring consumers' responses to the changes. The variation in the attributes follows an orthogonal design that exhibits no interattribute correlations across the questions. This approach enables the study to identify the effect of each attribute on the decisions of individuals in choosing a payment card. The study uses the Sawtooth software program to both design the questionnaire and analyze the results.

The main findings (first reported in Barr, Bachelder, and Dokko 2007 and explored in greater detail with refined modeling techniques in chapter 4) are twofold. First, many households without bank accounts expressed a desire to open one. In particular, the most attractive payment card achieved a hypothetical take-up rate of over 50 percent among unbanked LMI households and only slightly less than that rate among banked LMI households. This

Figure 2-3. *Relative Importance of Attributes on Choice of Product*

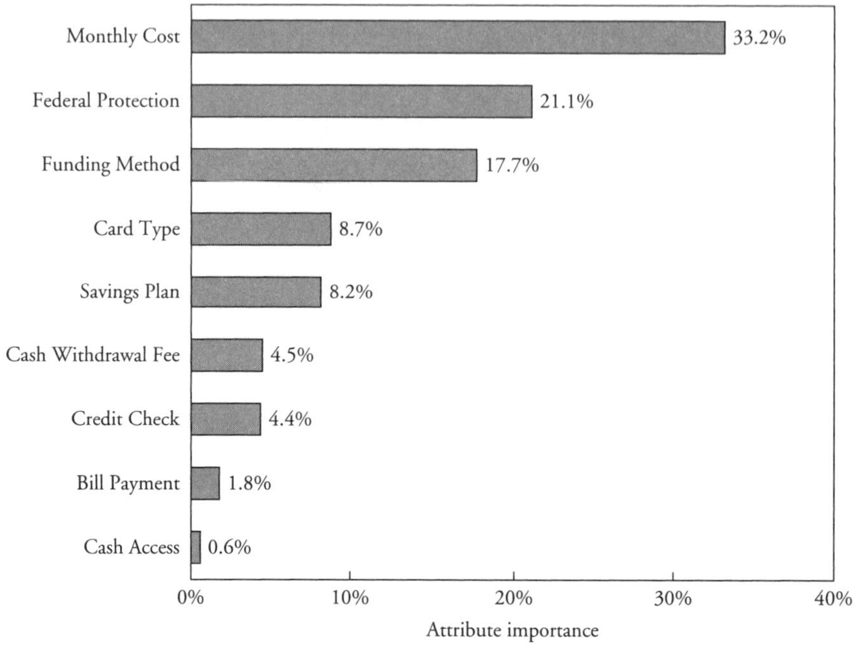

Source: Detroit Area Household Financial Services study.

finding suggests that there is a sizable opportunity for commercial banks to offer products that would be meaningful to LMI households. Second, the two most important features influencing individuals' decisions to pick a particular payment card are monthly cost and the availability of federal consumer protection with respect to the account (see figure 2-3), although there was significant heterogeneity in preferences among LMI households. This analysis could help inform depository institutions, payment-card providers, employers, and government agencies regarding the design of accounts and payment cards to bring low- and moderate-income households into the financial mainstream.

Banked and Unbanked Household Behavior: Income Receipt and Bill Payment

Contrary to the popular characterization of LMI households as operating in a cash economy, these households usually receive their income through other means (see table 2-3). Fifty-four percent of the sample reported having received a check, 21 percent cash, and 22 percent government cash benefits through a Bridge card, Michigan's electronic-benefits-transfer card, during the month preceding the interview. Another 5 percent received income from an electronic transfer to a place that was not a bank (for example, a check-cashing outlet), while only 1 percent received income through a payroll card from their employer.

Table 2-3. *Transactional Services: Income Receipt, Check Cashing, and Bill Payment*[a]

Percent unless otherwise noted

	All	Banked	Unbanked
How income is received			
Direct deposit	n.a.	62.9	n.a.
Check	54.3	50.5	63.6
Cash	20.7	17.1	29.5
Payroll card	1.2	0.8	2.2
Bridge card	21.6	14.0	40.5
Check casher	5.0	5.9	2.7
Other	4.3	4.1	4.8
Number of checks cashed in past month[b]	2.56	2.83	2.06
	(.35)	(.51)	(.11)
How income is converted			
Cashed checks[c]	n = 404	n = 265	n = 139
At a bank	93.4	96.1	83.1
Mean number	2.5	2.7	1.8
	(.11)	(.12)	(.16)
At a check casher	21.4	16.3	30.7
Mean number	2.2	2.0	2.3
	(.15)	(.22)	(.23)
At workplace	5.2	5.1	5.5
Mean number	2.5	2.4	2.6
	(.39)	(.52)	(.64)
Sign over to family or friend	8.5	4.6	15.4
Mean number	1.5	1.7	1.4
	(.25)	(.35)	(.22)
At supermarket or store	33.3	20.7	55.7
Mean number	2.1	1.9	2.2
	(.13)	(.18)	(.18)
Bill payment method[d]			
Personal check	. . .	62.1	. . .
Automated payment	. . .	32.3	. . .
Pay online	. . .	21.9	. . .
Over phone (with credit, charge, or debit card)	. . .	41.3	. . .
In cash	42.1	37.8	52.8
Money order	52.1	47.6	63.2
Payment center	36.6	33.2	45.2
Prepaid debit card	5.6	6.2	4.1
Purchased money order	68.3	64.8	77.1
Landlord accepts personal checks[e]	54.6	64.9	38.4
Sample size	938	668	270

Source: Detroit Area Household Financial Services study.

a. Standard errors are in parentheses.

b. Conditional on receiving income by check.

c. Conditional on having cashed a check at least once in the month preceding interview.

d. Personal check, automated payment, paying online, and paying by phone questions are only asked of banked respondents.

e. Asked only of renters.

Both banked and unbanked households use a mix of banking and AFS providers to receive their income and pay their bills. Unbanked households are more likely to use AFS providers than banked households, but they still rely significantly on banking services. Despite their lack of ready ability to cash checks at a bank, and as a function of their inability to receive direct deposit, unbanked households are more likely than banked households to be paid by check: nearly 64 percent of unbanked households report receiving income by check. Unbanked households are also, understandably, more likely than banked households to be paid in cash: nearly 30 percent are paid that way. Given their lower incomes and greater reliance on government support programs, unbanked households are also much more likely to receive income or food assistance through the Bridge card: more than 40 percent receive funds this way.

Unbanked households use a variety of formal and informal means to convert the income they receive by check into usable form. The dominant check-cashing strategy used by unbanked households is to go to a bank. Over 83 percent of unbanked households cash checks at a bank—most often the bank that issued the check. The next most common place where the unbanked cash checks was grocery and other stores: 56 percent of unbanked households report such a strategy. More than 30 percent of unbanked households use check cashers, and more than 15 percent of the unbanked sign over their checks to a family member or friend.

In paying bills, unbanked households cannot use personal checks, automatic payment through a bank, online payment using a credit card, or payment over the phone with a credit card. Instead of such services, 63 percent of unbanked households use money orders, 53 percent pay in cash, and 45 percent visit a payment center in person. Use of each of these bill payment services is about 15 percentage points higher for the unbanked than for the banked. Interestingly, use of AFS bill payment by the unbanked may also be related to whether mainstream bill payment would be accepted in their community. For example, only 38 percent of unbanked renters state that their landlords accept personal checks for payment of rent, while nearly two-thirds of banked renters are able to pay their rent by personal check. Future research might help to untangle the relationship between the payment options preferred by renting households and those accepted by landlords.

Banked respondents use a variety of services offered by their banks, as well as a range of AFS providers (table 2-3). Among banked LMI households, there is strong use of mainstream financial products. For example, 63 percent of the banked receive their income through direct deposit, about the same percentage that other data sources suggest is the case for the U.S. population as a whole (see Barr 2004). During the twelve months preceding the interview, banks played an important role in facilitating bill payments. Among the banked, 62 percent paid bills by check, and 41 percent used a credit or debit card over the phone. Thirty-two percent used automated bill payment, and 22 percent

Table 2-4. *Hardships Facing Respondents in the DAHFS in the Past Twelve Months*
Percent

Hardship	All	Banked	Unbanked
Poor health	7.9	6.7	11.0
Very difficult to live on household income	27.3	23.1	37.7
Major illness or medical expense	26.9	26.1	28.8
Evicted	5.9	4.1	10.5
Utility shut off	10.0	7.5	16.2
Phone disconnected	18.3	13.9	29.4
Filed for bankruptcy	3.9	3.9	4.1
Did not have enough food	16.8	13.1	25.9
Lacks health insurance	20.1	15.0	32.9
What is done when expenses exceed income			
Help from family and friends	53.0	50.7	56.7
Spend down assets	24.6	32.6	11.4
Borrow from the bank or use credit card	14.6	21.3	3.6
Sample size	938	668	270

Source: Detroit Area Household Financial Services study.

paid their bills online, most likely by allowing the recipient to access their bank accounts electronically.

Despite their access to checks and automated payment systems, the banked in the study are also likely to use AFS providers for their financial transactions. A surprisingly large fraction of the banked population, 65 percent, purchased money orders, and 48 percent used a money order to pay a bill, in the month preceding the interview. Moreover, 14 percent reported that they purchased a money order from a bank—in effect purchasing an alternative payment mechanism through a mainstream financial provider (not shown). In addition, 38 percent of banked households paid a bill in cash, and one-third visited a payment center in person to pay bills. Despite having access to a bank account, 6 percent of the banked also paid bills using a prepaid debit card, which can be purchased without a bank account. Although the overwhelmingly dominant check-cashing strategy for banked households is to use a bank, more than 16 percent of the banked population used a check casher, and 21 percent cashed a check at a supermarket or other store.

Financial Hardships among LMI Households

Low- and moderate-income households face serious obstacles to financial and physical well-being (table 2-4). Overall, 27 percent of the sample say that it is very difficult to live on their household's income. In addition, 27 percent had a major illness or paid a significant medical expense in the past twelve months.

Moreover, 6 percent of the respondents were evicted, 10 percent had a utility shut off, 18 percent had their phone disconnected, 17 percent experienced not having enough food to eat, and 4 percent filed for bankruptcy, a rate far above the national average. Almost all (about 90 percent) of LMI households experienced at least one of these hardships in the prior year.

The unbanked, who generally have lower incomes and hold lower levels of assets than the banked, are characterized by a much greater likelihood of facing financial hardships. Nearly 38 percent of the unbanked report that it is very difficult to live on the household's current income, compared with 23 percent of those with bank accounts. The unbanked are more than twice as likely as the banked sample to have been evicted and twice as likely to have not had enough food to eat or to have had a phone connection or utility shut off. The banked and unbanked are equally likely to have had a major illness or to have suffered a significant medical expense in the previous twelve months. However, the unbanked are much more likely to classify themselves as being in poor health; this could be the result of the two groups having different subjective self-classification scales or different views of what a "significant medical expense" entails. In any event, the unbanked consider themselves to be much less healthy than the banked population.

Financial Services and Savings

Low- and moderate-income households exhibit considerable diversity in their savings behaviors (table 2-5). Given financial hardships, ongoing needs, and low income, saving is difficult for many LMI households. Moreover, many LMI households lack access to ready mechanisms that enable saving, such as bank accounts with direct deposit and automatic savings plans or retirement plans at work. Nonetheless, more than half of LMI households in the sample contributed to savings in the year before the survey. Banked households are nearly twice as likely to have added to savings as unbanked households. Households also vary in the regularity of their saving. About 20 percent of respondents contribute to financial savings at least every month. A larger portion of respondents never contribute to savings (46 percent), while 11 percent contribute once or twice a year. In the year preceding the survey, the mean contribution to savings (among those who saved) was $2,474, and the median contribution was $1,000.

Households deploy different methods of saving, using both formal and informal mechanisms. For example, nearly half of households in the sample save through savings accounts and more than one-third through retirement vehicles, while 15 percent save through holding jewelry, electronics, appliances, or cash. Moreover, 75 percent of LMI households that file tax returns want to overwithhold their income (Barr and Dokko 2007; chapter 10, this volume). The data suggest that overwithholding is related to dynamic inconsistency and that wanting to

Table 2-5. *Savings*
Percent unless otherwise noted

	All	Banked	Unbanked
Savings horizon[a]			
This year	47.6	47.8	46.3
Next year	33.9	33.7	34.8
In five years	17.4	17.9	14.9
In ten years	7.3	7.3	7.1
In more than ten years	14.2	14.9	10.8
Facing major expense for which unable to save	37.0	36.7	37.7
Feels in deep financial trouble	18.4	14.6	28.0
Saving is not "worth it"			
Agree	16.4	16.6	16.4
Disagree	83.4	83.3	83.6
Hard to save because money goes to necessities			
Agree	85.1	81.7	93.5
Disagree	14.6	17.9	6.5
Hard to save because hard to resist spending			
Agree	64.9	61.3	73.8
Disagree	34.6	38.3	25.6
Frequency of saving			
In past year	54.1	62.7	32.8
More than once a month	10.4	12.8	4.5
Every month	19.2	23.2	9.4
Most months	4.0	4.0	4.0
About half of months	3.7	4.6	1.7
A few months	5.5	6.3	3.7
Once or twice	11.3	12.0	9.5
Never	45.9	37.3	67.2
Mean amount contributed (dollars)[b]	2,474	2,825	949
	(385)	(447)	(202)
Median amount contributed (dollars)	1,000	1,000	300
Asset holdings			
Savings account	49.2	67.8	0.0
Retirement savings	48.2	51.1	34.9
Life insurance	30.3	35.7	16.9
Money market funds	17.0	22.9	2.4
Jewelry, electronics	15.3	14.9	16.5
Car	73.0	79.6	56.5
Home	45.4	53.4	25.7
Reasons to save			
Financial security	78.2	79.1	74.3
Emergency or medical costs	69.9	68.7	75.8
Unanticipated job loss	50.9	48.1	64.3
Special events	52.8	49.3	69.2
Home improvements	49.3	49.1	50.3

(continued)

Table 2-5. *Savings (continued)*

Percent unless otherwise noted

	All	Banked	Unbanked
Furniture and appliances	33.5	30.7	46.9
Education and training	39.5	37.0	51.3
Invest in business	16.4	16.0	18.5
Retirement	48.2	51.1	34.9
Overwithhold to save	75.3	77.1	69.5
Save some or all of tax refund	50.2	53.2	40.1
Agree account helps or would help respondent save	. . .	81.5	67.4
Sample size	938	668	270

Source: Detroit Area Household Financial Services study.

a. Asked only of respondents who have saved in the past twelve months. Respondents are able to give multiple responses.

b. Standard errors are in parentheses.

use the withholding system, with its built-in capacity to generate illiquid savings, is a precommitment device against overconsumption. In addition, more than half of LMI tax filers report that they save some or all of their tax refund, suggesting that tax filing is an important savings opportunity for LMI households.

Households tended to express "pro-savings" attitudes. About 67 percent of respondents strongly agree that it is hard to save because most of their money goes toward basic necessities, such as food, rent, and housing. When asked if it is hard to resist the temptation to spend money, 41 percent "strongly agree," and only 8 percent strongly agree that saving money is "not worth it." Bank-account ownership may help some LMI households save. Of those who have a bank account, 85 percent believe that it helps them save. Among those who are unbanked, over two-thirds agree that an account would help them save.

"Savers" are in some ways different from those who do not save (table 2-6). Savers tend to be more educated and more likely to be currently employed. Strikingly, however, there are no significant differences among African Americans, whites, and other races or ethnicities when looking at savers and nonsavers. Bank-account ownership is an important factor that may distinguish savers from nonsavers. About 83 percent of savers have bank accounts, while 58 percent of nonsavers have an account. A poor credit history, surprisingly, is not related to savings behaviors (results not shown).

Income plays a significant role in both the regularity of savings and in the amount contributed to savings. Respondents who contribute to savings have a higher mean and median income than respondents who do not contribute. More than three-quarters of respondents who save are above the poverty line, while one-quarter remain below. Of those who contributed to savings in the past twelve months, the average amount of annual saving is $2,474 and the median

Table 2-6. *Characteristics of Savers*
Percent unless otherwise noted

	All	*Savers*	*Nonsavers*
Black	69.1	68.7	70.5
White	20.4	21.2	18.8
Arab	1.9	1.2	2.7
Other	8.6	8.9	8.0
Less than high school diploma	29.6	19.5	40.9
High school diploma or GED	23.0	20.2	26.8
Greater than high school diploma	47.4	60.3	32.3
Employed at interview	54.3	65.6	41.0
Unemployed at interview	5.8	3.1	9.1
Not in labor force at interview	39.9	31.3	49.9
Banked	71.3	82.6	57.9
Percent living below poverty line	33.2	23.6	44.5
Sample size	938	427	504

Source: Detroit Area Household Financial Services study.

amount is $1,000. Savers with incomes above the poverty level contribute an average amount of $2,852 and a median amount of $1,000. For savers who are below the poverty level, the amount contributed is dramatically lower—with a mean contribution of $1,317 and a median of $300.

While the debate over national savings policy is often focused exclusively on retirement saving, households save for a variety of reasons, and many LMI households have savings needs other than retirement; for example, they may save for investment, precautionary reasons, or future consumption. Savings policy for LMI households should encompass the range of the savings needs of these households. The Detroit survey demonstrates that most LMI households are saving for precautionary reasons. About 78 percent save to feel financially secure, 70 percent save for emergency and medical expenses, and 51 percent save for unanticipated job loss. Nearly three-quarters of respondents also save for consumption in the near future—in order to make purchases that year or the next. This includes special events (53 percent), house or home improvements (49 percent), or furniture and household appliance (33 percent). Still, a sizable portion of respondents also save for investment purposes. About 40 percent are saving to invest in education or training, while roughly 16 percent save to invest in business. Nearly half are saving for retirement.

Saving is challenging for low- and moderate-income households, many of whom face income volatility, start from a low base of asset holding, shoulder high debt-service burdens, and have ongoing informal financial obligations, such as the 45 percent of households that save in order to help family or friends in need. Strikingly, nearly one-quarter lost their job in the year preceding the interview, and 46 percent saw their income go down (or go up and down). One of the main reasons families find asset development a challenge is simply that they are poor and saving is difficult with little income. Roughly 86 percent of respondents find it hard to save because most of their money goes toward basic necessities. About 27 percent of respondents find it "very difficult" to live on current household income, while 44 percent find it "somewhat difficult." Nearly two-thirds of respondents experienced a financial hardship in the year preceding the survey, such as having utilities or phone service shut off, not having enough food, or being evicted, and about 18 percent view themselves as being in "deep financial trouble."

Nearly 30 percent of the sample respondents have monthly expenses that exceed income during most of the year. For half of these households, family and friends play a significant role in contributing to basic living expenses. If they can not rely on family or friends, 25 percent of respondents spend down assets, while 15 percent borrow from the bank or use their credit card. While 45 percent report that they are always able to cover their expenses out of current income, about 40 percent of households are in debt on their credit cards. The median debt burden among LMI households, excluding home and automobile, is $500, and the mean debt outstanding is more than ten times that amount. Looking forward, a significant portion of households (37 percent) anticipates a major expense over the next five to ten years for which they are unable to save.

Poor health and major illness can also negatively affect a household's ability to save. At the time of the interview, 28 percent of respondents had a health condition that inhibited their ability to work, and in the previous year 27 percent faced a major illness or medical expense. About 20 percent do not have insurance and therefore are likely to be extremely vulnerable to major medical expenses if an illness occurs.

Asset Holding among LMI Households

Despite the difficulty of asset accumulation, many LMI households are able to build savings. About 90 percent of the LMI households accumulate physical and financial assets in both formal and informal ways; 75 percent hold formal or informal financial assets. Nearly half have a savings account, 36 percent have retirement savings, and 30 percent have life insurance, while only 17 percent have money market funds, bonds, or CDs, and 15 percent save through holding cash, jewelry, gold, appliances, or electronics. Nonfinancial assets are more valuable than financial assets for LMI households. Roughly 75 percent of respondents own a car, and 45 percent own a home. Owning a car and home significantly increases the median value of assets for respondents—to about

$68,000—but that amount falls to $2,500 when the value of homes and auto-mobiles is excluded.

One would predict that LMI households would need liquid assets in case of emergencies, given their relative lack of insurance or other supports. Among the Detroit study respondents, a higher proportion of households holds imme-diately liquid assets as compared with assets with other liquidity levels. For households above the poverty line, the median amount of liquid asset holdings is $1,000, which might be helpful in the event of an unexpected emergency. However, with a median liquid asset holding of only $400, households below the poverty line may not be able to cover a serious emergency. Even lower pro-portions of poor households hold financial assets that are not immediately liq-uid and that generate higher rates of return. While the average amount of asset holdings increases from $1,636 to $4,277 when examining assets that are not immediately liquid, the proportion of those who hold these assets drops from 44 to 13.7 percent.

Generalizing from the Detroit study, national savings policy needs to be nuanced for LMI households, many of whom are simply too poor to save and must rely as much as possible on friends or family and the social safety net. For many of these households, that safety net appears to be weak, and financial crises often lead to further deterioration. At the same time, for some LMI house-holds, saving—and even asset accumulation—is possible. Rather than focus-ing on retirement saving, as national policy tends to do, savings policy for LMI households should focus on the wide range of their savings needs, including the need for liquid savings for emergencies as well as the need for illiquid savings for medium- and longer-term savings goals. Also, given the breadth of saving approaches taken by LMI households, savings policy needs to develop a range of alternative savings products to meet the needs of LMI households, includ-ing direct deposit initiatives, automatic saving plans, and tax-refund saving pro-grams. These issues are taken up in more depth below.

Debt Patterns among LMI Households

Although access to credit can help households smooth consumption, invest in human capital development, and build assets through home ownership and other investments, the high cost of credit presents another obstacle for low-and moderate-income households. Reduced access and increased cost of credit limit how much households can borrow, and higher-cost credit increases debt-service burdens, crowding out both current consumption and savings. Dis-saving through borrowing may be necessary for many LMI households, but its toll on these households needs to be better understood. The median debt outstanding (excluding home and automobile loans) among LMI households in the Detroit study is a mere $500, but the mean is more than ten times that amount.

Table 2-7. *Borrowing and Alternative Financial Services*
Percent unless otherwise noted

	All	Banked	Unbanked
Borrowing			
Percent looking to borrow	61.5	62.7	58.6
Percent actually borrowed	51.0	51.0	51.5
Method considered			
Bank	27.5	33.9	11.6
Finance company	13.6	16.6	6.3
Short-term credit	47.0	44.7	52.7
Cash advance from credit card	7.9	10.1	2.3
Borrowed from pension or retirement fund	6.9	8.4	3.1
Payday loan	4.4	4.9	3.4
Buy on layaway	25.7	27.2	21.9
Pawn anything	11.2	7.2	21.1
Rapid tax refund loan	21.8	18.9	29.1
Rent-to-own	5.3	5.4	5.2
Overdraft from account	20.3	24.1	10.9
Land contract on house	1.9	2.0	1.5
Sample size	938	668	270

Source: Detroit Area Household Financial Services study.

Households in the sample use a variety of alternative financial services providers to meet their credit needs (table 2-7), based in part on whether or not they have a bank account and on their available collateral. Rather than using each alternative service as a substitute, low-income borrowers use payday loans, pawnshops, refund anticipation loans, rent-to-own contracts, and other formal and informal credit services as complementary products. While payday lending services have driven growth in the AFS sector over the past fifteen years and garnered significant public attention, payday loan services are still a lending practice on the financial fringe for LMI households. As table 2-7 shows, only 4.4 percent of respondents say they recently sought out a payday loan. Part of the reason so few respondents approach payday lenders might be the restrictive eligibility qualifications, including holding a bank account and a steady job. African Americans are much more likely to use payday lenders than whites.

An open question in the literature on alternative financial services is whether these AFS providers act as substitutes for one another and for formal-sector financial services or whether borrowers use a range of services depending on the situation. The Detroit study suggests that the services are usually interrelated. Tables 2-8 and 2-9, for example, show that, overall, respondents who use other types of credit are also more likely to use payday loans. For instance, those using

Table 2-8. *Use of Payday Loans among Users of Other Alternative Financial Services*
Percent

Other AFS[a]	Payday loan use	
	By users of other AFS	By nonusers of other AFS
Pawnshop	16	3
Cash advance	14	4
RAL	9	3
Rent-to-own	16	4
Pension cash-out	12	4
Overdraft	13	2

Source: Detroit Area Household Financial Services study.
a. For all services, difference is significant at the 10 percent level after controlling for age, race, gender, and income.

a pawnshop are much more likely to use a payday loan (16 versus 3 percent). Those who used a credit card for a cash advance are much more likely to use a payday loan (14 versus 4 percent). Households that took out a refund anticipation loan (RAL) at tax time (see Barr and Dokko 2007) are much more likely to use a payday loan (9 versus 3 percent), as are rent-to-own users (16 versus 4 percent) and those who cashed out a pension or insurance policy in the past three years (12 versus 4 percent). Moreover, payday usage in the AFS sector and bank overdrafts in the formal sector are often complementary: those who have

Table 2-9. *Use of Other Alternative Financial Services among Payday Loan Users*
Percent

Other AFS[a]	Other AFS use	
	By users of payday loans	By nonusers of payday loans
Pawnshop	40	10
Cash advance	24	7
RAL	45	21
Rent-to-own	20	5
Pension cash-out	19	6
Secured card	37	9
Credit-card late fee	43	21
Overdraft	57	19

Source: Detroit Area Household Financial Services study.
a. For all but credit-card late fee, difference is significant at the 10 percent level after controlling for age, race, gender, and income.

used an overdraft from their bank account are more than five times more likely to use a payday lender than those who overdrew their accounts.

Uses of these various alternative financial services are interconnected with one another as well as with respect to payday borrowing. Table 2-10 shows a correlation matrix of alternative financial services. The highest correlation is between pawnshop use and payday borrowing. Payday borrowing is also correlated with using an overdraft from a bank account. Nearly every entry in the table is positive, suggesting that individuals who use one service are more likely to use another. Although use appears complementary, most of the correlations are not large, implying relatively weak direct relationships within the network of financial services.

In addition, certain credit-card behaviors are related to payday borrowing. Those who paid late fees on a credit card are more likely to have used a payday loan than those who have a credit card and have not missed payments (9.2 percent versus 3.4 percent). Nearly 8 percent of those who say they never pay off the entire balance on their credit card have looked into using a payday loan, compared with fewer than 4 percent of those who pay off their entire credit-card balance each month. Payday loans are used by 12.5 percent of those who pay only the minimum amount due. In addition, the least creditworthy card holders—those whose cards require a deposit, known as "secured" credit cards—are much more likely to use payday lending: 17 percent compared with 3 percent of the rest of credit-card users. These relationships to credit suggest that payday borrowers have a history of credit problems that make it difficult for them to acquire short-term credit elsewhere. In addition, the higher rate of credit problems among payday borrowers suggests that this group exhibits riskier borrowing behavior. Riskier credit-card behavior also translates into difficulty acquiring loans from mainstream providers; over 10 percent of those who were rejected by mainstream loan providers (banks, savings and loan companies, credit unions, finance and mortgage companies) seek payday loans. Although payday borrowers contribute to savings as frequently as nonborrowers, payday borrowers have lower levels of financial assets and home ownership rates than nonpayday borrowers. In short, payday borrowers tend to seek more borrowing opportunities than nonpayday borrowers, exhibit riskier credit behavior, have lower asset levels, and face higher rates of rejection from mainstream lenders.

Individuals report that they have taken out payday loans to pay for necessities (table 2-11). Of those who most recently looked into getting a payday loan, 60 percent say that they need the money for everyday expenses such as food and gasoline or for regular bills. About 5 to 11 percent of respondents cite paying off credit-card or bank debts, car expenses, education costs, and medical or dental expenses. Although this evidence is consistent with the view that payday

Table 2-10. *Correlation Matrix of Alternative Financial Services Usage*

	Payday loan	Pawn shop	Refund anticipation loan	Rent-to-own	Layaway	Cash advance on credit card	Overdraft	Cash out on a pension
Pawnshop	0.200							
Refund anticipation loans	0.124	0.151						
Rent-to-own	0.136	0.171	0.187					
Layaway	0.027	0.041	0.192	0.086				
Cash advance	0.133	0.073	-0.009	-0.014	0.105			
Overdraft	0.196	0.057	0.092	0.105	0.144	0.193		
Cash out pension	0.105	0.017	0.077	0.040	0.021	0.119	0.065	
Any AFS[a]	0.101	0.184	0.276	0.125	0.306	0.076	0.141	0.011

Source: Detroit Area Household Financial Services study.

a. Includes pawnshops, rent-to-own stores, refund anticipation loans, money orders, and layaway.

Table 2-11. *Use of Recent Loan, Conditioned on Having Most Recently Taken Out a Payday Loan*[a]

Percent

Use of loan	Percentage
Everyday expenses (bills, food, gas, and so on)	59.5
Gift to a relative or friend	3.2
Car or transportation	7.7
Auto repair	2.3
Vacation, entertainment, casinos, dog racing, leisure	3.2
Education, tuition	7.7
Legal expenses, tickets	3.2
Medical or dental expenses	5.9
Debt consolidation, credit card debt, bank debt	10.9
Just to have money, to have cash, "just to see if I could get it"	3.2

Source: Detroit Area Household Financial Services study.

a. Respondents were allowed up to two responses.

borrowers take out loans when their income cannot meet their expenses, it is possible that their prior spending on nonnecessities crowded out spending on necessities and thus led to high-cost borrowing through payday loans. Future research would need to include data on consumption patterns to better understand these borrowing decisions.

Respondents who use payday lenders often use them multiple times, including by "rolling over" existing loans into new ones. The most common number of loans or cash advances (for those with at least one) in the past year is two (31 percent), with three and four times being the next most common (19.9 and 14.2 percent). Estimates regarding repeat loans are far smaller than is found in other studies. The median number of loans in the sample is three in the past year, in stark contrast to studies such as that by Gregory Elliehausen and Edward Lawrence (2001, table 5-11), who report a median between five and six loans.

It is possible that the measure does not fully capture rollovers when respondents were asked, "How many times have you taken a loan . . . ?" Separately, the survey asked specifically about rollovers: of those who use a payday lender, 40.2 percent paid a fee to postpone paying back the loan, but the survey results do not permit analysis of how often; an additional 14.3 percent took a loan from one payday lender to pay back a loan from a different payday lender. Overall, the rollover experiences of the payday borrowers in the sample suggest that the costs of repeated borrowing may be high. Nonetheless, the study does not find evidence that rollovers are as extensive as reported elsewhere.

The most important reasons given for going to payday lenders among other credit options are the convenience and accessible hours of the payday outlet (23.6 percent), the expectation of being approved for the loan

Table 2-12. *Total Indebtedness and Net Assets, by Banked Status*[a]

Dollars unless otherwise noted

Characteristic	Banked	Unbanked
Total indebtedness		
Mean	35,056	8,365
	(7,407)	(1,392)
Median	10,230	0
Net assets (assets − debts)		
Mean	103,965	25,029
	(42,278)	(4,404)
Median	38,800	1,500
Sample size	668	270

Source: Detroit Area Household Financial Services study.

a. Standard errors in parentheses. "Total indebtedness" is an aggregated dollar value of all debts and liabilities. Net assets aggregates the value of assets and subtracts out the respondent's debts and liabilities.

(22 percent), and the need for a small amount of money or money to pay a bill (19.2 percent).

Despite the high costs, customers choose payday lenders over other possible sources of credit in part because they have been recently turned down by lower-priced alternatives and are confident that they will be approved for a payday loan. To the extent that borrowers need access to credit during emergencies, payday lenders may fill a critical need. At the same time, payday lenders charge high fees, and many borrowers find it difficult to repay payday loans when they come due. These borrowers often pay additional fees to postpone or "roll over" payments, or they borrow from one payday lender to pay back another. In this way, payday borrowers may get into further financial difficulties.

Overall Levels of Indebtedness and Net Worth

Given significant debt levels and low levels of asset holding, not surprisingly, net worth among LMI households is relatively low. Net worth is strongly connected to income. The mean and median net worths of respondents are significantly higher for those above the poverty level than for those below. The median net worth of those whose income is above the poverty line is about $38,000, while those with incomes below the poverty line hold about $1,000. Banked households have higher levels of debt and assets, and higher levels of net worth, than the unbanked, even relative to income. As table 2-12 shows, median indebtedness is approximately $10,000 among the banked and approaches $0 for the unbanked; the means are about $35,000 and $8,000, respectively. Given their higher level of asset holding, however, the banked have greater net worth (nearly $39,000) than the unbanked (only $1,500); the respective means are about $100,000 and $25,000.

Directions for Policy

The results of the Detroit study suggest that LMI households would benefit from a range of financial services products to meet their needs to receive their income, pay bills, and save. The private sector should provide straightforward and affordable bank accounts, or prepaid debit cards with similar functionality, deposit insurance, and federal protections. Rather than promoting traditional checking accounts, which often are high cost and high risk for these households, the initiative would encourage debit card–based bank accounts with no check writing, no overdraft, and no hidden or back-end fees. These accounts would not require a minimum balance or account opening balance, and given the no-overdraft restriction, they would not require complicated reviews to open. The accounts should also be made available to those who have had difficulty managing a checking account in the past, given that these accounts would not permit check writing. Funds could be accessed at automated teller machines and at the point of sale. Over time, the accounts could increase in functionality. The accounts could provide for bill payment, an automatic savings plan, and reasonable consumer credit options to compete with the AFS sector. For example, banks could offer a six-month, self-amortizing consumer loan up to $500 with direct debit from the account; such a loan would be relatively low risk and paid automatically, could be offered without the need for labor-intensive interaction with the customer, and could be offered at reasonable interest rates. The credit option could also include a savings component, in which monthly payments would include the borrower's contribution to a savings account (see Bair 2005; Barr 2004, 2007).

The primary goal of public policy changes to strengthen the financial security of LMI families should be to facilitate the provision of safe and affordable bank accounts that meet the transactional, savings, and short-term credit needs of these households. Given the relatively low profit margins available to the financial sector for offering such accounts, public policy needs to provide incentives to the financial sector to provide them and should also be focused on making it easier for LMI households to get access to them. In the remainder of this section, I offer three examples of policies that would promote these twin goals.

A New Tax Credit for Safe and Affordable Accounts for Working Americans

To overcome the financial services mismatch, Congress should enact a tax credit for financial institutions to offer safe and affordable bank accounts to LMI households (see Barr 2004, 2007). The tax credit would be offered on a pay-for-performance basis, with financial institutions able to claim tax credits for a fixed amount per account opened and used by a low- to moderate-income household. The tax-credit program would be administered by the Financial Management Service, which would track bank performance, in cooperation with the

Internal Revenue Service, which would administer the reduction in the bank's quarterly withholding tax to adjust for the credits earned. The initiative could be coupled with outreach to employers to encourage direct deposit and automatic savings plans.

A New Opt-Out, Direct-Deposit Tax-Refund Account

The Financial Management Service could administer a new tax-refund account plan to improve tax administration, encourage savings, and expand access to banking services, while reducing reliance on costly refund loans (see Barr 2007). Under the plan, unbanked low-income individuals who file their tax returns would have their tax refunds directly deposited onto a prepaid debit card. Taxpayers could choose to opt out of the system if they did not want to deposit their refund directly, but the expectation is that the accounts would be widely accepted since they would significantly reduce the costs of receiving one's tax refund. Once the tax-refund account is set up through the Internal Revenue Service mechanism at tax time, households would receive their refund in the account weeks earlier than if they had to wait for a paper check. Moreover, once it is established, the account could continue to be used long past tax time. Households could also use the account just like any other bank account—to receive their income, to save, to pay bills, and the like. By using an opt-out strategy and reaching households at tax time, this approach could dramatically, efficiently, and quickly reach millions of LMI households and bring them into the banking system.

State Strategies to Move Families into the Financial Mainstream

States can adopt access to financial services as a core element of welfare-to-work strategies. For example, states now use debit card–based products for many state benefits, but these cards often do not permit direct deposit of other sources of income, and they cannot be used for other purposes or retained when benefits end. In addition, the household does not develop any transactional or credit history and cannot use the card as a means of taking care of daily financial needs. States should use more-flexible, low-cost debit cards to help families achieve greater financial stability.

Conclusion

High-cost financial services, barriers to saving, lack of insurance, and credit constraints may contribute to poverty and other socioeconomic problems. Low-income individuals often lack access to the financial services they need from banks and thrifts and turn to alternative financial services providers such as check cashers, payday lenders, and money transmitters. Many low-income households live paycheck to paycheck and are vulnerable to emergencies that might endanger their financial stability. Often lacking access to insurance, reasonably priced credit, or regular savings plans, low-income households suffering emergencies endure worse outcomes. Moreover, the lack of longer-term savings options tailored to low-income households may undermine their ability to invest in human capital or build assets over time. More generally, heavy reliance on alternative financial services reduces the value of take-home pay as well as government assistance programs, such as the earned-income tax credit. Low-income households may be able to achieve greater financial stability if the market shifts to provide more functional financial products that meet their needs.

References

Aizcorbe, Ana M., Arthur B. Kennickell, and Kevin B. Moore. 2003. "Recent Changes in U.S. Family Finances: Evidence from the 1998 and 2001 Survey of Consumer Finances." *Federal Reserve Bulletin* 89 (January): 1–32.

Bair, Sheila. 2005. *Low-Cost Payday Loans: Opportunities and Obstacles.* Report prepared for the Annie E. Casey Foundation. Amherst: University of Massachusetts, Isenberg School of Management (www.aecf.org/upload/publicationfiles/fes3622h334.pdf).

Barr, Michael S. 2004. "Banking the Poor." *Yale Journal on Regulation* 21:121–237.

———. 2007. "An Inclusive, Progressive National Savings and Financial Services Policy." *Harvard Law and Policy Review* 1:161–84.

Barr, Michael S., Ed Bachelder, and Jane K. Dokko. 2007. "Consumer Choice in Payment Cards." Working Paper. University of Michigan, Ann Arbor.

Barr, Michael S., and Rebecca M. Blank. 2009. Introduction to *Insufficient Funds: Savings, Assets, Credit, and Banking among Low-Income Households,* edited by Rebecca M. Blank and Michael S. Barr, 1–24. New York: Russell Sage Foundation.

Barr, Michael S., and Jane K. Dokko. 2007. "Paying to Save." Working Paper 79. Ann Arbor: University of Michigan, John M. Olin Center for Law and Economics.

Bucks, Brian K., and others. 2009. "Changes in U.S. Family Finances from 2004 to 2007: Evidence from the Survey of Consumer Finances." *Federal Reserve Bulletin* 95 (February): A1–A56.

Caskey, John. 1994. *Fringe Banking: Check-Cashing Outlets, Pawnshops, and the Poor.* New York: Russell Sage Foundation.

Dunham, Constance R. 2001. "The Role of Banks and Nonbanks in Serving Low- and Moderate-Income Communities." In *Changing Financial Markets and Community Development: A Federal Reserve System Research Conference,* edited by Jackson L. Blanton, Sherrie L. Rhine, and Alicia Williams. Richmond, Va.: Federal Reserve Bank of Richmond.

Dunham, Constance R., Fritz J. Scheuren, and Douglas J. Willson. 1998. "Methodological Issues in Surveying the Nonbanked Population in Urban Areas." In *Proceedings of the American Statistical Association, Survey Research Methods Section* 20:611–16.

Elliehausen, Gregory, and Edward C. Lawrence. 2001. "Payday Advance Credit in America: An Analysis of Customer Demand." Monograph 35. Washington: Georgetown University, McDonough School of Business (www.fdic.gov/bank/analytical/cfr/2005/jan/CFRSS_2005_elliehausen.pdf).

FDIC (Federal Deposit Insurance Corporation). 2009. *FDIC National Survey of Unbanked and Underbanked Households* (www.fdic.gov/householdsurvey/full_report.pdf).

Green, Paul E., and V. Srinivasan. 1978. "Conjoint Analysis in Consumer Research: Issues and Outlook." *Journal of Consumer Research* 5:103–23 (www.jstor.org/stable/2489001).

Kish, Leslie. 1949. "A Procedure for Objective Respondent Selection within the Household." *Journal of the American Statistical Association* 44:380–87 (www.jstor.org/stable/2280236).

Luce, R. Duncan, and John W. Tukey. 1964. "Simultaneous Conjoint Measurement: A New Type of Fundamental Measurement." *Journal of Mathematical Psychology* 1:1–27.

Osili, Una Okonkwo, and Anna L. Paulson. 2009. "Immigrants' Access to Financial Services and Asset Accumulation." In *Insufficient Funds: Savings, Assets, Credit, and Banking among Low-Income Households,* edited by Rebecca M. Blank and Michael S. Barr, 285–317. New York: Russell Sage Foundation.

Scholz, John Karl, and Ananth Seshadri. 2009. "The Assets and Liabilities Held by Low-Income Families." In *Insufficient Funds: Savings, Assets, Credit, and Banking among Low-Income Households,* edited by Rebecca M. Blank and Michael S. Barr, 25–65. New York: Russell Sage Foundation.

Seidman, Ellen, Moez Hababou, and Jennifer Kramer. 2005. *A Financial Services Survey of Low- and Moderate-Income Households.* Chicago: Center for Financial Services Innovation (http://cfsinnovation.com/system/files/imported/managed_documents/threecitysurvey.pdf).

3

And Banking for All?

MICHAEL S. BARR, JANE K. DOKKO, AND BENJAMIN J. KEYS

The use of alternative financial services—such as check cashers, pawnshops, and payday lenders—among low- and moderate-income (LMI) households presents challenges to policymakers seeking to improve financial outcomes among those with few economic resources. That LMI households choose these alternative financial services, in spite of their monetary cost, suggests that they value these services and would find regulations banning them outright harmful. Policies such as "lifeline" banking have aimed to make traditional bank accounts more available, but banks have generally seen these programs as unattractive and have not marketed them widely; as a result, the programs have had low participation rates and have been too limited in scope to increase the number of households with bank accounts (Doyle, Lopez, and Saidenberg 1998; Prescott and Tatar 1999; Washington 2006).

Among the demand-side explanations for low bank-account take-up, one possibility is that users of alternative financial services may not be especially sensitive to relative prices, on average, making policy interventions that solely lower the monetary costs of banking services yield low take-up rates.[1] Another possibility is that other factors influencing the demand for financial services, such as income or nonmonetary factors (for example, inertia, trust, convenience), are more important or salient to LMI households. Using "holistic" data on household balance

---

1. An alternative, supply-side explanation for low participation rates may be that banks avoid low-cost products and low-revenue customers.

sheets, financial services decisions, and expenditures on financial services from the DAHFS survey, we show that, though annual outlays on financial services are low on average, LMI households incur substantial nonpecuniary costs to obtain and use banking services, suggesting that policies focused solely on lowering the costs of bank accounts might do little to increase bank-account ownership or discourage the use of alternative financial services. Instead, improving account functionality (including convenience) may be more likely to increase demand for banking services.

Broadly speaking, our household-level survey data on financial services behavior enable us to fully measure the portfolio of financial services used by LMI households to transact, save, and borrow, which previous work could not do. We obtain financial service usage patterns, estimates of annual financial services outlays, and household demographics, socioeconomic characteristics, and attitudes from this in-person survey. Our estimates of outlays are based on self-reported use of financial services and the self-reported fees paid for these services rather than posted fees alone, which distinguishes this study from previous work that extrapolates the financial burden of financial services based on posted fees. The LMI households in our sample reported spending, on average, about 1 percent of annual income on all financial services, which suggests that many LMI households are able to avoid regular use of the most expensive financial services options. The top spenders, however, take up a disproportionate share of spending. Moreover, the economic burden of financial services for LMI households is not well measured solely by their outlays, particularly if households curtail their use of welfare-enhancing financial services in response to the high posted fees they face.

When we compare annual reported outlays on financial services between observably similar "banked" and "unbanked" households, we find that annual outlays for transactional and credit products are higher for banked households than for the unbanked. As we show, banked households are more "economically active" than unbanked households, on average, which corresponds to higher financial service use and total outlays. That is, the banked have higher annual incomes, are more likely to be employed, and have stronger labor-force attachment. Accordingly, they make more transactions and have greater access to credit (for example, through credit cards). Surprisingly, most of the outlays for the median banked household are for alternative financial services. That the banked have higher annual outlays suggests that diminished economic activity of the unbanked may contribute to their lower outlays. In addition, higher spending on financial services may not necessarily be welfare reducing for banked households if it is accompanied by the benefits of financial services associated with greater economic activity.

Furthermore, we find that LMI households incur substantial nonpecuniary costs to obtain financial services—such as waiting in line to pay bills, lacking ready mechanisms to save, and burdening friends and family with borrowing needs. The nonpecuniary costs incurred by these households include time and distance costs.[2] For instance, 37 percent of households use an in-person bill-payment center to pay their bills (typically in cash) rather than more efficient and less time-consuming payment methods such as online bill payment. Thirty percent find a nonbank—rather than a bank—the most convenient location to obtain their financial services, which may indicate relatively higher convenience costs for using banks. In addition, the nonpecuniary costs for financial services of unbanked households are higher than for banked households. These results suggest that part of the burden of the financial services system is borne through nonpecuniary channels.

Finally, in addition to being related to economic activity, having a bank account and using banking services are also closely tied with income volatility (relative to expenses) and economic insecurity. The banked are more likely to report they are economically secure in being able to meet their expenses than the unbanked and less likely to be food insufficient; these outcomes are most likely owing to higher income and employment and lower income volatility. When income cannot cover expenses, low-income banked households are more likely to borrow from a bank or credit card or spend out of savings or investments. The unbanked are less secure in their ability to meet their expenses and to obtain food sufficiency. When their income cannot cover their expenses, these low-income unbanked households are relatively more likely to use informal sources, such as family and friends, to cover the shortfall. Thus having a bank account is related to choosing a different set of financial stability actions by low-income households.

These results, which are based on more holistic data than has previously been available, suggest that policies to increase the use of banking services among LMI households deserve a nuanced approach. While previous work has shown that simply lowering the cost of bank-account ownership has only modest effects at best, our work suggests that policymakers should assess bank accounts and products along both pecuniary and nonpecuniary dimensions. In addition to low fees, attributes such as convenience, speed, simplicity, and transparency may be attractive to unbanked LMI households. New products developed with these features in mind may be more successful than previous attempts to increase bank-account ownership.

---

2. We interpret these results as suggesting that the nonpecuniary costs of financial services are high. This is, of course, open to debate. On one hand, LMI households have low wages and may have a low opportunity cost of time, suggesting that time and distance costs are lower for this group than for higher-income households. On the other hand, market wages may not fully capture the shadow costs of time and distance for LMI households, who are often constrained in the labor market, their child care options, or other responsibilities and may thus face high nonpecuniary costs of financial services.

Background

The alternative financial services (AFS) sector in the United States has grown tremendously during the past two decades. Not only have the number of outlets providing check-cashing services, payday loans, and pawnshop loans increased, but also the dollar volume of transactions occurring in the AFS sector has increased (Caskey 1994; Barr 2004; Bair 2005; Stegman 2007; Fellowes and Mabanta 2008). Around $75 billion of money orders, the largest transactional alternative financial service, are purchased from outlets other than banks or post offices, while check cashers convert approximately $60 billion of checks each year (Federal Reserve System 2007; Fellowes and Mabanta 2008).[3] Payday lenders provide $40 billion of short-term loans annually, and until recently, paid tax preparers disbursed over $25 billion of tax refunds through refund anticipation loans (Stephens Inc. 2007; Internal Revenue Service 2006).[4]

Greater visibility of alternative financial services has prompted increased attention to them among researchers, policymakers, and consumer advocates. Though relatively small in the aggregate, the AFS sector plays a significant role in the provision of financial services to low- and moderate-income households. These households, a quarter of which have no formal banking relationship, use high-fee AFS to convert their paychecks into cash, make payments, and obtain credit (Barr 2004; Bucks, Kennickell, and Moore 2006). At the same time, households with bank accounts face annual fees, minimum balance requirements, and bounced-check fees, all of which may make bank-account ownership too costly for LMI households. A key policy concern is the extent to which LMI households' use of financial services burdens them with excessive fees, reduces access to or increases the costs of credit, or minimizes opportunities for ready mechanisms to save (Barr 2004). Such barriers may contribute to financial instability among these households.

Since John Caskey's (1994) seminal work on "fringe banking," the research on financial services for the poor has emphasized the inefficiencies and inequities in the financial services system (Barr 2004; Seidman and Tescher 2005; James and Smith 2006; Fellowes and Mabanta 2008). Because the financial services system is ill suited to serve LMI households, as earlier studies argue, these households face higher pecuniary and nonpecuniary costs than they otherwise would under a system redesigned to better suit their needs (Barr 2004).[5] The

3. See also MoneyGram International (2008).

4. Because of concerns regarding the effect on tax administration of refund anticipation loan practices, beginning with the 2011 tax-filing season the Internal Revenue Service no longer provides tax preparers with a debt indicator (for example, whether a portion of the taxpayer's refund will be offset by unpaid student loans or child support), limiting the ability of paid tax preparers to offer refund anticipation loans.

5. John Caskey (1994) and Michael Barr (2004) document that fees for financial services in the AFS sector are high relative to the mainstream financial products of banks or credit unions.

economic benefits of such a system potentially include fewer numbers of unbanked households; greater ability among LMI households to smooth their consumption through lower-cost savings, borrowing, or insurance instruments; reduced stress, time, and other nonpecuniary costs of financial services; and fewer economic and material hardships among those least able to pay.[6] For instance, having an account with direct deposit and automatic savings features may increase the ability of LMI households to develop savings, which can serve to buffer shocks and increase financial stability.

The potential gains from redesigning the financial services system for LMI households depend (though not exclusively) on these households' usage patterns and annual outlays. The benefit to households from more-functional and lower-fee products may be large if LMI households are very likely to use high-fee financial services and credit, if their outlays are onerous, or if they have little opportunity to develop savings. On the other hand, lower usage of high-fee services or outlays suggests that the scope for substantially improving the financial lives of LMI households through financial services innovation is likely to be more limited and nuanced.

Motivated in part by the government's mandate that all nontax federal payments be made electronically by January 1, 1999, a number of studies have explored the prevalence of unbanked individuals and their characteristics (Booz-Allen and Hamilton and Shugoll Research 1997; Prescott and Tatar 1999; Hogarth and O'Donnell 1999; U.S. General Accounting Office 2002).[7] Although these studies have used different survey methods and surveyed different cities and neighborhoods, the profile of the unbanked that has emerged is generally consistent (Dove Consulting 2000, 2008; Rhine, Greene, and Toussaint-Comeau 2006). The unbanked are consistently found to be younger, less likely to be employed, less likely to be married, and more likely to be from a minority or immigrant population (Caskey 1994). As we discuss in greater detail in the next sections, our study corroborates this demographic description of the unbanked.

While other studies use household-level data to provide estimates of usage and outlays and to address the burden of financial services for LMI households (Dunham, Scheuren, and Willson 1998; Dunham 2000; Vermilyea and Wilcox 2002; Berry 2004; Seidman, Hababou, and Kramer 2005), these earlier works lack comprehensive information on demographics, socioeconomic characteristics, financial-service and credit usage patterns, attitudes and preferences, and

6. For evidence on the effects of bank-account ownership in the United Kingdom, see Fitzpatrick (2009).

7. The electronic-funds-transfer mandate has not yet been fully achieved (U.S. Government Accountability Office 2008), but significant progress has been made with the introduction in 2008 of the Direct Express prepaid card and new regulations mandating use of direct deposit or Direct Express in the coming years. The Direct Express card is discussed more fully in chapter 12 of this volume.

full balance-sheet information in order to quantify more precisely the burden of financial services for LMI households. Without these important measures of economic and financial services activity, attitudes, and other factors, previous studies have been unable comprehensively to measure the financial services portfolios of LMI households and to analyze the pecuniary and nonpecuniary costs of these practices.

Data and Sample

This chapter relies on surveys collected in the Detroit Area Household Financial Services survey.[8] To provide readers with a sense of the questions used in this part of the survey, this section briefly describes the exact wording of a few of the questions that are used to construct some key variables. The full instrument is available from the authors. To classify individuals and households as banked or unbanked, we asked participants whether they had a checking or savings account at a bank, savings and loan, or credit union. Following the standard in the literature, anyone with a checking or savings account was classified as banked. In a separate question, they were asked whether anyone in the household besides themselves had a bank account. In this chapter, unless otherwise noted, banked status refers to that of the individual. To determine participants' roles in the financial choices of their household, we asked, "How much do you participate in making financial decisions for the household? A lot, some, or not at all?" Similarly, as is asked in the Survey of Consumer Finances, to gauge the degree to which households shop around for financial services we asked, "When making major decisions about saving, investment, credit, or borrowing, some people shop around for the very best deal while others don't. Looking at this scale [which ranged from "almost no shopping" to "great deal of shopping"] what number would you assign to you and your household?"

To measure the dollar amount spent on transaction and credit services, henceforth called "outlays," we asked participants about the types of financial services used and how much they paid for such services. In determining what time period to use in asking respondents about their use of financial services, we consulted questions designed for previous surveys, as well the frequency of use reported in earlier work, and worked closely with survey methodologists to develop the framing of the questions. For services such as refund anticipation loans, which are tied to the annual filing of tax returns, it made little sense to ask about use in the month preceding the survey interview, since tax filing is highly concentrated in certain calendar months. For other services like payday or title loans, previous research suggested that in a sample of 1,000 households, measuring usage monthly would have provided too narrow a window to allow observation of

8. For a full discussion of the survey data and the collection methodology, see chapter 2.

behavior. For other services, such as check cashing, a monthly window seemed to be appropriate in that, because its use was expected to be at least monthly, a shorter window would allow for measuring its use.

The longest window during which we measure the use of financial services is one year. We generally estimate annual outlays by multiplying the reported fee paid with the frequency of use; for instance, if usage is measured monthly, we then multiply the monthly outlay by 12 to arrive at the annual amount. To estimate credit-card interest, we take the outstanding credit-card balance, the self-reported response about how much of this balance is for transactional purposes rather than borrowing, self-reported repayment frequency, and the credit card's annual percentage rate to infer prospectively the amount of interest likely to be paid in a year.

A benefit of our approach to measuring outlays is potentially minimizing recall bias, as respondents are generally only required to recollect one month of financial services use. On the other hand, a limitation of our approach is the risk of making errors when scaling up monthly financial services usage across a full year. If average usage is more rare than once a month, we would overestimate annual outlays for those who report use in the previous month but understate usage for those who report no use in the previous month (in fact, understating to zero annual usage). It is not a priori obvious in which direction our estimated annual outlays would be biased, and there is no clear seasonal pattern in outlays in our household surveys (which were conducted over more than six months). The reliability of our measure thus depends on averaging across similar households and the stability of the relationships between financial services usage, bank-account ownership, and income across the year.

To measure the nonpecuniary costs of financial services, we surveyed participants on a range of factors. For example, we asked what type of establishment was most convenient for them. We also asked whether they had paid any of their bills at a payment center in the past twelve months, and we asked renters whether their landlord accepted personal checks; if not, they would have to get a money order or pay in cash.

Results

This chapter focuses on the pecuniary and nonpecuniary costs facing low- and moderate-income households of using alternative and mainstream financial services. As explained further below, reported outlays average 1 percent of respondent's income, suggesting that most households are able to avoid consistently paying the high posted fees of alternative financial services. Expenditures are concentrated among top spenders. Households generally face high nonpecuniary costs of financial services, and bank-account ownership is correlated with income stability. To place these costs in contexts, we note that low- and moderate-income households in the Detroit area face low employment rates and high rates of poverty (see table 3-1). Fifty-four percent of respondents are employed at the time of the survey interview, and the median household income in 2004 is $20,000. Around one-third of respondents have household incomes that place their households below the federal poverty line.

Accounts and Transaction Services

Twenty-nine percent of the sample does not have either a checking or savings account, in line with the LMI subsample of the national Survey of Consumer Finances that suggests that roughly 20 million families are unbanked (Bucks, Kennickell, and Moore 2006; Bucks and others 2009). Notably, these unbanked respondents are less economically active: they are less likely to be employed than the banked (42 percent versus 59 percent), have substantially lower median household income ($10,000 versus $25,000), and are much more likely to live in poverty (51 percent versus 26 percent). The regression results shown in table 3-2 present descriptive relationships between bank-account ownership and demographic characteristics. Those who are employed at the time of the survey interview are 12 percentage points more likely than the unemployed or those not in the labor force to have a bank account.

Respondents who report that they participate "a lot" or "some" in their households' financial decisionmaking are substantially more likely to have a bank account, suggesting that reported financial decisionmaking is correlated with reported behavior. To proxy for households' opportunity costs of time, we include an indicator variable for whether the household usually shops around "a lot" or "a little" for financial services (the omitted category is "some"). Those who shop around "a little," which may indicate a higher opportunity cost of time, are slightly less likely to have a bank account than those who shop around "a lot" or "some."

Notably, even when providing a full set of controls for income, education, and employment status (in column 3), we observe large, unexplained racial differences in bank-account ownership: African American respondents are 12 percentage points less likely to have a bank account than their nonblack counterparts in the survey. In fact, including the additional covariates has no impact on the magnitude of the estimated relationship between race and bank-account ownership. This striking racial difference persists even in the presence of better measures of financial activity and financial management than those previously available in other surveys.

Despite relatively low levels of economic activity, LMI households regularly use financial services, as can be seen in tables 3-3 and 3-4. Table 3-3 describes the usage patterns for transactional services among all, banked, and unbanked respondents. Consistent with the findings of John Caskey (1997) and Constance Dunham (2000), the use of mainstream transactional services among

Table 3-1. *Characteristics of Sample Members, by Banked Status*[a]
Percent unless otherwise noted

	Census	All	Banked	Unbanked
Black	70.5	69.1	65.3	78.3
White	21.8	20.4	23.1	13.6
Arab	n.a.	1.9	2.0	1.5
Other	7.7	8.6	9.5	6.5
Female	52.3	66.3	66.5	65.6
		(1.6)	(2.3)	(3.4)
Less than high school diploma	35.8	29.6	26.6	37.1
High school diploma or GED	31.0	23.0	19.1	32.7
Greater than high school diploma	33.2	47.4	54.3	30.2
Employed at interview	44.5[b]	54.3	59.3	41.9
Unemployed at interview[c]	8.2	5.8	3.9	10.7
Not in labor force at interview[d]	47.0	39.9	36.8	47.5
Age (years)	n.a.	43.5	44.9	40.0
		(1.0)	(1.1)	(1.2)
Born in the United States	92.7	92.1	90.5	95.9
		(1.9)	(2.4)	(1.4)
Single or never married	44.1	45.6	37.7	65.1
Married and living with spouse	24.5	19.7	24.0	9.1
Living with partner	n.a.	4.1	3.7	5.0
Separated, widowed, or divorced	31.3	30.6	34.6	20.9
Households with no children	n.a.	67.2	70.6	58.9
		(2.2)	(2.5)	(4.3)
Total household monthly income (dollars)	n.a.	2,248	2,703	1,156
		(334)	(439)	(399)
Annual household income in 2004 (dollars)	n.a.	28,435	33,224	17,078
		(2,118)	(2,573)	(1,467)
Median household income in 2004 (dollars)	24,146	20,000	25,000	10,000
Living below poverty line	31.5	33.2	26.2	50.5
		(2.4)	(2.5)	(3.9)
Sample size	626[e]	938	668	270

Source: Detroit Area Household Financial Services study.

a. Standard errors are in parentheses. Poverty guidelines come from the Department of Health and Human Services (http://aspe.hhs.gov/poverty/04poverty.shtml).

b. Based on civilian employment rate.

c. Percentage of people currently unemployed who are in the labor market.

d. Includes respondents who said they were retired, homemakers, or students, did not have the required documentation, or chose not to work.

e. Consists of census tracts in the Detroit metropolitan area (Wayne, Oakland, and Macomb Counties) with median income under $36,073 (80 percent of the Detroit metropolitan area's median $49,051).

Table 3-2. *Estimated Relationship between Bank-Account Ownership and Socioeconomic Outcomes Using Linear Probability Model*[a]

	Dependent variable is individual bank-account ownership		
	(1)	*(2)*	*(3)*
Age	0.004***	0.005***	0.005***
	(0.001)	(0.001)	(0.001)
Black	−0.100***	−0.111***	−0.121***
	(0.037)	(0.035)	(0.036)
Female	0.037	0.059	0.045
	(0.044)	(0.043)	(0.043)
Married	0.136***	0.079**	0.076**
	(0.036)	(0.035)	(0.037)
Citizen	−0.062	0.035	0.041
	(0.132)	(0.119)	(0.115)
Education			
Less than high school		−0.115***	−0.103***
		(0.031)	(0.032)
High school or GED		−0.174***	−0.164***
		(0.048)	(0.049)
Income		0.001**	0.001**
		(0.000)	(0.000)
Living below poverty line		−0.090	−0.080
		(0.055)	(0.055)
Employment status			
Employed		0.115***	0.119***
		(0.058)	(0.055)
Unemployed		−0.018	−0.002
		(0.051)	(0.049)
Financial participation			
A lot			0.225***
			(0.060)
Some			0.169**
			(0.071)
Shopping around			
A lot			−0.010
			(0.046)
A little			−0.059*
			(0.033)
Constant	0.615***	0.480***	0.298*
	(0.151)	(0.161)	(0.159)
R^2	0.05	0.15	0.17
Sample size	930	925	921

Source: Detroit Area Household Financial Services study.

a. Standard errors are in parentheses. All estimates are weighted. Clustered standard errors are reported to account for stratified sampling design. Reference category consists of individuals who are not black, male, not married, not U.S. citizens, have some college or more, are not in poverty, are out of the labor force, participate in financial decisionmaking "a little," and shop around for financial services "some."

*Statistically significant at the 10 percent level, two-tailed test.
**Statistically significant at the 5 percent level, two-tailed test.
***Statistically significant at the 1 percent level, two-tailed test.

Table 3-3. *Use of Transactional Financial Services in Month Preceding Survey Interview, by Banked Status*
Percent unless otherwise noted

	All	Banked	Unbanked
How income is received			
Direct deposit[a]	44.7	62.9	0
Check	54.3	50.5	63.6
Cash	20.7	17.1	29.5
Bridge card	21.6	14.0	40.5
Check casher	5.0	5.9	2.7
Cashes checks	41.2	50.0	19.5
Number of checks cashed[b]	2.6	2.8	2.1
How income is converted			
By cashing check[c]	n = 404	n = 265	n = 139
At a bank	93.4	96.1	83.1
At a check casher	21.4	16.3	30.7
At workplace	5.2	5.1	5.5
By signing over to family or friend	8.5	4.6	15.4
At grocery or liquor store	33.3	20.7	55.7
How bills are paid			
Personal check	44.2	62.1	0
Automated payment	23.0	32.3	0
Money order	52.1	47.6	63.2
Uses money orders	68	64	77
Uses nonbank wire transfers	23	22	26
Sample size	938	668	270

Source: Detroit Area Household Financial Services study.
a. Only asked of banked respondents.
b. Conditional on receiving income by check.
c. Conditional on having cashed a check at least once in the month preceding interview.

respondents is not large, and AFS use is nearly as widespread as mainstream use (the "All" column). Furthermore, having a bank account does not preclude the use of alternative financial services, and not having a bank account does not preclude using banks (for example, to cash checks).

Receiving income and paying bills are core financial services. Only 45 percent of LMI households in our study receive their income through direct deposit, although the figures for banked households are about the same as the 70 percent of Americans nationally who use direct deposit (Federal Reserve Board 2004). Other common methods include checks (54 percent), cash (21 percent), and Bridge cards (22 percent) (Michigan's electronic-benefits-transfer card). On average, 41 percent of respondents cash checks, and those who do so cash an average of 2.6 checks a month, banks being the dominant check-cashing institution, followed by grocery or liquor stores and check cashers. Money orders (52 percent) and personal checks (44 percent) are the most common methods of bill payment. More generally, 68 percent use money orders for both bills and other purposes. Finally, nearly one-quarter of the sample transfers money within the United States through wire transfer outlets, such as Western Union or MoneyGram.

Banked and unbanked respondents differ in their use of transactional services: generally speaking, the unbanked are less likely to use mainstream services and more likely to use AFS. The unbanked are more likely than the banked to receive their income through checks (64 percent versus 51 percent) or cash (30 versus 17 percent); they are also more likely to receive public assistance through a Bridge card (41 versus 14 percent), reflecting their relatively lower levels of self-sufficiency. The unbanked are more likely to cash checks, on average, but those who cash checks convert about the same number of checks each month as the banked.[9] Although banks are the modal institution cashing unbanked respondents' checks, the unbanked are less likely than banked households to frequent banks (83 versus 96 percent) and more likely to use check cashers (31 versus 16 percent) and grocery or liquor stores (56 versus 21 percent) to cash checks. The unbanked also are more likely to use money orders to pay bills or for other purposes and more likely to rely on friends or family to cash their checks on their behalf. Interestingly, the banked and unbanked are equally likely to use domestic wire transfers, suggesting that the use of these services may depend on the bank-account status of the receiving party rather than of the sending party.

Short-Term Credit

Respondents' use of credit products largely mirrors their use of transactional services: mainstream and AFS products are about equally used. Table 3-4 presents the usage patterns for credit products among all, banked, and unbanked respondents. Refund anticipation loans are the most common form of short-term borrowing (28 percent), followed by overdrawing an account (20 percent). Using pawnshops and taking credit-card cash advances are other commonly used borrowing methods (11 and 8 percent, respectively). Few survey respondents take out payday loans (3 percent). Because a bank account and proof of employment are required, most respondents may be too disadvantaged to qualify for such loans.[10] Overall, half of LMI households do not use any short-term credit products.

---

9. Though the point estimate for the average number of checks cashed by the unbanked is lower than for the banked, this difference is not statistically significant.

10. Consistent with this finding, Gregory Elliehausen (2006) and Matthew Fellowes and Mia Mabanta (2008) also note that generally speaking, payday customers earn more income than pawnshop borrowers.

Table 3-4. *Use of Credit Products in Three Years Preceding Survey Interview, by Banked Status*
Percent unless otherwise noted

Product	All	Banked	Unbanked
Short-term borrowing			
Refund anticipation loan	27.7	23.7	37.1
Pawnshop	11.2	7.2	21.1
Overdraft from account	20.3	24.1	10.9
Cash advance from credit card	7.9	10.1	2.3
Pension or retirement account	6.9	8.4	3.1
Rent-to-own	5.3	5.4	5.2
Payday loan	3.4	3.9	1.9
Title loan	1.1	1.3	0.7
Any short-term loan[a]	49.3	50.7	48.8
Has credit card	41	53	12
Sample size	938	668	270

Source: Detroit Area Household Financial Services study.
a. Unlike the previous categories, which are individual methods of borrowing, this category includes borrowing through any of the above methods.

Banked and unbanked respondents use short-term credit products to differing degrees: broadly, the unbanked are more likely to use products from the AFS sector and less likely to use mainstream products. However, because banked respondents also use alternative financial services, the usage patterns in table 3-4 suggest that merely having a bank account does not translate into exclusive participation in the financial mainstream. Use of refund anticipation loans and pawnshops is significantly higher among the unbanked than the banked (37 versus 28 percent and 21 versus 7 percent, respectively), while bank overdrafts and credit-card cash advances are used less by the currently unbanked than the banked (11 versus 24 percent and 2 versus 10 percent, respectively).[11] Notably, however, the unbanked are much less likely to have access to a credit card (12 versus 53 percent), and this lack of access may contribute to their use of other types of credit.

Aggregating all products in the mainstream and alternative sectors, however, banked and unbanked respondents make use of short-term borrowing at the same rate (even though banked households borrow more in dollar terms than the unbanked). This finding is somewhat surprising in that the unbanked are not as economically active as the banked. That is, lack of employment corresponds to

11. Because the horizon for the question is "use in the last three years," some respondents who are unbanked at the time of the survey may have used bank overdraft at some point in the three previous years.

Table 3-5. *Annual Outlays on Transactional and Credit Services, by Banked Status*
Units as noted

	All	Banked	Unbanked
Median transactional outlays (dollars)	99	101	83
As percent of annual income	1.2	0.4	1.5
As percent of outlays on AFS	58	67	73
Transactional outlays, 90th percentile (dollars)	324	336	301
Median credit outlays (dollars)	41	57	0
As percent of annual income	0.2	0.4	0
As percent of outlays on AFS	39	49	0
Credit outlays, 90th percentile (dollars)	397	453	184
Median total annual outlays (dollars)	185	206	123
As percent of annual income	1.2	2.7	1.0
As percent of outlays on AFS	53	36	62
Annual outlays, 90th percentile (dollars)	615	693	446
Sample size	938	668	270

Source: Detroit Area Household Financial Services study.

lower use of transactional services but not to lower use of short-term credit products. One explanation might be that the unbanked in the sample are more likely to experience hardships such as food insufficiency and eviction, and may borrow to cope with these hardships (or may be unable to cope without borrowing). Credit use is integral to these households' ability to manage their regular needs.

In addition to these usage patterns, we construct estimates of annual outlays on transactional and credit services in table 3-5 for all, banked, and unbanked respondents. These outlays represent the fees that households incur annually for the financial services they consume. The Detroit study measures the fees that households report they faced in their most recent transaction or borrowing. We annualize these fees and assume that the cross-sectional variation in fees roughly mirrors the time (month-to-month) variation, so that taking the cross-sectional average over the sample yields a good approximation of what we would report if we could have measured spending on financial services every month. Fees that households incur from the mainstream sector include annual bank-account fees, check-writing and check-cashing fees, insufficient-funds fees, bank overdraft charges, annual credit-card fees, and cash-advance fees. Alternative financial services fees include those from using money orders, check cashers, domestic remittances, payday loans, refund anticipation loans, pawnshops, and title loans.

Low- and moderate-income households face a vast array of high-fee services in both the mainstream and alternative sectors (Caskey 1994; Barr 2004;

Fellowes and Mabanta 2008). In addition, these fees are often complicated and confusing. Posted fees of financial services alone, however, do not fully depict how much households spend on financial services; the quantity of services consumed also matters. Our estimates of annual outlays incorporate both the respondents' reporting of incurred fees of financial services and the quantity of services consumed.

We find that outlays on financial services are, on average, low. As seen in table 3-5, median total annual outlays on transactions and short-term credit are only \$185.[12] Table 3-5 contextualizes the outlays as a percentage of annual income for households at the 50th percentile of the outlay distribution, which is estimated at around 1 percent. The table also reports the share of outlays spent in the AFS sector. We hold fixed the "median household" when contextualizing the outlays because, for example, households at the 50th percentile of the outlay distribution may be (and are) different from the households at the median of the annual income distribution. Because computing the median is not a linear operator, the estimates in the first column of table 3-5 are generally not weighted averages of the corresponding estimates for banked and unbanked respondents.

The median outlay for transactions is \$99, less than 1 percent of the annual income of the households at the 50th percentile of the transactional outlay distribution. Households at the median allocate roughly half of this amount to services obtained in the AFS sector. In addition, the share of outlays going to the AFS sector is roughly constant across the distribution of transactional outlays (not shown). Consistent with Edward Prescott and Daniel Tatar (1999) and Dunham (2000), the distribution of transactional outlays is very skewed to the right (see figure 3-1), and 10 percent of households spend more than \$324 annually on transactional services (or 1.5 percent of the annual income of these households). Put somewhat differently, 35 percent of all households' annual transactional outlays are concentrated among the top 10 percent of households.

Table 3-5 further shows that the median outlay for credit is \$41, which is a small share of annual income among the households at the 50th percentile of the credit outlay distribution. Less than half of this amount is for AFS products, and this share is roughly constant across the credit outlay distribution (not shown). Similar to the distribution for transactional outlays, the credit distribution is also very skewed to the right: 10 percent of households spend more than \$397 to obtain credit (between 3 and 15 percent of annual income).[13] Fifty-seven percent

12. In addition to annual outlays, we explored constructing quantity-adjusted outlays to account for differential intensity of use of financial services across households. We found constructing and interpreting the latter challenging, as financial services are not easily countable. For instance, refund anticipation loans, which can only be taken out once a year, are not expressed in the same "units" as cashing a check, which can occur multiple times per year.

13. The average among these households is around 5 percent.

Figure 3-1. *Distribution of Annual Outlays on Transactional Services*

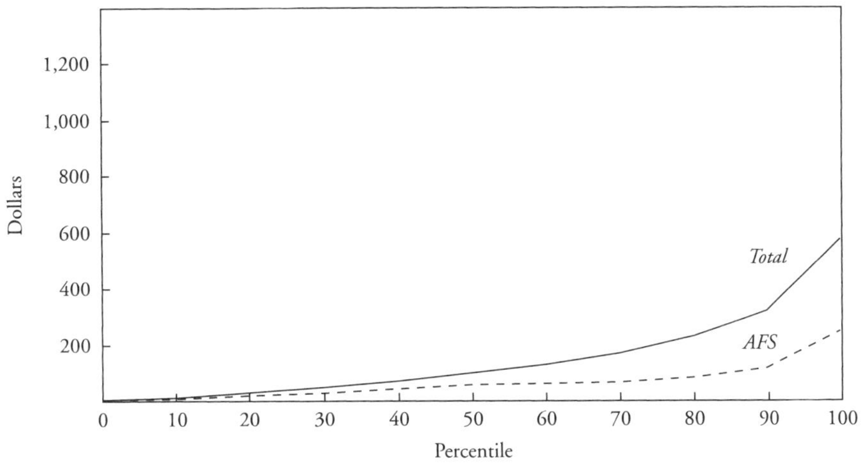

Source: Detroit Area Household Financal Services study.

of all households' annual credit outlays are concentrated among the top 10 percent of households (see figure 3-2).

Banked and unbanked differences in annual outlays are presented in table 3-5. Interestingly, median outlays on transactional and credit services for the banked respondents are higher than for the unbanked ($101 versus $83 and $57 versus $0, respectively).[14] This is also true at the 90th percentile of the two distributions of outlays. In spite of having access to (arguably) lower-fee financial services, the banked spend more than the unbanked. Looking first at transactional services, despite spending more, the banked spend a smaller share of their income than the unbanked (0.4 percent versus 1.5 percent), although overall, the levels of spending are quite low. As a share of income, the median banked household spends more than the median unbanked household on credit services, and this is entirely a by-product of having access to more forms of credit and borrowing more in dollar terms. That the banked spend more on financial services and credit contrasts with a model suggesting that bank-account ownership reduces total financial services outlays.[15]

14. Even when looking at the fees per transaction, the banked spend more than the unbanked because of their greater use of transactions requiring a nontrivial, one-time payment (for example, bank-account annual fees, tax preparation fees). These results are available upon request.

15. The median total annual outlays for the banked and unbanked differ by $80, but there is a large difference in the fraction of annual income that this constitutes (2.7 percent for banked compared with 1.0 percent for unbanked). This is largely a result of an anomalously low income for the median household. Other households near the median total outlays had larger annual incomes and as a percentage of total income fees were on the order of 1.3 to 1.4 percent.

Figure 3-2. *Credit Services*

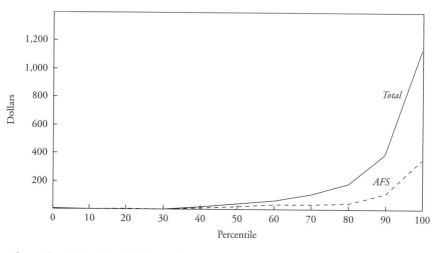

Source: Detroit Area Household Financial Services study.

In previous research, a common calculation to illustrate the high burden of fees entails calculating the hypothetical fees an unbanked household faces to convert $20,000 of income annually at a check cashing outlet. Based on the posted fees of check cashers, this household pays between $400 and $600 annually, or 2–3 percent of annual income and a nontrivial charge for a service that for many households is free. In contrast, survey evidence from the Detroit area suggests much smaller expenditures, as the median annual outlays for transactional and credit services are $99 and $41, respectively. While we acknowledge that these figures may be lower than actually incurred because of respondents' recall problems or other factors, a comparison of respondents' answers to pricing questions with actual pricing information obtained from financial service providers in the Detroit area suggests that these factors, on average, do not substantially bias reported fee levels paid, although under-reporting of usage is possible, as in other expenditure surveys.[16] Consistent with their usage patterns, LMI households allocate their spending to both AFS and mainstream products.

The banked and unbanked allocate their outlays differently between the mainstream and alternative sectors. Surprisingly, for the median banked household, 67 percent of transactional outlays go toward AFS rather than banking services (and this share is relatively constant across the transactional outlays distribution). In contrast, 73 percent of the median unbanked household's transactional

16. We conducted a mail survey to gain insight into Detroit-area formal and informal financial service providers' pricing structure and costs. Further details are available from the authors upon request.

outlays are spent in the AFS sector (largely reflecting the fact that the unbanked, by definition, are not a part of the financial mainstream). Higher up in the fee distribution, this fraction is lower but still high, at around 85–90 percent. With respect to credit, the median banked household allocates 49 percent of its annual credit outlays to AFS products, while the median unbanked household does not borrow.

The finding that the banked spend more than the unbanked is further supported by the data in table 3-6, which reports coefficients from ordinary least squares (OLS) and least absolute deviations (LAD, or median) regressions of annual outlays on a dummy for bank-account ownership and a vector of characteristics. In addition to the OLS coefficients, we report results from fitting the conditional median because the distribution of outlays is very skewed to the right and applying OLS may thus overstate the banked-unbanked differences in outlays. The control variables in columns 1 and 2 include age, an indicator variable equal to one if the respondent is black, a female dummy, a married dummy, and a citizenship dummy. The coefficient on having a bank account describes how spending differs, on average, between banked and unbanked households, holding other observable characteristics constant. This coefficient is about half as large ($67 versus $133) when estimating the conditional median function rather than the conditional mean.[17] The inclusion of additional covariates (education, employment status, income, and financial participation) reduces the OLS and LAD coefficients on banked status to $87 and $18, respectively, in columns 5 and 6. These coefficients remain significantly higher than for those individuals without bank accounts once one includes additional covariates.

Greater spending among the banked on financial services is robust to the inclusion of factors such as income. In addition, bank accounts may not necessarily mitigate the cost of financial services, particularly if the quantity of services consumed increases proportionally more than the costs of financial services upon becoming banked. On a final note, an important omitted variable in table 3-6 is a household's demand for transactional financial services and short-term credit, which is likely to differ among banked and unbanked households. This omission, along with many other unobserved differences between the banked and unbanked, as well as issues with specifying the conditional expectations or median functions, may account for the higher outlays among the banked.

To test the robustness of the finding that the banked spend more on both transactional services and short-term credit, tables 3-7 and 3-8 repeat the analysis in table 3-6 for these two types of outlays separately. Looking at both tables, the

17. With quantile regression, estimated coefficients indicate how the conditional median, for example, changes with a marginal change in the independent variable. However, although discrete changes in the independent variable may correspond to a shift into a different quantile, the 50th percentile of the distribution of outlays has both banked and unbanked respondents.

Table 3-6. *Regression-Adjusted Differences in Annual Outlays for Banked and Unbanked Respondents*[a]

			Dependent variable is total annual outlays			
	OLS (1)	LAD (2)	OLS (3)	LAD (4)	OLS (5)	LAD (6)
Has bank	133***	66.8***	94.0***	19.4	87.0***	17.8
account	(26.1)	(18.9)	(24.4)	(16.3)	(24.1)	(15.4)
Age	−3.19***	−3.01***	−2.63***	−1.47**	−2.86***	−1.67**
	(0.508)	(0.483)	(.659)	(0.624)	(0.627)	(0.576)
Black	82.1***	37.9*	74.4***	13.4	68.9***	9.33
	(22.1)	(22.2)	(22.3)	(17.8)	(20.6)	(18.0)
Female	−16.8	8.9	−2.2	38.6**	−5.6	35.4**
	(25.4)	(16.9)	(25.8)	(15.8)	(25.7)	(16.8)
Married	73.7***	71.4***	42.5	50.2**	45.8	38.9
	(24.2)	(22.7)	(28.0)	(25.3)	(28.6)	(24.1)
Citizen	−30.8	70.2	−11.6	123.6	−19.0	99.1
	(163)	(159)	(185)	(292)	(187)	(294)
Education						
Less than high			−52.2*	−27.6	−50.7*	−24.9
school			(28.1)	(18.4)	(29.1)	(17.1)
High school or			−30.1	−21.0	−29.1	−26.6
GED			(27.9)	(16.2)	(26.7)	(16.1)
Income			1.51**	2.04***	1.59***	1.92***
			(0.589)	(0.687)	(0.605)	(0.716)
Living below			−8.25	12.4	−6.11	12.5
poverty line			(30.8)	(24.1)	(30.2)	(24.1)
Employment status						
Employed			20.4	90.2***	12.4	82.9***
			(32.9)	(26.8)	(33.4)	(26.6)
Unemployed			−23.7	−8.6	−24.8	−10.1
			(40.8)	(20.4)	(41.6)	(21.2)
Financial participation						
A lot					104.0***	78.2***
					(29.3)	(23.2)
Some					55.3	57.3*
					(35.1)	(34.3)
Shopping around						
A lot					62.5*	8.3
					(33.6)	(23.2)
A little					36.2	−4.7
					(23.9)	(14.6)
Constant	288.0	159.0	254.0	−13.2	172.0	−37.1
	(171)	(159)	(189)	(290)	(192)	(292)
R^2	0.06	0.05	0.08	0.10	0.09	0.10
Sample size	930	930	925	925	921	921

Source: Detroit Area Household Financial Services study.

a. Standard errors are in parentheses. All estimates are weighted. For OLS regressions, clustered standard errors are reported to account for the stratified sampling design. For LAD regressions, bootstrap standard errors based on 1,000 replications are reported to account for the stratified sampling design. Pseudo R^2 reported for LAD regressions. Reference category consists of individuals who are not black, male, not married, not U.S. citizens, have some college or more, are not in poverty, are out of the labor force, participate in financial decision making "a little," and shop around for financial services "some."

*Statistically significant at the 10 percent level, two-tailed test.

**Statistically significant at the 5 percent level, two-tailed test.

***Statistically significant at the 1 percent level, two-tailed test.

Table 3-7. *Regression-Adjusted Differences in Annual Transactional Outlays for Banked and Unbanked Respondents*[a]

	Dependent variable is total annual transactional outlays					
	OLS	LAD	OLS	LAD	OLS	LAD
	(1)	(2)	(3)	(4)	(5)	(6)
Has bank account	34.4**	17.8	10.0	−6.14	4.4	−10.6
	(14.3)	(13.1)	(13.2)	(12.5)	(13.4)	(10.8)
Age	−2.40***	−1.97***	−2.09***	−1.34***	−2.11***	−1.56***
	(0.311)	(0.313)	(0.411)	(0.335)	(0.400)	(0.359)
Black	29.6***	22.6**	24.6*	22.0**	21.3*	18.2*
	(13.2)	(11.0)	(12.9)	(10.5)	(12.6)	(10.0)
Female	2.21	−0.85	13.50	13.10	9.54	6.40
	(12.5)	(11.6)	(12.1)	(10.8)	(12.0)	(10.1)
Married	22.7*	38.0***	−0.1	6.4	−0.7	9.7
	(12.6)	(13.8)	(13.7)	(11.2)	(13.6)	(10.3)
Citizen	−6.92	15.2	3.0	31.3	1.03	10.2
	(56.5)	(91.6)	(68.4)	(116.0)	(74.2)	(118.0)
Education						
Less than high school			−6.9	−23.8	−2.2	−10.4
			(15.1)	(10.5)	(15.8)	(11.1)
High school or GED			−2.0	−14.0	1.8	−13.4
			(16.2)	(10.5)	(15.8)	(11.3)
Income			1.03***	0.64**	1.03***	0.64
			(0.316)	(0.380)	(0.319)	(0.427)
Living below poverty line			−13.8	−23.0	−12.8	−25.0
			(14.7)	(13.9)	(14.7)	(15.5)
Employment status						
Employed			18.7	37.4**	16.8	22.3
			(20.3)	(15.8)	(21.2)	(16.5)
Unemployed			−20.5	−10.3	−19.8	−25.1*
			(21.0)	(13.6)	(21.9)	(14.6)
Financial participation						
A lot					55.7***	45.8***
					(17.5)	(15.7)
Some					31.7	18.4
					(23.7)	(18.5)
Shopping around						
A lot					18.4	12.1
					(20.3)	(15.9)
A little					−15.0	−15.1
					(10.4)	(9.4)
Constant	218***	152*	187***	106	150**	123
	(56.5)	(89.6)	(66.5)	(113.0)	(73.8)	(107.0)
R^2	0.05	0.04	0.09	0.08	0.10	0.09
Sample size	930	930	925	925	921	921

Source: Detroit Area Household Financial Services study.

a. Standard errors in parentheses. All estimates are weighted. For OLS regressions, clustered standard errors are reported to account for the stratified sampling design. For LAD regressions, bootstrap standard errors based on 1,000 replications are reported to account for the stratified sampling design. Pseudo R^2 reported for LAD regressions. Reference category consists of individuals who are not black, male, not married, not U.S. citizens, have some college or more, are not in poverty, are out of the labor force, participate in financial decisionmaking "a little," and shop around for financial services "some."

*Statistically significant at the 10 percent level, two-tailed test.

**Statistically significant at the 5 percent level, two-tailed test.

***Statistically significant at the 1 percent level, two-tailed test.

Table 3-8. *Regression-Adjusted Differences in Annual Short-Term Credit Outlays for Banked and Unbanked Respondents*[a]

	Dependent variable is total annual short-term credit outlays					
	OLS (1)	LAD (2)	OLS (3)	LAD (4)	OLS (5)	LAD (6)
Has bank account	99.0***	37.5***	84.0***	18.6**	82.5***	15.7**
	(17.60)	(9.61)	(16.90)	(7.34)	(16.70)	(6.39)
Age	−0.797**	0.000	−0.543	0.082	−0.750*	0.005
	(0.371)	(0.047)	(0.463)	(0.107)	(0.417)	(0.115)
Black	52.5***	−0.0	49.8***	8.4	47.6***	8.3
	(15.9)	(7.9)	(16.1)	(6.5)	(15.3)	(6.5)
Female	−19.0	0.0	−15.7	5.8	−15.1	4.8
	(22.5)	(1.1)	(22.7)	(4.7)	(23.1)	(4.9)
Married	51.0**	17.7	42.6*	25.4**	46.5**	28.5***
	(20.1)	(14.1)	(22.6)	(11.0)	(23.1)	(10.1)
Citizen	−23.9	20.7	−14.6	25.1	−20.0	28.7
	(121.0)	(28.1)	(135.0)	(19.3)	(133.0)	(18.6)
Education						
Less than high school diploma			−45.3*	−13.4*	−48.5**	−13.3**
			(23.3)	(6.9)	(23.7)	(5.9)
High school diploma or GED			−28.2	−10.6	−30.9	−11.7*
			(24.5)	(6.8)	(24.1)	(6.1)
Income			0.482*	0.307	0.560**	0.359
			(0.493)	(0.283)	(0.506)	(0.295)
Living below poverty line			5.51	21.23	6.69	3.15
			(28.50)	(7.04)	(27.80)	(7.47)
Employment status						
Employed			1.69	11.10	−4.33	13.70**
			(26.2)	(6.3)	(26.0)	(6.2)
Unemployed			−3.11	2.62	−5.08	2.64
			(31.4)	(4.3)	(31.6)	(4.6)
Financial participation						
A lot					48.20**	−1.49
					(19.80)	(7.41)
Some					23.6	−11.8
					(21.60)	(7.38)
Shopping around						
A lot					44.10*	2.85
					(24.50)	(6.41)
A little					51.20**	3.41
					(21.30)	(4.95)
Constant	70.3	−20.7	67.2	−36.8	21.8	−37.3*
	(131.0)	(27.8)	(143.0)	(20.0)	(140.0)	(20.2)
R^2	0.034	0.034	0.041	0.039	0.049	0.040
Sample size	930	930	925	925	921	921

Source: Detroit Area Household Financial Services study.

a. Standard errors are in parentheses. All estimates are weighted. For OLS regressions, clustered standard errors are reported to account for the stratified sampling design. For LAD regressions, bootstrap standard errors based on 1,000 replications are reported to account for the stratified sampling design. Pseudo R^2 reported for LAD regressions. Reference category consists of individuals who are not black, male, not married, not U.S. citizens, have some college or more, are not in poverty, are out of the labor force, participate in financial decisionmaking "a little," and shop around for financial services "some."

*Statistically significant at the 10 percent level, two-tailed test.

**Statistically significant at the 5 percent level, two-tailed test.

***Statistically significant at the 1 percent level, two-tailed test.

Table 3-9. *Nonpecuniary Costs of Financial Services*[a]

Percent

	All	Banked	Unbanked
Most convenient location for financial service			
Bank office	44.0	54.8	17.2
ATM	25.8	27.9	20.7
Check casher	4.8	1.7	12.5
Grocery or liquor store	25.4	15.6	49.6
Landlord accepts checks[b]	54.6	64.9	38.4
Uses bill payment center to pay bills	36.6	33.2	45.2
Most important for cashing checks[c]			
Convenience	50.8	52.0	48.7
Cost	19.5	20.0	18.6
Getting money quickly	29.7	28.0	32.7
Sample size	938	668	270

Source: Detroit Area Household Financial Services study.

a. Standard errors are in parentheses.

b. Asked only of renters.

c. Asked only of respondents who cash checks. Question reads, "When cashing your checks, which is most important—convenience, cost, or getting your money quickly?"

most saturated specifications in columns 5 and 6 suggest that outlays are higher among the banked only for short-term credit. Controlling for education, income, employment status, financial participation, and economic activity, broadly speaking, attenuates the coefficient on having a bank account for both the OLS and LAD specifications in table 3-7 (annual transactional outlays). However, for short-term credit outlays (table 3-8), the banked-unbanked OLS and LAD differences remain statistically and economically significant at $83 and $16, respectively. It may be the case that bank-account ownership increases access to, and therefore spending on, short-term credit. Also, the contrast between the results for transactional outlays and short-term credit lends further support to the unobserved selection issue; namely, that households with bank accounts may have a higher demand for borrowing.

Although annual outlays are low for the majority of LMI households, table 3-9 shows that the nonpecuniary costs of financial services are nontrivial. For 30 percent of respondents, a check casher or grocery or liquor store is the most convenient location for financial services. In other words, 30 percent may incur the "cost of inconvenience" to access a bank or ATM. The unbanked are much more likely than the banked to report that a check casher or grocery or liquor store is the most convenient location (62 versus 17 percent), which is consistent with their decision to not have a bank account. Among the renters, only 55 percent have landlords who accept checks, which, by restricting their payment options,

Table 3-10. *Banking, Hardships, and Emergency Funds over Three Months Preceding Interview*
Percent

	All	Banked	Unbanked
Income covered expenses every month	45.2	51.2	28.7
Experienced food insufficiency[a]	16.8	13.1	25.9
If income did not cover expenses, difference was made up by			
Borrowing from family and friends	53.0	50.7	56.7
Borrowing from a bank or credit card	14.6	21.3	3.6
Spending out of savings or investments	24.6	32.6	11.4
If needed, could borrow $500 for three months	66.7	71.5	54.9
If needed, could borrow $500 for three months from			
Family, friends, or church	81.4	76.6	96.8
Bank, credit union, or credit card	15.8	20.5	0.8
Employer	1.2	0.9	2.1
Other assets[b]	0.9	1.1	0.0
AFS[c]	0.8	0.9	0.4
If could not borrow from friends or family, would go next to			
Bank, credit union, or credit card	41.0	49.0	19.6
Employer	8.9	6.2	16.2
Other assets	1.4	1.9	0.0
AFS	6.3	7.5	3.2
Would not borrow	42.5	35.5	61.0
Sample size	938	668	270

Source: Detroit Area Household Financial Services study.

a. A household is classified as being food insufficient if the respondent or respondent's household reports that they sometimes or often did not have enough food to eat.

b. Other assets include life insurance, 401(k), IRA, home equity line of credit, brokerage account, or business assets.

c. AFS include finance company, check casher, payday loan, pawnshop, or title loan.

adds to the cost of paying their rent. A much smaller fraction of the unbanked has landlords that accept checks relative to those with bank accounts (38 percent versus 65 percent); the reduced ability to use checks to pay for common bills, such as rent, may be related to reduced demand for a checking account. Table 3-9 also shows that 37 percent of respondents (33 percent of banked, 45 percent of unbanked) use bill payment centers, which are typically associated with long lines, to pay their bills.[18] Estimates of annual outlays exclude these nonpecuniary costs, even though they may be nontrivial.

In table 3-10, we show that having a bank account and using banking services are closely tied with income volatility (relative to expenses) and economic insecu-

---

18. Fewer respondents (23 percent) use automated payment methods to pay their bills.

rity as measured by food insufficiency.[19] About half of banked respondents report that their income covered their expenses in the year preceding the survey interview, compared with 29 percent of unbanked respondents, most likely reflecting the latter's average lower incomes and lower rates of employment. Also, twice as many unbanked respondents report having been food insufficient during the year preceding the survey (26 versus 13 percent). Compounding these economic security issues is that the unbanked are less likely to have a buffer against economic shocks: 45 percent report they do not have a source from which to borrow $500 for three months, in contrast to 28 percent among the banked. In addition, an overwhelming majority of the unbanked (97 percent) relies on informal sources of borrowing and has little recourse if these informal sources are not available: 61 percent of those who would first turn to family, friends, or church report they would not borrow at all if these informal sources were unavailable. Though considerable additional research is needed to infer that having a bank account leads to greater economic stability, the strong correlation between these factors suggests that income is suggestive of the demand for financial services.[20] Indeed, in an open-ended, qualitative question about what would motivate someone without a bank account to open one, a common answer given by respondents was "more money" or "more income."

As LMI households have more volatile incomes than the rest of the population, so too does their participation in the mainstream financial sector fluctuate. As in Caskey (1997) and Bucks and others (2009), the estimates in table 3-11 suggest that having a bank account is not a permanent condition.[21] Seventy percent of unbanked respondents have previously had a bank account. Among the two-thirds who voluntarily closed an account, common reasons include facing high minimum-balance requirements or fees or worrying about bouncing checks. The unbanked are four times as likely as the banked to worry about bouncing a check. On the other hand, 15 percent of respondents (12 percent of the banked and 21 percent of the unbanked) have involuntarily had a bank close their accounts. Among this group, bouncing checks or overdrafts is a commonly cited reason for why the bank took action (53 percent among the banked, 65 percent among the unbanked). Another common reason is low balance or inactive accounts (63 percent of the banked, 29 percent of the unbanked). Taken together, the results

19. Following well-known surveys, such as the Survey of Income and Program Participation, the National Health and Nutrition Examination Survey, and the Current Population Survey, we asked respondents to report whether they or their households sometimes or often did not have enough to eat to code them as "food insufficient."

20. These differences between the banked and unbanked remain large and significant after controlling for annual income, employment, poverty, marital status, and age, suggesting that the measures of economic hardships in table 3-10 are important alternative manifestations of the role of income, above and beyond simply the level, in bank-account ownership.

21. The wording of the questions related to prior bank-account experiences in the survey instrument does not enable us to construct transition matrices.

Table 3-11. *Transitions into and out of Banking*
Percent

	All	Banked	Unbanked
Previously had bank account	91.5	100	70.3
Account voluntarily closed[a]	52.8	54.4	48.8
Reason for closing account			
High minimum balance or fees	23.2	24.4	20.6
Worry about bounced checks	7.7	4.2	16.3
Another bank more convenient	n.a.	27.4	n.a.
Prefer check cashers	n.a.	n.a.	0.8
Other	49.3	44.1	62.3
Account involuntarily closed	14.6	12.2	20.8[b]
Reason account was closed[c]			
Poor credit	n.a.	9.2	1.6
Bounced checks or overdrafts[d]	n.a.	52.9	64.7
Low balance/inactive account	n.a.	63.4	29.2
Fraud	n.a.	4.2	9.5
Other	n.a.	n.a.	4.5
Percent who grew up with banked adults in home	72.2	72.9	70.7
Sample size	938	668	270

Source: Detroit Area Household Financial Services study.

a. Other than when they have moved.

b. Among the unbanked, the percent that voluntarily closed an account and the percent that involuntarily closed an account do not add up to the percent that previously had an account because one respondent did not answer the question about why the account was closed.

c. The banked were allowed to provide more than one response whereas the unbanked were not, so we do not calculate or report sample statistics for all respondents.

d. This category also includes suspected fraud.

in table 3-11 suggest that having a bank account is not necessarily a means of permanently entering the financial mainstream, nor is being unbanked an insurmountable condition. Both banked and unbanked respondents are about equally likely to have grown up in households where the adults had bank accounts (73 versus 71 percent), suggesting that one's attachment to the financial mainstream is unlikely to be driven by purely intergenerational factors. Rather than supporting a view that LMI households are permanently either "in" or "out of" the banking sector, we find that account ownership and use is variable, and may be amenable to public and private sector innovation to increase usage.

Discussion and Policy Implications

Bank-account ownership and usage is highly related to income. African American households, however, are 12 percentage points less likely to have a bank account than their nonblack counterparts, even after controlling for income, education and employment. Lack of bank-account ownership is closely related to income volatility and economic insecurity, and unbanked households have fewer resources to fall back on and less ability to borrow to make ends meet. Bank-account ownership is not a permanent state, but rather largely a reflection of the household's current economic conditions.

While low- and moderate-income households are active users of mainstream and alternative financial services, annual outlays on these services are relatively low, at around 1 percent of annual household income. This estimate is lower than those implied by previous work using the posted fees of financial services alone, suggesting that LMI households are able to avoid regular use of the most expensive financial services options. The top spenders, however, take up a disproportionate share of overall spending.

We also show that although annual outlays on financial services are low, on average, some LMI households incur significant nonpecuniary costs to obtain and use banking services. These households often pay bills in person and incur large search costs to avoid the most expensive options. When asked what features of financial services would motivate them to change behavior, they cite convenience and speed before costs. Moreover, banked households use a wide range of alternative financial services, and most of the outlays of the median banked household are for alternative financial services. Thus our results suggest that policies to lower the fees of bank accounts might do little on their own to increase bank-account ownership or discourage the use of alternative financial services. In contrast, improving geographic convenience, hours of operation, transparency and simplicity, or, most important, the functionality of services provided might go further to increase bank-account ownership. Additional experimental field research is needed to estimate how important or effective these changes might actually be.

Banked and unbanked households use both banking and alternative financial services. Having a bank account is related to the set of steps households take to maintain financial stability when income cannot cover expenses. Banked households are more likely to turn to savings and bank credit to deal with fluctuations in income or expenses, while unbanked households rely more on friends and family or borrow or dip into savings. Furthermore, the evidence is consistent with LMI households' substituting among an array of financial services from the mainstream and alternative financial services sectors, which highlights the need for policymakers to look across the consumer financial services marketplace, rather than focusing on a particular product, when making decisions about regulation of banking, credit, and savings products and services.

From the perspective of supply, the administrative costs of collecting small-value deposits are high in relation to banks' potential earnings on the relatively small amounts saved, unless the bank can charge high fees; with sufficiently high fees, however, it is not clear that using a bank account makes economic sense for many LMI households. Indeed, the current structure of bank accounts is likely one of the primary reasons why LMI households do not have or use them. With respect to transaction accounts, high minimum-balance requirements, high fees for overdraft protection or bounced checks, and delays in check clearance dissuade LMI households from opening or retaining bank accounts. Moreover, banks use the private ChexSystems to screen out households who have had difficulty with accounts in the past.

These supply-side considerations suggest that one goal of policy ought to be to increase the scale and offset costs for the private sector in expanding the functionality of bank accounts for low-income households. As discussed in more detail elsewhere, policymakers can use a range of tools to expand the supply of more functional accounts to low-income households. For example, local Bank On initiatives can focus on improving the range of account offerings to low-income households, rather than merely on signing up households to existing accounts. Federal efforts, such as the Direct Express card for Social Security recipients, and recent Treasury pilots of tax-refund accounts, can focus on improving the functionality of offered prepaid cards. And state electronic benefit programs can focus on expanding the range of uses of these cards beyond state benefit receipt.

We can only speculate, based on the data presented in this chapter, that high-cost financial services may increase the economic challenges faced by LMI households. At low income levels and with limited access to credit, small fluctuations in income or expenses may create serious problems for financial management and household well-being. Further research is needed to assess rigorously how the financial services system compounds the difficulties these households face as they cope with income fluctuations that occur because of job changes, instability in hours worked, medical illnesses or emergencies, changes in family composition, or other factors that can unexpectedly change income or needs.

References

Bair, Sheila. 2005. *Low-Cost Payday Loans: Opportunities and Obstacles.* Report prepared for the Annie E. Casey Foundation. Amherst: University of Massachusetts, Isenberg School of Management (aecf.org/upload/publicationfiles/fes3622h334.pdf).

Barr, Michael S. 2004. "Banking the Poor." *Yale Journal on Regulation* 21:121–237.

Berry, Christopher. 2004. "To Bank or Not to Bank? A Survey of Low-Income Households." Working Paper BABC 04-3. Harvard University, Joint Center for Housing Studies (www.jchs.harvard.edu/publications/finance/babc/babc_04-3.pdf).

Booz-Allen and Hamilton and Shugoll Research. 1997. *Mandatory EFT Demographic Study.* Report prepared for the Financial Management Service. OMB 1510-00-68. U.S. Department of the Treasury.

Bucks, Brian, Arthur Kennickell, and Kevin Moore. 2006. "Recent Changes in U.S. Family Finances: Evidence from the 2001 and 2004 Survey of Consumer Finances." *Federal Reserve Bulletin* 92 (February): A1–A38.

Bucks, Brian K., and others. 2009. "Changes in U.S. Family Finances from 2004 to 2007: Evidence from the Survey of Consumer Finances." *Federal Reserve Bulletin* 95 (February): A1–A56.

Caskey, John. 1994. *Fringe Banking: Check Cashing Outlets, Pawnshops, and the Poor.* New York: Russell Sage Foundation.

———. 1997. *Beyond Cash-and-Carry: Financial Savings, Financial Services, and Low-Income Households in Two Communities.* Report prepared for the Consumer Federation of America and the Ford Foundation. Swarthmore, Penn. (December). (www.swarthmore.edu/Documents/academics/economics/beyond_cash_and_carry.pdf).

Dove Consulting. 2000. "Survey of Non-Bank Financial Institutions for the Department of Treasury." Report prepared for the U.S. Treasury Department (April 4).

———. 2008. "Banks' Efforts to Serve the Unbanked and Underbanked." Report prepared for the Federal Deposit Insurance Corporation (December).

Doyle, Joseph J., Jose A. Lopez, and Marc R. Saidenberg. 1998. "How Effective Is Lifeline Banking in Assisting the 'Unbanked'?" *Federal Reserve Bank of New York Current Issues in Economics and Finance* 4, no. 6: 1–6 (www.newyorkfed.org/research/current_issues/ci4-6.pdf).

Dunham, Constance. 2000. "Financial Service Usage Patterns for the Poor: Financial Cost Considerations." Working Paper. U.S. Department of Treasury, Office of the Comptroller of the Currency.

Dunham, Constance R., Fritz J. Scheuren, and Douglas J. Willson. 1998. "Methodological Issues in Surveying the Nonbanked Population in Urban Areas." In *Proceedings of the American Statistical Association, Survey Research Methods Section* 20:611–16.

Elliehausen, Gregory. 2006. "Consumers' Use of High-Priced Credit Products: Do They Know What They Are Doing?" Working Paper 2006-WP-02. Terre Haute: Indiana State University, Networks Financial Institute (http://ssrn.com/abstract=921909).

Federal Reserve Board. 2004. "Survey of Consumer Finances." Last updated October 5, 2011 (www.federalreserve.gov/econresdata/scf/scf_2004.htm).

Federal Reserve System. 2007. "The 2007 Federal Reserve Payments Study: Noncash Payment Trends in the United States, 2003–2006."

Fellowes, Matthew, and Mia Mabanta. 2008. *Banking on Wealth: America's New Retail Banking Infrastructure and Its Wealth-Building Potential.* Brookings (www.brookings.edu/~/media/Files/rc/reports/2008/01_banking_fellowes/01_banking_fellowes.pdf).

Fitzpatrick, Katie. 2009. "The Effect of Bank Account Ownership on Credit and Consumption: Evidence from the United Kingdom." Working Paper 2009-07. Federal Deposit Insurance Corporation (www.fdic.gov/bank/analytical/cfr/2009/wp2009/CFR_WP_2009_07_Fitzpatrick.pdf).

Hogarth, Jeanne M., and Kevin H. O'Donnell. 1999. "Banking Relationships of Lower-Income Families and the Governmental Trend toward Electronic Payment." *Federal Reserve Bulletin* 85 (July): 459–73 (www.federalreserve.gov/pubs/bulletin/1999/0799lead.pdf).

IRS (Internal Revenue Service). 2006. National Taxpayer Advocate's 2007 Objectives Report to Congress, Volume II: The Role of the IRS in the Refund Anticipation Loan Industry.

James, Lisa, and Peter Smith. 2006. "Overdraft Loans: Survey Finds Growing Problem for Consumers." Issue Paper 13. Durham, N.C.: Center for Responsible Lending (www.responsiblelending.org/overdraft-loans/research-analysis/ip013-Overdraft_Survey-0406.pdf).

MoneyGram International 2008. *Annual Report.* Form 10-K (March 25).

Prescott, Edward S., and Daniel D. Tatar. 1999. "Means of Payment, the Unbanked, and EFT '99." *Federal Reserve Bank of Richmond Economic Quarterly* 85, no. 4: 49–70.

Rhine, Sherrie L. W., William H. Greene, and Maude Toussaint-Comeau. 2006. "The Importance of Check-Cashing Businesses to the Unbanked: Racial/Ethnic Differences." *Review of Economics and Statistics* 88:146–57 (www.mitpressjournals.org/doi/pdf/10.1162/rest.2006.88.1.146).

Seidman, Ellen, Moez Hababou, and Jennifer Kramer. 2005. *A Financial Services Survey of Low- and Moderate-Income Households.* Chicago: Center for Financial Services Innovation (http://cfsinnovation.com/system/files/imported/managed_documents/threecitysurvey.pdf).

Seidman, Ellen, and Jennifer Tescher. 2005. "Unbanked to Homeowner: Improving Financial Services for Low-Income, Low-Asset Customers." In *Building Assets, Building Credit: Creating Wealth in Low-Income Communities,* edited by Nicolas Retsinas and Eric Belsky. Brookings and Joint Center for Housing Studies.

Stegman, Michael. 2007. "Payday Lending." *Journal of Economic Perspectives* 21 (Winter): 169–90 (www.jstor.org/stable/30033706).

Stephens Inc. 2007. *Industry Report: Payday Loan Industry.* Little Rock, Ark.

U.S. General Accounting Office. 2002. *Electronic Transfers: Use by Federal Payment Recipients Has Increased, but Obstacles to Greater Participation Remain.* GAO-02-913 (www.gao.gov/new.items/d02913.pdf).

U.S. Government Accountability Office. 2008. *Electronic Payments: Many Programs Electronically Disburse Federal Benefits, and More Outreach Could Increase Use.* GAO-08-645 (www.gao.gov/new.items/d08645.pdf).

Vermilyea, Todd, and James A. Wilcox. 2002. "Who Is Unbanked, and Why: Results from a Large, New Survey of Low- and Moderate-Income Adults." Report prepared for the Federal Reserve Bank of Chicago, Conference on Bank Structure and Competition (May).

Washington, Ebonya. 2006. "The Impact of Banking and Fringe Banking Regulation on the Number of Unbanked Americans." *Journal of Human Resources* 41:106–37 (www.jstor.org/stable/40057259).

4

Preferences for Plastic

MICHAEL S. BARR, JANE K. DOKKO,
AND ELEANOR McDONNELL FEIT

T his chapter characterizes the features of an account-based payment card—
including bank debit cards, prepaid debit cards, and payroll cards—that
elicit a high take-up rate among low- and moderate-income (LMI) households,
particularly those without bank accounts. We apply marketing research techniques, specifically choice modeling, to identify the design of specific financial
services products for LMI households, who often face difficulties acquiring or
maintaining standard bank accounts but need banking services. After monthly
cost, we find that, on average, nonmonetary features of a payment card, such
as the availability of federal consumer protection, are factors LMI consumers
weigh most heavily when choosing among differently designed payment cards.
We estimate a high take-up rate for a well-designed payment card. The sensitivity of the take-up rate with respect to cost varies by income and bank-account
ownership. These results can guide private and public sector initiatives to expand
the range of financial services available to LMI households, particularly as the
federal government embarks on a wide-ranging effort to move federal benefits
and tax refunds to electronic transmission and as federal regulators weigh new consumer protections for payment cards in the wake of the passage in 2010 of the
Dodd-Frank Wall Street Reform and Consumer Protection (Dodd-Frank) Act.

Bank-account ownership and financial inclusion are widely viewed as necessary conditions for improving the economic well-being of low- and moderate-
income households, yet 25 percent of households in the United States earning
under $20,600 a year do not have a bank account (Barr and Blank 2009; Bucks

and others 2009). As articulated by John Caskey (1994), Michael Barr (2004), and Michael Barr and Rebecca Blank (2009), LMI households need affordable bank accounts to make payments, obtain credit, save for short-term emergencies, and build longer-term assets. Increasing the capacity of LMI households to build savings as a buffer against emergencies may promote their financial stability and improve their income and employment opportunities. Without affordable and accessible banking services, these households frequently use nonbank substitutes: a typical LMI household spends around half of its annual outlays on financial services in the high-priced alternative financial services sector to obtain services, such as check cashing, wire transfers, and short-term credit, and does not accumulate significant savings (chapter 3, this volume). From a public-policy perspective, this financial exclusion and the use of high-priced alternative financial services undermine the government's mechanisms for income redistribution, reduce the employment incentives of programs such as the earned-income tax credit, and reduce the positive network externalities in electronic payment systems (Humphrey, Kim, and Vale 2001; Barr 2004).[1] An understanding of preferences for payment-card features can help improve the overall equity of the banking system by building on the efficiency gains from electronic payments.

A payment card, a broad term used in this chapter to include debit, prepaid debit, and payroll cards (but not gift cards), provides the user with an electronic method of receiving income, making purchases, paying bills, and withdrawing cash. Payment cards can also be set up to offer the card holder the opportunity to save, either by accumulating funds on the card or by linking to a separate deposit account. Payment cards typically do not enable check writing and can be set up without the ability to overdraw, thus minimizing risks and administrative costs for financial institutions and consumers.

In this study, we use the term *debit card* to describe basic cards that are linked to a bank account and can be used with a personal identification number (PIN) at an automated teller machine (ATM) and at retail stores that have PIN pads at the point of sale. A *payroll card* is set up by the card holder's employer and enables employees to electronically draw their pay from a pooled account. A *prepaid debit card* is also drawn from a pooled account but is loaded with funds by the consumer or a third party. Despite these differences, debit, payroll, and prepaid debit cards can be structured to have federal deposit insurance. Unlike the debit card that can be accessed with a PIN, payroll and prepaid debit cards are typically offered only through the MasterCard or Visa network and can generally be used at any retailer that is a part of these

---

1. For example, programs providing benefits to the poor could more efficiently transfer resources to the poor if LMI households were to receive funds and pay their bills using modern electronic funds transfer systems instead of checks that are expensive for the payment system to process and potentially subject to fraud.

networks, by the consumer signing rather than entering a PIN. Each of these payment cards poses different costs and risks to the financial institution providing the card.

Recent Initiatives to Improve Access to Banking and Payment Services

Aware of the benefits that accrue to LMI families that use depository services, policymakers have acted to improve access to these services. These efforts fall into two categories: First, regulators created a more favorable regulatory environment for the use of low-cost payment cards. Such policies attempt to balance account holders' requirements for reasonable cost, convenience, and consumer protections, on one hand, and banks' requirements for acceptable profitability and risk, on the other. Second, both the federal government and the states have entered into contracts with banks and other card providers to offer lower-cost, card-based deposit accounts or other card products to LMI households, usually in connection with public benefit programs.

Regulatory Environment for Low-Cost Payment Cards

The bulk of policymakers' progress to date in more adequately balancing the needs of both LMI households and mainstream financial institutions has focused on improving the regulatory environment for lower-cost account substitutes, particularly stored-value cards. An important early initiative to extend access to unbanked households was the Treasury Department's Electronic Transfer Account program, launched as a part of the wider EFT '99 initiative to promote electronic federal payments. Financial institutions that joined the program offered federal benefit recipients the option to open electronic transfer accounts, traditional bank accounts with standardized account features: account holders paid no more than $3.00 a month in maintenance fees and enjoyed protections equal to those of other account holders, including those covered under the Federal Reserve System's Regulation E (Barr 2004). The Treasury Department paid financial institutions a per-account sum to cover initial account costs (Barr 2004). Though nearly six hundred banks, credit unions, and thrifts had agreed to offer electronic transfer accounts by 2004, funding for EFT '99 public educational programs ran out in 2001 (Barr 2004), and as of 2002 the program had succeeded in reaching only 36,000 recipients, a mere 1 percent of unbanked federal beneficiaries (GAO 2002). As of September 2010, only 251,941 electronic transfer accounts had been opened over the program's life; of those, 121,191 accounts were active.[2]

2. Management of Federal Agency Disbursements, 75 *Federal Register* 80315, 80328 (December 22, 2010).

With the development and spread of debit-card payment technology, regulators began to promote stored-value cards as lower-cost alternatives to traditional bank accounts. The Federal Reserve Board recognized that employers could lower costs by disbursing payroll to stored-value cards rather than issuing checks.[3] Employees without bank accounts could also lower their costs of access by reducing the risks of carrying cash (Keitel 2011) and by eliminating check-cashing fees, which could consume, on average, 1.5 to 2.5 percent of take-home pay (Barr 2004). In 2006 the Fed increased the attractiveness of stored-value cards for workers without bank accounts by finalizing a rule extending to these card holders many of the core consumer protections offered to bank-account holders under Regulation E, including limits on card holder liability for unauthorized transactions.[4] The board also exempted payroll-card issuers from Regulation E's paper periodic-statement requirements, mandating instead that issuers provide transaction details electronically.[5]

Later, in 2008, the Federal Deposit Insurance Corporation (FDIC) increased depositor safeguards for some stored-value-card holders by providing that, subject to some requirements, holders of stored-value cards issued by banks using pooled accounts could enjoy federal deposit insurance coverage on an individual, rather than aggregate, basis.[6] This rule allowed employers and banks to lower costs through the use of an omnibus account without sacrificing individual depositor protections in the event of a bank failure, an important consumer protection that made individuals more comfortable using these cards. In December 2010 the Treasury Department further encouraged stored-value-card issuers to improve deposit protection by setting minimum standards that cards must meet to receive federal benefit deposits: card holders must receive deposit insurance coverage on a pass-through basis, and issuers must adhere to the consumer protections extended to payroll cards under Regulation E.[7] The rule also prohibits cards that receive federal benefits from subscribing to overdraft services.[8]

In addition to promoting lower-cost account substitutes, regulators have also sought to eliminate common disincentives to bank encountered by LMI households. Although many federal benefit payments are generally protected from

---

3. See, for example, Electronic Fund Transfers, 69 *Federal Register* 55996, 55998–99 (proposed September 17, 2004).

4. See Electronic Fund Transfers, 71 *Federal Register* 51437 (August 30, 2006) (codified as amended at 12 C.F.R. § 205.18 (2011)).

5. See ibid., 51442–44.

6. See Insurability of Funds Underlying Stored Value Cards and Other Nontraditional Access Mechanisms, 73 *Federal Register* 67155 (November 13, 2008).

7. Federal Government Participation in the Automated Clearing House, 75 *Federal Register* 80335 (December 22, 2010) (amending 31 C.F.R. § 210.5).

8. Ibid.

creditor garnishment,[9] while creditor claims and exempt funds are being evaluated banks must honor creditor garnishment judgments or risk judicial sanction; as a result, account holders are unable to access their funds at all until garnishment orders are amended to reflect protected payments.[10] Recipients who seek to avoid this situation by collecting benefit proceeds by check rather than using direct deposit to a bank account, suffer higher costs (through check-cashing fees) and impose higher costs on the government (through check issuance costs). To alleviate this situation, under Treasury leadership the major federal benefit agencies amended their respective regulations in early 2011 to require banks on receipt of a garnishment order to protect from seizure an amount equal to the total protected payments received over the past sixty days, or the entire account balance (whichever is smaller).[11]

Provision of Lower-Cost Payment Cards

All state governments and the federal government have created programs that allow some public benefit recipients electronic access to benefit proceeds without a bank account. Electronic disbursement lowers costs for both recipients and administrators: recipients carry less cash and pay less in check-cashing and money-order issuance fees (Keitel 2011; NCLC 2011), and administrators eliminate check-issuance expenses (FRB 2011; Keitel 2011). Also, lowering the cost of access to public benefits increases the effectiveness of these programs by allowing recipients to use a larger portion of the proceeds (Barr 2004).

State Programs

State-administered benefit programs serve approximately 48 million recipients,[12] and states have introduced payment-card programs to provide unbanked households with lower-cost access to these funds. As of 2011, at least thirty-eight states and the District of Columbia allow the benefits of cash assistance programs such as Temporary Assistance for Needy Families and the Low Income Home Energy Assistance Program to be issued through the electronic-benefit-transfer (EBT) system (FRB 2011; FNS 2003), a nationwide card-payment network created in 1996 to replace paper food coupons distributed under the federal food stamp

---

9. Some examples of creditor-protected benefits are Social Security benefits, Supplemental Security benefits, and Veterans Administration benefits. See Garnishment of Accounts Containing Federal Benefits, 75 *Federal Register* 20299, 20300 & n.1 (April 19, 2010) (collecting citations).

10. Ibid., 20300.

11. See Garnishment of Accounts Containing Federal Benefit Payments, 76 *Federal Register* 9939 (February 23, 2011) (amending scattered sections of 5 C.F.R., 20 C.F.R., 31 C.F.R., and 38 C.F.R.).

12. Includes Low-Income Home Energy Assistance Program, Supplemental Nutrition Assistance Program, Temporary Assistance for Needy Families, unemployment compensation, and the Women, Infants, and Children program. These figures count all program recipients separately, though one household may receive benefits from more than one program.

program.[13] Though the costs of accessing cash assistance through EBT cards vary by state (FRB 2011), card holders in most states may make at least one free withdrawal a month at an in-network ATM and may pay for purchases with EBT cards at accepting merchants without incurring fees.

Stored-value cards are also commonly used to distribute unemployment insurance benefits. As of May 2011, forty states allowed unemployment insurance beneficiaries to access benefits using a stored-value card (NCLC 2011). As with EBT-delivered cash-assistance programs, the costs of using these stored-value cards vary by state, but federal law requires card holders to have at least one method of accessing unemployment insurance proceeds without cost.[14] Moreover, these card holders are given protections under Regulation E similar to those provided to payroll-card holders.[15]

Federal Programs

The federal government has created similar programs to lower the costs of depository services for federal benefit recipients. Many households who receive federal benefits do not have accounts with mainstream financial institutions (Keitel 2011). To comply with federal laws requiring that federal agencies disburse non-tax payments electronically,[16] and to make accounts available at a "reasonable cost" for the electronic receipt of benefit proceeds,[17] the Treasury Department's Fiscal Management Service has created the Direct Express program, which allows participants to access benefit proceeds with a payment card. Direct Express card holders may make purchases without charge at a merchant point-of-sale terminal and may withdraw funds without charge through a network of surcharge-fee ATMs. The card's fee schedule allows card holders access to their funds at a total cost lower than that of managing funds in cash or with a typical prepaid card and provides protections similar to those extended to payroll-card holders under Regulation E.[18] As of 2010, the Direct Express program served more than 1.5 million federal benefit recipients (Keitel 2011). The success of the program contributed to the Treasury Department's decision in 2010 to mandate elec-

---

13. The nationwide electronic benefit transfer program began in the 1980s and 1990s through a series of state-initiated pilot programs. By 1996, five states had statewide programs in place; that same year, Congress mandated that all states distribute food stamp benefits electronically by 2002 (see Personal Responsibility and Work Opportunity Reconciliation (Welfare Reform) Act of 1996, Pub. L. No. 104–193, § 825(a), 110 Stat. 2105, 2324–26 (codified as amended at 7 U.S.C. § 2016(h) (2006 & Supp. IV 2010)). The nationwide rollout was completed in June 2004.

14. Ibid., 5–6.

15. See 12 C.F.R. § 205.15 (2011). Card programs administered by governments are generally exempt from Regulation E (15 U.S.C. § 1693b(d)(2)(B) (2006)), but programs for employment-related benefits do not fall under the exemption (15 U.S.C. § 1693b(d)(2)(A)(ii)).

16. See 31 U.S.C. § 3332(e)–(f).

17. Ibid., 31 U.S.C. § 3332(i)(2)(A).

18. See Management of Federal Agency Disbursements, 75 *Federal Register* 80315, 80321–23 (December 22, 2010).

tronic payment for nearly all new federal benefit recipients beginning May 1, 2011, and to require existing check payees to move to electronic payment by May 1, 2013, except for a narrow class of persons eligible for waivers.[19]

Outstanding Issues

Despite some progress, policymakers' efforts to increase the availability of payment cards have not yet solved the problems with financial access. Public and private payment-card programs are fragmented, and neither sector offers a broadly available product that is affordable, transparent, and reflects the preferences of low- and moderate-income households. Most states do not establish individually owned accounts linked to EBT cards for benefit recipients and instead use a private contractor to provide cards for recipients to access funds held by the state government in a pooled account (Barr 2004). Both state and federal cards currently lack full functionality, such as the ability for card holders to receive other income, pay bills electronically, or set up savings accounts. As currently structured, LMI households cannot use publicly offered payment cards to fulfill many of their financial services needs. Similar to publicly offered payment cards, payroll cards generally do not offer bill payment or savings mechanisms. The availability of these options usually depends on the employers, who, like state governments, use a single contractor to allow employees to withdraw funds from a pooled account.

Private sector payment-card programs offer a broader array of financial services but at a much higher price. For example, three popular cards in the market charge activation fees ranging from $3.00 to $19.95, as well as monthly maintenance fees between $1.95 and $9.95.[20] Additional charges apply for making purchases with the card, making ATM withdrawals, enrolling in a bill payment plan, reloading the card, overdraft (where permitted) and other uses of the card. If the card holder is not savvy, the fees of a payment card offered in the private sector can rival and even surpass those of check cashers and bank accounts.

In addition to high fees, shopping for and selecting a payment card can be complicated because the card's fixed and variable costs are complex and hidden. Also, the services offered on a card are often bundled. For example, one card charges a different set of fees depending on whether the card holder chooses to pay a large up-front activation fee or a lower monthly fee. Another card offers an entirely different menu of fees and services. Moreover, consumers' cognitive biases may make comparing the two cards difficult, as their respective costs depend on how the card holder anticipates loading the card with money and

19. Management of Federal Agency Disbursements, 75 *Federal Register* 80315 (December 22, 2010) (to be codified at 31 C.F.R., pt. 208).

20. Details available upon request.

how frequently purchases are expected to be made. Consumers may incorrectly forecast their behavior and pay significantly more than they expected to pay for the bundle of services that they purchased.

Federal consumer protection regulations for payment cards may leave gaps in coverage or create confusion.[21] The Federal Deposit Insurance Corporation's deposit regulations and the Federal Reserve's Regulations D and E stipulate deposit insurance and liability protection for some payment cards, but these rules do not necessarily apply to all types of payment cards or their holders in all situations. When a card is lost or stolen and the card holder does not report a stolen or missing card within two business days, the card holder is not fully protected. Also, a card holder's responsibility for charges made is capped at $50 only if the card holder is able to prove that he or she did not "recklessly" use or misplace the card. In some cases, deposit insurance may not pass through to a card holder if the account linked to the card is itself linked to a pooled account without individually assigned subaccounts (as may often be the case with a private payroll card). The card holder agreements of the most popular prepaid branded payment cards warn that in the event of a loss or theft, it is possible under certain circumstances for the holder to lose all the money that has been loaded onto the card.

Given that public and private payment cards form an incomplete spectrum of affordable and transparent financial services, the use of payment cards, though growing, is not widespread among LMI households (Romich, Gordon, and Waithaka 2009). This suggests that there is a possibility in the current payment-card marketplace to provide more affordable financial services through payment cards without hidden fees to LMI households. The federal government and the states are embarking on a series of steps to provide benefit payments and tax refunds electronically, as well as to expand access to financial services for LMI households. Policymakers are debating a variety of techniques to expand access, including public subsidies or efforts to reduce acquisition costs for the private sector through the development of large-scale programs for the direct deposit of tax refunds and government benefits onto such cards.[22] Similarly, federal, state, and local governments are increasingly galvanizing Bank On initiatives around the country, which provide low-cost starter bank accounts and financial education for unbanked households. These programs also seek to develop and deploy new bank products for unbanked households, including many that use debit, prepaid, and payroll-card technologies.

---

21. Although federal consumer protections do not apply to publicly offered payment cards, such as the electronic-benefits-transfer card, state government regulations ensure that card holders do not lose the money that is loaded on a card when it is lost or stolen.

22. Research on an early U.S. Treasury project in this area, the Electronic Transfer Accounts program, has found that banks are likely to need subsidies to cover the cost of opening an electronically based account but could profitably offer the account on a monthly recurring basis (Dove Associates and U.S. Department of the Treasury 1999).

This study contributes to this policy discussion by characterizing the features of an account-based payment card—including bank debit cards, prepaid debit cards, and payroll cards—that elicit a high take-up rate among low- and moderate-income households, particularly those without bank accounts. To the best of our knowledge, no large-scale study identifies how preferences for monetary and nonmonetary features of a payment card influence its use.[23] Previous research on electronic payment methods has focused on individuals' decisions to choose among different electronic payment methods, such as debit cards, credit cards, and electronic funds transfer (Hirschman 1982; Kennickell and Kwast 1997; Mantel 2000). Related research demonstrates the substantial sensitivity of consumers' use of an electronic payment method to its price (Humphrey, Kim, and Vale 2001; Amromin, Jankowski, and Porter 2007; Borzekowski, Kiser, and Ahmed 2008). In this prior research, it is unclear whether the nonmonetary aspects of electronic payment methods, such as how money is loaded onto the card, whether a card has lost-card protection, or how the card is branded, are quantitatively important. Also, the importance of nonmonetary costs relative to the monetary costs of electronic payments is not well understood. Recent research, however, emphasizes the relative importance of nonmonetary factors in influencing the financial decisions of the poor (Bertrand, Mullainathan, and Shafir 2006). An aggregated view of consumer preferences that does not distinguish between monetary and nonmonetary features leaves financial institutions, payment-card providers, employers, and government agencies uninformed on how to design payment cards to maximize take-up among LMI households.

This study contributes to an important policy discussion as the federal government embarks on a wide-ranging effort to move federal benefits and tax refunds to electronic transmission and federal regulators weigh new consumer protections for payment cards in the wake of the passage in 2010 of the Dodd-Frank Wall Street Reform and Consumer Protection Act. For example, early results from this study were provided to the Treasury Department to design and move forward with the Direct Express prepaid card, which is now used by more than 1 million individuals to receive their Social Security and other benefit payments. Similarly, early results helped the Treasury Department shape its pilot of a new prepaid debit card (MyAccountCard) for the receipt of tax refunds. This pilot, launched in January 2011, will provide important information regarding the card's use by LMI households. Specifically, on the basis of our preliminary results, the Treasury Department decided to test whether the presence of a savings plan would increase take-up rates. Similarly, the FDIC also launched in January 2011 a "safe accounts" pilot in which nine

---

23. See for example, Romich, Gordon, and Waithaka (2009) (presenting results from a qualitative survey of twenty-two users of prepaid cards).

banks are using an early version of our research results. These nine institutions will pilot accounts designed to appeal to LMI households in terms of key consumer protections, transactional features, and a savings option over the course of a year.

Moreover, that LMI households place high value on federal consumer protections suggests that the new Consumer Financial Protection Bureau, established under the Dodd-Frank Act, may want to focus resources on establishing clear protections in this market, in conjunction with the FDIC's rules on deposit insurance. Our results and existing research suggest that uniform consumer protection rules ought to reduce consumer confusion, increase take-up rates, and improve the functionality of these cards.

Though our study focuses on the payment-card preferences of LMI households, payment cards are by no means the only payment technology that can increase financial access for unbanked households. Indeed, in the developing world, payments using mobile phones promise to expand financial access in areas with no dedicated electronic financial infrastructure, such as ATMs or point-of-sale terminals (Porteous 2006).[24] Developing countries need not invest in older technologies and can instead "leapfrog" directly to mobile payment systems, which promise to increase capability and lower infrastructure costs (Porteous 2006; Evans and Schmallensee 2009).

However, this approach seems less likely to significantly improve financial access in the United States for LMI households in the near term. The United States has a large financial infrastructure, including large branch and ATM networks and nearly ubiquitous payment-card acceptance through point-of-sale terminals; in view of the existing alternatives, the increased utility that mobile payments provide over these existing options may not yet justify the significant up-front investment in mobile-payment infrastructure (see Contini and others 2011). Moreover, new "two-sided" network technologies suffer from what David Evans and Richard Schmallensee (2009) call a "chicken-and-egg" problem: Much of customers' utility from a mobile payment system would derive from the convenience of payment at the point of sale, say, through a contactless near-field-communications technology, as suggested by Darin Contini and colleagues (2011). However, with few existing users, merchants would be reluctant to incur the costs to accept the new payment system. Since few merchants accept the technology, few consumers adopt. Where mobile payment technologies have managed to build a user base, they are often only bridges between existing payment systems and the wireless communications network used by mobile phones: for example, customers may deposit a check by photographing it with a smartphone, and merchants may accept payment cards by swiping them through a

---

24. For example, in the Philippines, 70 percent of unbanked households use mobile phones (Beshouri and others 2010, exhibit 1).

dongle attached to a phone.[25] Since these mobile technologies currently rely on mainstream financial products to operate and often require expensive hardware, such hybrid solutions are unlikely to aid the unbanked in the short term, even if they hold promise for the longer term. In view of these factors, our research in this study focuses on technologies that can maximize customer take-up in the near term, particularly payment cards that use existing ATM and point-of-sale-terminal infrastructure.

Measuring Consumer Preferences for Payment Cards

Drawing on methods from marketing research, we develop a discrete-choice model of LMI households' preferences for payment cards as a function of the features of the payment card. We then use this model to predict take-up rates for payment cards with different combinations of monetary and nonmonetary features. By assigning costs to different payment-card designs, policymakers and financial institutions can assess the net benefits implied by the costs and take-up rates of various payment cards. The proposed analysis approach can be used by policymakers to determine which payment card is most profitable (or least unprofitable), given costs and demographics in a particular locale, and whether subsidies or other public intervention will be necessary to entice private institutions to offer payment cards.

The model we use allows us to compare (among other things) whether banked and unbanked respondents value the features in similar or different ways. This comparison is facilitated by the hierarchical multinomial logit specification used in the discrete-choice model. At the lower level in this model, we estimate a relationship between observed payment-card choices and unobserved consumer preferences for payment-card features (compare Rossi, Allenby, and McCulloch 2005; Train 2003). In the upper level of the model, these consumer preferences are modeled as a linear function of LMI households' characteristics, including income, age, race, gender, and whether they have a bank account. This structure enables us to analyze whether LMI households' preferences for payment-card features differ depending on income, age, race, and gender. It also allows us to extrapolate from a representative sample of LMI households in Detroit in order to predict take-up rates for other cities with different distributions of demographic and socioeconomic characteristics.

Data Collection

There are a number of different features that a payment card can offer that can change the cost of offering the card and the utility of services available to

25. Emily Glazer, "Use a Phone for Deposits on the Go," *Wall Street Journal,* July 6, 2011; Claire Cain Miller and Nick Bilton, "Cellphone Payments Offer Alternative to Cash," *New York Times,* April 28, 2010.

low- and moderate-income users. These features are summarized in table 4-1. This study collected data specifically designed to measure how the features in table 4-1 affect take-up rates for purchase of cards among LMI households.

The limited use of payment cards by LMI households in the marketplace makes it difficult to assemble market data to estimate preferences for the various features described in table 4-1, particularly given the need to explore the preferences of nonusers as well as users. As a result, the study estimates our model for payment-card take-up based on hypothetical choices made by LMI households in a survey (following the conjoint analysis or discrete-choice survey approach; see Louviere, Hensher, and Swait 2001). These hypothetical-choice questions are part of the Detroit Area Household Financial Services study, explained in detail in chapter 2. The DAHFS sample consists of 1,003 interviews. Of those, 788 answered all of the discrete-choice questions, as well as the five demographic and socioeconomic questions used in estimating the demand model.

In the discrete-choice portion of this survey, respondents were asked to look at a thirteen-page chart presenting payment-card options. As to each page, they were asked to indicate which of three alternative payment cards they found most attractive (see figure 4-1, for an example). Each card also included a fourth option of "none" or no purchase. The attributes and levels for the alternatives in each question followed an experimental design created using Sawtooth Software's Choice-Based Conjoint package (for background, see, for example, Sawtooth Software 2008).

Descriptive Statistics for the Sample

The DAHFS survey identifies a number of problems with bank-account ownership among LMI households. Among the 73 percent of respondents who have either a checking or savings account, 35 percent overdrew their accounts at least once during the year preceding the survey interview.[26] During this period, 13 percent paid a fee for going below their minimum balance. To identify which financial barriers are most important to the unbanked, we asked what improved feature of a bank account would make them most likely to open an account. Unbanked respondents cite less confusing fees (16 percent), lower minimum balances (14 percent), and the ability to get money faster (10 percent) as the main obstacles they would like to see removed. For 29 percent of the sample, lower fees were perceived as the primary facilitator to opening an account, while 20 percent considered more convenient bank hours and locations as their chief motivation in considering whether to open up an account.

---

26. The estimate of the proportion unbanked is consistent with previous large-scale surveys (Aizcorbe, Kennickell, and Moore 2003; Dunham, Scheuren, and Willson 1998; Seidman, Hababou, and Kramer 2005; Bucks, Kennickell, and Moore 2006; Bucks and others 2009).

Table 4-1. *Attributes and Levels in the Payment-Card Questions*

Attribute	Level
Credit-check requirement	
	No credit check
	Favorable credit report
Card type	
	Debit (ATM) card
	Payroll card
	MasterCard prepaid debit card
Lost card protection	
	Federal protection
	No protection
Deposits	
	Direct deposit
	Employer loads cards
	Card holder cashes check and loads card for $2.95 fee
Savings	
	Automatic savings plan
	No savings plan
Bill payment	
	Buy money orders with card
	Automatic bill payment available
	Pay bills in person with card
	Pay bills by phone or Internet with card
Get cash	
	Get cash at any ATM, from bank teller, and with purchase at store
	Get cash at participating ATMs and with purchase at store
Cash access fees	
	Four free transactions a month at the card issuer's ATMs; then $2.00 each
	$1.50 fee for each ATM cash withdrawal
	$2.50 fee for each ATM cash withdrawal
Monthly fees	
	None with direct deposit of paycheck
	$2.95
	$5.95
	$9.95

Source: Detroit Area Household Financial Services study.

Figure 4-1. *Sample Page from Discrete-Choice Questionnaire*

Please put an **X** under the *one* option you would choose from this card:

	Option 1	Option 2	Option 3	Option 4
Requirements	Favorable credit report	No credit check	No credit check	None
Card Type	MasterCard Prepaid Debit Card	Payroll Card	Debit (ATM) Card	I would not choose any of these options.
Lost Card Protection	No protection	Federal protection	Federal protection	
Deposits	You cash check and load card for $2.95 fee	Direct Deposit	Employer loads cards	
Savings	No savings plan	No savings plan	Automatic savings plan	
Bill Payment	Automatic bill payment available	Buy money orders with card	Pay bills in person with card	
Get Cash	Get cash at any ATM, from bank tellers and with purchases at stores	Get cash at participating ATMs and with purchases at stores	Get cash at any ATM, from bank tellers and with purchases at stores	
Cash Access Fees	$1.50 fee for each ATM cash withdrawal	4 free per month at the card issuer's ATMs; then $2.00 each	$2.50 fee for each ATM cash withdrawal	
Monthly Fees	$5.95 per month fee	$9.95 per month fee	$2.95 per month fee	
	○	X	○	○

SID # _ _ _ _ _ _ _

Respondents report difficulty maintaining a bank account. Despite being banked, 12 percent of account holders had a previous bank account closed by the bank (not owing to a move). Common reasons for a bank's closing of an account include a low balance or an inactive account or bounced checks and overdrafts. In addition, 55 percent of the banked respondents closed a previously held bank account voluntarily, most commonly owing to the convenience of another bank or excessive fees. Among the unbanked, 70 percent report they chose to close the account themselves, citing moving, worrying about bouncing checks, and having to pay fees as their reasons for closing the account. The remaining formerly banked portion (30 percent) reports that the bank closed the account mostly because of bounced checks and overdrafts.

In spite of LMI households' difficulty in acquiring or maintaining traditional bank accounts, there is interest among the unbanked to have a bank account. Of the unbanked respondents, 75 percent say they would like to open a bank account in the next year, and 33 percent say they have shopped around for a bank account. However, 17 percent report that a bank denied their application to open a bank account.[27] Determining what type of account (or its functional equivalent using a payment card) would be attractive to low-income households could thus help the private and public sectors to develop products that could serve these households better.

Model Specification

To analyze the responses to the hypothetical-choice questions in the discrete-choice portion of the survey, we use a hierarchical multinomial logit model (see Allenby and Ginter 1995; Train 2003). In this model, the choice made by consumer i in question t is related to the vector of product attributes, $\mathbf{X}_{ijt}$, for each alternative j through a vector of individual-level parameters, β_i. Specifically, the likelihood that alternative j is chosen is given by the multinomial logit model:[28]

$$p\left(y_{it} = j*|\beta_i,\{\mathbf{X}_{ijt}\}\right) = \frac{\exp\left(\beta_i\mathbf{X}_{ij*t}\right)}{\sum_j \exp\left(\beta_i\mathbf{X}_{ijt}\right)}. \tag{4-1}$$

The estimated parameters β_i indicate respondent i's strength of preference for the different levels of the attributes. These parameters are assumed to arise from a multivariate regression relating β_i to a vector $\mathbf{z}_i$ of known characteristics of consumer i. Specifically,

27. See chapters 2 and 3, this volume, for further details regarding the unbanked.

28. Throughout, we use the notation $p(y \mid x)$ to indicate the probability (or probability density function for continuous random variables) for y conditional on x. $N_K(\mu, \Sigma)$ is used to denote the multivariate normal distribution for a random vector of dimension K with mean vector μ and covariance matrix Σ.

$$p(\beta_i \mid \mathbf{z}_i, \Delta, \Sigma) = N_K(\Delta \mathbf{z}_i, \Sigma), \qquad (4\text{-}2)$$

where K is the number of attributes, Δ is the matrix of regression coefficients, and Σ is the covariance matrix of the error term. The matrix Δ describes the overall population preferences for the different product attributes and the covariance between those preferences and the characteristics of the individuals. The matrix Σ describes how individual preferences vary around the predictions of the regression model. This hierarchical structure allows us to understand how consumer preferences for payment cards vary with the demographics of the respondent. The data used to estimate the model consist of the product attributes in the discrete-choice questions $\{x_{ijt}\}$, the observed choices $\{y_{it}\}$, and respondent characteristics, $\{\mathbf{z}_i\}$.

For this application, we specified the x_{ijt} as effects coded for the attribute levels described in table 4-1 plus a dummy variable for the "none" option (or outside good), which resulted in seventeen estimated attribute preference parameters for each respondent. To specify $\mathbf{z}_i$ we chose five demographic variables from the survey that we believed were likely to be related to individuals' payment-card preferences and were relatively uncorrelated with one another. These included the age of the respondent (centered at forty, approximately the median age), the gender of the respondent, the log of the income (centered at $20,000 a year, approximately the median income), a dummy variable indicating whether the respondent has a bank account, and a dummy indicating that the respondent is not African American. We also included a dummy variable for the moderate-income sampling stratum versus the low-income stratum in $\mathbf{z}_i$. Thus each estimated parameter in Δ describes how preferences for the payment-card attributes vary with the demographics of the respondent.

Our approach to estimation is Bayesian with conditionally conjugate, diffuse, proper priors for Δ and Σ, which allows use of the usual Metropolis-within-Gibbs sampler for the hierarchical multinomial logit model (see Rossi, Allenby, and McCulloch 2005). The priors on Δ and Σ were

$$p(vec(\Delta)) = N_{KL}(0, \operatorname{diag}(1{,}000))$$

and

$$p(\Sigma) = \text{Inverted Wishart}(K + 2, I)$$

where K is the number of attributes and L the number of individual characteristics. The sampler was coded using the R statistical language. Convergence of the sampler was assessed by comparing two chains with different starting values. All parameters in Δ and Σ achieved Gelman-Rubin potential scale reduction factors of 1.1 or less. Posterior inference was based on 200,000 draws, thinned by 10 to reduce data storage requirements.

Parameter Estimates for the Discrete-Choice Model

The parameter estimates for the model suggest that there may be a significant opportunity to induce take-up of a payment card among LMI households, and in particular among those without bank accounts and those who live in low-income census tracts. In this section, we describe the features of a payment card that have the largest weight in determining individuals' decisions about payment cards. We also discuss demographic differences in the relative weight given to a particular payment-card feature as well as in the take-up rates of cards for different demographic groups. The parameter estimates for the model are shown in table 4-2. Estimates of the relationship between payment-card features and households show the relative importance of payment card features for the modal respondent (column 1) and differences between average preferences for the modal respondent and those for respondents who have higher income, are older, are male, are not African American, or live in a moderate-income census tract (columns 2 through 7).[29]

The most appealing payment card for the modal unbanked respondent, as shown in column 1 of table 4-2, is a debit card with no credit check requirements, with federal lost-card protection, that is loaded for a $2.95 fee and has unlimited cash withdrawals for $1.50 each, a savings plan, automatic bill payment, and no monthly fees. Preferences for payment-card attributes vary with respondent demographics, as shown in columns 2 through 7. Although almost all groups prefer a debit card to a prepaid MasterCard or payroll card, this distinction is not as important for those with bank accounts (who already have debit cards) and those who are older (who are more likely to have bank accounts and therefore debit cards). Similarly, federal deposit protection is preferable to no protection among all groups but is somewhat less important to those who are male, older, and have lower incomes relative to the modal respondent in column 1. These patterns suggest that preferences for the availability of federal protection among younger, female, and unbanked respondents (the reference category) are quite strong relative to other demographic groups.

Cards with savings plans are preferable to all groups but are less important to those who are male, and to those without bank accounts (who may not value the saving option as much as the transactional features of a payment card). There is statistically significant variation across respondent groups in preferences for the method of loading the card. Respondents who are unbanked and not African American, on average, prefer to have the employer load the card, while banked

---

29. The first column shows the intercept parameters in Δ. Given the coding scheme for the variables in z_i, these intercept terms correspond to the average attribute part-worths (that is, the marginal utility of the attribute) for the modal respondent in the sample who is unbanked. Parameters that are different from zero (that is, the 5th and 95th percentiles of the posterior density do not span zero) are highlighted in bold.

Table 4-2. *Parameter Estimates for Payment-Card Attributes, by Respondent Characteristics*[a]

Attribute	Modal respondent unbanked low-income tract (1)	Has bank account (2)	Log (income/$20,000) (3)	Age in decades (4)	Male (5)	Not African American (6)	Moderate-income census tract (7)	Unexplained heterogeneity (variance) (8)
Requirements								
No	0.26							
Yes	**−0.26** (0.05)	0.11 (0.06)	0.00 (0.01)	0.02 (0.02)	**0.12** (0.05)	0.01 (0.06)	−0.07 (0.06)	**0.20** (0.02)
Card type								
Debit	0.44	0.00	0.02	−0.13	−0.11	−0.30	−0.22	
Master card	**−0.60** (0.23)	**0.48** (0.24)	−0.04 (0.03)	**0.16** (0.07)	0.07 (0.22)	0.33 (0.2)	0.25 (0.23)	**0.19** (0.02)
Payroll	0.17 (0.13)	**−0.48** (0.14)	0.01 (0.02)	−0.03 (0.04)	0.03 (0.12)	−0.04 (0.12)	−0.03 (0.13)	**0.22** (0.02)
Protection								
No	−0.70	−0.05	−0.02	0.05	0.22	0.02	0.09	
Yes	**0.70** (0.06)	0.05 (0.07)	**0.02** (0.01)	**−0.05** (0.02)	**−0.22** (0.06)	−0.02 (0.07)	−0.09 (0.06)	**0.28** (0.03)
Deposits								
Fee	0.21	−0.38	0.02	−0.13	−0.01	−0.61	−0.34	
Direct deposit	−0.08 (0.13)	**0.38** (0.14)	−0.03 (0.02)	0.05 (0.04)	0.16 (0.13)	0.23 (0.13)	0.12 (0.13)	**0.27** (0.03)
Employer	−0.13 (0.12)	0.00 (0.13)	0.01 (0.02)	**0.09** (0.04)	−0.15 (0.11)	**0.38** (0.11)	0.21 (0.12)	**0.25** (0.03)
Savings								
No	−0.22	−0.15	−0.01	−0.01	0.14	0.04	0.07	
Yes	**0.22** (0.07)	**0.15** (0.07)	0.01 (0.01)	0.01 (0.02)	**−0.14** (0.07)	−0.04 (0.08)	−0.07 (0.08)	**0.27** (0.03)

Bill pay								
Money order	-0.16	0.05	-0.02	-0.03	0.05	0.02	0.15	
Automatic	**0.22** (0.08)	-0.01 (0.09)	**0.04** (0.01)	0.00 (0.03)	-0.12 (0.08)	0.03 (0.09)	-0.17 (0.09)	**0.27** (0.03)
By phone	-0.02 (0.08)	0.07 (0.08)	-0.01 (0.01)	0.01 (0.03)	-0.04 (0.09)	-0.12 (0.09)	0.01 (0.09)	**0.31** (0.04)
In person	-0.04 (0.1)	-0.12 (0.1)	0.00 (0.01)	0.01 (0.03)	0.12 (0.09)	0.07 (0.1)	0.01 (0.09)	**0.37** (0.05)
Get cash								
Participating	-0.04	0.06	0.00	-0.02	0.02	-0.06	0.11	
Any	0.04 (0.06)	-0.06 (0.07)	0.00 (0.01)	0.02 (0.02)	-0.02 (0.06)	0.06 (0.07)	-0.11 (0.07)	**0.26** (0.03)
Cash fee								
None	-0.06	-0.02	0.01	-0.01	0.08	0.13	0.09	
$1.50	**0.23** (0.09)	-0.01 (0.09)	-0.02 (0.01)	-0.01 (0.03)	-0.07 (0.09)	-0.05 (0.09)	-0.14 (0.09)	**0.36** (0.04)
$2.50	-0.17 (0.1)	0.02 (0.1)	0.00 (0.01)	0.02 (0.03)	-0.01 (0.09)	-0.08 (0.11)	0.05 (0.1)	**0.48** (0.05)
Monthly fee								
None	0.61	0.48	0.04	0.04	-0.07	0.15	0.17	
$2.95	**0.26** (0.12)	-0.07 (0.11)	-0.01 (0.02)	-0.01 (0.03)	-0.01 (0.13)	0.04 (0.13)	**0.26** (0.11)	**0.60** (0.07)
$5.95	-0.09 (0.13)	-0.22 (0.14)	-0.02 (0.02)	-0.05 (0.04)	-0.06 (0.13)	0.09 (0.13)	-0.19 (0.12)	**0.81** (0.09)
$9.95	**-0.78** (0.14)	-0.19 (0.15)	-0.02 (0.02)	0.02 (0.05)	0.15 (0.15)	-0.28 (0.15)	-0.24 (0.14)	**1.23** (0.15)
Outside good	**1.24** (0.35)	0.53 (0.35)	**-0.15** (0.06)	**0.76** (0.11)	0.70 (0.34)	**1.08** (0.38)	0.21 (0.4)	**19.20** (1.75)

Source: Detroit Area Household Financial Services study.

a. Standard errors are in parentheses. Estimates are posterior means from the discrete-choice survey. Parameters for which the 5th and 95th percentiles of the posterior do not span zero are highlighted in bold.

respondents prefer direct deposit. Respondents who are African American show significantly less preference for cards that are loaded by employers, which is consistent with sociological research finding a general distrust of employers among inner-city African Americans (Wilson 1987, 1996). All respondent groups prefer cards with no fees for withdrawing cash or no monthly fees, although those from moderate-income neighborhoods find the $2.95 monthly fee less dissuasive than those who live in low-income census tracts.

The last row in table 4-2 shows how preferences for the outside good vary for different respondent groups by comparison to the modal respondent. The outside-good parameters describe how likely the respondent is to choose one of the payment cards over the "none" option in the discrete-choice questions. Generally, lower values of the outside-good parameter indicate more interest in payment-card products. The estimated parameters indicate that people who are older, male, and not black are significantly less likely to find payment cards attractive. In other words, respondents whose demographic characteristics suggest they have greater access to bank accounts, and therefore an outside option, are less likely to report wanting a payment card (see table 3-1, this volume). Although not statistically significant, the estimated parameter in the last row of column 2 indicates that those who already have bank accounts are also less interested in payment cards.[30] We also find that people with relatively higher incomes within LMI communities are significantly more interested in payment cards, possibly owing to greater economic activity and a stronger demand for financial services.

The parameters in column 8 in table 4-2 describe how much variance we see in attribute preferences among respondents with the same demographic profile.[31] The high estimate for the variance in the outside-good parameter (19.20) indicates that there are large differences between respondents with similar demographics in their preference for the outside good. This suggests that even within each demographic group, some respondents are very interested in payment cards while others are not at all interested. This heterogeneity suggests it is unlikely that a single card can be developed to be universally acceptable to all LMI households and that multiple card offerings would be required to reach the broadest audience.

The hierarchical-model structure allows computation of attribute importance estimates for different combinations of socioeconomic variables. In the first two columns of table 4-3, we contrast the average relative attribute importance for

30. In our Detroit sample, bank-account ownership is highly correlated with age, race, and income, which may help explain the relatively large standard error on the estimated preference for the outside good among the banked (see chapter 3, this volume).

31. Column 8 in table 4-2 shows the parameter estimates for the diagonal elements in Σ. To capture correlations between attribute preferences, we estimated a full covariance matrix for Σ, but we do not report the off-diagonal elements. There were few correlations with posterior support far from zero. Full results are available upon request.

Table 4-3. *Relative Importance of Payment-Card Attributes, by Respondent Characteristics*
Percent

Attribute	Female African American $20K income age 40 unbanked Low-income tract (1)	Female African American $20K income age 40 banked moderate-income tract (2)	Male not African American $50K income age 40 banked moderate-income tract (3)
Requirements	9	6	2
Card type	17	8	11
Lost card protection	24	19	11
Deposits	6	13	25
Savings	7	9	3
Bill payment	6	3	3
Get cash	1	4	2
Cash access fees	7	2	6
Monthly fees	23	35	36

Source: Detroit Area Household Financial Services study.

a. Attribute importance is computed based on the estimated mean utility parameters for the demographic group. Attribute importance is the difference between the best and worst levels for that attribute as a percentage relative to other attributes.

the modal unbanked respondent living in a low-income census tract to that of the modal banked respondent living in a moderate-income census tract. The first group of respondents place equal weight on monthly fees and the availability of federal protection when they make their payment-card decisions. After these two features, the payment card's type (debit versus payroll versus MasterCard) is an important factor. Like the first group, the second group places the most importance on monthly fees and lost-card protection, but relative to the first group, they place a higher weight on the former and less weight on the latter. Also, the second group of respondents places less importance on the card type and more on the method of making deposits than the modal unbanked respondent in column 1. We also contrast these two low-income respondents with a middle-income male resident of a moderate-income census tract who is not African American, is age forty, and has a bank account (column 3). Like the first two groups, this group places the greatest importance on monthly fees. In contrast to the other two groups, middle-income respondents place less importance on lost-card protection and more on the method of making deposits. Also, for this group, the functional aspects of the payment card, such as the availability of a savings plan and the method for paying bills, carry less weight.

By showing the variation in attribute importance, the results in table 4-3 suggest how different purchase-card programs could be tailored to appeal to various demographic groups. The relative importance of purchase-card attributes indicates that female, African American, unbanked respondents weigh lost-card protection and monthly fees similarly highly in choosing purchase cards, while banked and higher-income, male respondents find monthly fees substantially more important than any other attribute.

Predicting Take-Up Rates

As discussed earlier, the discrete-choice model can be used by policymakers to estimate the fraction of LMI households who report they would sign up for a payment card if one were offered to them. We refer to this fraction as the take-up rate. The take-up rate can be estimated for any combination of the payment-card features described in table 4-1, based on the estimated likelihood of choosing a particular payment card versus choosing the outside good. (Given the relative scarcity of payment cards in the low-income marketplace, take-up rate estimates reported here assume that there would be only one card available to LMI households. However, the model could be used to estimate take-up rates and market shares were multiple payment cards available to a group of LMI households.) We have developed an interactive tool that can be used to explore take-up rates for different payment-card configurations and different subgroups of the Detroit LMI population.[32] Policymakers can use this tool to determine the take-up rate for any payment-card program, given the target market in their locality (race, age, gender, access to bank accounts, and so on).

To demonstrate the approach, we used the tool to determine the payment-card design that would maximize the take-up rate for the overall Detroit LMI population. The card maximizing the take-up rate is a debit card with federal lost-card protection, an automatic savings plan, and no credit check. The full profile for this card is described in the first column of table 4-4. We estimate that almost 52 percent of LMI respondents would enroll in a payment-card program designed in this particular way. The estimated take-up rate is slightly higher for those living in a low-income census tract compared to those in a moderate-income census tract (52.8 versus 50.8 percent). The last two columns of table 4-4 describe designs tailored to the unbanked and banked subgroups, which are largely the same as the best design for the overall LMI population.

If a card were optimized for the unbanked subset of Detroit LMI households, it would allow users to pay bills in person with the card, would be a debit card, and would achieve a 54 percent take-up rate among the unbanked. A card optimized for the banked Detroit LMI households would be a MasterCard instead of a debit card and would achieve a 53 percent take rate-up among the banked. Although a card optimized for the unbanked achieves a lower overall take-up rate than one optimized for the banked or for the overall LMI population (50.4, 51.2, and 51.8 percent, respectively), the estimates in table 4-4 suggest that tailoring

---

32. This tool is available upon request.

Table 4-4. *Ideal Payment-Card Design and Take-up Rates for Detroit LMI Population*

Purchase card attribute	Detroit LMI population (1)	Detroit LMI unbanked (2)	Detroit LMI banked (3)
Credit-check requirement	No credit check	No credit check	No credit check
Card type	Debit (ATM) card	Debit (ATM) card	MasterCard prepaid debit card
Lost card protection	Federal protection	Federal protection	Federal protection
Deposits	Direct deposit	Direct deposit	Direct deposit
Savings	Automatic savings plan	Automatic savings plan	Automatic savings plan
Bill payment	Automatic bill payment available	Pay bills in person with card	Automatic bill payment available
Get cash	Get cash at participating ATMs and with purchase at store	Get cash at any ATM, from bank teller and with purchase at store	Get cash at participating ATMs and with purchase at store
Cash access fees	$1.50 fee for each ATM cash withdrawl	$1.50 fee for each ATM cash withdrawl	$1.50 fee for each ATM cash withdrawl
Monthly fees	No monthly fees with Direct Deposit of your paycheck	No monthly fees with Direct Deposit of your paycheck	No monthly fees with Direct Deposit of your paycheck
Estimated take-up rate (percent)[a]			
Detroit LMI population	**51.8**	50.4	51.2
Resident of low-income census tract (stratum 5)	52.8	51.4	50.3
Resident of moderate-income census tract (stratum 6)	50.8	49.2	52.2
Banked Detroit LMI population	51.4	49.2	**52.5**
Unbanked Detroit LMI population	53.0	**53.3**	47.8

Source: Detroit Area Household Financial Services study.

a. In each column, bold indicates the take-up rate for the group in that column for which the payment card was optimized. The nonbold take-up rates on each column are the take-up rates for the other groups.

Figure 4-2. *Residents in Moderate- versus Low-Income Neighborhoods, Response of Take-Up Rates to Monthly Fees*

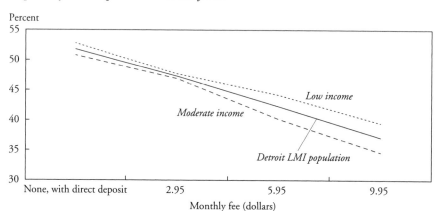

a card to the unbanked will sacrifice little in terms of the take-up rate among the banked.

The take-up rates shown in table 4-4 are estimated from the survey responses and therefore represent the likelihood that respondents would say that they would choose the card in a survey rather than the likelihood of their actual behavior. Take-up rates in the marketplace may be lower because respondents are not aware of the availability of payment cards or because they do not immediately take action as soon as a new product is available, or for other reasons.

The Effect of Price on Take-Up Rates

The interactive tool can also be used to predict how the response varies with changes in the design of the card. For instance, one can predict how take-up rates might change if monthly fees were added to the ideal card in the first column of table 4-4. (Such fees might offset the costs of providing payment cards.) Figure 4-2 shows that as monthly fees increase sharply, take-up rates drop off dramatically from 51.8 percent for the LMI population when there are no fees to 37.1 percent when the monthly fees are $9.95. The difference in the take-up rates for those who live in low-income compared with those who live in moderate-income census tracts increases (39.5 versus 34.6 percent) when fees are $9.95, indicating that demand for payment cards is less elastic in households that live in low-income census tracts. We also find that those living in moderate-income census tracts, who are more likely to have bank accounts, are more sensitive to fees, suggesting greater substitutability between the payment card and a bank account for these households. Similarly, in figure 4-3, we show the decline in take-up rates for banked and unbanked respondents as monthly fees increase. The take-up rates for the banked are more sensitive to monthly fees than for the

Figure 4-3. *Banked versus Unbanked, Response of Take-Up Rates to Monthly Fees*

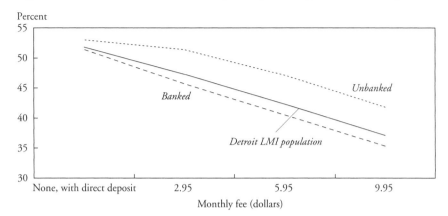

Percent

unbanked. Even when monthly fees are $9.95, nearly 45 percent of unbanked households say they would take the card.

Details of the Take-Up Rate Calculations

In the model, the take-up rate depends on the demographics of the consumers, and so we can compute take-up rates specific to any particular demographic profile. This allows policymakers to compute take-up rates specifically for any local target population. Following the Bayesian approach, we compute the average likelihood of the choice over the posterior. Specifically, the average take-up rate for a target design x for a respondent with demographics z_i is computed as

$$\text{take-up rate} = p\left(y_i = \text{target design}\right) = \int_{\Delta,\Sigma} p\left(y_i | x, \beta_i\right) p\left(\beta_i | z_i, \Delta, \Sigma\right) p\left(\Delta, \Sigma\right) d\Delta d\Sigma,$$

where $p(y_i | x, \beta_i)$ is the likelihood that i will choose the target design x over the outside good (based on equation 4-1), $p(\beta_i | z_i, \Delta, \Sigma)$ is as given in equation 4-2, and $p(\Delta, \Sigma)$ is the posterior density of the model parameters. The integral is estimated by sampling from the posterior draws.

To estimate the take-up rate for a population of respondents, we average the take-up rate over some distribution of the demographic variables. For example, to estimate the take-up rate overall among LMI households in Detroit, we use the distribution of z_i observed in the survey sample. One advantage of the hierarchical modeling approach is that we can also estimate take-up rates for another population of respondents (for example, for a different city) by averaging over some other distribution of z_i.[33] If $p(z_i)$ is the distribution of demographics for the

33. This assumes that the relationship between demographics and preferences holds between the target population and the survey population used to estimate the model, and it should be taken with care.

population we wish to estimate a take-up rate for, then the take-up rate for the population is given by

$$\text{take-up rate} = p(y_i = \text{target design})$$
$$= \int\limits_{z_i, \Delta, \Sigma} \int p(y_i | x, \beta_i) p(\beta_i | z_i, \Delta\Sigma) p(\Delta\Sigma) \, d\Delta d \, \Sigma p(z_i) \, dz_i.$$

The take-up rates for the overall Detroit LMI population, for example, are shown in the first row of the bottom panel of table 4-4.

Costs and the Profitability of Payment Cards

The design in the first column of table 4-4 represents the ideal payment card from the Detroit LMI consumer's perspective. However, government agencies and private financial institutions who are designing payment-card programs need to weigh the likely take-up rates against the costs of offering different features. When private firms design products for the market, the central objective is profit, and their analysis must consider the potential revenues that would be generated by fees at the different resulting take-up rates. However, government agencies are considering developing payment-card programs in an effort to improve the welfare of LMI households, and so they will weigh the costs of payment-card features against a broader metric, including the potential benefits to LMI households.

One approach to weighing costs of a payment-card program against the social benefits to an LMI household from having a payment card is to optimize the per-household cost of the program—that is, the ratio of the costs to the number of households who sign up for the program. Costs for payment-card programs can be summarized as the fixed cost of developing a program, C_0; the cost of setting up an individual account, s, and the monthly cost (net of revenues from fees) of servicing an account, $c(x)$. The take-up rate can be estimated using our discrete-choice model as the total number of individuals in the target population, M, times the take-up rate $\rho(x)$. The per-household net present cost for the program is then

$$\frac{C_0}{M\rho(x)} + s + \sum_{t=1}^{T} \delta^t c(x),$$

where δ is the discount factor and T is the planning horizon. If the fixed costs of the program, C_0, are sufficiently large, then the cost of adding attractive features to the program may be offset by the economies of scale gained by increasing the take-up rate, $\rho(x)$.

By combining their own internal cost data with the tool used here, policymakers and private firms can optimize payment-card designs to achieve the lowest possible per-household net present cost.[34] The hierarchical Bayes model allows this tool to adjust for any local demographic distribution (for example, percentage of African Americans, percentage of low- versus moderate-income households) so that the take-up rate predictions are specific to the group targeted by a particular program. This tool is available from the authors upon request.

Policy Implications and Recommendations

This chapter characterizes the features of account-based payment cards—including bank debit cards, prepaid debit cards, and payroll cards—that elicit a high take-up rate among low- and moderate-income households, particularly those without bank accounts. We apply discrete choice modeling to identify the design of specific financial services products for LMI households, who often face difficulties acquiring or maintaining standard bank accounts but need banking services. After monthly cost, we find that, on average, nonmonetary features of a payment card, such as the availability of federal protection and the type of card, are factors LMI consumers weigh most heavily when choosing among differently designed payment cards. We estimate a high take-up rate for a well-designed payment card. The sensitivity of the take-up rate with respect to cost varies by income and bank-account ownership. These results can guide private and public sector initiatives to expand the range of financial services available to LMI households, particularly as the federal government embarks on a wide-ranging effort to move federal benefits and tax refunds to electronic transmission and as federal regulators weigh new consumer protections for payment cards in the wake of the passage in 2010 of the Dodd-Frank Wall Street Reform and Consumer Protection Act. Results from the Detroit Area Household Financial Services study suggest several areas for improvement.

Consider Effects of Debit-Interchange Rules on Low- and Moderate-Income Households

Some policies may impose unintended costs in ways that may limit access to deposit services with mainstream financial institutions. For example, in 2010 Congress enacted section 920 of the Electronic Fund Transfer Act,[35] requiring that the interchange transaction fees that large debit-card issuers may receive

---

34. One way policymakers can use this tool is to project the revenues from a particular card and compare this figure with the likely costs. In turn, this comparison can help policymakers determine the size of the subsidy a depository institution would need, if any, in order to profit from issuing a payment card, or the amount the government could charge the depository institution for marketing the card to recipients.

35. Dodd–Frank Wall Street Reform and Consumer Protection Act, Pub. L. No. 111-203, sec. 1075(a)(2), 124 Stat. 1376, 2068–74 (2010) (to be codified at 15 U.S.C. § 1693o–2).

for debit transactions be "reasonable and proportional" to the issuer's per-transaction cost. The rules enacted under section 920 will reduce interchange fees from an average of $0.44 per transaction[36] to about $0.24 per transaction,[37] a 45 percent decrease. This change lowers the profitability of debit cards and of banking accounts, which are subsidized by debit-card interchange revenue. Banks are expected to act to maintain overall profitability by making deposit transaction pricing more explicit, increasing account maintenance charges, and reducing or ending debit-card reward programs.

There may also be some shift in usage from signature debit cards (with higher interchange fees) to PIN (personal identification number) debit (with lower interchange fees) because the latter will be less hard hit by the cap on interchange fees. Retailers may reduce prices over time as interchange costs go down. The overall social-welfare effects of these changes are not obvious. Beyond these measures, additional bank efforts to reduce costs are most likely to fall on those customers who generate the least marginal profit: namely, customers from LMI households. Though parts of section 920 seek to lessen its impact on LMI households by exempting government-sponsored payment programs and certain reloadable prepaid cards,[38] the rule may work to exclude more LMI households from ownership of bank accounts. Policymakers may need to undertake other measures to offset any reduction in access for LMI households that may be induced by this provision.

Lower Costs of Public-Benefit Transfer Cards

Governments could do more to lower the costs of transacting with state-government-sponsored benefit cards. Though federal regulations forbid the levy of fees on food assistance benefits accessed through the electronic benefits transfer system, there are no similar protections for cash assistance disbursed through the system (FRB 2011). As a result, merchants and payment network operators may charge fees for EBT cash transactions at an ATM or point-of-sale terminal. Similarly, several unemployment insurance stored-value cards carry a variety of penalty fees, such as overdraft fees, denied transaction fees, and inactivity fees (NCLC 2011). State governments could negotiate for reduced fees when extending benefit-card program management contracts or absorb some fees as a cost of administering the program, rather than passing them on

---

36. Debit Card Interchange Fees and Routing, 75 *Federal Register* 81722, 81725 (December 28, 2010).

37. The rule promulgated to enforce section 920 caps interchange fees for affected issuers at $0.21 plus 0.05 percent of the transaction value. Assuming an average debit-card transaction size of about $38, this translates to about $0.24 per transaction. Debit Card Interchange Fees and Routing, 76 *Federal Register* 43394, 43467 (July 20, 2011) (to be codified at 12 C.F.R. § 235.3(b)).

38. 15 U.S.C. § 1693o–2(a)(7) (2006 & Supp. IV 2010).

to households. In any event, states should work to simplify cost structures and improve disclosures for benefit cards.

Broaden Protections for Lower-Cost Account Substitutes

General-purpose reloadable prepaid cards (GPR cards) are an attractive alternative to traditional bank accounts for a number of customer niches (Keitel 2011), especially unbanked and underbanked households. However, unclear consumer protections and high fees prevent GPR cards from attracting more LMI households. First, a patchwork of overlapping regulatory powers has created uneven consumer protections for card holders. Some GPR-card holders receive pass-through federal deposit insurance, while others receive only minimal insurance because their deposits are aggregated with other card holders up to the insurance cap, while still others carry no insurance at all (Newville and Koide 2011); some GPR cards, such as payroll cards and cards issued in compliance with the Treasury Department's rule on federal benefit transfers, receive protections under Regulation E, while other cards are exempt (Newville and Koide 2011). Second, the variety of fees accompanying GPR cards makes comparison shopping difficult (Jun 2010; Newville and Koide 2011). The high value our survey respondents placed on federal protection suggests an important role for federal consumer-protection regulation across the card-based marketplace. Governments can enhance the viability of GPR cards by requiring pooled accounts to provide individually owned subaccounts that are eligible for pass-through insurance, expanding to all GPR cards the Regulation E protections currently given to payroll-card holders and improving fee disclosures to aid informed decisionmaking.[39]

Create Incentives for Lower-Cost Private Payment Cards

The high estimated take-up rate for a low-fee payment card is encouraging for policymakers and financial institutions interested in offering a broader range of payment-card products to LMI households. Policymakers and financial institutions can use our predicted take-up rates to weigh against cost estimates to determine the optimal design of the payment card that achieves the lowest possible per-household net present cost.[40] The predicted take-up rates will also help in determining whether the optimal payment card would be profitable. In the case where the optimal payment card is not profitable to the private sector but there are social benefits of expanding financial services to LMI households, subsidies to private institutions or a publicly funded payment card may be appropriate. One

---

39. See Barr (2004), Jun (2010), and Newville and Koide (2011) for a fuller discussion of these recommendations.

40. Whether the products should be made available through government initiatives or by the private sector is a question left unanswered, as we do not have proprietary data from financial institutions on the costs of offering payment card services.

form of these subsidies might be for the government to provide a one-time sub-sidy to financial institutions for opening the account linked to a payment card, as previous research suggests that once an account is open, banks are able to profit from it on a monthly basis if there are recurring payments of a sufficient size and if the account is held for a sufficiently long period of time (Dove Associates and U.S. Department of Treasury 1999). Another strategy would be for the govern-ment to reduce per-unit acquisition costs by presenting the opportunity for one or more financial institutions to offer prepaid debit cards or other electronic accounts to benefit recipients and those who receive tax refunds. A third strategy would be to increase attention on research, development, and dissemination of new products, such as by offering prizes for innovative development.

The FDIC, the Treasury Department, and a number of states are currently exploring many of these options. The FDIC's "safe accounts" pilot mentioned earlier in this chapter is one example. Early results from this research were pro-vided to the Treasury Department to shape its Direct Express card, which now helps more than a million Social Security and other federal benefit recipients, to launch its pilot program for electronic payment of tax refunds in January 2011, and to shape its Bank On initiatives, which seek to encourage innovation in meeting the financial services needs of LMI households through local efforts around the country. Similarly, this research could be used by state governments seeking to expand the use and functionality of electronic-benefit-transfer cards among households receiving state benefits or tax refunds.

Directions for Further Research

While the results presented in this chapter are encouraging for government policymakers as well as depository institutions and other firms interested in offer-ing payment cards or electronic-based financial services more broadly, they are derived from a hypothetical discrete-choice survey. The take-up rates estimated presume that consumers are fully aware of the attributes of the payment card, whereas in reality, substantial marketing and communication, which are costly, may be necessary to impart this awareness to consumers.[41] Moreover, further research is needed to understand how behavioral psychology factors, such as construal and situational factors and how the payment card's features or costs are presented, may inhibit or advance the actual take-up of a payment card (Bertrand, Mullainathan, and Shafir 2006). Additional research is also neces-sary to identify whether payment cards and the availability of mainstream financial services indeed improve the welfare of low- and moderate-income households.

---

41. We are grateful to an anonymous referee for pointing this out.

References

Aizcorbe, Ana M., Arthur B. Kennickell, and Kevin B. Moore. 2003. "Recent Changes in U.S. Family Finances: Evidence from the 1998 and 2001 Survey of Consumer Finances." *Federal Reserve Bulletin* 89 (January): 1–32.

Allenby, Greg M., and James L. Ginter. 1995. "Using Extremes to Design Products and Segment Markets." *Journal of Marketing Research* 32:392–403 (www.jstor.org/stable/3152175).

Amromin, Gene, Carrie Jankowski, and Richard Porter. 2007. "Transforming Payment Choices by Doubling Fees on the Illinois Tollway." *Economic Perspectives* 31 (Summer): 22–47.

Barr, Michael S. 2004. "Banking the Poor." *Yale Journal on Regulation* 21:121–238.

Barr, Michael S., and Rebecca M. Blank. 2009. Introduction to *Insufficient Funds: Savings, Assets, Credit, and Banking among Low-Income Households,* edited by Rebecca M. Blank and Michael S. Barr, 1–24. New York: Russell Sage Foundation.

Bertrand, Marianne, Sendhil Mullainathan, and Eldar Shafir. 2006. "Behavioral Economics and Marketing in Aid of Decision Making among the Poor." *Journal of Public Policy and Marketing* 25:8–23.

Beshouri, Christopher, and others. 2010. "Mobile Money for the Unbanked: Unlocking the Potential in Emerging Markets." *McKinsey on Payments,* June (www.mckinsey.com/clientservice/Financial_Services/Knowledge_Highlights/Recent_Reports/~/media/Reports/Financial_Services/MoP8_Mobile_money_for_the_unbanked.ashx).

Borzekowski, Ron, Elizabeth K. Kiser, and Shaista Ahmed. 2008. "Consumers' Use of Debit Cards: Patterns, Preferences, and Price Response." *Journal of Money, Credit, and Banking* 40:149–72.

Bucks, Brian K., Arthur B. Kennickell, and Kevin B. Moore. 2006. "Recent Changes in U.S. Family Finances: Evidence from the 2001 and 2004 Survey of Consumer Finances." *Federal Reserve Bulletin* 92 (February): A1–38.

Bucks, Brian K., and others. 2009. "Changes in U.S. Family Finances from 2004 to 2007: Evidence from the Survey of Consumer Finances." *Federal Reserve Bulletin* 95 (February): A1–A56.

Caskey, John. 1994. *Fringe Banking: Check-Cashing Outlets, Pawnshops, and the Poor.* New York: Russell Sage Foundation.

Contini, Darin, and others. 2011. "Mobile Payments in the United States: Mapping Out the Road Ahead." Banking PayPers Series. Federal Reserve Bank of Boston (www.bos.frb.org/bankinfo/firo/publications/bankingpaypers/2011/mobile-payments-mapping.pdf).

Dove Associates and U.S. Department of the Treasury. 1999. *ETA Initiative, Final Report.* U.S. Department of the Treasury (www.fms.treas.gov/eta/reports/final.pdf).

Dunham, Constance R., Fritz J. Scheuren, and Douglas J. Willson. 1998. "Methodological Issues in Surveying the Nonbanked Population in Urban Areas." In *Proceedings of the American Statistical Association, Survey Research Methods Section* 20:611–16.

Evans, David S., and Richard Schmallensee. 2009. "Innovation and Evolution of the Payments Industry." In *Moving Money: The Future of Consumer Payments,* edited by Robert E. Litan and Martin Neil Baily, 36–76. Brookings.

FNS (Food and Nutrition Service). 2003. *Food Stamp Electronic Benefit Transfer Systems: A Report to Congress.* U.S. Department of Agriculture (www.fns.usda.gov/snap/ebt/pdfs/2003_congress.pdf).

FRB (Board of Governors of the Federal Reserve System). 2011. *Report to the Congress on Government-Administered, General-Use Prepaid Cards.* Federal Reserve Board (www.federal reserve.gov/publications/other-reports/files/government-prepaid-report-201107.pdf).

GAO (U.S. General Accounting Office). 2002. *Electronic Transfers: Use by Federal Recipients Has Increased but Obstacles to Greater Participation Remain* (www.gao.gov/new.items/d02913.pdf).

Hirschman, Elizabeth C. 1982. "Consumer Payment Systems: The Relationship of Attribute Structure to Preference and Usage." *Journal of Business* 55:531–45 (www.jstor.org/stable/2352992).

Humphrey, David B., Moshe Kim, and Bent Vale. 2001. "Realizing the Gains from Electronic Payments: Costs, Pricing, and Payment Choice." *Journal of Money, Credit, and Banking* 33:216–34.

Jun, Michelle. 2010. *Prepaid Cards: Second-Tier Bank Account Substitutes.* San Francisco, Calif.: Consumers Union (www.consumerfed.org/pdfs/SVC-CU-Report-9-10-update.pdf).

Keitel, Philip. 2011. *Conference Summary: Federal Regulation of the Prepaid Card Industry: Costs, Benefits, and Changing Industry Dynamics.* Federal Reserve Bank of Philadelphia (www.philadelphiafed.org/payment-cards-center/events/conferences/2011/C2011-Federal-Regulation-of-Prepaid-Card-Industry.pdf).

Kennickell, Arthur, and Myron Kwast. 1997. "Who Uses Electronic Banking? Results from the 1995 Survey of Consumer Finances." Paper prepared for the Annual Meetings of the Western Economic Association, Seattle.

Louviere, Jordan J., David A. Hensher, and Joffre Swait. 2001. *Stated Preference Methods: Analysis and Applications.* Cambridge University Press.

Mantel, Brian. 2000. "Why Do Consumers Pay Bills Electronically? An Empirical Analysis." *Economic Perspectives* 24 (Winter): 32–47.

NCLC (National Consumer Law Center). 2011. *Unemployment Compensation Prepaid Cards: States Can Deal Workers a Winning Hand by Discarding Junk Fees.* Boston (www.nclc.org/images/pdf/pr-reports/uc-prepaid-card-report.pdf).

Newville, David, and Melissa Koide. 2011. *Prepaid Cards and Consumer Protections.* Chicago: Center for Financial Services Innovation (http://cfsinnovation.com/?q=node/440682/lightbox2&url=sites/default/files/CFSI_PrepaidPolicy_July2011.pdf).

Porteous, David. 2006. "Financial Infrastructure and Financial Access." In *Building Inclusive Financial Systems: A Framework for Financial Access,* edited by Michael S. Barr, Anjali Kumar, and Robert E. Litan, 117–41. Brookings.

Romich, Jennifer, Sarah Gordon, and Eric N. Waithaka. 2009. "A Tool for Getting By or Getting Ahead? Consumers' Views on Prepaid Cards." Working Paper 2009-WP-09. Terre Haute: Indiana State University, Networks Financial Institute (http://ssrn.com/abstract=1491645).

Rossi, Peter E., Greg M. Allenby, and Robert McCulloch. 2005. *Bayesian Statistics and Marketing.* West Sussex, U.K.: John Wiley & Sons.

Sawtooth Software. 2008. "Proceedings of the Sawtooth Software Conference, October 2007" (www.sawtoothsoftware.com/download/techpap/2007Proceedings.pdf).

Seidman, Ellen, Moez Hababou, and Jennifer Kramer. 2005. *A Financial Services Survey of Low- and Moderate-Income Households.* Chicago: Center for Financial Services Innovation (http://cfsinnovation.com/system/files/imported/managed_documents/threecitysurvey.pdf).

Train, Kenneth E. 2003. *Discrete Choice Methods with Simulation.* Cambridge University Press.

Wilson, William Julius. 1987. *The Truly Disadvantaged: The Inner City, the Underclass, and Public Policy.* University of Chicago Press.

———. 1996. *When Work Disappears: The World of the New Urban Poor.* New York: Alfred Knopf.

5

Which Way to the Bank?

MICHAEL S. BARR, JANE K. DOKKO, RON BORZEKOWSKI, AND ELIZABETH K. KISER

Currently, in the United States, geographic access to retail banking services is unequal across communities. In particular, households living in wealthier communities tend to travel shorter distances to bank branches and have more branches available in their neighborhoods from which to choose. Low- and moderate-income neighborhoods, on the other hand, tend to have fewer bank branches and more "fringe banking," through alternative financial services (AFS) providers such as check cashers, payday lenders, pawnshops, and grocery or liquor stores providing transactional financial services and short-term lending (Caskey 1994). Furthermore, holding the observable economic characteristics of neighborhoods constant, communities with a higher fraction of minority residents have fewer bank branches and more AFS providers. Many public and private sector initiatives have sought to improve the types of financial services available across communities in order to increase bank-account ownership and reduce the use of high-fee AFS, particularly among low- and moderate-income (LMI) households.[1] Nevertheless, the geographic distribution of bank branches and AFS providers across neighborhoods remains disparate across neighborhoods.

Higher incidence of bank-account ownership and reduced use of alternative financial services by low- and moderate-income households are generally viewed

---

1. The Community Reinvestment Act, state and local regulations governing payday lenders, and community-development financial institutions are examples of public and private sector initiatives seeking to improve the landscape of financial services across communities.

as welfare-improving outcomes.[2] Around one-fifth of households in the lowest quintile of the income distribution, roughly 9 million households, do not have a bank account; these households may substitute high-fee AFS for basic banking services (Barr 2004; Bucks, Kennickell, and Moore 2006). However, for these LMI households, bank accounts may be costlier than AFS because of minimum-balance requirements, overdraft charges, and fees for check writing and use of automated teller machines. Greater geographic access to bank branches reduces one of the costs of bank-account ownership. If households are more likely to have bank accounts when facing lower costs, then there are welfare gains from expanding bank-account ownership by improving geographic access.

Whether increasing geographic access to banks (or reducing it to AFS providers) influences households' financial services decisions depends on whether the geographic heterogeneity in access to financial services has a causal effect on bank-account ownership and financial service use. This research question is a topic of ongoing debate. As other studies have shown, the cross-sectional correlation between geographic access and financial service use suggests that, all things being equal, neighborhoods with fewer bank branches and more AFS providers tend to have more households without bank accounts. In other words, the unbanked tend to be more concentrated in neighborhoods with a higher share of AFS providers and with higher geographic costs of bank-branch access. This cross-sectional correlation undoubtedly does not show the causal effect of geographic access if, for instance, businesses locate in areas where the demand for their services is highest and if households freely choose their residences based in part on the bundle of financial services available in a community. Rather than indicating whether geographic access to banks causally contributes to the likelihood of being unbanked, this cross-sectional correlation is likely to absorb the joint location decisions of businesses and households, thereby overstating the importance of geographic access for increasing the financial welfare of unbanked and underbanked LMI households.

The data that we use to investigate the question of geographic access are from the Detroit Area Household Financial Services (DAHFS) study and from geographic information we collected on bank and other depository institutions and AFS providers, as described more fully below. The Detroit metro area is an ideal place to research the role of geographic access because it has neighborhoods with high concentrations of poverty as well as moderate- and middle-income communities. Moreover, because there are few state-level restrictions on AFS institutions, all types of providers operate while facing few (if any) binding fee or usury regulations.

---

2. In a behavioral economics view of the world, that might not necessarily be the case. For example, one could argue that individuals may choose to not have bank accounts in order to limit their opportunities to obtain credit and their borrowing opportunities (Laibson 1997).

To disentangle the simultaneity between business and household location decisions in Detroit, we implement an instrumental variables strategy using historical bank-branch locations and municipal zoning laws as arguably exogenous determinants of bank-branch and AFS-provider locations, respectively. For the historical bank-branch instrumental variable, a key identifying testable assumption is that bank branches exhibit more persistence over time in a neighborhood than do households. In other words, bank-branch locations in 1994 predict these locations in 2006, but households in 2006 did not base their location decisions on what their neighborhoods looked like in 1994. Similarly, for municipal zoning laws, we attempt to identify rules that influence the supply of financial services but not the residential decisions of the households in our survey. These instrumental variables help identify the effect of the locations of bank branches and AFS providers on the subpopulation's decision to live near one of these institutions, based on the variation in the supply of banks and AFS (Imbens and Angrist 1994; Angrist, Imbens, and Rubin 1996). In other words, these instrumental variables help to identify exogenous variation in the geographic costs of access to financial services, on the margin, for low- and moderate-income Detroit households. In this framework, the results from these instrumental variables apply only to those on the margin, not to the average low- or moderate-income Detroit household, and so should be interpreted with caution.

Our main findings are threefold. First, 38 percent of LMI households in the DAHFS study live near (that is, within a half mile of) at least one bank branch, and 96 percent of these households live near an AFS provider. Low- and middle-income LMI households who live near and far from these institutions appear not to differ systematically in terms of their observable characteristics. Second, in both the ordinary least squares (OLS) and instrumental variable (IV) specifications, households' proximity to bank branches has little to no relationship with either the probability of having a bank account or the likelihood of using AFS. Third, OLS results suggest that proximity to an AFS provider lowers the probability of having a bank account but has no effect on using alternative financial services. Our results imply that policies that solely expand geographic access to bank branches are unlikely to attract LMI households to the mainstream banking sector. Rather, policies to encourage bank-account ownership should also focus on expanding the range of products offered by depository institutions.

Data and Sample

The data for this chapter are from the DAHFS study, together with geographic information we collected on the location of financial service providers in the Detroit metropolitan area. In the DAHFS study, the sample members were selected based on a stratified random sample of the Detroit metropolitan area (Wayne, Oakland, and Macomb Counties). We first selected eighty-five segments from census tracts with median incomes that are 0–60 percent (low income), 61–80 percent (moderate income), and 81–120 percent (middle income) of the Detroit area's median household income of $49,057. We then randomly selected households from these eighty-five randomly selected segments. We oversampled low- and moderate-income strata and undersampled the middle one. Hence, households are more likely to be drawn from the low- and moderate-income strata. Stratum definitions do not, however, restrict the income levels of the households to those that fall within these ranges.[3] Upon selecting a household, the Survey Research Center randomly selected an adult to interview from that household (Kish 1949). The DAHFS data set thus generalizes to both the adult individuals and the households living in census tracts with median incomes less than 120 percent of the Detroit area's median.

The Detroit study's data set consists of individuals who completed the interview between July 2005 and March 2006; almost 90 percent of the interviews occurred before January 2006. We interviewed 1,003 households and attained a 65 percent response rate. Upon completion of the data collection, the Survey Research Center constructed sampling weights that are inversely proportional to a respondent's probability of selection. All estimates reported in this chapter are weighted, and all standard errors are clustered at the segment level to account for the intrasegment correlation across individuals.

The subsample studied in this chapter consists of 938 respondents from the low- and moderate-income strata. As described in earlier chapters, these households use financial services in both the mainstream and AFS sectors. Nearly one-third of respondents do not have a bank account, and money orders are the most commonly used alternative financial service. Eighty-one percent of respondents use AFS, and this proportion is only somewhat higher among the unbanked. Many in this sample of LMI households belong to socially disadvantaged groups. Almost half of respondents have attended some college. Two-thirds of the sample is female.[4]

Location of Financial Service Providers

We obtained geographic location information on depository institutions and AFS providers during the relevant time frames from a variety of sources. Banking institutions operating in the Detroit area are drawn from the Federal Deposit Insurance Corporation's Institution Directory as of June 2006 (FDIC 2006).

3. With sampling weights, our sample represents the population of Detroit metropolitan area residents living in low-, moderate-, and middle-income census tracts.

4. In other work, we have compared the DAHFS sample with the U.S. census characteristics of households from the low- and moderate-income census tracts in the Detroit area (Barr and Dokko 2008).

Using the county listings of banks registered with the agency, we obtained 1,064 branch locations from individual corporate websites. Using the directory of state-chartered credit unions maintained by Michigan's Office of Financial and Insurance Regulation and the credit unions' web pages, we identified the branch locations of 191 credit unions (State of Michigan, Department of Labor and Economic Growth 2006). The branch locations of federally chartered credit unions were also collected and verified using Internet resources and the web pages of individual credit unions (NCUA 2006).

The locations of 3,418 check cashers, payday lenders, pawnbrokers, grocery and corner stores providing financial services, tax preparation centers, accountants, and money transmitters were compiled for the relevant time frames from two commercial data vendors (InfoUSA and Dunn & Bradstreet), Internet resources, and the Yellow Pages. Applying standard industrial classification criteria (SIC codes) enabled us to identify businesses providing financial services in addition to other services, such as selling groceries or liquor. For firms that were not clearly identifiable as financial service providers based on their SIC codes, phone calls were made to ascertain whether the firms provided financial services, and what services they provided. We also conducted a mail survey of a subset of AFS providers.[5]

Distance between Households and Financial Service Providers

As described above, households were sampled from eighty-five distinct segments or census block groups. To compute the distance between each household and financial service providers, we positioned each household as if it were located at the centroid of a given census block group. Using the latitude and longitude of each centroid and the latitude and longitude of each bank and AFS location, we measured the distance from each household to each provider.

Using these distances, we are able to construct several different measures of households' distance to service providers. In this chapter, we use the number of banks or AFS providers within a half mile of the household. That distance was chosen as a reasonable estimate of proximity—a distance from which consumers can easily access the provider. We have performed robustness checks using 1,000 feet and even extending the distance to one mile with little change to the results. We have also tested other measures such as using the actual distance to the nearest bank, and those too are very similar to the results reported here.

Descriptive Findings on the Use of Financial Services

As mentioned earlier, nearly one-third of the sample does not have a bank account, and AFS use is quite high. As can be expected, AFS use is higher among the unbanked, by 6 percentage points (86 percent versus 80 percent). With

---

5. Further details on the data collection of financial service providers are available upon request.

Table 5-1. *Mainstream and Alternative Financial Services Use among
Low- and Moderate-Income Households in Detroit*
Percent

Service	All	Banked	Unbanked
Bank account	71	100	0
Check casher[a]	29	27	33
Money order[a]	68	64	77
Payday loan[b]	3	4	2
Pawnshop[c]	11	7	21
Refund anticipation loan[c]	22	19	29
Any AFS[d]	81	80	86
Bank within half mile	38	38	38
Sample size	938		

Source: Detroit Area Household Financial Services study.
a. In previous month.
b. In previous year.
c. In previous three years.
d. Any AFS defined as check cashing, money order, cash advance, layaway, pawnshop, tax anticipation, rent-to-own, or payday loan.

the exception of payday loans, the unbanked are more likely to use a variety of alternative financial services than the banked.[6] Nearly three-quarters of households have a car, consistent with Detroit being the Motor City. Interestingly, the banked and unbanked are equally likely to live within a half mile of a bank branch (table 5-1).

Table 5-2 shows that while the demographic and socioeconomic characteristics of households living near and far from bank branches are roughly similar, neighborhoods with and without nearby bank branches are somewhat different based on tract-level information from the 2000 census. Put differently, individual-level characteristics vary less than neighborhood characteristics, suggesting that studies using neighborhood characteristics alone to make inferences about the role of geographic access may be incomplete. Census data suggest that neighborhoods with nearby bank branches have higher median home values, are slightly older, and have a higher fraction of white households. The correlation of these attributes of Detroit neighborhoods with bank-branch access corroborates other findings in the literature. However, as table 5-3 shows, both types of LMI households, that is, those living nearer to and farther from bank branches, are equally likely to have bank accounts and have quite similar patterns of AFS use, which deviates from the previous literature's findings.

6. The exception of payday loans is not surprising as one of the requirements to qualify for a payday loan is to have a bank account.

Table 5-2. *Demographic Features of Households Living, by Proximity to Bank*
Percent unless otherwise noted

	All	Bank within half mile	Bank more than half mile away
Age			
25–34	21	21	21
35–44	22	22	21
45–54	22	18	25
55–64	10	12	9
65 and older	13	13	13
Female	66	65	67
Race-ethnicity			
Black	69	61	74
Hispanic	4	5	3
Other	8	12	5
Has a car	73	71	74
Married	24	24	23
Has some college	47	51	44
Employed at time of interview	54	53	55
Mean family size	2.3	2.2	2.4
Household income			
Lowest quartile	11	11	11
Second quartile	11	12	11
Third quartile	11	11	10
Highest quartile	12	9	14
2000 census characteristics			
Population	3,567	3,295	3,647
Population density	6,953	7,163	7,435
Percent single-family housing	54.9	45.5	58.5
Median house value (dollars)	63,911	64,252	55,826
Median year house built	1949	1950	1949
Percent white	30.1	32.8	19.3
Number of banks within half mile	0.8	2.2	0.0
Sample size	938		

Source: Detroit Area Household Financial Services study.

Table 5-3. *Geography and Use of Mainstream and Alternative Financial Services*
Percent

	All	Bank within half mile	Bank more than half mile way
Bank account	71	71	71
Check casher[a]	29	27	30
Money order[a]	68	68	68
Payday loan[b]	3	4	3
Pawnshop[c]	11	11	12
Refund anticipation loan[c]	22	20	22
Any AFS[d]	81	79	83
Sample size	938		

Source: Detroit Area Household Financial Services study.
a. In previous month.
b. In previous year.
c. In previous three years.
d. Any AFS defined as check cashing, money order, cash advance, layaway, pawnshop, tax anticipation, rent-to-own, or payday loan.

Estimation and Results

It is very likely that both households and banks choose their locations with the other in mind. Households may wish to locate in areas that provide the financial services they desire, and banks and other providers locate offices to best serve household demand. This pattern of economic decision making will result in endogeneity concerns when using the distance measures as regressors: these measures are likely correlated with unobserved variation in the households.

To address this concern, we create two sets of instruments. For the measures related to banks, we use the bank location in 1994 as an instrument for the bank measure in 2006. To be more specific, for each household, we compute the same measure—the number of banks within a half mile—for each household using the banks that were present in June 1994. These are taken from the Federal Deposit Insurance Corporation's Summary of Deposits for that year, which we have cleaned and geocoded. As a result of the fixed costs needed to build a bank (for example, vault construction costs), bank locations tend to be persistent, and therefore bank locations in 2006 are highly correlated with bank locations in 1994. However, it is unlikely that a household's choice of location and other neighborhood attributes is correlated with these historical measures, since only the current feature of the neighborhood should matter for current households. We similarly used municipal zoning laws to address AFS provider location decisions (results available upon request).

Identification Strategy

To identify the effect of geographic access to bank branches, we are interested in estimating

$$BANK_{ij} = \alpha_0 + \alpha_1 BB_{ij} + \gamma_1 \mathbf{X}_{ij} + \gamma_2 \mathbf{W}_j + \varepsilon_{ij}, \qquad (5\text{-}1)$$

where $BANK_{ij}$ is an indicator for whether individual i in neighborhood j has a bank account, $\mathbf{X}_{ij}$ is a vector of individual-level characteristics, $\mathbf{W}_j$ is a vector of neighborhood characteristics, and ε_{ij} is an error term. BB_{ij} is an indicator equal to one if individual i lives in a neighborhood j that is within a half mile of a bank branch and zero otherwise. The coefficient α_1 measures the additional likelihood of having a bank account, holding individual and neighborhood characteristics constant.

Because individuals' preferences for financial services and banks' profit-maximizing strategies to locate in neighborhoods with likely consumers are unobserved, $E[BB_{ij}\varepsilon_{ij}|\mathbf{X}_{ij},\mathbf{W}_j] \neq 0$, and applying ordinary least squares (OLS) to equation 5-1 is likely to yield biased estimates of α_1. In particular, if there is positive sorting between households and bank branches, then the OLS estimate of α_1 is likely to be biased upward.

To obtain consistent estimates of α_1 and a causal interpretation of the role of geographic access, we apply an instrumental variables strategy. The first-stage and reduced-form equations are

$$BB_{ij} = \delta_0 + \delta_1 HB_{ij} + \eta_1 \mathbf{X}_{ij} + \eta_2 \mathbf{X}_j + v_{ij},$$

and

$$BANK_{ij} = \pi_0 + \pi_1 BB_{ij} + \alpha_1 \mathbf{X}_{ij} + \alpha_2 \mathbf{W}_j + \mu_{ij},$$

where HB_{ij} is an indicator for whether individual i's neighborhood j had a bank branch in 1994. If HB_{ij} is uncorrelated with the error term ε_{ij} and historical bank-branch locations have no independent effect on $BANK_{ij}$, then the instrumental variables strategy will yield a consistent estimate of α_1. These conditions are likely to hold when bank branches exhibit more persistence over time in a neighborhood than do households.

We are also interested in the effect of geographic access to bank branches on the likelihood of using AFS:

$$AFS_{ij} = \beta_0 + \beta_1 BB_{ij} + \gamma_1 \mathbf{X}_{ij} + \gamma_2 \mathbf{W}_j + \varepsilon_{ij}, \qquad (5\text{-}2)$$

where AFS_{ij} is an indicator for whether an individual uses AFS. If the costs of geographic access influence AFS use, then we expect β_1 from equation 5-2 to be significantly different from zero. The direction of this relationship has implications for whether bank accounts and AFS are substitutes or complements. If $\beta_1 > 0$, then it is more likely that individuals use bank accounts and AFS as complements, taking different services from each source. On the other hand, if $\beta_1 < 0$, then it is more likely that individuals treat bank accounts and AFS as substitutes. Since we also believe that there is an endogeneity issue with BB_{ij} in estimating the effect of bank-branch access on AFS use, we apply a similar instrumental variable strategy to estimating equation 5-2. Finally, we are interested in estimating the effect of geographic access to AFS providers on bank-account ownership, and we apply a similar econometric analysis.

Model Results

Table 5-4 presents the results of estimating equation 5-1 using OLS and IV. Column 1 presents the simple cross-sectional correlation between geographic access to bank branches and bank-account ownership seen in table 5-1. Column 3 includes individual-level covariates to the estimation, while column 5 also adds neighborhood-level covariates. In all three specifications, proximity to bank branches is not correlated with bank-account ownership. To address the endogeneity concerns that the OLS estimates in columns 1, 3, and 5 are biased upward owing to positive sorting, we also present the analogous IV estimates in columns 2, 4, and 6, which can be interpreted as the effect of bank-branch proximity on account ownership. The IV estimates are consistent with the view that geographic proximity has little to no marginal effect on bank-account ownership. Not only are the coefficients on the geographic proximity variable small and statistically insignificant from zero in columns 2, 4, and 6, but their standard errors are not particularly large, suggesting that the lack of an effect is measured with relative precision. We interpret the lack of an effect as indicating that households find bank accounts, as currently structured, relatively unattractive such that simply lowering the costs of having a bank account by reducing geographic distance to bank branches does not induce additional take-up.

Our results for the effect of bank proximity on AFS use, shown in table 5-5, are similar to the results for the effect of bank proximity on bank-account ownership. Both OLS and IV estimates suggest that simply lowering the costs of bank-account ownership through closer geographic proximity to bank branches has little to no marginal effect on AFS use. The inclusion of individual-level and neighborhood covariates does not change this finding. It appears that cross price elasticity is close to zero.

By contrast, proximity to AFS providers does matter for bank-account ownership. Tables 5-6 and 5-7 report the relationship between AFS provider proximity and financial service use. In table 5-6, the OLS estimates suggest that households living in close proximity to AFS institutions are less likely to have a bank account. The magnitude of this coefficient decreases with the inclusion of individual-level

Table 5-4. *Influence of Geographic Proximity to a Bank on Bank Account Ownership: OLS and IV Estimates*

	OLS1	IV1	OLS2	IV2	OLS3	IV3
	(1)	(2)	(3)	(4)	(5)	(6)
Bank within	.001	.012	−.014	−.057	.004	.028
half mile	(.043)	(.042)	(.037)	(.039)	(.037)	(.049)
Age						
25–34			.065	.053	.079	.106*
			(.063)	(.055)	(.064)	(.063)
35–44			.054	.038	.077	.103*
			(.059)	(.058)	(.059)	(.059)
45–54			.080	.085	.094	.132**
			(.060)	(.057)	(.058)	(.060)
55–64			.214***	.219***	.232***	.270***
			(.065)	(.062)	(.062)	(.065)
65 and older			.279***	.316***	.279***	.322***
			(.070)	(.066)	(.068)	(.071)
Female			.064	.048	.070*	.085**
			(.040)	(.039)	(.041)	(.043)
Race-ethnicity						
Black			−.085**	−.113***	−.104**	−.068
			(.035)	(.030)	(.047)	(.053)
Hispanic			−.036	−.070	−.012	.010
			(.086)	(.076)	(.086)	(.085)
Other			.089*	.111**	.070	.090*
			(.048)	(.046)	(.048)	(.048)
Has a car			.161***	.179***	.157***	.168***
			(.039)	(.036)	(.038)	(.040)
Married			.092**	.101***	.097**	.098***
			(.038)	(.038)	(.039)	(.038)
Has some			.133***	.156***	.126***	.131***
college			(.030)	(.029)	(.029)	(.030)
Employed			.133***	.131***	.118**	.126**
at time of			(.050)	(.044)	(.050)	(.050)
interview						
Mean family			−.034**	−.043***	−.039***	−.034**
size			(.015)	(.015)	(.015)	(.014)
Income						
Lowest			−.113*	−.034	−.090	−.091
quartile			(.063)	(.052)	(.061)	(.060)
Second			−.090	−.111*	−.083	−.075
quartile			(.067)	(.063)	(.066)	(.064)
Third			.069	.077	.074	.070
quartile			(.061)	(.059)	(.061)	(.060)
Highest			.107**	.106**	.099**	.102**
quartile			(.047)	(.044)	(.049)	(.048)

(continued)

Table 5-4. *Influence of Geographic Proximity to a Bank on Bank Account Ownership: OLS and IV Estimates* (continued)

	OLS1	IV1	OLS2	IV2	OLS3	IV3
	(1)	(2)	(3)	(4)	(5)	(6)
Population					9.16e-07	2.17e-06
					(.00002)	(.00002)
Population density					3.28e-06	3.55e-06
					(6.54e-06)	(6.53e-06)
Percent single-family housing					.0007	.0006
					(.0007)	(.0007)
Median house value					1.71e-06***	1.69e-06***
					(4.88e-07)	(4.89e-07)
Median year house built					−.00005	.0001
					(.00004)	(.00009)
Percent white					−.001	−.0009
					(.0007)	(.0007)
Constant	.712***	.716***	.433***	.457***	.408***	
	(.026)	(.020)	(.076)	(.072)	(.080)	
Observations	938	938	938	938	938	938

Source: Detroit Area Household Financial Services study.
*Statistically significant at the 10 percent level.
**Statistically significant at the 5 percent level.
***Statistically significant at the 1 percent level.

and neighborhood covariates. In column 3, households with nearby AFS providers are about 9 percentage points less likely to have a bank account. Here, if we take the OLS estimates at their face value, it seems that the cross price elasticity is negative, suggesting that bank accounts and AFS may be substitutes. The OLS estimates in table 5-7 show little responsiveness of AFS use to proximity to an AFS provider (perhaps because nearly all LMI households in the study both live near and use AFS). The results in tables 5-6 and 5-7 are also consistent with AFS use being an inferior good, which decreases in demand as income rises, while services from depository institutions are normal goods, with positive income effects.

Conclusion

Providers of alternative financial services are pervasive in LMI communities, while bank branches are relatively rare. Proximity to an AFS provider reduces bank-account ownership, but proximity to a bank branch does not increase it. These results suggest that increasing bank-branch penetration alone is unlikely

Table 5-5. *Influence of Geographic Proximity to a Bank on AFS Use: OLS and IV Estimates*

	OLS1	IV1	OLS2	IV2	OLS3	IV3
	(1)	(2)	(3)	(4)	(5)	(6)
Bank within half mile	−.033	−.023	−.005	−.005	−.010	−.004
	(.030)	(.026)	(.031)	(.037)	(.030)	(.041)
Age						
25–34			.077	.047	.083	.126**
			(.052)	(.050)	(.053)	(.058)
35–44			.056	.013	.059	.100*
			(.054)	(.050)	(.055)	(.058)
45–54			.041	.030	.045	.105*
			(.050)	(.050)	(.048)	(.058)
55–64			−.125**	−.148**	−.126**	−.064
			(.063)	(.058)	(.059)	(.070)
65 and older			−.193***	−.238***	−.197***	−.127*
			(.064)	(.061)	(.062)	(.072)
Female			.034	.044	.039	.062
			(.038)	(.034)	(.038)	(.042)
Race-ethnicity						
Black			.125***	.124***	.102**	.163***
			(.026)	(.025)	(.039)	(.062)
Hispanic			.045	.066	.050	.085
			(.068)	(.065)	(.069)	(.070)
Other			−.168**	−.148**	−.173**	−.134*
			(.066)	(.064)	(.069)	(.069)
Has a car			.031	.036	.042	.059
			(.034)	(.033)	(.034)	(.036)
Married			.042	.032	.049	.052
			(.036)	(.036)	(.037)	(.037)
Has some college			.021	.015	.017	.027
			(.026)	(.025)	(.026)	(.028)
Employed at time of interview			.017	.021	.022	.035
			(.042)	(.041)	(.041)	(.042)
Mean family size			−.004	−.0003	−.001	.007
			(.011)	(.010)	(.010)	(.012)
Income						
Lowest quartile			−.078	−.083	−.086	−.090
			(.059)	(.054)	(.057)	(.057)
Second quartile			.004	.007	.003	.016
			(.050)	(.047)	(.048)	(.050)
Third quartile			.025	.038	.023	.015
			(.061)	(.057)	(.061)	(.059)
Highest quartile			−.035	−.010	−.036	−.034
			(.051)	(.049)	(.052)	(.050)

(continued)

Table 5-5. *Influence of Geographic Proximity to a Bank on AFS Use: OLS and IV Estimates (continued)*

	OLS1	IV1	OLS2	IV2	OLS3	IV3
	(1)	(2)	(3)	(4)	(5)	(6)
Population					2.85e-06	2.58e-06
					(1.00e-05)	(1.00e-05)
Population density					−2.25e-06	−9.53e-07
					(4.35e-06)	(4.34e-06)
Percent single-family housing					−.001*	−.002*
					(.0007)	(.0008)
Median house value					−9.04e-08	−1.57e-07
					(4.47e-07)	(4.60e-07)
Median year house built					.00006*	.0003***
					(.00003)	(.00007)
Percent white					−.0007	−.0003
					(.0006)	(.0007)
Constant	.827***	.849***	.692***	.693***	.686***	
	(.019)	(.012)	(.066)	(.069)	(.060)	
Observations	938	938	938	938	938	938

Source: Detroit Area Household Financial Services study.
*Statistically significant at the 10 percent level.
**Statistically significant at the 5 percent level.
***Statistically significant at the 1 percent level.

Table 5-6. *Influence of Geographic Proximity to an AFS Institution on Bank-Account Ownership: OLS and IV Estimates*

	OLS1	OLS2	OLS3
	(1)	(2)	(3)
AFS within half mile	−211***	−.132***	−.087*
	(.022)	(.025)	(.051)
Age			
25–34		.069	.080
		(.063)	(.063)
35–44		.054	.076
		(.059)	(.059)
45–54		.076	.089
		(.060)	(.058)
55–64		.215***	.232***
		(.065)	(.061)
65 and older		.273***	.275***
		(.072)	(.069)
Female		.064	.070*
		(.039)	(.041)

Table 5-6. *Influence of Geographic Proximity to an AFS Institution on Bank-Account Ownership: OLS and IV Estimates (continued)*

	OLS1	OLS2	OLS3
	(1)	*(2)*	*(3)*
Race-ethnicity			
Black		−.078**	−.103**
		(.036)	(.047)
Hispanic		−.032	−.018
		(.085)	(.084)
Other		.094**	.074
		(.048)	(.048)
Has a car		.160***	.157***
		(.039)	(.038)
Married		.093**	.097**
		(.038)	(.038)
Has some college		.134***	.127***
		(.030)	(.030)
Employed at time of interview		.125***	.114**
		(.048)	(.049)
Mean family size		−.035**	−.040***
		(.015)	(.015)
Income			
Lowest quartile		−.101*	−.083
		(.061)	(.060)
Second quartile		−.082	−.077
		(.066)	(.066)
Third quartile		.074	.078
		(.059)	(.059)
Highest quartile		.107**	.101**
		(.047)	(.049)
Population			−1.12e-06
			(.00002)
Population density			5.44e-06
			(6.53e-06)
Percent single-family housing			.0006
			(.0006)
Median house value			1.53e-06***
			(4.86e-07)
Median year house built			−.00005
			(.00003)
Percent white			−.001
			(.0007)
Constant	.915***	.555***	.498***
	(.009)	(.085)	(.107)
Observations	938	938	938

Source: Detroit Area Household Financial Services study.
*Statistically significant at the 10 percent level.
**Statistically significant at the 5 percent level.
***Statistically significant at the 1 percent level.

Table 5-7. *Influence of Geographic Proximity to an AFS Institution on AFS Use: OLS and IV Estimates*

	OLS1	OLS2	OLS3
	(1)	(2)	(3)
AFI within half mile	−.015	−.031	−.038
	(.024)	(.034)	(.051)
Age			
25–34		.078	.085
		(.052)	(.053)
35–44		.056	.059
		(.054)	(.056)
45–54		.040	.044
		(.050)	(.048)
55–64		−.124**	−.127**
		(.063)	(.059)
65 and older		−.195***	−.198***
		(.064)	(.062)
Female		.034	.039
		(.038)	(.038)
Race-ethnicity			
Black		.127***	.102***
		(.025)	(.039)
Hispanic		.046	.047
		(.067)	(.071)
Other		−.167**	−.173**
		(.065)	(.067)
Has a car		.031	.042
		(.034)	(.034)
Married		.042	.048
		(.036)	(.037)
Has some college		.021	.016
		(.026)	(.026)
Employed at time of interview		.015	.020
		(.042)	(.041)
Mean family size		−.005	−.001
		(.011)	(.010)
Income			
Lowest quartile		−.075	−.083
		(.059)	(.057)
Second quartile		.006	.005
		(.050)	(.047)
Third quartile		.026	.026
		(.061)	(.061)
Highest quartile		−.034	−.034
		(.050)	(.051)

Table 5-7. *Influence of Geographic Proximity to an AFS Institution on AFS Use: OLS and IV Estimates (continued)*

	OLS1	OLS2	OLS3
	(1)	(2)	(3)
Population			2.81e-06
			(1.00e-05)
Population density			−1.62e-06
			(4.66e-06)
Percent single-family housing			−.001*
			(.0008)
Median house value			−1.55e-07
			(4.89e-07)
Median year house built			.00005*
			(.00003)
Percent white			−.0007
			(.0005)
Constant	.829***	.720***	.725***
	(.018)	(.077)	(.080)
Observations	938	938	938

Source: Detroit Area Household Financial Services study.
*Statistically significant at the 10 percent level.
**Statistically significant at the 5 percent level.
***Statistically significant at the 1 percent level.

to bring LMI households into the financial mainstream. Improving bank service offerings would likely attract more LMI households than denser branch coverage. Payment-card programs are promising ways to improve access to financial services at relatively low cost. The results discussed in this chapter suggest that the lack of a physical branch network, a salient drawback of most payment-card programs, is not an insuperable barrier to adoption among LMI households. At the same time, having a local branch in a community is likely to have other benefits not discussed in this chapter, such as increasing the availability of credit for small business or community development.

References

Angrist, Joshua D., Guido W. Imbens, and Donald B. Rubin. 1996. "Identification of Causal Effects Using Instrumental Variables." *Journal of the American Statistical Association* 91:444–55 (www.jstor.org/stable/2291629).

Barr, Michael S. 2004. "Banking the Poor." *Yale Journal on Regulation* 21:121–237.

Barr, Michael S., and Jane K. Dokko. 2008. "Paying to Save: Tax Withholding and Asset Allocation among Low- and Moderate-Income Taxpayers." FEDS Working Paper 2008-11. Federal Reserve Board (www.federalreserve.gov/pubs/feds/2008/200811/200811pap.pdf).

Bucks, Brian K., Arthur B. Kennickell, and Kevin B. Moore. 2006. "Recent Changes in U.S. Family Finances: Evidence from the 2001 and 2004 Survey of Consumer Finances." *Federal Reserve Bulletin* 92:A1–A38.

Caskey, John P. 1994. *Fringe Banking: Check-Cashing Outlets, Pawnshops, and the Poor.* New York: Russell Sage Foundation.

FDIC (Federal Deposit Insurance Corporation). 2006. "Institution Directory" (www2.fdic.gov/idasp/main.asp).

Imbens, Guido W., and Joshua D. Angrist. 1994. "Identification and Estimation of Local Average Treatment Effects." *Econometrica* 62:467–75 (www.jstor.org/stable/2951620).

InfoUSA. 2005. "Business Mailing List." December.

———. 2006. "Business Mailing List." January.

Kish, Leslie. 1949. "A Procedure for Objective Respondent Selection within the Household." *Journal of the American Statistical Association* 44:380–87 (www.jstor.org/stable/2280236).

Laibson, David. 1997. "Golden Eggs and Hyperbolic Discounting." *Quarterly Journal of Economics* 112:443–77 (www.jstor.org/stable/2951242).

NCUA (National Credit Union Administration). 2006. "Credit Union Queries" (www.ncua.gov/indexdata.html).

State of Michigan, Department of Labor and Economic Growth. 2006. "Credit Union Directory" (www.cis.state.mi.us/fis/indsrch/crdtun/creditunioncriteria.asp).

6

Borrowing to Make Ends Meet

MICHAEL S. BARR, JANE K. DOKKO, AND BENJAMIN J. KEYS

M any low- and moderate-income (LMI) households use short-term credit
products provided by firms that operate outside the mainstream banking sector (Barr 2004, 2005). These products include payday loans, pawnshop
services, refund anticipation loans (RALs), and rent-to-own. Low- and moderate-
income households also access short-term credit through credit cards, as well as
through nontraditional types of credit-card products, such as secured credit cards
or cash-advance options, and by using overdraft services provided by banks. The
finance charges and fees associated with short-term credit products can be high
(Drysdale and Keest 2000).[1] Furthermore, some short-term loans, such as payday
loans, can be rolled over or extended to provide additional time to pay back the
loan, often at a substantial fee, essentially equivalent to the cost of another loan
(Drysdale and Keest 2000). Use of payday lending products may result in a broad
range of credit problems for borrowers (Melzer, forthcoming).

In spite of these high fees and attendant problems, these products have pro-
liferated in the marketplace. For example, the number of payday lending outlets
grew from 10,000 to 22,000 between 2000 and 2004, and the estimated payday
loan volume in 2003 was $40 billion (Flannery and Samolyk 2005). Refund

---

1. For example, the fees associated with a typical payday loan of two-week duration typically
amount to $15–20 for each $100 loaned, or an APR of 390–520 percent (Drysdale and Keest
2000). The fees on refund anticipation loans are similarly high: evidence suggests that the average
price of an RAL for a family with children that files a return and is eligible for an earned-income
credit is $130 (Berube and Kornblatt 2005).

anticipation loans consumed $740 million of Americans' tax-refund dollars in 2003 (Berube and Kornblatt 2005). With their increased prevalence, these alternative products have faced greater regulatory scrutiny.

Nondepository and depository institutions providing alternative short-term credit products have historically needed to comply with a patchwork of federal and state regulations (Barr 2004). At the federal level, the Truth in Lending Act (TILA) generally governs disclosure of loan pricing according to a uniform standard defining, for example, the annual percentage rate (APR) of interest on the loan. However, evidence arguably suggests that consumers may not understand the costs of short-term borrowing in such terms (Mann and Hawkins 2007),[2] and there is little evidence regarding AFS-provider compliance with TILA.[3] Though many states have enacted substantive and procedural laws governing short-term consumer credit, these laws often treat particular forms of credit extension differently from one another,[4] and some forms of credit are not subject to such regulation at all. Some state regulation may reduce the costs of credit and improve credit access and outcomes, while others may unintentionally reduce the availability of credit, increase costs, or shift activity among different products. Some studies have found that restrictions on one form of AFS reduce supply of that product and do not increase the demand for other AFS products (see McKernan, Ratcliffe, and Kuehn 2010), while others have found that restriction of one AFS products leads to costly increases in use of other AFS products (see Zinman 2010). To further complicate matters, depending on the issuer of the loan, federal or state regulations may apply, with different governmental agencies regulating different types of lenders.

With the passage of the Dodd-Frank Wall Street Reform and Consumer Protection Act and the creation of the Consumer Financial Protection Bureau, policymakers have the opportunity to develop a coherent approach to regulation of short-term credit products offered by AFS and bank providers. Improved disclosures that permit individuals to assess costs and benefits across differ-

---

2. Ronald Mann and Jim Hawkins (2007) note that the relatively high probability that payday loans will be rolled over, for example, makes it difficult for consumers, even those who understand the finance charge and APR disclosures, to make an accurate estimate of the amount they will ultimately pay.

3. A survey of payday lender practices in the Columbus, Ohio, area finds that many lenders violated TILA's requirements in refusing to disclose finance charges or the APR before contract formation (Johnson 2002). A study of 100 payday lending sites advertising on the Internet reveals that 43 percent of sites did not make finance charges or APRs available until after potential borrowers had completed a loan application (Fox and Petrini 2004).

4. Michigan, for example, puts a relatively low 3 percent monthly interest rate (around 36 percent APR) on pawn transactions, Mich. Comp. Laws Ann. § 446.209 (West 1996 & Supp. 2011), while allowing payday loans made at effective APRs of over 300 percent; see Mich. Comp. Laws Ann. § 487.2153(1)(a) (permitting a service fee of 15 percent for loans of up to $100; for a two-week loan, this is equivalent to an APR of around 391 percent).

ent types of products and providers, for example, might improve outcomes. Similarly, the bureau could examine sales practices across these different products and services and provide for comprehensive supervision and enforcement across the market.

Better regulation of short-term credit products may be critical to LMI households' ability to make sound borrowing decisions, but it is difficult to specify the parameters of such a regulatory regime without an understanding of the complex financial decisions that these households undertake. This chapter provides an overview of types of federal and state regulation of short-term credit products and then uses the data from the Detroit Area Household Financial Services study (DAHFS) to cast light on the interactions among these different sectors. The analysis we provide should help policymakers craft better regulation of this sector.

To analyze the financial services behaviors and attitudes of LMI households, we designed and implemented the DAHFS study. Previous research on short-term credit options generally has focused narrowly on one type of provider (for example, payday lender or pawnshop) and lacked household-level data (Stegman and Faris 2003; Berube and Kornblatt 2005; Flannery and Samolyk 2005; DeYoung and Phillips 2006; Morgan and Strain 2007). The Detroit study permits a holistic, portfolio-wide approach. The data suggest that households use various sources for alternative credit, depending in part on their available collateral and borrowing needs. Rather than treating each source as a substitute, LMI borrowers appear to use payday loans, pawnshops, refund anticipation loans, and other services as complementary products. Unlike loans from mainstream providers (banks and credit unions), which, when used by LMI households, are mostly applied to home improvement or repairs and mortgage or car payments, AFS loans are used to pay off bills, to cover recurring expenses, or to consolidate debts. Individuals who use AFS credit are more likely to be in financial trouble and to have experienced financial hardships in the past year. Borrowers in these different sectors also differ in their attitudes toward debt. For example, AFS users are more likely than bank borrowers to believe that borrowing is an acceptable way to make up for short-term reductions in income.

These results have important implications for the effective regulation of short-term credit markets. Understanding households' preferences and behavior related to borrowing and saving is essential for analyzing how firms and households would respond to government regulation designed to address problems in this sector. The use of short-term credit, particularly for living expenses and emergencies, suggests caution about overregulating, and thereby excessively restricting access, without considering the costs involved. Moreover, regulation of singular parts of the AFS sector may be counterproductive when borrowers' portfolios include multiple short-term credit products in both the AFS and bank sectors.

At the same time, a marketwide review of short-term credit products across the AFS and bank sectors could potentially lead to better regulation, effective enforcement, improved disclosures, and other measures that hold the prospect of improving outcomes for consumers.

Policy and Regulatory Context

In recent years, state and federal policymakers have paid increasing attention to problems in the alternative financial services market. Some have focused on the high fees and repeated rollovers in the payday industry, while others have zeroed in on the high cost of refund anticipation loans. States have long been concerned with pawnshops and rent-to-own companies (see Caskey 1995; Martin and Huckins 1997). Regulation of the alternative financial services sector has largely evolved by treating the myriad short-term credit products as distinct and unique products without understanding the relationship among them. Moreover, AFS regulation has proceeded without regard to the mainstream market for bank credit, such as overdraft protection and credit cards. Conversely, bank and credit-card regulation has proceeded without regard for the relationship between these products and other sources of credit.

The patchwork of regulation may add to the cost and confusion regarding these products and services. Moreover, the lack of mainstream products and services tailored to LMI households may contribute to the dysfunctional menu of financial-services options. We argue that policymakers ought to make decisions regarding these products on the basis of data regarding how households actually use the range of products and services. With the creation of the Consumer Financial Protection Bureau, pursuant to the 2010 Dodd-Frank Wall Street Reform and Consumer Protection Act, policymakers have the ability, for the first time, to develop marketwide policies, supervision, and enforcement, covering bank and nonbank sectors alike.

Payday Lending

A payday loan is a transaction whereby a borrower receives cash, say $250, in return for writing a check for a larger amount to be cashed on the date of his or her next paycheck, usually two weeks from the date the loan is made (Drysdale and Keest 2000). In an updated form of the traditional transaction, no check is written; instead, the borrower signs an authorization that permits the lender to debit his bank account on a future date for the amount of the loan plus the finance charge (Mann and Hawkins 2007). The typical cost for a payday loan is $15 for each $100 borrowed.

A patchwork of federal and state regulation determines the availability, disclosure, and cost of payday loans, a rapidly growing industry in the AFS sector. At the federal level, the Truth in Lending Act imposes disclosure requirements on payday loans.[5] Payday lenders must disclose the finance charge and APR of the loan to borrowers before the transaction occurs.[6] The intent of TILA is to ensure that payday borrowers know the terms of the loan so as to understand its cost and to facilitate comparison between lenders.[7] Nonetheless, research suggests that payday borrowers may not understand the terms of their short-term loans (Mann and Hawkins 2007).[8] Moreover, the lender is not required to make additional disclosures when the loan is "rolled over"—that is, when the lender agrees to defer cashing the check for another two-week term in return for an additional fee; the sum charged for rolling over has not been held to be a finance charge within the meaning of TILA.[9] Since rollovers constitute a sizable proportion of payday transactions, borrowers do not always receive TILA's disclosure requirements in many of their interactions with lenders.

At the federal level, Congress has placed substantive restrictions on payday lenders in the so-called Talent-Nelson amendment to the 2007 defense authorization bill, which caps the legal APR on payday loans to armed forces members and their families at 36 percent.[10] The justification for the law's limitation to military personnel was that it would prevent debt problems from creating disciplinary and security-clearance issues (Rossman 2007).[11] Some payday lenders, at the time of the amendment's passage, stated that they would voluntarily cease lending to these individuals.[12] The extent to which interest-rate caps on payday loans limit overall access to credit is open to dispute. Michael Stegman and Robert Faris (2003), for example, point out that prohibiting payday lending might serve to increase loan-shark operations, which operate entirely out of regulatory purview. A study conducted in North Carolina after expiration of the state's law authorizing payday loans has found that consumers were not lacking for other sources of short-term credit and felt, on balance, little regret that payday loans

5. See 12 C.F.R. pt. 226, Supp. I, subpt. A, § 226.2(a)(14), ¶ 2 (2011).

6. See 12 C.F.R. §§ 226.17–226.18.

7. 15 U.S.C. § 1601(a) (2006) ("It is the purpose of this subchapter to ensure the meaningful disclosure of credit terms so that the consumer will be able to compare more readily the various credit terms available to him and avoid the uninformed use of credit, and to protect the consumer against inaccurate and unfair credit billing and credit card practices").

8. Gregory Elliehausen (2006) contends that while payday borrowers are not aware of or cannot recall the APRs of their loans, awareness of the finance charge, which borrowers do note, is sufficient to make informed decisions in the short-term credit context.

9. *Jackson* v. *Am. Loan Co.,* 202 F.3d 911, 912 (7th Cir. 2000); see also 12 C.F.R. § 226.20.

10. John Warner National Defense Authorization Act for Fiscal Year 2007, § 670, Pub. L. No. 109-364, 120 Stat. 2083, 2266 (2006) (codified at 10 U.S.C. § 987(b)).

11. Under military regulations, financial troubles can cause military personnel to lose their security clearances. Uncontrolled debt is the most common reason why security clearances are revoked. Revocations owing to financial troubles increased ninefold from 2002 to 2006 (Rossman 2007).

12. In response to Defense Department investigations into military families' use of payday lending, Advance America Cash Advance Centers, the nation's biggest payday loan company, announced in 2006 that it would no longer offer payday loans to active-duty troops or their families (Goulet 2007).

were unavailable (CCC 2007). Other research, however, suggests that the typical payday borrower has few alternatives to payday loans and appreciates their convenience (Elliehausen and Lawrence 2001).

Until recently, state regulation of payday lending was hampered by partnerships between payday lenders and out-of-state banks. To circumvent the usury laws of the borrower's home state, the payday outlet would pay the out-of-state bank a fee to act as the nominal lender, while the payday outlet would retain the actual economic interest in the loan it made (Barr 2004; Mann and Hawkins 2007).[13] As states had no authority to regulate the lending practices of national or out-of-state banks, they were powerless to prevent lenders from offering payday loans with interest rates far exceeding state limits. Since then, federal bank regulators have effectively shut down these arrangements through their safety-and-soundness supervisory authorities.[14] This example underscores the potential for conflict between state and federal regulation of these credit products (King, Parrish, and Tanik 2006). State regulation of payday lending is sometimes circumvented by alternative arrangements between borrowers and lenders to avoid imposed limits on rollovers (Feltner and Williams 2004) and by a lack of resources for data collection and enforcement (Mann and Hawkins 2007).

The states tend to adopt one of two approaches to payday lending. Eleven states effectively outlaw payday lending by allowing no exceptions to their usury laws (King, Parrish, and Tanik 2006).[15] States that have effectively banned payday lending, such as New York, have done so by aggressively enforcing usury limits through litigation and official regulatory action (Mann and Hawkins 2007). By contrast, thirty-six states have laws specifically authorizing payday lending at interest rates much higher than their usury limit (King, Parrish, and Tanik 2006). Such "safe-harbor" laws, such as Michigan's Deferred Presentment Transactions Act, allow lenders to charge a set fee for each $100 borrowed.[16] Some states

13. Under the U.S. Supreme Court's decisions in *Marquette National Bank of Minneapolis* v. *First of Omaha Service Corp.*, 439 U.S. 299 (1978), and *Smiley* v. *Citibank (South Dakota), N.A.,* 517 U.S. 735 (1996), the out-of-state bank was not required to comply with the interest-rate cap of the borrower's home state. The payday outlet effectively rented, for a fee, the bank's charter for the purpose of extending loans at interest rates well above those which would otherwise be allowed by its own state's laws. This arrangement has been dubbed "rent-a-charter."

14. The OCC (2001), which regulates national banks, cautioned banks against "franchising" their names and attributes to financial institutions without the banks' involvement in the services provided, warning that banks associated with predatory or abusive third-party financial practices could lose their charters. The Federal Deposit Insurance Corporation (FDIC 2005), which regulates state banks, imposed substantial capitalization requirements on state banks partnering with lending institutions in other states.

15. New York's usury law, for example, forbids interest rates above 16 percent. N.Y. Banking L. § 14-a(1) (McKinney 2008).

16. Michigan allows payday lenders to charge 15 percent of the amount borrowed up to the first $100, 14 percent of the second $100, and so on, up to $600. Mich. Comp. Laws Ann. § 487.2153 (West 1996 & Supp. 2011).

that allow payday lending attempt to discourage repeat borrowing (Mann and Hawkins 2007). Regulations take the form of limits on the number of times a borrower may renew or roll over a payday loan;[17] mandated "cooling-off" periods during which borrowers may not take out new loans after having paid off previous ones;[18] limits on the number of loans consumers may simultaneously undertake (perhaps from more than one lender);[19] and the creation of a real-time database that lenders must consult before lending to ensure borrowers do not take out more than one loan at a time.[20]

Payday-lending regulation is usually proposed to weed out perceived abuses in the marketplace. Although economists typically view less choice as welfare reducing, recent empirical research suggests that payday lending may have negative welfare consequences,[21] and behavioral models of decisionmaking point out that more choice may not necessarily be welfare enhancing (Ernst, Ferris, and King 2004; King and Parrish 2007). Regulation is also justified on the grounds that consumers will tend to overestimate their ability to repay and underestimate the likelihood that they instead will be caught in a "debt trap" of rollovers (Mann and Hawkins 2007). Some argue that the fees charged lead to excessive profits for lenders; however, other research suggests that per-loan margins are not unreasonably large (Skiba and Tobacman 2008).

Pawnshops

Pawn transactions are also subject to the disclosure requirements of TILA. When an individual sells an item to a pawnbroker in return for a sum of money and retains the right to redeem the item for a greater sum (the redemption price) within a specified period of time, disclosures are required.[22] The amount financed is the initial sum paid to the consumer; the finance charge is the difference between that sum and the redemption price; and the APR is calculated by the period of time for which the borrower has the right to redeem the pledge.[23] Despite the role of TILA in making the terms of credit more transparent, the value of the object held as collateral must be determined, which is inherently subjective and performed by the pawnbroker. By adjusting the accepted collateral value, pawnbrokers can effectively change APRs.

17. For example, Colo. Rev. Stat. Ann. § 5-3.1-108 (LexisNexis 2010).

18. For example, Ind. Code Ann. §§ 24-4.5-7-108, -401 (West 2006 & Supp. 2010) (prohibiting lender's making a loan within seven days after repayment of the borrower's fifth consecutive payday loan).

19. For example, Mich. Comp. Laws Ann. § 487.2153(2).

20. Ibid.

21. For example, research has shown that first-time applicants for payday loans who are approved are significantly more likely to subsequently enter Chapter 13 bankruptcy than first-time applicants who were rejected and denied payday loans (Skiba and Tobacman 2008).

22. See Truth in Lending, 61 *Federal Register* 14952, 14956 (April 4, 1996) (codified at 12 C.F.R. pt. 226 Supp. I, ¶ 17(c)(1)-18).

23. Ibid.

At the state level, pawnbrokers are generally not treated as lenders under usury and small-loans statutes (Drysdale and Keest 2000). In some states, pawnbrokers are completely exempt from usury ceilings,[24] while in other states pawn transactions are subject to special rates.[25] Pawnshops may also be subject to regulation at the municipal level—Florida, for example, allows municipalities to enact more restrictive regulations than those set forth in the state law.[26] A number of jurisdictions have zoning regulations specific to pawnshops that restrict the number of providers in a certain location.[27]

Payday outlets and pawnshops can be substitutes. Some researchers have found an inverse relationship between the prevalence of pawnshops and the availability of other forms of short-term credit (Peterson and Falls 1981). Individuals turned down for a payday loan have been found somewhat more likely to use a pawnshop for short-term credit than similar individuals who were approved for the loan (Skiba and Tobacman 2008).

Refund Anticipation Loans

Refund anticipation loans are loans taxpayers draw against their expected tax refunds when they file their taxes through professional tax preparers (Drysdale and Keest 2000). The tax preparer does not make the loan itself; rather, it markets the RAL on behalf of a financial institution making the loan. Both entities take their cut: the tax preparer charges, in addition to a normal fee for preparing a tax return, a "handling" or "processing" fee, and the bank charges its fee for the loan. Refund anticipation loans are available at physical tax preparation outlets as well as on the Internet. Like payday loans, RALs are collateralized by future income. Their volume increased in the late 1990s and reached a peak in 2004, when 12.38 million loans were taken out (Wu, Fox, and Woodall 2006). Since that time, volume has decreased to 7.2 million in 2009, and because of increased regulation it is expected to decrease further (Wu 2011).

Refund anticipation loans are subject to TILA requirements.[28] Accordingly, the cost of the RAL must be disclosed as an APR and separated from the cost of

24. For example, Colo. Rev. Stat. Ann. § 5-1-202(4) (LexisNexis 2010) (providing that Colorado consumer credit rates, charges, and disclosure requirements do not apply to pawnbrokers).

25. See, for example, Ga. Code Ann. § 44-12-131 (LexisNexis 2002) (limiting finance charges on pawn transactions to a special rate of 25 percent of the principal amount for each thirty-day period for the first ninety days, and 12.5 percent per thirty-day period thereafter); Fla. Stat. § 539.001(11) (2010) (limiting finance charges on pawn transactions to a special rate of 25 percent of the principal amount for each thirty-day period).

26. Fla. Stat. § 538.17 ("Nothing in this chapter shall preclude political subdivisions of the state and municipalities from enacting laws more restrictive than the provisions of this chapter").

27. For example, Detroit, Mich. City Code §§ 61-3-252(3), 61-3-253(8), 61-12-87, 61-12-94, 61-12-221 (2011).

28. Truth in Lending; Update to Official Staff Commentary, 55 *Federal Register* 13103, 13119 (April 9, 1990) (codified at 12 C.F.R., pt. 226, Supp. I, ¶ 17(c)(1)-17).

the concomitant tax preparation services. Yet it is unlikely that taxpayers are able to distinguish the cost of these services apart from one another (Barr and Dokko 2006). Furthermore, not all RAL fees are included in the APR calculation, so even when disclosed according to TILA requirements, the APR likely understates the loan's total cost. Excluding some RAL fees from the APR calculation also precludes an apples-to-apples comparison of the costs of a RAL with other short-term credit products.

The Internal Revenue Service (IRS) has promulgated certain requirements with which tax preparers must comply in offering or preparing applications for RALs. An e-file provider that prepares tax returns may not make the RAL itself, though it may act as an intermediary for the financial institution making the loan (IRS 2011). An e-file provider acting as an intermediary may not charge a processing fee that varies with the size of the RAL. Moreover, the e-file provider may not accept payment from the financial institution underwriting the RAL for acting as the intermediary.[29] Finally, e-file providers offering RALs or preparing applications for RALs taken from other financial institutions must disclose to the taxpayer all fees charged and the amount of refund money the taxpayer will receive; that a RAL is an interest-bearing loan; that a RAL is not a substitute for, nor a faster way of receiving, a tax refund; and that, if the refund is not received by the lender within the expected time frame, the taxpayer may be liable for additional interest charges on the RAL (IRS 2011).

Because of recent changes, RAL lending is expected to decrease sharply in the near future. First, RAL underwriting relied heavily on information from the IRS on whether a customer's tax refunds would be offset by other claims, such as unpaid student loan debt or child support; however, the IRS has announced it will no longer furnish these "debt indicators" beginning in the 2011 tax-filing season (IRS 2010). Without this information, RAL lenders can no longer know whether loans are sufficiently secured by the refund and will require more information regarding the borrower's ability to repay the difference. Second, bank regulators have acted in the wake of the IRS policy change to prohibit RAL lending by their supervised institutions. For example, H&R Block, a large provider of tax preparation services, did not offer RALs during the 2011 tax-filing season after the Office of the Comptroller of the Currency (OCC) directed HSBC, H&R Block's RAL partner, to stop offering RALs (H&R Block 2010). H&R Block announced later in 2011 that it would not seek a new partner and would no longer facilitate RALs (H&R Block 2011). Also, the Federal Deposit Insurance Corporation (FDIC) directed Republic Bank & Trust, a RAL partner for two other large tax preparers, to end its RAL business, alleging that the bank's

---

29. By implication, e-file providers may accept a flat fee for each RAL processed from the financial institution.

underwriting practices were deficient without the debt indicator and threatened the bank's safety and soundness.[30] The FDIC also levied a $2 million fine on Republic Bank on the basis of alleged violations by its tax loan business.[31] These enforcement actions will also likely encourage other financial institutions to wind down or end their RAL businesses.

The vast majority of states do not have specific RAL laws (Wu, Fox, and Woodall 2006).[32] Like payday lenders, RAL providers have often engaged in arrangements with out-of-state banks to evade local usury laws (Drysdale and Keest 2000). Most states that regulate RALs provide only for disclosure requirements similar to those under TILA,[33] although North Carolina authorizes its banking commissioner to declare specific RAL fees unconscionable.[34] Connecticut is the only state that has enacted an interest-rate cap on RALs; it bars RAL facilitators (tax preparers) from processing a RAL with an APR over 60 percent.[35]

Rent-to-Own

Rent-to-own businesses sell consumer goods through installment payments; however, the finance charges on such purchases far exceed those on mainstream retail financing (Drysdale and Keest 2000). A rent-to-own transaction is usually structured as a "lease terminable at will" to avoid falling under state usury laws (Drysdale and Keest 2000), a distinction sanctioned by the law of many states.[36] In fact, rent-to-own transactions typically are found not to be subject to the Fair Debt Collection Practices Act, TILA, and states' retail installment-sales acts (Burnham 1991). Laws governing rent-to-own transactions typically limit the degree to which the sum of rental payments may exceed the cash price of the object purchased.[37] However, "cash price" is usually defined as the price at which the rent-to-own outlet would sell the item for a single payment and need not be related to the fair market value of the item (Drysdale and

---

30. See Amended Notice of Charges for an Order to Cease & Desist; Notice of Assessment of Civil Money Penalties, Findings of Fact & Conclusions of Law; Order to Pay; & Notice of Hearing, Republic Bank & Trust Co., No. FDIC-10-079b (Fed. Deposit Ins. Corp., May 3, 2011), 14–16.

31. Ibid., 18. Republic Bank continues to issue RALs while the orders are under administrative review (see NCLC 2011).

32. Only eight states (California, Connecticut, Illinois, Minnesota, Nevada, North Carolina, Washington, and Wisconsin) have laws specific to RALs.

33. For example, Wis. Stat. § 422.310 (2009).

34. N.C. Gen. Stat. Ann. § 53-249 (LexisNexis 2009) (requiring RAL lenders to submit annually a fee schedule to the banking commissioner, who maintains the authority to deem interest rates unconscionable, and prohibiting lenders from deviating from the approved fee schedule).

35. Conn. Gen. Stat. § 42-480(d), (e) (2009).

36. See, for example, Colo. Rev. Stat. Ann. § 5-10-301 (LexisNexis 2010) (defining the consumer as "lessee" and the rent-to-own outlet as the "lessor"); Iowa Code § 537.3604 (2011) (defining a rent-to-own transaction as a "consumer rental purchase agreement").

37. For example, Iowa Code § 537.3608.

Keest 2000).[38] These laws therefore provide scant protection against high effective interest rates. Only a few states, such as Minnesota, define rent-to-own transactions as credit sales falling under the protection of state usury laws.[39]

Credit Cards

The Credit Card Accountability, Responsibility, and Disclosure (CARD) Act of 2009 enacts a number of key changes to the credit-card market.[40] For example, the act provides for improvements in plain-language disclosures on credit-card agreements. It requires credit-card companies to notify consumers forty-five days in advance of certain major changes to card terms, such as interest rates and fees. The act provides for consumer de-biasing: credit-card disclosures now include information on the time and cost of making only the minimum payment, as well as the time and cost of paying off the balance within three years. Moreover, consumers are provided with monthly and year-to-date figures on interest costs and fees incurred, so that they can more readily compare their anticipated costs with their actual usage patterns. The act requires firms to obtain consumers' consent—an opt-in—for over-limit transactions. It bans practices such as certain retroactive rate hikes on existing balances, late-fee traps (including midday due times, due dates less than twenty-one days after the time of mailing statements, and changes of due dates from month to month), and double-cycle billing.

These practices have in common that consumers cannot readily shape their behavior to avoid the charges; the fees or practices in question are not readily shopped for in making a choice among credit cards; and disclosures are of little help. Because consumers generally do not understand how payments are allocated across different account balances even after improved disclosures (see FRB 2007, 2008), the act requires that a consumer's payments above the minimum amount due be applied first toward higher-cost balances. Based on the understanding that consumers do not shop for penalty fees and that they often misforecast their own behavior, the act requires that late fees or other penalty fees must be "reasonable and proportionate," as determined by implementing rules; that in any event the fees may not be larger than the amount charged that is over the limit or late; and that a late fee or other penalty fee cannot be assessed more than once for the same transaction or event. Furthermore, the act takes steps to make it easier for the market to develop mechanisms for consumer comparison

---

38. Some state rent-to-own laws also limit the amount and frequency of late fees on tardy payments and provide for an "early purchase option" whereby the consumer may purchase the item for the unpaid balance of the cash price as stated in the rental-purchase agreement, plus all past due payments and fees. See, for example, N.Y. Pers. Prop. Law §§ 501(3)(e), 504 (McKinney Supp. 2011).

39. *Miller* v. *Colortyme, Inc.*, 518 N.W.2d 544, 547–48 (Minn. 1994).

40. Credit Card Accountability Responsibility and Disclosure (CARD) Act of 2009, Pub. L. No. 111-24, 123 Stat. 1734.

shopping by requiring the public posting to the Federal Reserve of credit-card contracts in machine-readable formats; private firms or nonprofits can develop tools for experts and consumers to use to evaluate these various contracts. The new Consumer Financial Protection Bureau will undoubtedly have occasion to review these and other requirements for credit cards in the future.

Overdraft

Traditionally, customer payment orders in excess of the funds available in the customer's bank account, whether by check or by debit card, were declined. However, some banks allowed managers to, on an ad hoc basis, honor some payments (usually checks) that would otherwise overdraw the account, as a customer accommodation, usually in recognition of a long-standing customer relationship or general creditworthiness (FDIC 2010). Banks extended these convenience overdrafts without formal credit scoring and without separate credit agreements. These payments spared the customer the inconvenience and embarrassment, as well as potential liability, of issuing bad checks and allowed the bank to earn, in most cases, insufficient funds fees (FDIC 2010).[41] Over time, banks transformed these overdraft programs into bank-wide policies, automatically honoring payments made by any customer who met basic criteria up to a bank-wide limit, typically $100 to $500 in excess of available balances.[42] Banks also began to market these services to customers as overdraft protection programs.[43] The number of automated overdraft protection programs grew rapidly from 2001 to 2007,[44] and as usage grew, overdraft fees have become a significant source of income for banks.[45]

Regulators' concern that some overdraft program features could amount to "unfair or deceptive acts or practices" prohibited by the Federal Trade Commission Act—particularly the marketing of such programs in a way that may lead customers to believe that the service acts like a normal line of credit—prompted the release by the OCC, the Federal Reserve Board (FRB), the FDIC, and the National Credit Union Administration of the Joint Guidance on Overdraft Pro-

---

41. In 2008, the average insufficient funds fee was just over $26; some banks charge additional fees for every day the account remains overdrawn (GAO 2008).

42. See Joint Guidance on Overdraft Protection Programs, 70 *Federal Register* 9127, 9128 (February 24, 2005).

43. Ibid.

44. In a study of some FDIC-supervised banks, 41 percent of banks operated an automated overdraft program in 2006–07; 68 percent of these banks began their automated programs after 2001 (FDIC 2008).

45. According to estimates made in 2009, the U.S. banking system collects $38.5 billion a year in consumer overdraft fees. Damian Paletta, "Fed Slaps Curbs on Overdraft Fees," *Wall Street Journal,* November 13, 2009 (http://online.wsj.com/article/SB1000142405274870381160457453206 3720902686.html).

tection programs in 2005.[46] The joint guidance listed best practices for overdraft protection programs, such as communicating transparently; permitting customers to opt out; and monitoring excessive customer use.[47]

Although regulators first worked jointly to produce an interagency overdraft program guideline, the regulatory approach has since fragmented. In 2009 the FRB introduced additional opt-in and customer notice requirements for overdraft fees.[48] In late 2010, the FDIC issued a separate Overdraft Payment Supervisory Guidance communicating its supervisory expectations with respect to overdraft programs (FDIC 2010) with requirements more stringent than those imposed by the FRB. For example, the supervisory guidance requires banks to monitor customer overdrafts for excessive or chronic customer use;[49] contact customers who have overdrawn their accounts six or more times in any rolling twelve-month period; and discuss less costly alternatives to overdraft protection with these customers (FDIC 2010). The supervisory guidance also asks banks to "consider eliminating overdraft fees for transactions that overdraw an account by a de minimis amount" and requires that overdraft fees, if charged on such amounts, be "reasonable and proportional to the amount of the original transaction." The OCC has also released for public comment its proposed Supervisory Guidance for Overdraft Products,[50] which requires prudent limits on the amount of overdrafts allowed and monitoring of account holders for excessive use.[51]

These divergent regulatory requirements have resulted in incomplete consumer protections for overdraft products. Though the FDIC's supervisory guidance strengthens consumer protections, these additional protections need not be disclosed to customers, unlike those requirements found in the FRB's Regulation E, which the FRB has incorporated into its model customer disclosures.[52] Moreover, unlike Regulation E violations, which could attract a cease-and-desist order,[53] it is unclear what sanctions will follow from failure to comply with the guidance. Although the FDIC alludes to cease-and-desist orders, the guidance mentions that its requirements will be factored into examination ratings (FDIC 2010). The Dodd–Frank Wall Street Reform and Consumer Protection Act addresses these issues by consolidating rule-making authority in the Consumer

46. Joint Guidance on Overdraft Protection Programs, 70 *Federal Register* 9127, 9130–31 (February 24, 2005).

47. Ibid., 9127.

48. Electronic Fund Transfers, 74 *Federal Register* 59033 (November 17, 2009) (codified as amended at 12 C.F.R. §§ 205.12, 205.17 (2011)).

49. Ibid., 4.

50. Guidance on Deposit-Related Consumer Credit Products, 76 *Federal Register* 33409 (June 8, 2011).

51. Ibid., 33410–12.

52. See 12 C.F.R. pt. 205, app. A-9 (2011).

53 See 12 U.S.C. § 1818(b) (2006).

Table 6-1. *Use of Short-Term Credit, by Payday Borrowing Status*
Percent

Service	Not a payday borrower	Payday borrower	Total
Pawnshop	10	40	11
Cash advance on credit card	7	24	8
Refund anticipation loans	21	45	22
Rent-to-own	5	20	5
Cash out pension or life insurance	6	19	7
Secured credit card	9	37	10
Any AFS[a]	39	100	42
Bank account	71	78	71
Bank account overdraft	19	57	20
Money order	68	80	68
Credit card	41	43	41
Credit card with late fee	21	43	22
Sample size	895	43	938

Source: Detroit Area Household Financial Services study.

a. Any AFS includes pawnshop, payday loan, refund anticipation loan, rent-to-own, pension cash-out, secured credit card, cash advance on credit card.

Financial Protection Bureau[54] and by further vesting the bureau with the power to prohibit unfair, deceptive, or abusive acts or practices.[55]

Empirical Results

Overall, the use of short-term credit is common among low- and moderate-income households. In particular, many such households use alternative short-term credit products, such as payday lenders, pawnshops, refund anticipation loans, rent-to-own, pension or life insurance policy cash-out, secured credit cards, and cash advances on credit cards (table 6-1). Over 40 percent of the sample use some form of alternative credit at least once during the three years preceding the survey interview. Over 20 percent take out a refund anticipation loan, 11 percent use a pawnshop, 10 percent have a secured credit card, and 8 percent take out a cash advance on a credit card. Other credit options such as rent-to-own (5 percent) and title loans (2 percent, not shown) are less common. In contrast, 28 percent of LMI households looked into obtaining a loan from a bank in the three years preceding the survey interview (not shown).

54. See Dodd–Frank Wall Street Reform and Consumer Protection (Dodd-Frank) Act, sec. 1084(3), Pub. L. No. 111-203, 124 Stat. 1376, 2081–82 (2010) (amending 15 U.S.C. § 1693b); id. sec. 1092(3), 124 Stat. at 2095 (striking 15 U.S.C. § 57a(f)(6)).

55. See 15 U.S.C. § 5531 (Supp. IV 2010).

Payday borrowing is a fringe practice among LMI households in the Detroit area. Only 4 percent of respondents say they "looked into getting a loan of $100 or more from a check casher, payday-loan store, or other place that gives you a payday loan" during the three years preceding the survey interview. Only 3 percent report having taken the payday loan from the lender during the year before the survey interview. Part of the reason that so few respondents approach payday lenders may be the restrictive qualifications for loan eligibility. As a general requirement, a source of steady income and a checking account are necessary to qualify for a payday loan. As table 6-1 suggests, however, payday borrowers are much more likely than non–payday borrowers to use a wide variety of other forms of short-term credit.

Demographics of Short-Term Borrowers

The demographics of the users of short-term credit are, by and large, similar to those of the overall sample in the DAHFS study, suggesting that demographic variation does not explain whether LMI households use these short-term credit products. Put differently, users of short-term credit seem to be, on net, demographically similar to LMI households at large. Median household size is the same for all LMI households and for AFS borrowers, with two family members, and blacks are no more likely to use these services than whites. Women are somewhat more likely than men to use an alternative credit source, with 44 percent of women using one of the AFS credit options and 36 percent of men doing so (results not shown).

Borrowers who use alternative financial services, however, are more likely to be employed than their nonborrowing LMI counterparts (see table 6-2). While 72 percent of the sample are working age (25–60), 81 percent of AFS borrowers are in that age category. Also, LMI households who borrow from alternative lenders are more educated than non–AFS borrowers: those with more than a high school diploma make up 54 percent of AFS borrowers and 47 percent of all respondents. The connection between education and AFS use derives in part from the requirements needed to obtain credit, particularly having steady income.

Interactions among Short-Term Credit Products

Table 6-3 shows a correlation matrix of short-term credit products that suggests they are interconnected. The strongest correlation is between pawnshop use and payday borrowing, which is consistent with the usage patterns presented in table 6-1. Payday borrowing use is also correlated with using an overdraft from a bank account. Nearly every entry in the table is positive, suggesting that individuals who use one short-term credit product are likely to use another. Although usage appears complementary, most of the correlations are not large and are statistically insignificant from zero, implying relatively weak direct relationships.

Table 6-2. *Demographic Characteristics of AFS Short-Term Credit Users*[a]
Percent

Characteristic	Users	Nonusers	Total
Age			
18–24	9.7	13.4	11.9
25–60	80.6	65.5	71.8
61 and older	9.7	21.1	16.3
Race			
African American	72.1	66.2	68.6
White	20.0	20.4	20.3
Asian American	0.6	3.3	2.1
Hispanic	3.4	3.7	3.5
Arab American	0.9	2.5	1.9
Other	3.1	3.9	3.6
Employment status			
Currently employed	62.8	48.2	54.3
Recently employed	15.6	11.4	13.2
Not employed	21.6	40.4	32.5
Educational attainment			
Less than high school diploma	23.6	33.9	29.6
High school diploma	22.5	23.4	23.0
More than high school diploma	53.9	42.7	47.4
Sample size	392	546	938

Source: Detroit Area Household Financial Services study.

a. AFS includes pawnshop, payday loan, refund anticipation loan, rent-to-own, pension cash-out, secured credit card, cash advance on credit card.

Table 6-3. *Relationship between AFS Short-Term Credit Products*[a]

	Payday loan	Pawnshop	RAL	Rent-to-own	Layaway	Cash advance on credit card	Overdraft
Payday loan							
Pawnshop	0.200						
RAL	0.124	0.151					
Rent-to-own	0.136	0.171	0.187				
Layaway	0.027	0.041	0.192	0.086			
Cash advance	0.133	0.073	−0.009	−0.014	0.105		
Overdraft	0.196	0.057	0.092	0.105	0.144	0.193	
Pension cash-out	0.105	0.017	0.077	0.04	0.021	0.119	0.065

Source: Detroit Area Household Financial Services study.

a. AFS includes pawnshop, payday loan, refund anticipation loan, rent-to-own, pension cash-out, secured credit card, cash advance on credit card.

The data also suggest that the AFS sector is a source of borrowing for those with certain credit-card behaviors. There are no significant differences in AFS use for those with and without a credit card—about 40 percent of both groups use AFS products. However, those who have paid late fees on a credit card are more likely to have used an AFS product than those who have not missed payments (33 versus 14 percent). Around 52 percent of those who report they never pay off the entire balance on their credit card have looked into using an alternative financial service, compared with 26 percent of those who pay off their entire balance each month. Alternative credit products are used by 77 percent of those who pay only the minimum amount due. In addition, the least creditworthy card holders, those whose cards require a deposit—known as secured credit cards—are much more likely to use other forms of AFS credit.

These findings about the borrowing patterns confirm that low- and moderate-income borrowers use many different credit products. The results are also consistent with AFS borrowers' having a history of credit problems, which may preclude borrowing from mainstream providers. Generally speaking, the results are broadly consistent with riskier borrowing behavior among AFS borrowers. Riskier borrowing behavior also corresponds to reported difficulties in acquiring loans from mainstream providers. More than 45 percent of AFS borrowers also applied for a loan from a mainstream provider (banks, savings and loan, credit union, finance, and mortgage companies) during the three years preceding the survey interview, whereas only 30 percent of nonusers requested a loan. Over 25 percent of AFS users who approached a mainstream lender for a loan were turned down, compared with 14 percent of nonusers. In short, AFS users tend to seek more borrowing opportunities than nonusers, exhibit riskier credit behavior, and face higher rates of rejection from mainstream lenders. The results from this section confirm that households use a variety of credit options to navigate the various different creditworthiness standards, collateral options, payment mechanisms, and finance charges available in the short-term credit market.

Borrower Experiences, Behavior, and Attitudes

Financial difficulties are common among users of alternative financial services (table 6-4). More than 80 percent of AFS users report that they were in financial trouble in the previous year, whereas 66 percent of nonusers report this about their financial security. Nine percent of users were evicted in the twelve months preceding the survey interview, 22 percent had their phone cut off, and over 13 percent had their utilities shut off. Around 29 percent experienced a major medical illness or expense in the twelve months before being interviewed. In addition, 4 percent filed for bankruptcy in the year preceding the survey interview, while around 22 percent have ever filed for bankruptcy.

This evidence on the hardships of AFS borrowers suggests that they may have a greater need for borrowing than nonusers. Their financial difficulties, however,

Table 6-4. *Hardships Experienced by Alternative Financial Services Users*
Percent

Financial situation	Users	Nonusers	Total
Financially secure	17.9	34.4	27.5
Some financial trouble	59.0	50.5	54.1
Deep financial trouble	23.0	15.1	18.4
Experienced in the past twelve months			
Recent bankruptcy	4.4	3.6	3.9
Eviction	8.9	3.8	5.9
Phone cut-off	21.9	15.8	18.3
Utilities shut-off	13.2	7.7	10.0
Major medical expense or illness	29.3	25.1	26.9
Foreclosure threatened	11.1	2.4	5.6
Turned down for loan with bank, savings and loan, or mortgage company	30.6	26.6	28.7
Ever filed for bankruptcy	22.4	16.1	18.7
Sample size	392	546	938

Source: Detroit Area Household Financial Services study.

a. AFS includes pawnshop, payday loan, refund anticipation loan, rent-to-own, pension cash-out, secured credit card, cash advance on credit card.

make them a riskier group from the perspective of mainstream and alternative lenders and may in part explain why they are turned down at a higher rate and face higher costs of borrowing. Furthermore, without knowing the underlying cause of their financial problems, it is difficult to assess whether their hardships are the cause of AFS borrowing or are a manifestation of some other behavior or attitude. More specifically, AFS borrowers, who are more likely to borrow from other sources, may do so for myriad reasons, including greater hardship, poorer financial planning, uncontrolled spending habits, or limited access to less costly sources of credit.

A comparison of the attitudes of users and nonusers of alternative financial services, shown in table 6-5, also confirms that the former group is made up of individuals and households with a preference for borrowing. Not surprisingly, those who take out AFS loans are also less averse to debt, which is consistent with our view that AFS users tend to seek all types of loans (AFS and mainstream) at a higher rate than nonusers. For instance, 87 percent of AFS users agree that it is "all right for someone . . . to borrow to cover rent and food when income is cut," whereas 70 percent of nonusers agree with that statement. Users of AFS are also more likely to find it acceptable to borrow for a car, to pay for educational expenses, or to cover the cost of a major illness. They are also more willing to borrow to finance the purchase of goods they cannot currently afford, though the overall proportions are small and not statistically

Table 6-5. *Attitudes toward Borrowing, Saving, by Short-Term Credit Use*[a]
Percent

Attitude	Users	Nonusers
If I did not pay my bills on time		
My credit rating would worsen	93.1	91.0
A bank would not let me borrow	88.5	80.2
Nothing would happen	12.4	15.5
I can walk away from it by filing for bankruptcy	29.6	28.3
I would be ashamed if I filed for bankruptcy	53.6	64.8
Most of my money goes to necessities	90.1	82.0
It is hard to resist temptation to spend money	69.1	62.4
Saving money just isn't worth it	13.3	18.9
Bankruptcy affects my ability to borrow	79.6	74.7
It is all right to borrow		
To cover rent and food	86.6	70.2
To finance a fur coat, stereo, jewelry, and so on	6.5	3.9
To buy a car	61.6	52.5
To pay for educational expenses	79.1	68.7
To cover the cost of a major illness	86.3	73.4

Source: Detroit Area Household Financial Services study.

a. AFS includes pawnshop, payday loan, refund anticipation loan, rent-to-own, pension cash-out, secured credit card, and cash advance on credit card.

different from each other (7 percent of AFS borrowers versus 4 percent of nonborrowers). They are less likely to feel ashamed or embarrassed if they were to file for bankruptcy, although it is hard to interpret this finding, given that those who do not identify a bankruptcy stigma are also more likely previously to have filed for bankruptcy.

Conclusion

Low- and moderate-income households use a range of alternative and mainstream short-term credit products to meet their needs. Credit access provides an important means for smoothing consumption for low-income households facing emergencies or income volatility, and with little savings and low asset levels. Households with no slack often turn to short-term credit to make ends meet. Many of these products, however, are associated with high fees. In some cases, fees are not transparently conveyed. In addition, a number of the products we studied are structured in a way that makes it easy for households to systematically overborrow. For example, payday borrowers often underestimate the need to roll over their payday loan at the time it is due, and credit-card holders often underestimate the extent to which they will carry balances from month to month or pay late or over-limit fees.

Moreover, short-term credit products are regulated in a piecemeal fashion that creates confusion and the potential for regulatory arbitrage. Because the regulatory structure imposes nonuniform borrowing standards, households face difficulty in ascertaining the costs associated with different loan products. Furthermore, because the different AFS markets are not connected, lenders cannot adequately, or at low cost, establish a household's ability to repay the loan or their overall indebtedness. And because restrictions on some AFS credit products lead households seeking borrowing opportunities to other products that are perhaps not as well regulated, households may potentially end up with fewer and poorer choices in the short-term credit market. Ultimately, for these reasons, low- and moderate-income households may unnecessarily face high pecuniary and non-pecuniary costs in the short-term credit market relative to a regulatory environment that integrates the different short-term credit products.

The current regulatory environment for short-term AFS credit is not well suited to address either the heterogeneous usage patterns or the socioeconomic diversity among LMI households. Given that these households use different short-term credit products, that are or are not covered by TILA, they may encounter a wide array of pricing disclosures that are expressed in different forms, or perhaps not at all. The complexity of eligibility requirements across the loan types may also confuse households to the point that they use the "wrong" type of short-term credit to satisfy their collateral and borrowing needs.

In light of the preference for borrowing among AFS users, piecemeal regulation of one product but not others is unlikely to influence overall levels of borrowing (and may indeed leave households worse off). Also, the nontransparency of loan characteristics makes it easy for households to make errors in the allocation of resources across time periods. For example, AFS users are more likely to report they save to pay down loans or to get out of debt (54 versus 41 percent; results not shown). They also feel unprepared for future expenses—44 percent of AFS users expect to face a major expense for which they feel unable to save (compared with 32 percent of nonusers). Regulation ought to ensure that households face accurate information as they make their saving and borrowing decisions. Regulatory reform ought to focus on a unified approach to all forms of short-term credit. Coordination across federal, state, and local regulations should help to reduce regulatory burden and improve consumer outcomes.

The Consumer Financial Protection Bureau has an important opportunity to look holistically at the short-term credit markets offered by both banks and AFS providers. Policymakers ought to focus on reforms across the range of credit products. For example, improved disclosure regulation applied properly to the range of mainstream and alternative credit options, from bank overdraft and credit cards to payday lending and refund loans, could help to foster LMI households' ability to comparison shop across alternative and mainstream credit sources. Regulations that move credit products away from hidden fees and into transparent prices, as under the CARD Act of 2009, would help reduce systematic resource allocation errors among households. The Consumer Financial Protection Bureau could also use behaviorally informed techniques, similar to the CARD Act's requirement regarding the consequence of making only the minimum monthly payment, that make it easier for individuals to understand the consequences of choosing among different credit products and usage patterns.

References

Barr, Michael S. 2004. "Banking the Poor." *Yale Journal on Regulation* 21:121–237.

———. 2005. "Credit Where It Counts: The Community Reinvestment Act and Its Critics." *New York University Law Review* 80:513–652.

Barr, Michael S., and Jane K. Dokko. 2006. "Tax Filing Experiences and Withholding Preferences of Low- and Moderate-Income Households: Preliminary Evidence from a New Survey." In *Recent Research on Tax Administration and Compliance,* compiled and edited by James Dalton and Beth Kilss, 193–210. U.S. Department of the Treasury, Internal Revenue Service.

Berube, Alan, and Tracy Kornblatt. 2005. *Step in the Right Direction: Recent Declines in Refund Loan Usage among Low-Income Taxpayers.* Brookings (www.brookings.edu/~/media/Files/rc/reports/2005/04childrenfamilies_berube/20050412_eitcdecline.pdf).

Burnham, Scott J. 1991. "The Regulation of Rent-to-Own Transactions." *Loyola Consumer Law Reporter* 3:40–45.

Caskey, John P. 1995. "Explaining the Boom in Check-Cashing Outlets and Pawnshops." *Consumer Finance Law Quarterly Report* 49:4–12.

CCC (University of North Carolina Center for Community Capital). 2007. *North Carolina Consumers after Payday Lending: Attitudes and Experiences with Credit Options.* Chapel Hill, N.C. (www.ccc.unc.edu/documents/NC_After_Payday.pdf).

DeYoung, Robert, and Ronnie J. Phillips. 2006. "Strategic Pricing of Payday Lenders: Evidence from Colorado, 2000–2005." Working Paper 2006-WP-05. Indiana State University, Networks Financial Institute (www.networksfinancialinstitute.org/Lists/Publication%20Library/Attachments/70/2006-WP-05_Young-Phillips.pdf).

Drysdale, Lynn, and Kathleen E. Keest. 2000. "The Two-Tiered Consumer Financial Services Marketplace: The Fringe Banking System and Its Challenge to Current Thinking about the Role of Usury Laws in Today's Society." *South Carolina Law Review* 51:589–670.

Elliehausen, Gregory. 2006. "Consumers' Use of High-Priced Credit Products: Do They Know What They Are Doing?" Working Paper 2006-WP-02. Indiana State University, Networks Financial Institute (http://ssrn.com/abstract=921909).

Elliehausen, Gregory, and Edward C. Lawrence. 2001. "Payday Advance Credit in America: An Analysis of Consumer Demand." Monograph 35. Georgetown University, McDonough School of Business Credit Research Center (www.fdic.gov/bank/analytical/cfr/2005/jan/CFRSS_2005_elliehausen.pdf).

Ernst, Keith, John Farris, and Uriah King. 2004. *Quantifying the Economic Cost of Predatory Lending.* Durham, N.C.: Center for Responsible Lending (http://cfsinnovation.com/system/files/imported/managed_documents/crlpaydaylendingstudy.pdf).

FDIC (Federal Deposit Insurance Corporation). 2005. *Guidelines for Payday Lending.* Financial Institution Letter FIL-14-2005 (www.fdic.gov/news/news/financial/2005/fil1405a.html).

———. 2008. *FDIC Study of Bank Overdraft Programs* (www.fdic.gov/bank/analytical/overdraft/FDIC138_Report_Final_v508.pdf).

————. 2010. *Overdraft Payment Programs and Consumer Protection: Final Overdraft Payment Supervisory Guidance.* Financial Institution Letter FIL-81-2010 (www.fdic.gov/news/news/financial/2010/fil10081.pdf).

Feltner, Tom, and Marva Williams. 2004. "New Terms for Payday Loans: High Cost Lenders Change Loan Terms to Evade Illinois Consumer Protections." Report 25. Chicago: Woodstock Institute (http://woodstockinst.org/document/alert_26.pdf).

Flannery, Mark, and Katherine Samolyk. 2005. "Payday Lending: Do the Costs Justify the Price?" Working Paper 2005-09. Federal Deposit Insurance Corporation (www.fdic.gov/bank/analytical/cfr/2005/wp2005/CFRWP_2005-09_Flannery_Samolyk.pdf).

Fox, Jean Ann, and Anna Petrini. 2004. *Internet Payday Lending: How High-Priced Lenders Use the Internet to Mire Borrowers in Debt and Evade State Consumer Protections.* Washington: Consumer Federation of America (www.consumerfed.org/pdfs/Internet_Payday_Lending 113004.PDF).

FRB (Federal Reserve Board). 2007. *Design and Testing of Effective Truth in Lending Disclosures* (www.federalreserve.gov/dcca/regulationz/20070523/execsummary.pdf).

————. 2008. Consumer Testing of Mortgage Broker Disclosures: Summary of Findings.

GAO (U.S. Government Accountability Office). 2008. "Bank Fees: Federal Regulators Could Better Ensure That Consumers Have Required Disclosure Documents prior to Opening Checking or Savings Accounts." Report GAO-08-281 (www.gao.gov/new.items/d08281.pdf).

Goulet, Dawn. 2007. "Protecting Our Protectors: The Defense Department's New Rules to Prevent Predatory Lending to Military Personnel." *Loyola Consumer Law Review* 20:81–99.

H&R Block. 2010. "HSBC Terminates Agreement to Provide RALs at Direction of OCC." News release, December 24 (www.hrblock.com/press/Article.jsp?articleid=49252).

————. 2011. "H&R Block Decides Not to Offer Refund Anticipation Loans in 2012." News release, September 13 (www.hrblock.com/press/Article.jsp?articleid= 52784).

IRS (Internal Revenue Service). 2010. "IRS Removes Debt Indicator for 2011 Tax Filing Season." News release, August 5 (www.irs.gov/newsroom/article/0,,id=226310,00.html).

————. 2011. *Handbook for Authorized IRS E-File Providers of Individual Income Tax Returns.* Publication 1345. U.S. Department on the Treasury.

Johnson, Creola. 2002. "Payday Loans: Shrewd Business or Predatory Lending?" *Minnesota Law Review* 87:1–152.

King, Uriah, and Leslie Parrish. 2007. *Springing the Debt Trap: Rate Caps Are Only Proven Lending Reform.* Durham, N.C.: Center for Responsible Lending (www.responsiblelending.org/payday-lending/research-analysis/springing-the-debt-trap.pdf).

King, Uriah, Leslie Parrish, and Ozlem Tanik. 2006. *Financial Quicksand: Payday Lending Sinks Borrowers in Debt with $4.2 Billion in Predatory Fees Each Year.* Durham, N.C.: Center for Responsible Lending (www.responsiblelending.org/payday-lending/research-analysis/rr012-Financial_Quicksand-1106.pdf).

Mann, Ronald J., and Jim Hawkins. 2007. "Just until Payday." *UCLA Law Review* 54:855–912.

Martin, Susan Lorde, and Nancy White Huckins. 1997. "Consumer Advocates vs. the Rent-to-Own Industry: Reaching a Reasonable Accommodation." *American Business Law Journal* 34:385–428 (doi:10.1111/j.1744-1714.1997.tb00899.x).

McKernan, Signe-Mary, Caroline Ratcliffe, and Daniel Kuehn. 2010. "Prohibitions, Price Caps, and Disclosures: A Look at State Policies and Alternative Financial Product Use." Urban Institute (November).

Melzer, Brian T. Forthcoming. "The Real Costs of Credit Access: Evidence from the Payday Lending Market." *Quarterly Journal of Economics,* forthcoming 2012.

Morgan, Donald P., and Michael Strain. 2007. "Payday Holiday: How Households Fare after Payday Credit Bans." Staff Report 309. Federal Reserve Bank of New York (www.newyork fed.org/research/staff_reports/sr309.pdf).

NCLC (National Consumer Law Center). 2011. "Consumer Advocates Applaud H&R Block Decision to Forego RALs and Urge Republic, Jackson Hewitt, and Liberty to Stop Making High Cost Loans." News release, September 14 (www.nclc.org/images/pdf/whats_new/ pr_advocates-applaud-block-dropping-rals.pdf).

OCC (Office of the Comptroller of the Currency). 2001. *Third-Party Relationships: Risk Management Principles.* Bulletin 2001-47. U.S. Department of Treasury (www.occ.gov/news-issuances/bulletins/2001/bulletin-2001-47.html).

Peterson, Richard L., and Gregory A. Falls. 1981. "Impact of a Ten Percent Usury Ceiling: Empirical Evidence." Working Paper 40. Purdue University, Krannert School of Management, Credit Research Center (http://faculty.msb.edu/prog/CRC/pdf/wp40.pdf).

Rossman, Stuart T. 2007. "Selected Hot Topics in Auto, Mortgage, and Subprime Lending." In *12th Annual Meeting of the Consumer Financial Services Litigation Institute,* edited by Alan S. Kaplinsky and others, 41–64. New York: Practicing Law Institute.

Skiba, Martin Paige, and Jeremy Tobacman. 2008. "Do Payday Loans Cause Bankruptcy?" Unpublished manuscript (February 19) (www.economics.ox.ac.uk/members/jeremy.tobacman/ papers/rd.pdf).

Stegman, Michael A., and Robert Faris. 2003. "Payday Lending: A Business Model That Encourages Chronic Borrowing." *Economic Development Quarterly* 17:8–32 (doi:10.1177/ 0891242402239196).

Wu, Chi Chi. 2011. *End of the Rapid Rip-Off: Epilogue for Quickie Tax Loans.* Boston, Mass.: National Consumer Law Center (www.nclc.org/images/pdf/high_cost_small_loans/ral/ report-ral-2011.pdf).

Wu, Chi Chi, Jean Ann Fox, and Patrick Woodall. 2006. *Another Year of Losses: High-Priced Refund Anticipation Loans Continue to Take a Chunk Out of Americans' Tax Refunds.* Boston, Mass.: National Consumer Law Center (www.consumerfed.org/pdfs/2006_RAL_r eport.pdf).

Zinman, Jonathan. 2010. "Restricting Consumer Credit Access: Household Survey Evidence on Effects around the Oregon Rate Cap." *Journal of Banking and Finance* 34(3).

7

High-Cost Home Ownership

MICHAEL S. BARR, JANE K. DOKKO, AND BENJAMIN J. KEYS

In spite of the recent impetus to reform home mortgage markets, particularly as they affect low- and moderate-income (LMI) households, little systematic evidence is available about how potential abuses in mortgage lending manifest in the mortgages held by those households. While racial discrimination in mortgage markets has a long history in the United States, the role of mortgage brokers in lending has only recently increased and become controversial.[1] In this chapter, we uncover two groups of LMI home borrowers who are subject to differential mortgage pricing: black borrowers and borrowers who use mortgage brokers pay more for mortgage loans than other borrowers, after controlling for a wide variety of factors.

To the best of our knowledge, the Detroit Area Household Financial Services (DAHFS) study is the first household-level survey to report data on different dimensions of high-cost mortgage pricing, such as balloon payments, up-front points and fees, "teaser" rates, and prepayment penalties, along with whether a household uses a mortgage broker.[2] The data set links household and mortgage characteristics to describe mortgage pricing among LMI households, their credit-

1. Until recently, 60 to 70 percent of loans were originated through the broker channel. Some economists argue that mortgage brokers contributed to the subprime boom and bust by aggressively marketing high-cost and potentially confusing mortgages to low-income borrowers (Quigley 2008).

2. Susan Woodward and Robert Hall (2010) use loan-level data with mortgage pricing variables but not many household-level characteristics, while Andrew Haughwout, Christopher Mayer, and Joseph Tracy (2009) merge data from LoanPerformance (LP) and the Home Mortgage Disclosure Act to examine racial differences in subprime mortgage pricing.

worthiness and attitudes about borrowing, and their use of mortgage brokers. Especially noteworthy is that the survey was conducted at the height of the subprime lending boom in 2005 and 2006 and in a state—Michigan—where antipredatory lending statutes were relatively weak.

We establish a profile of the demographic characteristics of home owners in LMI neighborhoods in the Detroit area.[3] We then estimate differences in mortgage pricing for these home owners and include as much available information about the borrower as possible to account for the demand-driven explanations that are correlated with race or with using a mortgage broker for the high costs some home owners pay. We focus on the intensive margin of differences in pricing rather than on how lenders may limit access to credit, ration credit, or require prohibitively high down payments. The characteristics of mortgages may differ across borrowers because of their income, the size of their down payment, their taste for risk, their creditworthiness, and their willingness to shop around for the best terms. While our approach cannot completely rule out these demand-driven explanations, our descriptive results are most consistent with supply-driven origins for differences in loan terms.

We find that within similar low-income neighborhoods, black home owners pay higher interest rates—110 basis points, on average—than similar nonblack home owners and are more than twice as likely as nonblack home owners to have prepayment penalties or balloon payments attached to their mortgages, even after we control for age, income, gender, creditworthiness, and a proxy for default risk. In addition, we observe that borrowers who used a mortgage broker are over 60 percent more likely to pay more in points or fees than those who did not use a broker.

The heterogeneity in pricing that we observe across racial groups and across transaction types (broker versus nonbroker) is unexplained after accounting for many demand-driven explanations that we present in greater detail later in the chapter. However, there may be other potentially important sources of heterogeneity that are unobservable to us but may be observed by the lender, such as more-precise measures of income volatility or earlier documentation of income and assets (see Edelberg [2007] for a discussion of these issues). Our approach cannot distinguish between racial differences in pricing and the presence of omitted financial characteristics that are correlated with race but are not included in our data. Nonetheless, a well-functioning mortgage market should eliminate the disparate treatment of minority borrowers and borrowers who use mortgage brokers.

Our analysis sheds light on the average home owner's experience in Detroit's LMI neighborhoods, which are similar to many Rust Belt communities such as

---

3. This includes Wayne, Oakland, and Macomb Counties.

Cleveland, Ohio, or Gary, Indiana.[4] The differences in loan terms by race, particularly in the up-front costs, which are not formally collected by fair lending enforcement mechanisms such as the Home Mortgage Disclosure Act (HMDA), suggest that collecting and scrutinizing a broader set of loan terms might be a way to extend our analysis to other types of communities.[5] The prevalence of brokers in this market and the finding that so many borrowers are presented with just a single mortgage option (and therefore know little about alternatives) potentially provide empirical support for models of predatory lending in which lenders use an informational advantage to their benefit (for example, Bond, Musto, and Yilmaz 2009). These results provide new insights into the ways in which brokers operate in LMI communities and help researchers understand the full costs of home ownership to LMI borrowers.

Data and Summary Statistics

No other randomized survey contains such a rich set of information pertaining to LMI household experiences regarding financial services and home ownership, including measures of creditworthiness and mortgage default risk (see Barr, Dokko, and Keys 2009 for a more detailed description of the data and sample). Unlike other data sets that do not directly observe up-front costs such as points and fees (for example, Haughwout, Mayer, and Tracy 2009), the DAHFS study has the unique advantage of providing sufficient information to obtain a more detailed picture of the total costs of a mortgage. Questions about housing, home ownership, and mortgage finance make up a portion of the overall survey. All information from the survey is based on self-reports of respondents' mortgages and experiences and therefore is not validated by administrative data; however, interviewers encouraged respondents to consult their mortgage and tax documents when answering more financially detailed questions. Consistent with the findings of Brian Bucks and Karen Pence (2008), not all home owners knew all aspects of their mortgage contracts. These responses are treated as missing and were excluded from the analysis.[6]

---

4. Low- and moderate-income communities in coastal cities, such as New York and Los Angeles, are quite different from Detroit in having Hispanic and immigrant populations as well as different housing markets.

5. Specifically, the APR required to be reported under the Home Mortgage Disclosure Act includes up-front costs such as points and fees, but lenders are not required to disclose these separately. In addition, the APR is disclosed only for high-cost originations.

6. Twenty-five percent of black home owners reported that they did not know their annual percentage rate, in contrast to 18 percent of nonblacks. Nine percent of black home owners did not know whether they had an adjustable-rate mortgage compared with 4 percent of nonblacks. For prepayment penalties, just under 20 percent of blacks and nonblacks did not know whether they had one, while just over one in ten households did not know whether they had a balloon payment. None of these differences are statistically significant.

Demographics in the Detroit Area Household Financial Services Study

Reflecting the demographics of the Detroit area, 69 percent of those surveyed in the LMI subsample of the DAHFS study are African American, 20 percent are white, while the remaining 10 percent are Hispanic, Arab American, Asian American, or other categories (see table 7-1). Because of this distribution of race, with an overwhelmingly African American sample consistent with LMI demographics in the Detroit area, we focus on black and nonblack comparisons of mortgage pricing terms. The respondents, like many Detroit residents, are long-term residents; over 90 percent have lived in the Detroit area for more than ten years.

Demographics of Home Owners

In the DAHFS study, 922 out of 938 respondents answered questions about their housing situation. Nearly half of respondents in the sample, 45 percent, own their homes. This proportion is well below the national average of 69 percent and the Midwest average of 73 percent (Joint Center State for Housing Studies 2007) but is roughly consistent with the nationwide home ownership rate for blacks (49 percent) and for LMI households (see Bucks and others 2009). The relatively low rates of home ownership in the sample reflect the difficulty LMI households in general, and minorities in particular, have in accumulating assets.

As shown in table 7-1, older households are much more likely to own their homes. Respondents over the age of sixty are twice as likely as eighteen- to twenty-four-year-olds to own their homes, with an ownership rate of 69 percent compared with just 33 percent for the younger cohort. White respondents in the DAHFS survey are 20 percent more likely than blacks to own their homes. The rate of home ownership among whites in LMI areas, 59 percent, is still well below nationwide home ownership rates. Married households and those with higher education levels are also much more likely to own their homes relative to their less educated and unmarried counterparts. Only 42 percent of female-headed households in the sample own their homes. Home owners also have significantly larger annual incomes than renters; owners' average income is nearly double that of renter households.

On the basis of the Detroit survey data, we calculate a measure of home equity, which is defined by the self-reported "hypothetical selling price" minus any outstanding amount remaining on all mortgages, including second liens.[7] The median level of home equity is $45,000, a substantial amount of money for families with moderate income and few or no alternative sources of wealth. The

---

7. The hypothetical selling price is the owner's response to the question "If you were to sell your house today, how much would it be worth?" and thus is most likely measured with some error (Bucks and Pence 2008). Home equity lines of credit are not included in this calculation of home equity.

Table 7-1. *Demographic Characteristics of DAHFS Sample*[a]

Percent unless otherwise noted

				Own	
	All	*Rent*	*Own*	*Outright*	*Mortgage*
Age					
18–24	11.9	66.9	33.2	29.0	71.0
25–60	71.8	57.3	42.7	26.1	73.9
61 and up	16.3	31.4	68.7	66.2	33.8
Race					
African American	68.6	58.3	41.7	38.7	61.3
White	20.3	41.0	59.0	33.7	66.3
Asian	2.1	69.2	30.8	34.7	65.3
Hispanic	3.5	56.7	43.3	41.7	58.3
Arab	1.9	32.0	68.0	0.0	100.0
Other	3.6	60.1	39.9	28.8	71.2
Educational attainment					
Less than high school diploma	29.6	61.5	38.5	47.9	52.1
High school diploma or equivalent	23.0	58.9	41.2	37.9	62.1
More than high school diploma	47.4	48.1	51.9	30.4	69.7
Gender					
Male	35.8	48.1	51.9	36.8	63.2
Female	64.2	58.1	41.9	35.8	64.2
Time in Detroit					
Less than 2 years	1.8	80.3	19.7	0.0	100.0
2–5 years	3.3	71.1	28.9	0.0	100.0
5–10 years	4.1	59.9	40.1	16.7	83.3
More than 10 years	31.3	49.0	51.0	42.1	57.9
Whole life	59.5	55.5	44.5	35.7	64.3
Marital status					
Married	19.7	27.7	72.3	24.6	75.4
Cohabiting	4.1	61.0	39.0	19.8	80.2
Divorced or separated	21.6	57.8	42.2	34.1	65.9
Widowed	9.0	36.2	63.8	67.3	32.7
Never married	45.6	68.1	31.9	39.7	60.3
Home ownership status					
Rent	54.6	. . .	. . .	. . .	. . .
Own	45.4	. . .	. . .	. . .	. . .
Home owners' mortgage status					
Own outright	35.2	. . .	. . .	. . .	. . .
Have mortgage	62.1	. . .	. . .	. . .	. . .
Have land contract	2.7	. . .	. . .	. . .	. . .

Table 7-1. *Demographic Characteristics of DAHFS Sample*[a] (*continued*)
Percent unless otherwise noted

	All	Rent	Own	Own Outright	Own Mortgage
Annual household income					
Mean (dollars)	28,163	19,399	39,530	33,006	45,506
Median (dollars)	20,000	12,500	30,000	23,000	38,000
Monthly mortgage or rent payment					
Mean (dollars)	. . .	497	660	. . .	. . .
Median (dollars)	. . .	500	650	. . .	. . .
Annual home payment[b]					
Mean (dollars)	. . .	5,958	7,920	. . .	. . .
Median (dollars)	. . .	6,000	7,800	. . .	. . .
Ratio of annual payment to annual income					
Mean	. . .	0.80	0.29	. . .	. . .
Median	. . .	0.36	0.19	. . .	. . .
Sample size	938	503	419	237	135

Source: Detroit Area Household Financial Services study.

a. This chapter uses data only from the households living in low- and moderate-income neighborhoods. Sample weights are used to make the sample representative of the Detroit-area LMI population. Payment-to-income ratio calculated by using annual household income and annual rent or mortgage payment. Of 938 respondents, 922 answered the own or rent question.

b. Calculated based on monthly mortgage or rent payments.

median purchase price of housing is $38,000, while the median stated selling price is $88,900, significantly below the Midwest average but consistent with actual sales prices in Detroit.[8] The median amount remaining on a mortgage is $54,000.

By one measure, annual housing costs are much less burdensome for home owners than for renters. While the median mortgage payment is higher than median rent in our sample ($650 a month versus $500 a month), this comparison does not capture the fact that home owners earn significantly more income each year. Defining housing outlay as the annual payment toward housing (either mortgage payment or rent) divided by annual income, median housing outlays for home owners with mortgages are only 20 percent of annual income, and this figure does not include home owners who own their homes outright and so have only maintenance, insurance, and property-tax costs. In contrast, median housing

8. The median sales price in July 2005 in the Midwest was $178,000, according to the *Daily Real Estate News.* "Home Sales Dip in June as Market Stabilizes" (www.realtor.org/rmodaily.nsf/pages/News2006072502 [July 25, 2006]). According to the Michigan Association of Realtors, average sales prices in Oakland and Macomb Counties were $234,000 and $175,000, respectively, in January to July 2005. The Detroit Board of Realtors reported an average sale price of $73,307 for the sales made in 2005, more in line with our reported estimates (Michigan Association of Realtors 2005).

outlays for renters are almost double this amount; renters in the DAHFS survey pay on average 36 percent of their annual income toward housing. This juxtaposition actually may understate the value of home ownership for some households, since the mortgage payments are reported without considering the increase to after-tax income from the mortgage interest deduction or the fact that the payments include the payment of principal, which increases the home owner's net worth.

An alternative way to view the relationship between payments and income is to compute annual payment to income ratios. Home owners earn twice as much as renters, yet mortgage payments are only 1.3 times greater than monthly rent. Consequently, the annual payment to annual income ratio is much lower for home owners than for renters, whose housing payments make up a larger portion of their household income. In this respect, home ownership seems advantageous in the sense that a higher percentage of income can be distributed toward nonhousing expenses.

Reasons for Delaying Payment and Measuring the Risk of Default

In addition to household demographics, the DAHFS survey collected information on the creditworthiness of home owners. Specifically, measures of creditworthiness include whether the household has a bank account, whether the household was denied a loan during the three years before the survey interview, whether the household typically pays less than the minimum amount on a credit-card bill, whether the household has ever filed for bankruptcy, whether the household has ever had a bank account closed because of poor credit, and whether the household is behind on any vehicle loans.[9] These are some of the measures that credit bureaus use to create summary indexes of creditworthiness, such as the FICO (Fair Isaac Corporation) score.[10] However, our measures are taken at the time of the survey rather than when the mortgage was approved, so it is possible that the survey measures do not fully capture the borrower's creditworthiness as observed by the lender when the mortgage was originated.

In our sample of home owners, 84 percent of households have a bank account. Nonblack households are 5.5 percent more likely to have an account. Six percent of the sample was denied a loan in the past three years. Fewer than 1 percent report that they pay less than the minimum on their credit cards, and only 1 percent say that they had a bank account closed because of poor credit. Of home

9. Using a common factor of these creditworthiness measures derived from factor analysis as a control variable (rather than each variable individually) yields qualitatively similar results (available upon request).

10. We recognize that these variables do not fully cover all of the information used by credit bureaus, such as credit-card or student loan delinquencies. However, these variables are highly correlated with the information that a credit bureau would use. We also surveyed home owners about borrowing behaviors and attitudes that are typically unobserved by credit bureaus to gauge profligate spending habits, tendencies toward financial irresponsibility, and perceived stigma of indebtedness. Including these variables in the analysis does not qualitatively change our conclusions.

owners in the sample, 15 percent report that they filed for bankruptcy at some point; 3 percent are behind on their vehicle loans.

We use borrowers' self-reports of whether they have problems paying their mortgage as a measure of (ex post) default risk. In the survey, we ask whether households have delayed their mortgage payment for one month or longer or are past due on their mortgage at the time of the survey interview. We combine these two reasons into one indicator variable that is intended to capture the likelihood of delinquency and default, in addition to our measures of creditworthiness. Ex post default risk serves as a proxy for a more complete model of ex ante risk used in lenders' risk-based pricing models and matrices. If lenders possessed all information about the determinants of default, this variable would be, on average, little different from one measuring ex ante default risk, such as a credit score.

There are two caveats to using self-reports of problems paying the mortgage as a measure of ex ante default risk. First, if lenders charge higher prices to blacks based on race, and this leads more black home owners to default, then ex post default risk would be positively correlated with the likelihood of being black (Apgar, Duda, and Gorey 2005). In this case, controlling for ex post default would lead us to understate the differences in pricing between blacks and nonblacks. Second, most missed payments do not lead to foreclosure, as borrowers cure. While the self-reported measures might overstate the level of default risk, we do not expect the degree of overstatement to be systematically different for blacks and whites, leaving the difference in self-reported default risk little different from the true difference. All told, the inclusion of this variable is a conservative approach to control for unobservable risk characteristics of the household, which may be available to the lender at the time of mortgage origination.

It is fairly common for home owners in the DAHFS survey to have problems paying their mortgages between the time of loan origination and the survey interview. Roughly one-third of home owners who are still paying their mortgages say that they have delayed payment for a month or more (see table 7-2). Forty percent of those who ever delayed paying their mortgage cite a job loss or unemployment as the reason for falling behind, while 24 percent say that they had too many other bills to pay, 8 percent cite unexpected medical expenses, and 12 percent cite emergencies. Those who have delayed payment also are more likely to be black; 34 percent of black home owners fell behind at some point compared with 25 percent of nonblack home owners.

Mortgage Pricing

In the DAHFS survey, many home owners hold mortgages that have the characteristics of a subprime loan. Over 10 percent of the home owners in our sample have interest rates above 10 percent, which is the Housing and Urban Development–Treasury definition of D class subprime lending (4 percentage points above prime) (U.S. Department of Housing and Urban Development

Table 7-2. *Mortgage Characteristics in the DAHFS*
Percent unless otherwise noted

	All owners	Black	Nonblack	Difference[a]	Adjusted difference[b]
Number of mortgages currently outstanding					
Zero	2.2	1.6	3.1	−1.5	. . .
One	89.5	88.4	91.1	−2.7	. . .
Two	8.3	10.0	5.8	4.2	. . .
Loan obtained through a mortgage broker	58.4	57.4	60.0	−2.7	−2.9
Broker offered loans from more than one lender	32.6	34.6	29.9	4.7	−5.5
Points or fees paid up front	28.5	29.5	27.0	2.5	0.0
Amount paid (dollars)	2,255	2,829	1,488	1,341*	1,112
Amount currently owed (dollars)	56,024	54,964	57,575	−2,611	−1,394
Current annual rate of interest (APR) on mortgage	7.4	7.8	6.7	1.1**	1.1**
Has adjustable-rate mortgage (ARM)	29.3	32.1	25.1	7.0	3.8
Amount of most recent payment (dollars)	660	654	668	−14	−14
Payment includes property taxes and insurance	59.8	56.4	64.7	−8.3	−6.6
Payment record					
Ahead of schedule	13.1	11.2	15.9	−4.7	. . .
Behind schedule	5.4	5.8	5.0	0.8	. . .
On schedule	81.5	83.1	79.1	4.0	. . .
Mortgage has prepayment penalty	23.3	28.6	15.3	13.3**	15.8**
Mortgage has balloon payment	11.1	14.8	5.7	9.1**	9.3**
Mortgage payment ever delayed for a month or more	30.4	33.8	25.4	8.4	6.5
Refinanced the original mortgage	49.2	47.3	51.9	−4.6	−7.2
Reasons for refinancing					
Get better terms	36.4	37.7	34.7	3.0	. . .
Borrow additional money on home equity	17.5	17.2	17.9	−0.7	. . .
Both	46.2	45.2	47.5	−2.3	. . .

Table 7-2. *Mortgage Characteristics in the DAHFS (continued)*

Percent unless otherwise noted

	All owners	Black	Nonblack	Difference[a]	Adjusted difference[b]
Refinanced because a broker or lender recommended it	20.2	18.9	21.9	−3.0	0.0
Sample size	419	263	156		

Source: Detroit Area Household Financial Services survey.

a. Black minus nonblack.

b. Adjusted difference is noted if, controlling for age, gender, income, creditworthiness, and loan performance, the adjusted difference between black and nonblack owners is significant at the 10 percent level. Creditworthiness is measured by indicators for whether the home owner has a bank account, has been denied a loan, has filed for bankruptcy, has had a bank account closed owing to poor credit, pays less than the minimum due on a credit card, or is behind on a vehicle loan. Loan performance measures are whether the owner has ever delayed a mortgage payment and whether the owner is currently behind on the mortgage payment. Significance is qualitatively unchanged if the difference between black and nonblack owners is estimated.

*Significant at the 10 percent level.

**Significant at the 5 percent level.

and U.S. Department of the Treasury 2000).[11] In contrast, on July 1, 2005, when we began collecting survey responses, the prime offer rate was 5.5 percent, according to the Federal Home Loan Mortgage Corporation. More than half the sample pay above prime interest rates; the median reported annual percentage rate (APR) is 6.9 percent.[12] On average, the current annual interest being charged on a mortgage for all respondents is 7.4 percent (table 7-2).

Sixty percent of home owners with a mortgage used a mortgage broker. Although one of the financial functions of a mortgage broker is to provide buyers and sellers with opportunities to find the best fit in mortgage product and price, only one-third of those who used a mortgage broker were offered a loan from more than one lender. Put another way, two-thirds of those who used a mortgage broker most likely received little benefit from the shopping services brokers provide, despite their high costs. However, it might be that had these households not used a broker, they would not have been able to obtain any loan. We explore this possibility in more detail later in this chapter.

11. Among those home owners paying interest rates above 10 percent, 35 percent purchased their homes after 2000 during a period with low interest rates. In our data, we are not able to discern why those with high interest rates who bought their homes before 2000 did not refinance amid widespread availability of lower interest rates.

12. We refer to the annual rate of interest reported by the borrower as the APR. However, borrowers could be reporting the note rate rather than the APR. The APR combines the note rate with other fees charged by the lender and expresses them as a yearly percentage. Our estimated APR differences across demographic groups are biased only if groups differentially report their note rate instead of their APR.

The costs of obtaining a mortgage are seemingly high. Approximately 29 percent of mortgage-holding respondents paid points or fees to acquire the loan; it does not appear that these points resulted in a reduction in interest rate. Median amounts are 2 points or $2,000 in fees, significant costs for access to the credit market. Over one-fourth of the home owners in our sample have adjustable-rate mortgages (ARMs). At the time of the survey, the median APR was 6.9 percent, with a mean of 7.4 percent. In the region, one-year ARMs were 4.8 percent in July 2005, while five-year ARMs were at 5.5 percent. Our finding of rates well above those posted suggests that home owners, on average, are paying higher-than-average market rates for mortgage borrowing.

Nearly one-fourth (23 percent) of respondents in the sample of LMI home owners have prepayment penalties written into their mortgages, which results in an additional fee if these borrowers decide to repay their mortgage (by either paying off the balance or refinancing) within, typically, the first two to three years after origination of the loan. In comparison, at the national level, only 2 percent of prime loans include a prepayment penalty, whereas an estimated 80 percent of subprime loans include this surcharge (Farris and Richardson 2004; Goldstein and Son 2003). In our study, 11 percent of home owners have a balance payable, or balloon payment, when their loans are due. While the inclusion of balloon payments in mortgage contracts is controversial, one benefit is that they allow borrowers to pay less each month at the expense of a large future payment. However, balloon payments may mask the true costs of home ownership to the extent that borrowers take out larger loan balances or pay higher rates or fees for the same monthly payment as a mortgage without a balloon payment. Balloon payments may prove difficult to make or refinance at the time they are due.

Among those who report being behind on their payments at the time of the survey interview, 31 percent have a prepayment penalty, and 20 percent face a balloon balance at the end of their mortgage contract. Consistent with these correlations, Roberto Quercia, Michael Stegman, and Walter Davis (2005) report that mortgages with prepayment penalties attached are 20 percent more likely to be foreclosed than those mortgages without, and the effect for balloon payments is even larger; such loans are 50 percent more likely to foreclose. The relationship between these high-cost mortgage features and the likelihood of default is an equilibrium outcome when lenders tailor mortgages to borrowers based on their risk characteristics.

Heterogeneity in Mortgage Pricing

Differences in race and the use of a mortgage broker are two channels through which differences in mortgage pricing arise among LMI home owners. Our approach compares observably similar borrowers who differ along one of these dimensions. We compare differences in prices paid by black and nonblack borrowers as well as those paid by borrowers using and not using a mortgage broker, and we assess whether these differences are attributable to differences in demographic characteristics, employment, income, creditworthiness, and default risk. These comparisons provide unbiased estimates of the differences in mortgage pricing if these groups are also, on average, unobservably similar (such as in terms of their default risk or the moral stigma they associate with not repaying their debt).[13] But if, for example, blacks are more (or less) likely to default on their mortgages, a simple comparison of interest rates between blacks and nonblacks would overstate (or understate) the true difference in pricing. However, in the DAHFS study's cross-sectional sample of borrowers, as in any cross section, we do not observe all information about the borrower, particularly the information that lenders use to price loans. Instead, we describe the variables available in the DAHFS study and discuss how including these variables addresses the biases that are likely to arise.

Racial Disparities

Overall, our results support the view that observably similar blacks and whites receive different loan terms along most, though not all, dimensions of their mortgage contracts. First, we find that black home owners have interest rates that are 1.1 percentage points higher than those of whites (see table 7-2). Because blacks and whites differ in many observable dimensions, in tables 7-3 and 7-4 we present regression-adjusted differences in mortgage pricing between these two groups of home owners.[14] Since we are simply interested in characterizing the average differences in pricing between blacks and nonblacks, we use ordinary least squares to estimate these differences. In table 7-3 the interest rate difference seen in table 7-2 is unaffected by adjusting for income, loan size, home value, origination date, creditworthiness, and default risk.[15] In other words, this point estimate of 110 basis points does not vary with the inclusion of the borrower characteristics that a lender would observe to gauge default risk. The magnitude of this result on controlling for default risk is particularly striking, since blacks are more likely to delay their mortgage payment or be behind on their mortgage, and the point estimate does not decrease once we include this variable. This result suggests that blacks obtain loans with higher interest rates, on average, and the disparity is not explained by the observable creditworthiness or default risk of the borrower.[16]

13. Borrowers using brokers would be unobservably similar to those not using brokers if mortgage-broker usage were randomly assigned.

14. The number of observations in each column varies owing to individuals opting to report that they "don't know" certain terms of their mortgage.

15. We do not have information on the loan-to-value ratio of the loan at origination, so we use measures of the current amount outstanding and the value of the loan if sold today as comparable (albeit imperfect) controls.

16. We also include a variable measuring how much borrowers generally shop around for financial services. The inclusion of this variable leads to effectively identical results.

Table 7-3. *Regression Version of Mortgage Characteristics Table: Amount of Fees and APR*[a]

	Amount of fees			APR		
	(1)	(2)	(3)	(4)	(5)	(6)
Black	1,001	781.8	736.1	1.165***	1.126***	1.009***
	(750.4)	(879.5)	(1,007)	(0.339)	(0.353)	(0.352)
Female	195.9	53.87	1942	-0.350	-0.124	-0.127
	(968.3)	(894.4)	(1,423)	(0.396)	(0.454)	(0.471)
Age 25–60	-1472	-1658	-2877	0.450	0.600	0.315
	(1,099)	(1,543)	(2,398)	(0.569)	(0.577)	(0.572)
Age 61 and older	n.a.	n.a.	n.a.	-0.347	-0.145	-0.369
				(0.930)	(1.062)	(1.054)
Married	-772.2	-1,505	-2,103	-0.213	-0.288	-0.323
	(910.3)	(1,054)	(1,286)	(0.414)	(0.452)	(0.438)
Income	n.a.	-0.0762	-0.0527	n.a.	-8.64e-05	-9.63e-05*
		(0.104)	(0.0908)		(5.22e-05)	(5.09e-05)
Income^2	n.a.	1.52e-06	-1.56e-07	n.a.	1.38e-09	1.58e-09*
		(1.72e-06)	(1.39e-06)		(8.62e-10)	(8.55e-10)
Income^3	n.a.	-0	0	n.a.	-0*	0*
		(0)	(0)		(0)	(0)
Delayed paying mortgage	n.a.	n.a.	49.79	n.a.	n.a.	0.915**
			(739.3)			(0.417)
Banked	n.a.	n.a.	-2,692	n.a.	n.a.	-0.0645
			(3,610)			(0.787)

	(1)	(2)	(3)	(4)	(5)	(6)
Been denied a loan	n.a.	n.a.	5,755	n.a.	n.a.	0.691
			(4,148)			(0.672)
Pay less than minimum on credit card	n.a.	n.a.	n.a.	n.a.	n.a.	1.727
						(2.841)
Ever bankrupt	n.a.	n.a.	756.1	n.a.	n.a.	0.567
			(2,101)			(0.412)
Ever account closed because of poor credit	n.a.	n.a.	−1,592	n.a.	n.a.	−1.787***
			(2,423)			(0.679)
Behind on vehicle loan	n.a.	n.a.	−567.1	n.a.	n.a.	0.689
			(2,245)			(1.006)
Purchase price	0.0428	0.0371	0.0491	−6.18e-06	−7.01e-06	−8.70e-06
	(0.0375)	(0.0291)	(0.0345)	(5.50e-06)	(5.61e-06)	(5.69e-06)
Value if sold today	−0.0137	−0.0152	−0.00529	2.99e-06	1.31e-06	4.84e-06
	(0.0136)	(0.0154)	(0.0166)	(4.37e-06)	(4.94e-06)	(5.31e-06)
Loan remaining	−0.0167	−0.0184	−0.0492	−9.03e-06	−5.61e-06	−8.01e-06
	(0.0240)	(0.0246)	(0.0302)	(6.82e-06)	(7.06e-06)	(7.28e-06)
Refinance	961.8	1,014	2,774*	−0.687**	−0.761**	−0.660*
	(639.9)	(729.2)	(1,385)	(0.344)	(0.357)	(0.365)
Date of purchase controls?	Yes	Yes	Yes	Yes	Yes	Yes
Observations	39	37	37	173	163	163
R^2	0.295	0.406	0.573	0.174	0.217	0.264

Source: Detroit Area Household Financial Services study.

a. Robust standard errors in parentheses. DAHFS sample weights used in all regressions.

*Significant at the 10 percent level.

**Significant at the 5 percent level.

***Significant at the 1 percent level.

Table 7-4. *Regression Version of Mortgage Characteristics Table: Prepayment Penalty and Balloon Payment*[a]

	Prepayment penalty			Balloon payment		
	(7)	(8)	(9)	(10)	(11)	(12)
Black	0.122*	0.151**	0.133*	0.0821*	0.0920*	0.0951*
	(0.0666)	(0.0742)	(0.0732)	(0.0458)	(0.0514)	(0.0493)
Female	-0.0443	-0.0813	-0.0828	0.0586	0.00679	0.00670
	(0.0704)	(0.0751)	(0.0776)	(0.0482)	(0.0525)	(0.0521)
Age 25–60	-0.149	-0.107	-0.158	-0.111	-0.0855	-0.0890
	(0.131)	(0.137)	(0.144)	(0.123)	(0.122)	(0.144)
Age 61+	-0.372**	-0.386**	-0.440***	-0.0442	-0.0347	-0.0699
	(0.152)	(0.161)	(0.165)	(0.145)	(0.155)	(0.139)
Married	0.0701	0.101	0.0994	0.0331	0.0711	0.0737
	(0.0696)	(0.0781)	(0.0801)	(0.0484)	(0.0552)	(0.0547)
Income	n.a.	-1.91e-06	-.16e-06	n.a.	-2.26e-06	-4.25e-06
		(5.66e-06)	(5.80e-06)		(4.92e-06)	(4.68e-06)
Income^2	n.a.	-0	0	n.a.	-0	-0
		(9.34e-11)	(9.28e-11)		(7.15e-11)	(6.75e-11)
Income^3	n.a.	0	0	n.a.	0	0
		(0)	(0)		(0)	(0)
Delayed paying mortgage	n.a.	n.a.	0.0469	n.a.	n.a.	0.166***
			(0.0804)			(0.0636)
Banked	n.a.	n.a.	0.0351	n.a.	n.a.	0.0343
			(0.119)			(0.103)

	(1)	(2)	(3)	(4)	(5)	(6)
Denied a loan	n.a.	n.a.	-0.203*	n.a.	n.a.	-0.0904
			(0.103)			(0.0592)
Pay less than minimum on credit card	n.a.	n.a.	0.417	n.a.	n.a.	0.737***
			(0.496)			(0.113)
Ever bankrupt	n.a.	n.a.	0.151	n.a.	n.a.	-0.0777
						(0.412)
Ever account closed because of poor credit	n.a.	n.a.	0.000386	n.a.	n.a.	-0.126
			(2101)			
			(0.444)			(0.0669)
Behind on a vehicle loan	n.a.	n.a.	0.0827	n.a.	n.a.	-0.173**
			(0.186)			(0.0669)
Purchase price	-1.55e-06**	-1.40e-06	-1.61e-06*	5.59e-07	6.89e-07	5.06e-07
	(7.64e-07)	(8.76e-07)	(8.96e-07)	(5.45e-07)	(5.64e-07)	(5.36e-07)
Value if sold today	-1.36e-06*	-1.31e-06	-1.20e-06	-1.01e-06**	-7.95e-07	-5.63e-07
	(7.73e-07)	(7.98e-07)	(8.24e-07)	(4.97e-07)	(4.99e-07)	(4.94e-07)
Loan remaining	2.70e-06***	2.46e-06**	2.25e-06**	3.14e-07	2.55e-07	2.98e-07
	(9.28e-07)	(1.00e-06)	(1.04e-06)	(7.07e-07)	(7.90e-07)	(8.43e-07)
Refinance	0.0617	0.0473	0.0481	-0.118**	-0.0990*	-0.0990*
	(0.0705)	(0.0764)	(0.0782)	(0.0510)	(0.0519)	(0.0526)
Date of purchase controls?	Yes	Yes	Yes	Yes	Yes	Yes
Observations	188	174	174	197	183	183
R^2	0.136	0.149	0.187	0.100	0.115	0.224

Source: Detroit Area Household Financial Services study.

a. Robust standard errors in parentheses. DAHFS sample weights used in all regressions.

*Significant at the 10 percent level.

**Significant at the 5 percent level.

***Significant at the 1 percent level.

This sizable black-white difference in interest rates is larger than previous estimates that control for default risk (Courchane 2007) or those found in studies of data reported under HMDA, which contains information on both high-priced mortgages and race. The APRs for high-priced originations in the 2005 and 2006 HMDA data differ between blacks and whites by 49 to 56 basis points (see Avery, Brevoort, and Canner 2007, table 12). However, this disparity accounts only for the intensive margin of the difference in high-cost loans, as loans with APRs below the high-price threshold need not report their APR. The black-white difference in the likelihood of appearing in the high-cost sample (that is, the extensive margin) is 29.8 percent, since 47 percent of blacks receive loans classified as higher-priced as opposed to only 17.2 percent of whites (see Avery, Brevoort, and Canner 2007, table 11). Our sample is of all mortgages, not just high-priced mortgages, so it is plausible that the combination of both the intensive margin and the extensive margin would lead to estimated black-white differences in interest rates that are much larger than the difference that was observed on the intensive margin alone.

Next, we examine points and fees, balloon payments, and prepayment penalties, since in principle the inclusion of these mortgage terms may result in lower interest rates. Overall, we do not find this to be the case. Inclusion of these terms does not lower interest rates for black households, who pay higher fees and are more likely to have balloon payments and prepayment penalties than nonblack borrowers.

Blacks pay roughly twice the amount in fees or points that whites pay (table 7-2). African American respondents paid roughly $2,829 up front in fees, whereas nonblack respondents paid roughly $1,488. Owing to very small sample sizes, this difference is not statistically significant after controlling for demographics, income, and creditworthiness. However, the magnitude of the adjusted difference is very similar to the unadjusted difference and remains economically large at more than $1,100.

The presence of prepayment penalties also varies considerably by race. Nearly 29 percent of blacks have prepayment penalties compared with roughly 15 percent of white respondents, a statistically significant difference (see table 7-2). This difference remains statistically meaningful even after controlling for income, age, gender, and various measures of creditworthiness (regression results are reported in table 7-4). Also, as shown in table 7-2, a higher fraction of black home owners (15 percent) have balloon payments written into their mortgage contracts, compared with white home owners (6 percent). This difference is also statistically significant after controlling for other demographic characteristics, loan size, house value, income, and creditworthiness (regression results are reported in table 7-4).

Overall, these high-cost loan practices differ substantially along racial lines. These disparities are consistent with the findings of Robert Avery, Kenneth Brevoort, and Glenn Canner (2006), who analyze HMDA data on mortgages originated in 2005 and find that African Americans disproportionately obtained high-cost mortgages relative to their share of mortgages received. Our results also support the finding of race-based disparities in audit-based studies, which focus on a different dimension of the mortgage process: the loan approval stage (for example, Ross and Yinger 2002; or Bocian, Ernst, and Li 2006). Kerwin Charles and Erik Hurst (2002) find that black households are less likely to apply for mortgages and, conditional on applying, are less likely to be approved. That we find racial differences in loan terms in a cross section of home owners who have successfully received a mortgage loan suggests that race-based disparities persist even after differential treatment during the approval process. Also note that in a cross section of home owners, such as this one, riskier borrowers are not as likely to be observed as in samples drawn from loan originations, since, conditional on having taken a mortgage at some point, they might have already defaulted, are no longer home owners, and therefore are not observed in the data. As a result, if blacks have, on average, greater default risk than whites, then a comparison by race of those remaining in the sample will understate the differences in pricing arising at origination.[17]

Mortgage Broker Use

We next explore differences in loan pricing based on the use of mortgage brokers. While brokers are criticized for aggressively selling high-cost mortgages with potentially predatory loan terms (see Jackson and Burlingame 2007), in theory, one function of a broker is to match borrowers with competitively priced mortgage offers from lenders. Indeed, Amany El Anshasy, Gregory Elliehausen, and Yoshiaki Shimazaki (2006) estimate that subprime borrowers using a broker obtain APRs that are 15 to 190 basis points lower than those obtained by using a retail lender. However, in our data, we observe that borrowers who use a mortgage broker are 60 percent more likely to pay points or fees than are those who do not use a broker. As table 7-5 shows, 36 percent of home owners who purchased through a broker paid points and fees, whereas only 21 percent of home owners who did not use a broker did so. The average difference in the size of these fees is over $800. We also observe interest rates that are 40 basis points higher as well as a greater prevalence of balloon payments among those who used a mortgage broker; owing to sample-size limitations, the differences in interest rate and balloon payment are not statistically different from zero. That is, despite being more likely to pay points and fees, borrowers using a mortgage broker do not seem to obtain lower interest rates.

Our findings are consistent with the work of Howell Jackson and Laurie Burlingame (2007), who find that average yield spread premiums were on the order of $1,500 to $1,800 in additional costs to the borrower and that these costs were not offset by lower up-front fees. In addition, over two-thirds of home owners who used a broker were offered only one mortgage product (see table 7-2),

17. Samples drawn from loan originations, such as HMDA data, are not susceptible to this bias.

Table 7-5. *Mortgage Characteristics: The Role of Brokers*[a]

Percent unless otherwise noted

	Broker	Nonbroker	Difference[b]	Adjusted difference[c]
Fraction of home owners	58.4	41.6	16.8	
Paid points or fees	35.5	21.3	14.2**	13.6**
Mean fee amount (dollars)	2,356	2,032	324	827
Has adjustable rate	31.7	25.7	6.0	8.4
Mean interest rate	7.6	7	0.7**	0.4
Mean purchase price (dollars)	68,613	55,264	13,348	11,492**
Mean year of purchase	1993.3	1993.3	0.0	0.8
Has prepayment penalty	24.4	22.5	1.9	0.1
Has balloon payment	14.6	6.7	7.9**	5.1
Ever delayed payment	33.3	27.4	5.9	4.7

Source: Detroit Area Household Financial Services study.

a. Sample consists of DAHFS respondents who have a mortgage.

b. Brokered minus nonbrokered.

c. Adjusted difference is noted if the adjusted difference between brokered and nonbrokered loans is significant at the 10 percent level. Controls are age, race, gender, income, marital status, and creditworthiness indicators. Creditworthiness is measured by indicators for whether the home owner has a bank account, has been denied a loan, has filed for bankruptcy, has had a bank account closed owing to poor credit, pays less than the minimum due on a credit card, or is behind on a vehicle loan. Loan performance measures are whether the owner has ever delayed a mortgage payment and whether the owner is currently behind on the mortgage payment.

**Significant at the 5 percent level.

which undermines the view that brokers provide borrowers with a diverse range of loan options.

Furthermore, we find that there is no difference in the likelihood of using a broker based on age, race, or income in our sample of home owners, which suggests that there is no support for differential demand-driven use of brokers across demographic groups.[18] Indeed, the estimated coefficients on the demographic variables are small in magnitude (as well as statistically insignificant). The borrowers who used a broker do not differ statistically in terms of creditworthiness measures. Thus it seems unlikely that brokers helped marginal borrowers to obtain access to credit they otherwise would have been unable to acquire. Because blacks and whites are equally likely to use brokers, it is unlikely that the racial differences in pricing arise in our sample through the broker channel. Specifically, the coefficient on being black remains significant in regressions, including the interaction of race and broker use, while the coefficient on the interaction

18. In contrast, El Anshasy, Elliehausen, and Shimazaki (2006) find that race, education, and income are highly predictive of broker use. Their results arc based on a sample of subprime borrowers rather than both prime and subprime borrowers living in low- and moderate-income neighborhoods. Still, it may be that black and white borrowers use different types of mortgage brokers. However, given the limitations of the survey questions about broker use, we are unable to investigate this issue further.

term is statistically insignificant (result not shown). These results present new puzzles about how LMI borrowers use mortgage brokers and lenders and about the mechanisms by which LMI borrowers incur costs in obtaining a mortgage.

Conclusion

This chapter makes use of a unique survey data set of LMI households to identify two mechanisms through which high-cost mortgages can arise: racial differences in pricing and the role of mortgage brokers. We find that within similar low-income neighborhoods, black home owners pay higher interest rates than similar nonblacks do—110 basis points on average—and are more than twice as likely to have prepayment penalties or balloon payments attached to their mortgages as nonblack home owners are, even after controlling for age, income, gender, cred-itworthiness, and a proxy for default risk. In addition, we observe that borrowers who use a mortgage broker are over 60 percent more likely to pay points or fees than those who did not use a broker but do not obtain better interest rates. Over-all, the results suggest that across some dimensions of pricing, similar borrowers are treated differently by mortgage lenders and brokers.

The observed differential treatment in the mortgage market is puzzling for at least three reasons. First, advances in mortgage underwriting technology have standardized the mortgage origination process for many lenders (Collins, Belsky, and Case 2004). The underwriting software does not include race as an input in either mortgage approval rates or pricing. Second, information on pricing has become less costly to obtain since the supply of mortgage brokers has increased dramatically over the past fifteen years. Furthermore, the Internet has made interest-rate comparisons and price quotes readily available. Together, these developments ought to have enhanced competition and standardized contracts across borrowers with similar risk profiles. Finally, fair lending laws prohibit dis-criminatory practices and have been in place for decades (see, for example, Ross and Yinger 2002 or Barr 2005). However, while differences in pricing may have decreased over time, they nonetheless persist (Apgar and Calder 2005), including among those we surveyed in Detroit in 2005 and 2006.

Our descriptive findings are most consistent with supply-driven origins for differences in loan terms. Our rich data set can account for differences in the demand for mortgages across borrowers because of income, desired mortgage size, creditworthiness, and default risk. By including as much available infor-mation about the borrower as possible, we have attempted to address demand-driven explanations that are correlated with race or using a mortgage broker.

Our results suggest that enhanced fair-lending enforcement and improved mortgage-market regulation may be in order. One direction in which fair lend-ing laws could be bolstered is through enhanced disclosure policies, coupled with financial education. Differences in pricing between blacks and nonblacks could potentially arise through different disclosure practices and conventions apart from the required TILA disclosures. That is, it may be that other aspects of the transaction or behavior by lenders, brokers, and borrowers swamp the effect of required TILA disclosures. In the DAHFS study, black borrowers were less informed than nonblack borrowers on their APR and on whether their mortgage has an adjustable rate, a prepayment penalty, or a balloon payment. Further research is needed to understand the relationship between race and disclosure practices and whether certain types of disclosure practices lead to higher-priced loans. Improved TILA disclosures or other measures that are attentive to the sales context facing particular borrowers may reduce these disparities.

Another direction is to improve regulation of the brokers and lenders (see Barr, Mullainathan, and Shafir 2008). For example, a ban on yield spread premiums that vary by the terms of the loan, as recently contained in the Dodd-Frank Act, should help to reduce disparities that are produced through the broker channel. New rules under the Act requiring that lenders assess a borrower's ability to pay; escrow requirements; risk retention standards for lenders; restrictions on prepayment penalties and bans on steering; licensing of mortgage brokers; and other measures under the act should help improve broker and lender conduct.

The Consumer Financial Protection Bureau has the opportunity to improve disclosures, further police mortgage broker and lender conduct, and ban unfair, deceptive, or abusive acts or practices. The bureau can empirically test disclosures and permit private sector pilots of improved disclosures with safe harbors for compliance. The bureau is also charged with merging outdated and confusing mortgage disclosure forms. Rules regarding "qualified mortgages" may also help to improve outcomes in the marketplace. To the extent that differences in pricing arise because of decisions made by borrowers who do not understand loan terms or fee structures because of excessively opaque financial products or because of deceptive practices, the more that consumers are exposed to straightforward mortgages with sound underwriting the easier it may be for them to make borrowing decisions that better meet their needs. Sound mortgage regulation will be essential to avoid a repeat in the practices that contributed to the devastating financial crisis of 2007–09.

References

Apgar, William C., and Allegra Calder. 2005. "The Dual Mortgage Market: The Persistence of Discrimination in Mortgage Lending." In *The Geography of Opportunity: Race and Housing Choice in Metropolitan America,* edited by Xavier de Souza Briggs, 101–26. Brookings.

Apgar, William C., Mark Duda, and Rochelle Nawrocki Gorey. 2005. "The Municipal Cost of Foreclosures: A Chicago Case Study." Housing Finance Policy Research Paper 2005-1. Minneapolis, Minn.: Homeownership Preservation Foundation (www.995hope.org/wp-content/uploads/2011/07/Apgar_Duda_Study_Full_Version.pdf).

Avery, Robert B., Kenneth P. Brevoort, and Glenn B. Canner. 2006. "Higher-Priced Home Lending and the 2005 HMDA Data." *Federal Reserve Bulletin* 92 (September): A123–A166.

———. 2007. "The 2006 HMDA Data." *Federal Reserve Bulletin* 93 (December): A73–A109.

Barr, Michael S. 2005. "Credit Where It Counts: The Community Reinvestment Act and Its Critics." *New York University Law Review* 80:513–652.

Barr, Michael S., Jane K. Dokko, and Benjamin J. Keys. 2009. "And Banking for All?" Finance and Economics Discussion Series 2009-34. Federal Reserve Board.

———. 2011. "Exploring the Determinants of High-Cost Mortgages in Low- and Moderate-Income Neighborhoods." In *The American Mortgage System: Crisis and Reform,* edited by Susan M. Wachter and Marvin W. Smith, 60–86. University of Pennsylvania Press.

Barr, Michael S., Sendhil Mullainathan, and Eldar Shafir. 2008. "Behaviorally Informed Home Mortgage Credit Regulation." In *Borrowing to Live: Consumer and Mortgage Credit Revisited,* edited by Nicolas P. Retsinas and Eric S. Belsky, 170–202. Joint Center on Housing Studies at Harvard University and Brookings Institution Press.

Bocian, Debbie Gruenstein, Keith S. Ernst, and Wei Li. 2006. *Unfair Lending: The Effect of Race and Ethnicity on the Price of Subprime Mortgages.* Durham, N.C.: Center for Responsible Lending (www.responsiblelending.org/mortgage-lending/research-analysis/rr011-Unfair_Lending-0506.pdf).

Bond, Philip, David K. Musto, and Bilge Yilmaz. 2009. "Predatory Mortgage Lending." *Journal of Financial Economics* 94:412–27.

Bucks, Brian, and Karen Pence. 2008. "Do Borrowers Know Their Mortgage Terms?" *Journal of Urban Economics* 64:218–33 (doi:10.1016/j.jue.2008.07.005).

Bucks, Brian K., and others. 2009. "Changes in U.S. Family Finances from 2004 to 2007: Evidence from the Survey of Consumer Finances." *Federal Reserve Bulletin* 95 (February): A1–A56.

Charles, Kerwin Kofi, and Erik Hurst. 2002. "The Transition to Home Ownership and the Black-White Wealth Gap." *Review of Economics and Statistics* 84:281–97 (www.jstor.org/stable/3211777).

Collins, Michael, Eric Belsky, and Karl E. Case. 2004. "Exploring the Welfare Effects of Risk-Based Pricing in the Subprime Mortgage Market." Working Paper BABC 04-8. Harvard University, Joint Center for Housing Studies (www.jchs.harvard.edu/publications/finance/babc/babc_04-8.pdf).

Courchane, Marsha J. 2007. "The Pricing of Home Mortgage Loans to Minority Borrowers: How Much of the APR Differential Can We Explain?" *Journal of Real Estate Research* 29:399–439.

Edelberg, Wendy. 2007. "Racial Dispersion in Consumer Credit Interest Rates." FEDS Working Paper 2007-28. Federal Reserve Board (www.federalreserve.gov/pubs/feds/2007/200728/200728pap.pdf).

El Anshasy, Amany, Gregory Elliehausen, and Yoshiaki Shimazaki. 2006. "The Pricing of Subprime Mortgages by Mortgage Brokers and Lenders." Working Paper. Washington: George Washington University (www.ca-amp.org/documents/GW_brokerstudy_06.pdf).

Farris, John, and Christopher A. Richardson. 2004. "The Geography of Subprime Mortgage Prepayment Penalty Patterns." *Housing Policy Debate* 15:687–714 (doi:10.1080/10511482.2004.9521517).

Goldstein, Debbie, and Stacy Strohauer Son. 2003. *Why Prepayment Penalties Are Abusive in Subprime Home Loans.* Policy Paper 4. Durham, N.C.: Center for Responsible Lending (www.responsiblelending.org/mortgage-lending/research-analysis/PPP_Policy_Paper2.pdf).

Haughwout, Andrew, Christopher Mayer, and Joseph Tracy. 2009. "Subprime Mortgage Pricing: The Impact of Race, Ethnicity, and Gender on the Cost of Borrowing." In *Brookings-Wharton Papers on Urban Affairs: 2009,* edited by Gary Burtless and Janet Rothenberg Pack, 33–63. Brookings.

Jackson, Howell E., and Laurie Burlingame. 2007. "Kickbacks or Compensation: The Case of Yield Spread Premiums." *Stanford Journal of Law, Business, and Finance* 12:289–361.

Joint Center for Housing Studies. 2007. "The State of the Nation's Housing, 2006." Harvard University (www.jchs.harvard.edu/publications/markets/son2006/son2006.pdf).

Michigan Association of Realtors. 2005. "Residential Sales Statistics, December 2005 YTD." Lansing, Mich. (December) (www.mirealtors.com/Content/Upload/AssetMgmt/Site/HOUSING/Dec05stats.pdf).

Quercia, Roberto G., Michael A. Stegman, and Walter R. Davis. 2005. "The Impact of Predatory Loan Terms on Subprime Foreclosures: The Special Case of Prepayment Penalties and Balloon Payments." Working Paper. University of North Carolina, Chapel Hill, Center for Community Capitalism (www.ccc.unc.edu/documents/foreclosurepaper2005.pdf).

Quigley, John. 2008. "Compensation and Incentives in the Mortgage Business." *Economists' Voice* 5, no. 6: art. 2 (doi:10.2202/1553-3832.1431).

Ross, Stephen L., and John Yinger. 2002. *The Color of Credit.* MIT Press.

U.S. Department of Housing and Urban Development and U.S. Department of the Treasury. 2000. *Joint Report on Predatory Lending* (http://archives.hud.gov/reports/treasrpt.pdf).

Woodward, Susan E., and Robert E. Hall. 2010. "Diagnosing Consumer Confusion and Sub-Optimal Shopping Effort: Theory and Mortgage-Market Evidence." Working Paper 16007. Cambridge, Mass.: National Bureau of Economic Research (www.nber.org/papers/w16007).

8

Living on the Edge of Bankruptcy

MICHAEL S. BARR AND JANE K. DOKKO

The debate over federal bankruptcy reform, including the Bankruptcy Abuse Prevention and Consumer Protection Act of 2005, and recent legislative efforts to permit home mortgage principal to be reduced through bankruptcy in the wake of the foreclosure crisis of the last several years, reflects policymakers' beliefs on the causes of bankruptcy and inspired a spirited dialogue among academics about households' decisions to file for bankruptcy (Keys 2010; Sullivan, Warren, and Westbrook 1989, 2000, 2003; Warren and Tyagi 2003; White 1998; Fay, Hurst, and White 2002; Jacoby, Sullivan, and Warren 2001; Gross and Souleles 2002; Gan and Sabarwal 2005; Mann 2005). Those favoring tougher bankruptcy laws that intend to make it more difficult to file or get relief argue that lenient bankruptcy laws increase the incentive to file; they argue that a decline in bankruptcy's stigma has eroded moral restraints on filing. In their view, households engage in profligate borrowing knowing that they can evade paying debts by strategically filing for bankruptcy. Opposing scholars argue that bankrupt debtors face crushing financial burdens, often caused by adverse trigger events such as illness or divorce; they contend that many people who could file for bankruptcy do not file, indicating that stigma may be an important deterrent. In the view of many of these scholars, practices in the home mortgage and credit-card industry have increased the likelihood that households will overborrow (Mann 2005), and the 2005 bankruptcy reforms may have contributed to the increase in foreclosures on subprime mortgages (Morgan, Iverson, and Botsch, forthcoming).

Data have been lacking to permit an extensive comparison of the financial-services behaviors, attitudes, and economic outcomes among low-, moderate-, and middle-income households who file for bankruptcy and those who do not. Our aim in this chapter is to fill this particular gap. The story that emerges from our data is essentially this: low- and moderate-income (LMI) households have insufficient income or assets to overcome the financial difficulties that come their way. Put another way, they have no slack. Many of them experience concurrent, serious adverse events and a range of financial hardships. Bankruptcy is but one of the outcomes associated with this persistent financial instability. There are meaningful differences between households who would benefit from filing and those who would not. These differences are muted, however, when one looks at who is actually filing, and many households who would benefit from filing for bankruptcy do not file. This result suggests that the decision to file may not be based solely on the strategic question of whether bankruptcy filing would be financially beneficial. Our research design and methodology do not allow us to untangle causation. Rather, our data confirm that the decision to file is a complex one for households, and one of myriad economic decisions made by households experiencing other financial difficulties. In sum, many of the households we study experience serious financial hardships and deploy a range of methods to cope with them, including filing for bankruptcy.

Previous Research

Over the past twenty years, bankruptcy filings have significantly increased, prompting researchers to seek the causes. Four causes of bankruptcy have emerged from this research: adverse trigger events, strategic timing, the decline of stigma, and market structure. While each of the theories has brought insight to the policy debate on bankruptcy reform, a number of questions concerning the appropriate empirical framework in which to ascertain the causes of bankruptcy filing remain.

The adverse-events theory posits that the decision to file for bankruptcy is driven by financial shocks exogenous to the decision to file. In particular, job loss, severe reductions in income, divorce or widowhood, and high, uninsured medical costs from injury or serious illness instigate bankruptcy filings among households with low asset levels. Debt levels under this theory are not jointly determined with the bankruptcy-filing option; rather, debt levels reflect the difficulties households face in meeting the costs of housing, health care, and the like as they weather adverse shocks.

The empirical approach to evaluating the adverse-events theory relies on a cross-sectional correlation between adverse events and bankruptcy filings (Sullivan, Warren, and Westbrook 1989, 2000, 2003; Domowitz and Sartain

1999). For households already living in a financially precarious position, job loss, divorce or widowhood, high medical costs, and negative shocks to income can "trigger" the bankruptcy decision. The data from Theresa Sullivan, Elizabeth Warren, and Lawrence Westbrook (1989, 2000, 2003) are from individuals who have filed for bankruptcy. In their data set, most households with children who filed for bankruptcy experienced an adverse event preceding filing.

There are several methodological issues underlying the research on adverse events as triggers to bankruptcy. First, without data on households who experience adverse events but do not file for bankruptcy, it is impossible to establish the first-order correlation between adverse events and bankruptcy since there are many households experiencing the former but not the latter. In bankruptcy policy terms, this lack of evidence may not matter, for if those who do file for bankruptcy are in extreme distress, there is little reason to toughen bankruptcy laws to dissuade them from filing; however, if prefiling behaviors, such as levels of credit-card indebtedness, are amenable to intervention, then understanding the precise nature of household financial decisionmaking and behavior remains critical. Benjamin Keys is able to analyze data that include adverse event information among filers and nonfilers (Keys 2010).

Second, there may be behaviors, attitudes, and events that are linked to adverse events and bankruptcy that are not captured by the data. Consider the following example: Suppose that stress at a job triggers bankruptcy; that is, a social planner who could manipulate on-the-job stress could increase bankruptcy filings by increasing that stress among certain individuals. In a survey, on-the-job stress may not be possible to measure but may be correlated with job loss, divorce, and other adverse events. Since on-the-job stress is related to bankruptcy independent of adverse events, studying the triggers of bankruptcy among filers becomes extremely sensitive to the timing of bankruptcy vis-à-vis other adverse events. More specifically, if half of those experiencing on-the-job stress experience adverse events before filing for bankruptcy while the other half experience the two in the reverse order, the cross-sectional correlation between adverse events and bankruptcy, among those filing for bankruptcy, will be misleading. Half the sample will attribute bankruptcy to an adverse event, while the other will attribute it to a phenomenon that is not measured in the data. The truth (in this hypothetical) is that on-the-job stress is the underlying cause, but by studying the cross-sectional correlation between adverse events and bankruptcy, the researcher has not discovered the nature of that underlying cause.

In contrast to the adverse-events theory, the strategic-timing theory asserts that the decision to file for bankruptcy is endogenous to the behaviors of the filer. The debtor makes a rational choice regarding filing by determining the net financial benefit from filing. In its strong form, the debtor's borrowing levels are jointly determined with the decision to file; debtors incur more debt because of the option to file. In its weak form, the theory simply suggests that households are more likely to file when there is a greater financial benefit from doing so; in this form, the financial-benefit theory can operate alongside the adverse-events theory.

Michelle White (1998) and Scott Fay, Erik Hurst, and White (2002) argue that households are more likely to file when their net worth after bankruptcy is greater than their net worth before bankruptcy. In their view, the amount of debt discharged and assets exempted under relevant laws can play a significant role in an individual's decision to file. The empirical support for the strategic-timing theory presented in White (1998) and Fay, Hurst, and White (2002) relies on a cross-sectional correlation between the financial benefit of bankruptcy and actually filing for bankruptcy, holding other characteristics of the household fixed. Fay, Hurst, and White (2002) argue that their results not only support the strategic-timing theory but also reject the adverse-events theory.

The research design in White (1998) and Fay, Hurst, and White (2002) relies on cross-sectional variation in the net financial benefit of bankruptcy to explain bankruptcy filings. There are several methodological concerns worth mentioning. First, as these authors note, a small percentage of those who would benefit from filing actually file. It is difficult to imagine the strategic-timing theory having much explanatory value with respect to why households file for bankruptcy if it has so little explanatory value with respect to why households choose not to file. One would have to introduce other, nonrational models of behavior—stigma, lack of understanding of financial benefits, and the like—and these models do not fit comfortably within a theory based on rational agents strategically filing for bankruptcy.

Second, the variable measuring the net financial benefit of bankruptcy is a nonlinear function of a household's assets, debts, state of residence, and the way these assets and debts are distributed across different exempt and nonexempt categories. In other words, this net financial benefit variable depends on the household's financial status and decisionmaking process, including any adverse events and the decision to file for bankruptcy. If, as in an earlier example, on-the-job stress increases the financial benefit of bankruptcy (by changing a household's asset and debt levels and structure), then the cross-sectional correlation between the financial benefit and filing for bankruptcy tells us little about the process by which households decide to file for bankruptcy. In addition, if on-the-job stress also contributes to the likelihood of adverse events, we would expect the financial benefit of bankruptcy and the likelihood of adverse events to be highly correlated. This correlation is likely to confound Fay, Hurst, and White's (2002) test of the adverse-events theory, which provides a reason why their test may fail to reject the null hypothesis that adverse events are not (conditionally) correlated with bankruptcy filing.[1] Finally, Fay, Hurst, and White (2002)'s assertion that local variations in bankruptcy filing can be explained by reduced stigma in communities with more filers may reflect instead other unobserved characteristics of these communities.

Li Gan and Tarun Sabarwal (2005) acknowledge this theoretical indeterminacy between the adverse-events and strategic-timing theories and propose to apply a statistical test (Hausman 1978) to ascertain the endogeneity of the financial benefit of bankruptcy. The valid applicability of the Hausman test, however, relies on the assumption that adverse events are exogenous to the bankruptcy decision and to a household's asset and debt holdings. If, as in an earlier example, on-the-job stress affects both but is not observed in the data, the Hausman test is no longer a valid test of endogeneity. In addition, even if adverse events were exogenous, the Hausman test is best interpreted as a test of whether the endogeneity of financial benefit influences the consistency of the effect of financial benefits on bankruptcy (see Johnston and DiNardo 1996, 339). The Hausman test is not a test for whether the endogeneity is present.

Often combined with the financial-benefit or strategic-timing theory of bankruptcy, but logically orthogonal to it, is the notion that bankruptcy filings have increased because of a decline in stigma from filing. David Gross and Nicolas Souleles (2002, 345) infer a "decline in social stigma or information costs" because their explanatory variables do not account for the magnitude in changes in bankruptcy-filing rates. They do not present direct evidence regarding stigma, and there is little reason to credit their explanation for increased filings over other theories, particularly given that their data cover only two years, a rather short period within which such a change in social mores might occur.

The market-structure theory advanced by Ronald Mann (2005) rejects a focus on the individual decision to file in favor of an approach that examines the link between credit-card borrowing and bankruptcy. Mann argues that strategies of credit-card companies to use complicated rate structures and high rates induce high levels of credit-card indebtedness that put households at risk of bankruptcy. Mann's (2005) empirical results rely on cross-country variation in credit-card indebtedness to identify the effect of market structure on bankruptcy. This research design faces many of the same methodological issues discussed earlier in that there are many unobservable determinants of both credit-card indebtedness

---

1. More specifically, the lack of statistical significance when testing the adverse-events theory does not indicate that adverse events are statistically uncorrelated with bankruptcy given the presence of multicollinearity. In addition, their test of the adverse-events theory essentially amounts to a "horse race" between adverse events and the financial benefit of bankruptcy. This horse race is not a valid means of ascertaining which theory the data support if there are nonlinearities or interaction effects among these variables in the true model. There is no a priori reason to assume that the effects of financial benefits are linear. As discussed above, adverse events and financial benefits are likely to be interrelated.

and bankruptcy rates. In addition, Mann's (2005) empirical results cannot rule out either the adverse-events or strategic-timing theories.

Results

For our analysis of the Detroit Area Household Financial Services survey data, we divided respondents into four categories based on bankruptcy filing: all respondents, those who have ever declared bankruptcy, those who recently declared bankruptcy, and those who have never declared. "Recently declared" consists of respondents who declared bankruptcy in the twelve months preceding their interview. Respondents in each of these groups share many similarities in terms of financial condition, employment status, and demographic traits at the time of interview.

Financial Benefit

We calculate the net financial benefit of bankruptcy under eighteen different scenarios. These scenarios vary according to assumptions about the sample member's marital status, federal and state statutes selected, and best- or worst-case exemption possibilities. For marital status, exemption limits differ depending on whether the individual is single or married and whether the primary residence is under respondent's name. If respondent's house is under a spouse's name, household exemption limits do not apply, and financial benefits associated with the primary residence are excluded from our calculations. Household exemption limits and other asset exemption limits also change depending on the statute elected; we determine the new net worth of households under federal law, state law, and new state law that went into effect during our study period. For the best- and worst-case scenarios, we apply the most favorable and most unfavorable exemption limits assuming specific asset holdings.[2] Based on research and fee quotes from lawyers, we estimate filing costs at the relevant time to have been $1,200, an amount that does not vary across sample members. While this amount was included in our calculation of costs, it did not change the overall distribution of those who would financially benefit under any of the eighteen scenarios.

---

2. These scenarios arise with our data because, in the interest of time and clarity, for a few of the assets we ask about multiple assets with a single question. The bankruptcy statutes, however, apply different exemption standards to these assets, which we only measure as an aggregated unit. To bound the true exemption an individual is likely to take, we first assume that the aggregated amount is held in the asset with the lowest exemption level (worst-case scenario). We then construct the best-case scenario by assuming that the aggregated amount is held in the asset with the highest exemption level. For example, the value of life insurance policies, "other" financial instruments, and "other" savings is asked in a single question. Under bankruptcy law, a filer may exempt a life insurance policy up to $9,850, while other savings are nonexempt. Therefore, the best-case scenario includes an exemption of $9,850 for "other assets," and the worst-case scenario does not exempt anything.

By our estimates, between 10 and 17 percent of our sample would financially benefit if they declared bankruptcy today. The percentage that would benefit varies according to assumptions made about how assets are held if a sample member is married, the federal or state statute elected, asset classes held, and other circumstances. Despite their low incomes and precarious financial situations—and the financial benefit of bankruptcy filing for 10 to 17 percent of them—only 4 percent of our sample have recently declared bankruptcy. This fraction is much higher than the national average of less than 1 percent (White 1998; Fay, Hurst, and White 2002). We find that the fraction of our sample filing for bankruptcy in a given year is considerably smaller than those who would benefit from filing. We also measure the percentage of our sample who ever filed for bankruptcy. Some 15 percent of households have filed for bankruptcy at some point in their lives. About 1 percent of households has filed more than once.

Demographic Characteristics of Filers and Nonfilers

Overall, as shown in table 8-1, filers and nonfilers in our sample share many similarities. They are equally likely to be black or female, and the average age in the two groups is similar. Their employment status at the time of the interview is also similar. Filers and nonfilers report similar levels of average earnings, as well as average monthly and annual household income. They are equally likely to participate often in making their households' financial decisions.

There are some interesting differences among filers and nonfilers. Respondents who have ever declared bankruptcy are about 12 percentage points more likely to have greater than a high school diploma than those who have never declared bankruptcy. Filers are 9 percentage points more likely to be separated, widowed, or divorced. We do not have information regarding the date of separation, divorce, or widowhood and are unable therefore to relate these to timing of bankruptcy. Despite similarities in the average household monthly and annual income, the median household income of those who have filed for bankruptcy, at $28,000, is $10,000 higher than for those who have never filed. Also, 25 percent of those who have filed currently live below the poverty line, compared with a poverty rate of 35 percent for those in our sample who have never declared bankruptcy. One interpretation of these results is that there is more (cross-sectional) variation in income among nonfilers than filers, income inequality being more prevalent among the former.

Table 8-2 presents the demographic and descriptive characteristics among sample members who would benefit from bankruptcy, as well as among sample members who would not benefit. Individuals who would benefit are as likely to have more than a high school diploma as those who would not benefit. In addition, there are no differences in the marital status of the two groups. Individuals who would benefit have lower average earnings and incomes than those who would not benefit. Among the former, monthly earnings average $560 less at

Table 8-1. *Demographic Characteristics of Sample, by Bankruptcy Filing*[a]
Percent unless otherwise noted

Characteristic	All	Ever declared	Declared but not recently	Declared in last twelve months	Never declared
Black	69.1	71.4	71	72.7	68.1
	(1.5)	(3.9)	(4.5)	(7.3)	(1.7)
White	20.4	17.0	16.6	18.0	20.8
	(1.3)	(3.2)	(3.7)	(6.3)	(1.4)
Arab American	1.9	3.3	3.7	2.4	1.6
	(0.4)	(1.5)	(1.9)	(2.5)	(0.4)
Other	8.6	7.1	7.2	6.9	8.9
	(0.9)	(0.2)	(2.6)	(4.2)	(1.0)
Female	66.3	63.3	60.9	70.3	66.7
	(1.6)	(4.1)	(4.9)	(7.5)	(1.7)
Less than high school diploma	29.6	18	14.3	28.6	31.7
	(1.5)	(3.3)	(3.5)	(7.4)	(1.7)
High school diploma or GED	23.0	24	23.8	24.5	22.8
	(1.4)	(3.7)	(4.3)	(7.1)	(1.5)
Greater than high school diploma	47.4	58.0	61.9	46.9	45.5
	(1.6)	(4.2)	(4.9)	(8.2)	(1.8)
Age (years)	43.5	44.0	45.7	38.9	43.4
	(0.5)	(1.20)	(1.4)	(2.0)	(0.6)
Born in the United States	92.1	93.4	93.6	92.5	91.8
	(1.9)	(2.1)	(2.4)	(4.3)	(1.0)
Single or never married	45.6	37.5	36.9	39.4	46.8
	(1.6)	(4.1)	(4.8)	(8.0)	(1.8)
Married and living with spouse	19.7	20.2	22.7	13.4	19.5
	(1.3)	(3.4)	(4.2)	(5.6)	(1.4)
Living with partner	4.1	4.3	2.6	9.4	4.0
	(0.6)	(1.7)	(1.6)	(4.8)	(0.7)
Separated, widowed, or divorced	30.6	37.9	37.9	37.8	29.2
	(1.5)	(4.1)	(4.9)	(8.0)	(1.6)
Household has no children	67.2	66.2	66.2	66.2	67.5
	(2.2)	(4.0)	(4.7)	(7.8)	(1.7)
Currently employed	54.3	61.9	61.4	63.3	52.8
	(1.6)	(4.1)	(4.9)	(7.9)	(1.8)
Participates often in financial decisions	75.0	74.6	79.0	62.0	75.0
	(1.4)	(3.7)	(4.1)	(7.9)	(1.5)
Respondents' monthly earnings (dollars)	1,337	1,288	1,392	970	1,350
	(131)	(167)	(210)	(225)	(152)
Mean household monthly income (dollars)	2,248	1,977	2,150	1,443	2,306
	(334)	(268)	(343)	(290)	(264)

(continued)

Table 8-1. *Demographic Characteristics of Sample, by Bankruptcy Filing*[a] (*continued*)

Percent unless otherwise noted

Characteristic	All	Ever declared	Declared but not recently	Declared in last twelve months	Never declared
Mean household annual income (dollars)	28,435 (2,118)	34,023 (3,457)	36,341 (4,441)	27,124 (3,753)	27,358 (1,136)
Median household annual income (dollars)	20,000	28,000	27,064	30,000	18,000
Living below poverty line[b]	33.2 (2.4)	25.0 (3.7)	24.6 (4.3)	26.2 (7.2)	34.7 (1.7)
Sample size	938	141	105	37	794

Source: Detroit Area Household Financial Services study.

a. Standard errors are in parentheses.

b. Poverty guidelines come from the Department of Health and Human Services (http://aspe.hhs.gov/poverty/04poverty.shtml).

$855, monthly household income is $1,250 less, and annual household income is a little over $9,000 less. Median annual household income is $15,000 among those who would benefit, $5,000 less than the median among those who would not. Poverty rates, however, are roughly the same in both groups.

Assets and Debts

Overall, respondent households have low assets relative to average American households (see table 8-3). Average assets are about $108,000 and median assets stood at only $38,400. Nearly 60 percent of the respondents hold no funds in any kind of bank account at the time of the interview. An overwhelming majority of individuals own a vehicle, which is the predominant asset in our LMI sample. As with most Americans, the asset with the highest value is the home, which has an average value of $112,000 among home owners. Over 10 percent of all respondents do not hold any formal or informal assets.

Table 8-3 displays the average asset and debt holdings, the median levels of each, and the percentage holding each type of asset or debt by bankruptcy-filing status. The distribution and average levels of assets differ somewhat between bankruptcy filers and nonfilers. Overall, a complex picture emerges. Filers are 12 percentage points more likely to have an individual retirement account. With respect to all other assets, filers and nonfilers are equally likely to hold them. Among bankruptcy filers, respondents have, on average, about $500 in their checking or savings account; those who had not filed have about $2,000. Those

Table 8-2. *Demographics of Sample, by Benefit from Bankruptcy*[a]
Percent unless otherwise noted

Characteristic	All	Would benefit	Never benefit
Black	69.1	68.2	68.7
	(1.5)	(4.1)	(1.6)
White	20.4	18.6	20.5
	(1.3)	(3.4)	(1.4)
Arab American	1.9	2.6	1.7
	(0.4)	(1.4)	(0.5)
Other	8.6	10.6	8.3
	(0.9)	(2.7)	(1.0)
Female	66.3	68.2	65.9
	(1.6)	(4.1)	(1.7)
Less than high school diploma	29.6	28.9	29.7
	(1.5)	(4.0)	(1.6)
High school diploma or GED	23.0	27.1	22.3
	(1.4)	(3.9)	(1.5)
Greater than high school diploma	47.4	44.0	48.0
	(1.6)	(4.4)	(1.8)
Age (years)	43.5	42.3	43.7
	(1.0)	(1.4)	(0.6)
Born in the United States	92.1	90.0	92.4
	(1.9)	(2.6)	(0.9)
Single or never married	45.6	45.1	45.5
	(1.6)	(4.4)	(1.8)
Married and living with spouse	19.7	24.6	18.9
	(1.3)	(3.8)	(1.4)
Living with partner	4.1	3.6	4.14
	(0.6)	(1.6)	(0.7)
Separated, widowed, or divorced	30.6	26.7	31.1
	(1.5)	(3.9)	(1.6)
Household has no children	67.2	62.7	68.0
	(2.2)	(4.3)	(1.6)
Currently employed	54.3	49.2	55.1
	(1.6)	(4.4)	(1.8)
Participates often in financial decisions	75.0	80.8	74.0
	(1.4)	(3.3)	(1.5)
Respondents' monthly earnings (dollars)	1,337	855	1,416
	(131)	(119)	(151)
Mean household monthly income (dollars)	2,248	1,174	2,425
	(334)	(160)	(262)

(continued)

Table 8-2. *Demographics of Sample, by Benefit from Bankruptcy*[a] (*continued*)
Percent unless otherwise noted

Characteristic	All	Would benefit	Never benefit
Mean household annual income (dollars)	28,435	20,549	29,757
	(2,118)	(2,000)	(1,239)
Median household annual income (dollars)	20,000	15,000	20,000
Living below poverty line[b]	33.2	39.0	32.2
	(2.4)	(4.3)	(1.6)
Sample size	938	134	804

Source: Detroit Area Household Financial Services study.

a. Standard errors are in parentheses.

b. Poverty guidelines come from the Department of Health and Human Services (http://aspe.hhs.gov/poverty/04poverty.shtml).

who have filed for bankruptcy hold median assets of $53,000, compared with $32,000 for those who have never filed, though the average asset amounts are the same for both groups.

About three-quarters of the sample have some form of debt. On average, respondents have $1,548 in credit-card debt, and about 40 percent of respondents have some credit-card debt. Nearly a quarter of the sample have a car loan, averaging over $10,000 among those with loans. Sixteen percent of respondents hold student loans, which average $13,500 among this group. Twenty-one percent have unpaid medical bills, averaging around $3,000, conditional on having this debt. The average debt level in our LMI sample is $26,500, with the median at $3,400. This wide divergence between the mean and the median suggests considerable skewness in the right tail of the distribution of debt.

There are some differences between filers and nonfilers in the distribution and average amounts of their debts. Overall, filers are more likely to have some form of debt and have more sources of debt. Filers are 9 percentage points more likely to hold credit-card debt, 4 percentage points more likely to have mortgage debt, and over 10 percentage points more likely to have outstanding student loans. Medical bills are 7 percentage points more prevalent among filers than nonfilers. Among filers, the median level of indebtedness is $11,500, while for nonfilers, it is far lower, at $3,000.

We make no causal claims about these findings on indebtedness. These findings are consistent with a view that individuals filing for bankruptcy are prone to borrowing as well as with a view that the difficulty of making loan payments under financial stress contributes to bankruptcy. Furthermore, we cannot provide evidence on when our sample members incurred these debts vis-à-vis when

Table 8-3. *Assets, Debts, and Income, by Bankruptcy Filing*[a]
Dollars unless otherwise noted

	All	Ever declared	Declared, but not recently	Declared in past twelve months	Never declared
Asset					
Amount in checking and savings accounts	1,636 **43.9**	490 **39.2**	627 **43.0**	96 **28.2**	1,843 **44.7**
Value of house	44,614 **40.3**	40,958 **37.6**	46,531 **40.0**	24,989 **28.9**	45,344 **35.0**
Other real estate	8,274 **6.4**	7,620 **6.4**	7,489 **5.7**	7,998 **7.9**	8,415 **5.9**
Vehicles	10,338 *3,000* **73.9**	13,406 *6,000* **94.3**	14,342 *8,000* **92.4**	10,724 *3,400* **94.7**	9,775 *3,000* **90.8**
Business or farm	876 **3.3**	565 **3.5**	305 **2.9**	1,311 **5.3**	934 **3.1**
Stocks or investments	7,495 **11.0**	5,720 **12.8**	5,265 **11.4**	7,025 **15.8**	7,834 **10.6**
IRAs	9,525 **28.0**	10,761 **32.6**	12,499 **31.4**	5,781 **34.2**	9,330 **20.4**
Retirement account	4,485 **14.0**	3,173 **14.2**	4,086 **14.3**	560 **13.2**	4,646 **9.4**
Money market funds	4,277 **13.7**	7,291 **12.8**	9,685 **12.4**	432 **13.2**	3,753 **10.0**
Jewelry, gold, other goods	1,282 **14.0**	1,690 **14.9**	2,200 **16.2**	227 **10.5**	1,213 **13.7**
Other assets	15,527 **24.8**	25,543 **29.8**	31,114 **27.0**	9,581 **36.8**	13,664 **20.2**
Additional savings	190 **1.5**	16 **2.1**	21 **2.9**	0 **0**	222 **1.6**
Total assets	108,520 *38,400*	117,234 *52,900*	134,164 *60,200*	68,722 *50,000*	106,972 *31,600*
Has at least one asset	89.2	91.7	94.6	83.5	88.7
Mean number of assets	3.0	3.2	3.3	2.8	3.0
Debt					
Credit card	1,548 **38.1**	1,257 **44.9**	1,424 **48.6**	780 **34.5**	1,602 **36.1**
Mortgage	16,941 **26.6**	22,126 **30.0**	24,761 **32.4**	14,576 **22.9**	16,047 **26.0**
Second mortgage	461 **2.0**	882 **5.7**	1,190 **7.7**	0 **0**	387 **1.3**

(continued)

Table 8-3. *Assets, Debts, and Income, by Bankruptcy Filing (continued)*
Dollars unless otherwise noted

	All	Ever declared	Declared, but not recently	Declared in past twelve months	Never declared
Equity loan	1,120	855	1,141	0	1,170
	5.0	**3.8**	**5.0**	**0**	**5.3**
Other home loan	457	763	937	263	404
	2.7	**5.5**	**6.9**	**1.6**	**2.2**
Car loan	2,428	3,338	4,080	1,213	2,250
	24.7	**33.6**	**39.7**	**16.2**	**23.0**
Title loan	1.62	0	0	0	1.91
	0.19	**0**	**0**	**0**	**0.20**
Student loan	2,093	4,310	3,752	5,892	1,649
	15.5	**24.2**	**23.7**	**29.4**	**13.8**
Medical bills	637	591	588	600	647
	20.8	**27.0**	**28.7**	**22.1**	**19.7**
Legal bills	106	113	138	40	105
	1.9	**2.3**	**0.7**	**7.1**	**1.9**
Other loan	877	1,291	1,579	453	806
	11.6	**10.9**	**12.3**	**6.9**	**10.1**
Total debt	26,490	37,143	41,379	24,534	24,964
	3,394	*11,500*	*18,000*	*5,000*	*3,000*
Has at least one debt	74.2	85.4	87.3	79.9	72.3
Mean number of debts	2.0	2.5	2.8	1.9	1.9
Income					
Respondents' monthly earnings	1,337	1,288	1,392	970	1,350
Total household monthly income	2,249	1,977	2,150	1,443	2,306
Annual household income in 2004	28,435	34,023	36,341	27,124	27,358
Debt-to-income ratio	1.17	1.67	1.81	1.19	1.08
	0.20	*0.54*	*0.54*	*0.29*	*0.18*
Sample size	938	141	105	37	794

Source: Detroit Area Household Financial Services study.

a. Means are not conditional on having asset. Nonzero medians are in italics. Percentage of respondents with asset or debt are in bold.

they filed for bankruptcy. It may be the case that they were able to obtain loans even after they filed for bankruptcy.

Table 8-4 presents similar asset and debt statistics but organizes the data by whether respondents would or would not benefit from filing. Here, the contrasts between the beneficiaries and nonbeneficiaries are stark, which is not surprising since qualifying respondents as beneficiaries is a nonlinear function of their asset and debt holdings. Individuals who would not benefit from filing for bankruptcy, on average, hold more types of assets and have significantly higher levels of asset holdings ($121,000 versus $34,000). Conversely, individuals who would benefit from filing for bankruptcy are more likely to hold some form of debt, carry more types of debt, and have higher median levels of debt. Though not statistically significant, the point estimate of the average level of indebtedness is higher among those who would benefit from filing for bankruptcy.

Table 8-4 suggests why the methodology in White (1998) and Fay, Hurst, and White (2002) may not be appropriate either to show that the financial benefit of bankruptcy serves as an incentive to file or to preclude the adverse-events hypothesis. By construction, the channel by which the financial benefits of bankruptcy vary across individuals occurs primarily through asset and debt levels and holdings. Hence the variation in whether an individual financially benefits reflects the variation in assets and debts, which may have independent effects on the likelihood of filing for bankruptcy. To the extent that unobserved events, like on-the-job stress as in our previous example, or unobserved behaviors influence levels of assets and debts, they will also affect the likelihood an individual would benefit from filing for bankruptcy. In other words, the financial incentives to file for bankruptcy are endogenous to the individual. This means that a cross-sectional correlation between this measure and the actual filing decision may be driven by other, unobserved factors correlated with asset and debt levels.

Hardships

We measure a range of financial hardships experienced by respondents in the twelve months preceding the interview, including major medical expenses, food insecurity, eviction, utilities being cut off, the telephone being disconnected, and threats of foreclosure. Table 8-5 reports the incidence of these hardships. Even among those who have never filed for bankruptcy, hardships are prevalent. Over 60 percent of respondents who never declared bankruptcy report experiencing at least one of these hardships over the past year. Over a quarter report a major medical expense; 17 percent report not having enough food to eat; 18 percent report having their phone disconnected; 10 percent had their utilities cut off; 6 percent were evicted; and 2 percent were threatened with foreclosure.

Table 8-4. *Assets, Debts, and Income, by Benefit from Bankruptcy*[a]
Dollars unless otherwise noted

	All	Would benefit	Never benefit
Asset			
Amount in checking and savings accounts	1,636	205	1,874
	43.9	**32.5**	**45.8**
Value of house	44,614	24,884	48,226
	40.3	**22.9**	**43.1**
Other real estate	8,274	56	9,640
	6.4	**0.4**	**7.4**
Vehicle	10,338	3,326	11,504
	3,000	*1,400*	*4,000*
	73.9	**70.5**	**74.5**
Business or farm	876	394	956
	3.3	**3.3**	**3.3**
Stocks or investment	7,495	21	8,737
	11.0	**3.1**	**12.3**
IRA	9,525	4,121	10,424
	28.0	**19.8**	**29.3**
Retirement account	4,485	1,423	4,994
	14.0	**9.3**	**14.9**
Money market fund	4,277	147	4,963
	13.7	**6.2**	**15.0**
Jewelry, gold, other goods	1,282	276	1,449
	14.0	**9.7**	**14.7**
Other assets	15,527	1,038	17,935
	24.8	**13.5**	**16.6**
Additional savings	190	72	210
	1.5	**1.2**	**1.6**
Total assets	108,520	33,963	120,911
	38,400	*3,187*	*56,247*
Has at least one asset	89.2	93.0	98.5
Mean number of assets	3.01	2.16	3.15
Debt			
Credit card	1,548	4,117	1,121
	0	*500*	*0*
	38.1	**58.2**	**44.7**
Mortgage	16,941	17,185	16,901
	26.6	**21.4**	**17.4**
Second mortgage	461	1,070	361
	2.0	**4.3**	**1.6**
Equity loan	1,120	1,572	1,044
	5.0	**5.8**	**4.9**
Other home loan	457	69	522
	2.7	**1.3**	**2.9**
Car loan	2,428	2,288	2,451
	24.7	**22.1**	**25.1**

(continued)

Table 8-4. *Assets, Debts, and Income, by Benefit from Bankruptcy*[a] (*continued*)
Dollars unless otherwise noted

	All	Would benefit	Never benefit
Title loan	1.62	0	1.89
	0.19	**0**	**0.22**
Student loan	2,093	2,078	2,095
	15.5	**21.6**	**14.5**
Medical bills	637	2,300	360
	0	*137*	*0*
	20.8	**54.8**	**15.2**
Legal bills	106	149	99
	1.9	**3.2**	**1.7**
Other loan	877	1,226	817
	11.6	**17.7**	**10.6**
Total debts	26,490	31,209	25,709
	3,394	*7,000*	*3,000*
Has at least one debt	74	100	70
Mean number of debts	2.02	2.71	1.91
Measure of income			
Respondent's monthly earnings	1,337	855	1,416
Total household monthly income	2,249	1,174	2,425
Annual household income in 2004	28,435	20,549	29,757
Debt-to-income ratio	1.17	2.74	0.90
	0.20	*0.67*	*0.14*
Sample size	938	134	804

Source: Detroit Area Household Financial Services study.

a. Means are not conditional on having the asset. Nonzero medians are in italics. Percentage of respondent with asset or debt in bold.

Respondents who have recently declared bankruptcy report even higher levels of adverse events than those who have never filed for bankruptcy. Of those who declared bankruptcy within the past twelve months, 100 percent report having experienced one or more of these hardships during that period. Over a third of respondents who recently declared bankruptcy experienced a job loss, while nearly 30 percent of these respondents had major medical expenses. Twenty-two percent of this group experienced food insecurity; 24 percent report having had their phone cut off; 23 percent had their utilities cut off; 18 percent were evicted; and 3 percent were threatened with foreclosure.

As seen in table 8-6, financially benefiting from filing for bankruptcy is correlated with experiencing hardships. Among those who would benefit from filing, 37 percent had a major medical expense, 25 percent were food insecure, 24 percent had their phone disconnected, 19 percent had their utilities cut off, and 13 percent were evicted. These rates are all lower among the group that

Table 8-5. *Adverse Events Experienced during Past Twelve Months,*
by Bankruptcy Filing[a]
Percent

Event	Ever declared	Declared in past twelve months	Never declared
Job loss[b]	18.2	36.8	23.7
	(3.3)	(7.9)	(1.5)
Food insecurity	15.7	22.3	17.0
	(3.1)	(6.8)	(1.3)
Major medical expense	36.3	29.5	25.2
	(4.2)	(7.6)	(1.5)
Eviction	6.9	18.0	5.8
	(2.2)	(6.3)	(0.8)
Utilities cut off	12.7	23.1	9.5
	(2.9)	(6.9)	(1.0)
Phone disconnected	18.5	23.8	18.3
	(3.3)	(7.0)	(1.4)
Threat of foreclosure	6.2	3.2	1.8
	(2.1)	(2.9)	(0.5)
Experienced at least one	70.9	100.0	60.7
Mean number of adverse events	1.4	2.6	1.0
	(0.1)	(0.2)	(0.0)
Sample size	137	38	798

Source: Detroit Area Household Financial Services study.

a. Standard errors in parentheses. Data are weighted and restricted.

b. Aggregated from multiple questions: Those currently working for pay were asked if they have been "unemployed and looking for work at any time during the last 12 months." For respondents not currently working for pay, the month and date that they stopped working for their last employer was compared with the date they completed the survey. Respondents who stopped working within the past twelve months were flagged. Then they were identified as experiencing job loss if, in response to "why are you not currently working," they said either they quit, were fired, were laid off, were unemployed, did not have proper documentation, or other. Those who responded that they are retired, homemakers or caring for their own children, or students, or choose not to work were coded as zeros since they are not currently looking for work.

would not benefit from filing: 25 percent had a major medical expense, 16 percent were food insecure; 17 percent had their phone disconnected; 9 percent had their utilities cut off; and 5 percent were evicted. These findings are consistent with the view that hardships and financially benefiting from bankruptcy are jointly determined.

Attitudes and Knowledge

Table 8-7 reports the attitudes of all households, filers, and nonfilers. Overall, respondents have accurate perceptions about the financial consequences of filing for bankruptcy and of exhibiting delinquent financial behavior. Most

Table 8-6. *Adverse Events Experienced during Past Twelve Months, by Benefit from Bankruptcy*[a]

Percent

Event	All	Would benefit	Never benefit
Job loss[b]	22.9	21.3	23.2
	(1.4)	(3.6)	(1.5)
Bankruptcy	3.9	4.8	3.8
	(0.6)	(1.8)	(0.7)
Food insecurity	16.8	24.5	15.5
	(1.2)	(3.7)	(1.3)
Major medical expense	26.9	36.9	25.1
	(1.5)	(4.2)	(1.5)
Eviction	5.9	13.0	4.7
	(0.8)	(2.9)	(0.8)
Utilities cut off	10.0	18.5	8.5
	(1.0)	(3.3)	(1.0)
Phone disconnected	18.3	24.4	17.3
	(1.3)	(3.7)	(1.3)
Threat of foreclosure	2.5	2.0	2.6
	(0.5)	(1.2)	(0.6)
Experienced at least one	61.3	69.7	59.8
Mean number of adverse events	1.1	1.4	1.0
	(0.0)	(0.1)	(0.0)
Sample size	938	136	802

Source: Detroit Area Household Financial Services study.

a. Sample is weighted and restricted. Standard errors are in parentheses.

b. Data are aggregated from multiple questions: Those currently working for pay were asked if they have been "unemployed and looking for work at any time during the last 12 months." For respondents not currently working for pay, the month and date that they stopped working for their last employer was compared with the date they completed the survey. Respondents who stopped working within the past twelve months were flagged. Then they were identified as experiencing job loss if, in response to "why are you not currently working" they said either they quit, were fired, were laid off, were unemployed, did not have proper documentation, or other. Those who responded that they are retired, homemakers or caring for their own children, students, or choose not to work were coded as zeros since they are not currently looking for work.

individuals (77 percent) in our study believe that filing for bankruptcy affects their credit. Moreover, when asked about the consequences of not paying their rent or bills on time, more than two-thirds of individuals disagree with the statement: "I know that I can walk away from that debt by filing for bankruptcy." Over 90 percent of sample members agree with the view that not paying their bills on time would result in worsening their credit rating. Similarly, over 80 percent of respondents believe that banks will not lend to them if they do not pay their bills on time. When asked the converse, only 14 percent of respondents believe that "nothing would happen" if they did not pay their bills on time.

Table 8-7. *Attitudes toward Bankruptcy, by Bankruptcy Filing*[a]
Percent

Attitude	All	Ever declared	Declared, but not recently	Declared in past twelve months	Never declared
Thinks bankruptcy affects credit	77.0 (1.4)	62.0 (4.2)	55.0 (5.0)	82.7 (6.4)	79.5 (1.5)
I can walk away from debts[b]					
Strongly agree	13.8 (1.1)	17.4 (3.2)	14.4 (3.5)	26.1 (7.2)	13.0 (1.2)
Somewhat agree	14.7 (1.2)	26.0 (3.7)	25.0 (4.3)	29.0 (7.4)	12.7 (1.2)
Somewhat disagree	15.5 (1.2)	12.6 (3.0)	11.3 (3.2)	16.0 (6.0)	16.0 (1.3)
Strongly disagree	54.5 (1.6)	44.1 (4.2)	49.3 (5.0)	29.0 (7.5)	56.0 (1.8)
I'd be ashamed if I had to file for bankruptcy[c]					
Strongly agree	43.4 (1.6)	23.3 (3.6)	19.4 (4.0)	34.6 (7.8)	47.0 (1.8)
Somewhat agree	16.6 (1.2)	10.8 (2.6)	12.1 (3.3)	4.8 (3.5)	17.4 (1.3)
Somewhat disagree	15.1 (1.1)	18.8 (3.0)	20.6 (4.0)	13.5 (5.6)	14.5 (1.2)
Strongly disagree	24.5 (1.4)	48.0 (4.3)	47.9 (5.0)	47.1 (8.2)	20.4 (1.4)
If I do not pay my bills on time, my credit rating will become worse					
Strongly agree	79.4 (1.3)	82.1 (3.3)	82.3 (3.9)	81.7 (6.4)	79.2 (1.4)
Somewhat agree	12.1 (1.0)	7.6 (2.3)	6.6 (2.5)	10.3 (5.0)	12.9 (1.2)
Somewhat disagree	3.4 (0.6)	4.1 (1.7)	4.9 (2.2)	1.8 (2.2)	3.2 (0.6)
Strongly disagree	4.6 (0.7)	6.2 (2.0)	6.2 (2.4)	6.2 (4.0)	4.4 (1.0)
If I do not pay my bills on time, banks will not lend to me					
Strongly agree	66.9 (1.5)	68.4 (4.0)	63.2 (4.8)	83.4 (6.1)	66.7 (1.6)
Somewhat agree	15.8 (1.2)	18.8 (3.3)	20.7 (4.0)	13.2 (5.6)	15.3 (1.3)
Somewhat disagree	9.5 (1.0)	8.5 (2.4)	10.9 (3.1)	1.8 (2.2)	9.7 (1.0)
Strongly disagree	6.6 (0.8)	4.3 (1.7)	5.0 (2.2)	1.7 (2.1)	7.0 (0.9)

(continued)

Table 8-7. *Attitudes toward Bankruptcy, by Bankruptcy Filing*ᵃ *(continued)*
Percent

Attitude	All	Ever declared	Declared, but not recently	Declared in past twelve months	Never declared
If I do not pay my bills on time, nothing will happen					
Strongly agree	7.1	2.8	1.8	5.8	7.9
	(0.8)	(1.4)	(1.3)	(3.9)	(1.0)
Somewhat agree	6.9	8.5	8.9	7.4	6.7
	(0.83)	(2.4)	(2.9)	(4.3)	(0.9)
Somewhat disagree	11.5	13.9	12.4	18.4	11.0
	(1.0)	(2.9)	(3.3)	(6.4)	(1.1)
Strongly disagree	73.6	73.5	75.3	68.4	73.7
	(1.4)	(3.8)	(4.3)	(7.6)	(1.6)
Sample size	938	141	105	37	794

Source: Detroit Area Household Financial Services study.

a. Standard errors are in parentheses.

b. Question reads: "I know I can walk away from that debt by filing for bankruptcy. (Do you strongly agree, somewhat agree, somewhat disagree or strongly disagree?)" That debt refers to a hypothetical situation that states, "What do you think would happen if you did not pay your rent or bills on time?"

c. Question reads: "I would feel ashamed or embarrassed if I had to file for bankruptcy. (Do you strongly agree, somewhat agree, somewhat disagree or strongly disagree?)"

With respect to knowing the financial consequences of filing for bankruptcy and exhibiting delinquent financial behavior, the ever filers and never filers exhibit relatively similar patterns in their responses. However, nonfilers and those who have recently declared bankruptcy are more likely to believe that filing for bankruptcy affects their credit than are those who have declared less recently (80 and 83 percent versus 55 percent). Respondents recently filing for bankruptcy are more likely to believe that filing for bankruptcy enables them to walk away from their debts (55 percent versus 26 percent for nonfilers), although this belief diminishes (to 39 percent) among those who filed less recently. Recent filers are more likely than nonfilers or those who have declared bankruptcy, but not recently, to agree that banks may not lend to them if they do not pay their bills on time (97 versus 82 and 84 percent). From these correlations alone, we cannot assess whether individuals who file for bankruptcy learned about the consequences from their experiences or whether those who had these beliefs about the consequences were more likely to file for bankruptcy (perhaps owing to other related financial knowledge).

In our sample, 60 percent of households have an aversion to bankruptcy and agree with the following statement: "I would feel ashamed or embarrassed if I had to file for bankruptcy." Among those who have never declared, the aversion to bankruptcy seems stronger than among those who have declared (64 versus

34 percent). This finding, however, cannot tell us whether shame plays a role in "causing" bankruptcy. Most obviously, we do not know how filers felt about bankruptcy before filing, and thus we cannot assess whether those who would not feel shame are more likely to file or whether bankruptcy has changed their attitudes about filing.

Financial Services

As seen in table 8-8, most respondents have bank accounts and credit cards and are connected to the financial mainstream, but many do not. Seventy-five percent of respondents have a bank account, charge card, or credit card. Less than a quarter of bank-account holders face account fees or minimum-balance requirements. Nearly half the sample used an alternative financial service during the twelve months preceding the interview.[3]

Though bank-account terms are similar across filers and nonfilers, credit-card use and terms exhibit some heterogeneity across bankruptcy filers and nonfilers. Over 40 percent of the sample have a credit card, and this fraction does not vary across filers and nonfilers. While 27 percent of credit-card holders pay an annual fee, filers are 25 percentage points more likely to pay than nonfilers (48 versus 23 percent). In addition, more filers pay a deposit to secure their credit cards (18 versus 8 percent).

Credit-card behaviors also differ across filers and nonfilers in certain dimensions. For instance, filers are less likely than nonfilers to pay off their credit-card balance in full every month (21 versus 33 percent). Recent filers have one fewer credit card on average than nonfilers. Nonfilers appear to have better knowledge of the institutional rules concerning credit cards. They are over 10 percentage points more likely to believe that paying the minimum amount due on a credit card each month will increase the balance each month. They are less likely to exhibit riskier credit-card behavior; for example, they are less likely to have transferred a balance from one credit card to another in the previous twelve months (11 versus 16 percent).

Use of alternative financial services is higher among filers than nonfilers. Over 60 percent of filers used such services during the year preceding the interview, while 47 percent of nonfilers did so. Though a lack of statistical precision makes it impossible to tell how the distribution of alternative services use differs between filers and nonfilers, the point estimates suggest that payday loans account for a large part of the difference between filers and nonfilers in the use of alternative financial services.

3. Alternative financial services include purchasing something on layaway, taking a loan at a pawnshop, taking a refund anticipation loan, purchasing a rent-to-own item, and taking out a payday loan.

Table 8-8. *Connection to Financial Services, by Bankruptcy Filing*[a]
Percent unless otherwise noted

Characteristic	Ever declared	Declared in past twelve months	Never declared
Access to account			
Has bank account	73.9	70.2	70.7
	(3.8)	(7.5)	(1.6)
Has credit card	47.5	32.9	39.9
	(4.3)	(7.7)	(1.7)
Has charge card	20.3	8.0	28.1
	(3.5)	(4.5)	(1.6)
Has debit or payroll card	50.0	50.0	45.0
	(4.3)	(8.2)	(1.8)
Has any account[b]	80.4	75.1	76.6
	1.9	*1.6*	*1.8*
	(0.0)	(0.2)	(0.1)
Account information			
Shopped around for a bank account	36.0	25.8	37.4
	(4.8)	(8.4)	(2.0)
Account has monthly fees	21.6	32.0	17.6
	(4.5)	(9.7)	(1.8)
Checking account has minimum-balance requirement	29.9	28.9	28.2
	(5.0)	(9.4)	(2.2)
Savings account has minimum-balance requirement	26.1	37.1	28.4
	(5.6)	(14.6)	(2.4)
Bank closed an account	19.1	20.0	10.9
	(3.9)	(7.7)	(1.3)
Use of financial services			
Used money order in past twelve months	79.5	79.2	66.2
	(3.5)	(6.7)	(1.7)
Used ATM to take out cash in past month	47.7	51.0	42.2
	(4.3)	(8.2)	(1.7)
Have done banking online	23.0	12.2	21.9
	(4.2)	(6.3)	(1.7)
Received credit counseling in past twelve months	1.2	0	3.3
	(0.9)	(0)	(0.6)
Credit card questions			
Card has an annual fee	47.6	40.7	22.6
	(6.3)	(13.6)	(2.4)
Paid a late fee in past twelve months	32.9	42.1	19.4
	(5.8)	(13.2)	(2.3)
Number of credit cards	2.2	1.4	3.0
	(0.2)	(0.3)	(0.3)
Credit card required deposit	18.3	14.6	8.2
	(4.8)	(9.4)	(1.6)
Annual percentage rate on card	15.2	13.8	12.9
	(0.9)	(2.0)	(0.5)
Has had interest rate changed	28.1	38.6	36.2
	(5.8)	(13.5)	(2.9)

(continued)

Table 8-8. *Connection to Financial Services, by Bankruptcy Filing*[a] *(continued)*
Percent unless otherwise noted

Characteristic	Ever declared	Declared in past twelve months	Never declared
Knew interest rate could change	54.6	73.2	61.9
	(11.7)	(22.2)	(4.8)
Has transferred a balance from one card to another in past twelve months	10.5	4.4	15.8
	(3.8)	(5.5)	(2.1)
Respondent pays entire balance			
Every month	20.7	31.0	32.8
	(5.0)	(12.4)	(2.7)
Some months	44.6	38.9	39.0
	(6.2)	(13.0)	(2.8)
Never	34.8	30.2	28.2
	(5.9)	(12.3)	(2.6)
How much respondent usually pays			
Minimum	24.1	19.1	16.5
	(6.0)	(12.4)	(2.6)
Less than minimum	3.2	10.7	1.4
	(2.5)	(9.8)	(0.8)
More than minimum	72.6	70.1	82.1
	(6.2)	(14.5)	(2.7)
Respondent thinks paying minimum will make balance			
Go down	22.5	36.2	25.5
	(5.2)	(12.8)	(2.5)
Stay the same	40.0	44.7	26.4
	(6.1)	(13.3)	(2.6)
Go up	37.5	19.1	48.1
	(6.1)	(10.5)	(2.9)
Use of alternative financial services			
Cash advance	15.7	13.4	6.5
	(3.1)	(5.6)	(0.9)
Layaway	26.0	23.1	25.6
	(3.8)	(6.9)	(1.5)
Pawnshop	19.9	16.3	9.7
	(3.4)	(6.1)	(1.0)
RAL	26.5	23.7	21.0
	(3.8)	(7.0)	(1.4)
Rent-to-own	10.6	10.0	4.4
	(2.7)	(4.9)	(0.7)
Payday loan	9.5	7.2	2.3
	(2.5)	(4.3)	(0.5)
Uses at least one service[c]	61.1	55.2	46.8
	1.1	*0.94*	*.69*
	(0.1)	(0.2)	(3.2)
Sample size	137	38	798

Source: Detroit Area Household Financial Services study.
a. Standard errors are in parentheses. Sample is weighted and restricted.
b. Mean number of accounts is in italics.
c. Mean number of services used is in italics.

Conclusion

Bankruptcy affects a large portion of LMI households in the Detroit area at some point in their lives. While the bankruptcy filing rate of 4 percent in the year preceding the survey may seem low by absolute standards, our estimate is higher than the national averages cited in previous research (White 1998; Fay, Hurst, and White 2002). Furthermore, 15 percent of respondents in our sample have declared bankruptcy at some point in their lives, and 9 percent of this group (or 1 percent of the entire sample) have filed more than once. At the same time, many LMI households who experience adverse events and would benefit from filing for bankruptcy do not do so.

Our characterization of LMI households who do and do not file for bankruptcy paints a complex picture of these households. Most strikingly, in the LMI population, filers and nonfilers are similar in many observable socioeconomic dimensions. The ways in which they differ do not suggest that there exists a simple set of reasons for why households file for bankruptcy. Our results show that at a given point in time, nonfilers may be a more diverse group in terms of their income though, on average, income is the same in both groups. In addition, the asset and debt holdings in these two groups neither support nor refute the view that profligate borrowing contributes to bankruptcy. The decision to file or not to file for bankruptcy cannot be traced to a single factor, either financial benefit or life-event trigger. Many households who would benefit from filing do not, and many households who experience adverse events do not file as well.

A comparison of individuals who would and would not financially benefit from bankruptcy suggests that the process of filing for bankruptcy and the institutions regulating this decision are complex. There is a clear link between asset and debt levels and whether an individual financially benefits from declaring bankruptcy, and there is a clear correlation between hardships and whether an individual financially benefits. To the extent that asset and debt levels and hardships are both related to the bankruptcy-filing decision, our findings emphasize that there are many observed and unobserved codeterminants of the financial benefits of bankruptcy and the decision to file. Untangling these myriad relationships ought to contribute to the policy debate over bankruptcy reform as well as related areas of credit-card and home mortgage regulation, consumer financial laws, and savings policy.

References

Domowitz, Ian, and Robert L. Sartain. 1999. "Determinants of the Consumer Bankruptcy Decision." *Journal of Finance* 54:403–20 (www.jstor.org/stable/222422).
Fay, Scott, Erik Hurst, and Michelle J. White. 2002. "The Household Bankruptcy Decision." *American Economic Review* 92:706–18 (www.jstor.org/stable/3083362).

Gan, Li, and Tarun Sabarwal. 2005. "A Simple Test of Adverse Events and Strategic Timing Theories of Consumer Bankruptcy." Working Paper 11763. Cambridge, Mass.: National Bureau of Economic Research (www.nber.org/papers/w11763).

Gross, David B., and Nicolas S. Souleles. 2002. "An Empirical Analysis of Personal Bankruptcy and Delinquency." *Review of Financial Studies* 15:319–47 (www.jstor.org/stable/2696806).

Hausman, J. A. 1978. "Specification Tests in Econometrics." *Econometrica* 46:1251–71 (www.jstor.org/stable/1913827).

Jacoby, Melissa B., Teresa A. Sullivan, and Elizabeth Warren. 2001. "Rethinking the Debates over Health Care Financing: Evidence from the Bankruptcy Courts." *New York University Law Review* 76:375–418.

Johnston, Jack, and John E. DiNardo. 1996. *Econometric Methods.* 4th ed. New York: McGraw-Hill/Irwin.

Keys, Benjamin J. 2010. "The Credit Market Consequences of Job Displacement." FEDS Working Paper 2010-24.

Mann, Ronald J. 2005. "Global Credit Card Use and Debt: Policy Issues and Regulatory Responses." Legal Series Paper 490. Berkeley, Calif.: Berkeley Electronic Press (http://law.bepress.com/expresso/eps/490/).

Morgan, Donald P., Benjamin Iverson, and Matthew Botsch. Forthcoming. "Subprime Foreclosures and the 2005 Bankruptcy Reform." *Economic Policy Review.* Federal Reserve Bank of New York.

Sullivan, Theresa A., Elizabeth Warren, and Jay Lawrence Westbrook. 1989. *As We Forgive Our Debtors.* Oxford University Press.

———. 2000. *The Fragile Middle Class: Americans in Debt.* Yale University Press.

———. 2003. "Who Uses Chapter 13?" In *Consumer Bankruptcy in Global Perspective,* edited by Johanna Niemi-Kiesiläinen, Iain Ramsay, and William C. Whitford, 269–82. Oxford, U.K.: Hart Publishing.

Warren, Elizabeth, and Amelia Warren Tyagi. 2003. *The Two-Income Trap.* New York: Basic Books.

White, Michelle. 1998. "Why Don't More Households File for Bankruptcy?" *Journal of Law, Economics, and Organization* 14:205–31 (doi:10.1093/jleo/14.2.205).

9

Expensive Tax Refunds

MICHAEL S. BARR AND JANE K. DOKKO

The U.S. federal income-tax code has an enormous potential to shape the economic and financial decisions of tax-paying households. Tax rates, compliance laws, and the withholding system all create incentives, as do the methods by which the U.S. Treasury collects tax receipts and disburses tax refunds. The role of third-party service providers in the tax system is less well understood, even though tax preparation firms have a prominent role in the U.S. tax system. Nationally, more than half of taxpayers use paid preparers to submit their tax returns. Low- and moderate-income (LMI) households are among those who use the paid tax preparation system. In fact, among low-income households who file, more than two-thirds use paid tax preparation services. Thus understanding the role of third-party providers in the tax system is critical to understanding how our tax system affects low-income households.

Tax preparation service providers can potentially both help and hurt taxpayers. On the positive side, tax preparation firms may increase the likelihood that taxpayers will hear about and take advantage of tax incentives designed to reach them. For example, over 20 million low- and moderate-income households file for approximately $35 billion in refunds and reduced tax liability under the earned-income tax credit (EIC), designed to reward work by low-income taxpayers. On the negative side, tax preparation firms can add to the efficiency costs of the tax system and reduce the amount of redistribution through the EIC and other tax credits and expenditures. Furthermore, tax preparation is a high-fee service in itself, and low-income households often face additional, ancillary fees associated with filing. For example, many low-income households lack bank accounts and may also pay a nontrivial fee to cash their government refund check at a check casher or other establishment. In addition, a large portion of households receiving the EIC take out costly refund anticipation loans and similar products in order to receive the proceeds of their tax refund more quickly or to pay for tax services. Understanding the institutional context in which tax-refund distribution occurs, including households' attitudes toward the withholding system, is important for understanding the efficiency and distributional aspects of the tax system.

In this chapter, using data from the Detroit Area Household Financial Services (DAHFS) study, we examine the tax-filing experiences of LMI households. The study documents households' current tax-filing behavior, their attitudes about the withholding system, their use of tax refunds to consume and save, and the mechanisms by which they would like to receive their refunds. Overall, there is little empirical evidence on the tax-filing experiences of LMI households. Toward this end, the study documents the prevalence of the use of tax preparation services and the receipt of both tax refunds and refund anticipation loans (RALs). It describes the reasons taxpayers cite for taking out RALs and the uses to which they put their tax refunds. Using individuals' responses to a hypothetical scenario in which individuals choose the time profile of how they pay their taxes and receive their refunds, this chapter begins to explore the extent to which households use the withholding system as a financial planning tool.

The evidence on LMI households' tax-filing experiences helps to shed light on a number of important policy questions. For example, our analysis informs the policy debate over tax complexity (Holtzblatt and McCubbin 2004; Barr 2004; President's Advisory Panel on Federal Tax Reform 2005). In addition, our evidence helps to assess whether households' overwithholding, use of paid tax preparers, and use of refund anticipation loans is better understood through rational-actor models or through behavioral economic lenses. In particular, we begin to explore whether default rules, framing, and heuristics play a role in LMI households' tax-filing behaviors (Thaler 1990). Moreover, our analysis can assist in the formulation of consumer financial protection regulation and national savings policies.

Policy Context and Previous Research

Paid tax preparers provide valuable services to taxpayers but charge high fees, leaving the net benefits ambiguous. On behalf of households facing conflicting and complex rules under different tax provisions for determining household status and dependents, tax preparers interface with the tax code. They also serve households who worry about increased Internal Revenue Service (IRS) audits (particularly among EIC filers) and IRS delays in receiving their refunds

(Holtzblatt and McCubbin 2004). Tax preparers may expand the take-up rate for the EIC and other tax credits designed to redistribute income to households by advertising the availability of refunds and expertise in filing returns to maximize the client's use of available tax credits (Kopczuk and Pop-Eleches 2005). Commercial tax preparers also can serve as a vehicle through which to encourage savings, including retirement savings (Barr 2004; Duflo and others 2005).

On the other hand, commercial tax preparers charge high fees, and the use of refund anticipation loans imposes additional fees. In addition to RALs, tax preparers offer other high-fee financial services, such as loans to pay taxes owed or prepaid debit cards with complex fee structures. Unbanked households often must pay a third party, often the tax preparer, to convert their refund checks into cash. Finally, paid tax preparers may reduce the salience of an administratively complicated tax system, thereby reducing the urgency of the need for tax reform (Friedman and Friedman 1998; Finkelstein 2007).

Tax filers who have prepaid taxes (through withholding from their paycheck) in excess of what they owe at the end of the year are issued a tax-refund check by the IRS.[1] Many LMI households are eligible for the EIC and related credits that result in a net refund, absent changes in withholding. Overwithholding is also a common phenomenon at many other income levels. Given their low incomes and pressing financial needs, however, overwithholding by LMI taxpayers is particularly puzzling. By overwithholding, households, in effect, deny themselves access to their take-home pay until they receive a lump-sum tax refund.

A number of factors may influence this pattern of overwithholding among LMI households. First, it is likely to be difficult for such households to adjust their withholding payments to match their income-tax liability. Very few households use the advanced earned-income credit, through which a large portion of their anticipated tax refund could be moved earlier to increase regular take-home pay. The structure of the EIC and its advanced counterpart may be too complicated; employees may be reluctant to ask their employers to implement the provision; and employers may be reluctant to adjust their withholding (or ignorant of how to do so). Moreover, complicated employment patterns over the year, with multiple jobs, may make it difficult to adjust withholding.

Second, uncertainty about tax liability may deter income smoothing through the withholding system. Taxpayers may fear that adjusting withholding would result in an underpayment of taxes, with significant sums owed (perhaps with penalties) at the end of the tax year. For low-income households, the risk of underwithholding, resulting in lump-sum tax liability, may be too great. Some

---

1. In the United States, the IRS collects taxes on earned income by requiring employers to remit a portion of the employees' paychecks as a prepayment of the taxes owed at the end of the year. If the amount prepaid is greater than the taxes owed, then the employee has overwithheld and is entitled to a tax refund in the amount of the difference.

households may also be uncertain as to how to make a payment to the IRS (or may encounter administrative difficulties doing so) if they do not have a bank account. In addition, the complexity of eligibility rules for the EIC and other tax credits, particularly as such rules relate to family structure, may increase the uncertainty involved in determining the appropriate amount of withholding.

Third, as behavioral economic research suggests, taxpayers may like the non-smooth timing of how they receive their income, the lump-sum nature of tax refunds, and their default withholding patterns. In many contexts, individuals prefer rising (or nonsmooth) income and consumption profiles, holding the present value of these profiles constant (Loewenstein and Thaler 1989; Loewenstein and Sicherman 1991; Frank and Hutchens 1993; Neumark 1995). Individuals may also use "mental accounts" to set aside income received as a lump sum in order to finance large purchases (Loewenstein and Thaler 1989; Thaler 1990). Given a bias for the status quo, individuals may find deviating from the default withholding pattern (corresponding to filling out a W-4 form crudely) both difficult and unpleasant. Based on the services offered by the leading tax preparation firms, tax preparers are keenly aware of LMI individuals' potential motives for overwithholding. An understanding of these motives informs how the tax-filing experience interacts with households' consumption and saving decisions (Shapiro and Slemrod 1995; Souleles 1999).

Regardless of whether households intentionally overwithhold, respond to uncertainty, or simply adhere to the tax system's default rules (because of inertia), LMI households do in effect use the institutional features of the with-holding system to save in the short term (that is, for a period of about one year or less). The poor have few assets and find it difficult to save out of current income (see Barr 2004 for a summary of the literature). In light of high-fee alternative financial and banking services, as well as the barriers to saving that LMI households face, the withholding system may provide a mechanism for saving.[2] Furthermore, their attitudes about the withholding system may reflect an awareness that they are able to save by overwithholding and subsequently receive a sizable (lump-sum) tax refund. Research has noted the importance of mental accounts in influencing households' marginal propensity to consume income, finding that the smaller the marginal propensity to consume, the larger the tax refund (Loewenstein and Thaler 1989; Thaler 1990; Souleles 1999). As a large lump-sum payment, the EIC and related tax refunds could present a saving opportunity for LMI households that they may not otherwise have (Souleles 1999; Barr 2004; Tufano, Schneider, and Beverly 2005; Duflo and others 2005; Rhine and others 2005).

---

2. See Barr (2004), Duflo and others (2005), and Bertrand, Mullainathan, and Shafir (2004) for further discussion of these constraints and their contributions to poverty and other socioeconomic conditions.

Description of Survey, Sampling, and Data

In this chapter, we present results from the tax module of the Detroit Area Household Financial Services survey, which consists of twenty-one questions, some with multiple parts. These questions pertain to experiences the respondents had in filing their taxes. This means that the DAHFS study does not necessarily capture all of the experiences of the household. The question asked of tax filers concerning their withholding preferences reads as follows:[3]

> Next we have a question about how people think about tax refunds. In this question, you have a choice of how you get your income. The total amount of your tax refund or money owed will be the same for each option. But you can choose whether you get the money spread out over the year or all at the end. I will read the question and your answer choices—you can read along from this page. . . . For this question, please assume that you receive a regular paycheck from an employer. Which of the following describes how you would like to receive your income?
>
> —a paycheck that is $100 smaller each month than your current one with a tax refund that is $1,200 larger at the end of the year
> —a paycheck that is the same as your current one with no additional refund and no need to pay any additional taxes at the end of the year
> —a paycheck that is $100 larger each month than your current one with a tax refund that is $1,200 smaller at the end of the year

If the respondent chose the third option, the survey proceeded with a follow-up question to ascertain whether framing the question in terms of a tax refund differs from the respondent having to owe a tax liability: Would you want a paycheck that is $100 larger each month than your current one if you owed $1,200 more in taxes at the end of the year?

Results

Table 9-1 documents the tax-filing experiences of the survey sample. Of the 938 LMI respondents in the "low" and "moderate" income strata used here, 73 percent report they filed a tax return in 2004 or 2003. The tax-filing experiences of

---

3. A respondent is a tax filer if he or she filed a tax return in 2004 or 2003. It is possible that a financially uninvolved spouse or a dependent might respond "no" to the question of whether he or she filed a tax return, even though the respondent's household may have filed. Because of data quality concerns, the survey asks the respondent about his or her own tax experiences, rather than the households' experiences. Respondents who did not file a return would probably not be able to recall survey items, such as whether the household filed for the earned-income tax credit or the size of its tax refund.

Table 9-1. *Average Tax-Filing Experiences of Banked and Unbanked Respondents, by EIC Filing Status*[a]

Percent, except as indicated

Characteristic	All	Banked	Unbanked
Filed a tax return in 2003 or 2004	73	79	57
Received a refund	82	81	84
Amount of federal refund (dollars)	2,078	2,100	2,004
	(102)	(135)	(144)
Filed for EIC	41	38	51
Received EIC	33	30	43
Filing method			
Used paid tax preparer	66	66	67
Filed by mail	10	11	7
Filed by computer or phone	8	9	3
Used free service to file	4	3	8
Got help from a friend	5	4	9
Other	7	7	6
Type of paid tax preparer used[b]			
National chain	45	40	60
Local firm	22	24	17
Accounting firm	17	19	11
Other	16	17	12
Used preparer and received RAL[c]	38	30	65
Cost of tax preparation with RAL[d] (dollars)	177	171	187
	(10)	(12)	(15)
Cost of tax preparation without RAL[e] (dollars)	112	115	93
	(7)	(8)	(18)
Sample size	938	668	270

Source: Detroit Area Household Financial Services study.

a. Standard errors are in parentheses.

b. Percentages are based on the sample of respondents using paid tax preparers.

c. Percentages are based on respondents using a paid tax preparer to file taxes in 2003 or 2004.

d. Averages are computed for respondents who took out an RAL.

e. Averages are computed for respondents using a paid tax preparer but not taking out an RAL

respondents reflect their socioeconomic disadvantages. About 82 percent of tax filers received a refund, and the average refund was a little over $2,000 among those receiving a refund. Approximately 41 percent of tax filers were aware that they had applied for the EIC, and 33 percent of them report having received it. (We expect that others were simply not aware of the specific provisions connected to the filing of their tax return.)

The DAHFS study confirms administrative data that a large portion of LMI taxpayers use paid preparers: 65 percent of our sample of low- and moderate-income tax filers use a paid preparer to file their returns.[4] About 38 percent of taxpayers using a paid preparer took out a RAL, or "fast refund" product, which translates to 25 percent of all tax filers or 37 percent of all taxpayers receiving a tax refund. Tax preparation services are costly relative to income and refund size among this sample of LMI respondents. On average, RAL users of paid preparers paid $177 for RAL and tax preparation services, which represents 8 percent of the average refund of such households ($2,105). Among those who use paid preparers but do not take RALs, the cost of tax preparation alone is $112, which represents 7 percent of the average refund of these households ($1,595).[5]

Banked and unbanked individuals have different tax-filing experiences, even though, conditional on filing, the two groups are equally likely to receive a tax refund. Banked households are 13 percentage points less likely to file for and receive the EIC than unbanked households. Though banked and unbanked individuals are nearly equally likely to use paid tax preparation services, the latter group is about 20 percentage points more likely to use a national chain, like H&R Block or Jackson Hewitt, rather than a local firm or accountant, to file their taxes. Moreover, unbanked households are twice as likely to take out a RAL. More than 60 percent of unbanked households using a paid preparer took out a RAL, compared with 30 percent of banked households who used paid preparers. These differences persist when controlling for income and employment (results not shown). These results are consistent with the notion that unbanked households are influenced in their decision to take out a RAL because they need to wait much longer than banked households to receive their refund. Typically, the IRS disburses refund checks by mail in four to six weeks of filing one's taxes, which is about one month longer than for banked households filing electronically and using direct deposit. Still, unbanked households make up only 38 percent of RAL users as a whole, suggesting that banked households also use RALs in significant numbers.

Table 9-2 lists reasons that individuals cite for taking out RALs. About 90 percent of RAL recipients state they took out the loan because they wanted the money faster, and most of these correlate highly with the nearly 80 percent of households who say they took out a RAL to pay their bills or other debt faster. That is, they borrowed to pay down other debt. While the annual percentage rate of a RAL is an order of magnitude higher than the interest rates for most (if not

---

4. According to IRS data (on file with the authors), in tax year 2003, in Macomb, Oakland, and Wayne Counties, 72.3 percent of EIC filers paid for preparation services; 38.0 percent of EIC filers received a RAL; and 52.5 percent of EIC filers who used a paid preparer received a RAL.

5. During survey development, respondents were not able to distinguish the amount that they paid to tax preparers for tax preparation as distinct from the cost of RALs, so the final questionnaire asks about combined costs. The DAHFS study reports the total cost for tax preparation and RALs; this chapter later imputes separate costs.

Table 9-2. *Reasons for Obtaining an RAL, by Banked Status*[a]
Percent

Characteristic	All	Banked	Unbanked
Wanted refund sooner			
Very important	55	54	56
Somewhat important	33	30	37
Not at all important	13	16	7
Needed to pay tax preparer			
Very important	16	14	19
Somewhat important	31	28	35
Not at all important	53	58	46
Wanted to pay bills faster			
Very important	60	51	73
Somewhat important	17	18	17
Not at all important	23	31	1
Wanted to be sure about getting the refund			
Very important	32	27	39
Somewhat important	24	28	18
Not at all important	44	45	43
Other reason	11	10	13
Sample size	156	95	61

Source: Detroit Area Household Financial Services study.

a. Conditional on receiving a refund anticipation loan (RAL). Respondents are banked if they responded yes to having a checking account, a savings account, an account with a debit card but no checks, or any other account held at a bank, savings and loan, or credit union. Unbanked respondents responded no to having any of these types of accounts.

all) types of consumer credit, RAL takers may face other costs on outstanding debt (such as late fees).[6] These other costs would have to be quite high, however, to justify taking out a RAL to pay down outstanding debt. Interestingly, to the extent that these individuals are paying down debt, they are in effect borrowing money in order to increase net savings. In addition, some 56 percent of households take out a RAL because they want certainty about getting their refund. Nearly half of respondents report that an important reason for taking out a RAL is simply to pay the tax preparer for tax preparation and filing services. That is, low incomes and liquidity constraints may prevent taxpayers from paying to file in order to receive their large, lump-sum refunds, absent taking out an expensive RAL.

6. For a historical overview of consumer-credit interest rates, see the Federal Reserve Board's G.19 statistical release. Calculations of the dollar-weighted average interest rate on all outstanding nonmortgage debt are available from the authors upon request.

Table 9-3. *Use of Tax Refund by Banked Status and Receipt of RAL*[a]
Percent

Characteristic	All	Banked	Unbanked	Received RAL	No RAL
Received a refund	84	83	87	95	80
Saved all of refund[b]	10	11	5	5	12
Spent all of refund	50	47	60	56	47
Saved some, spent some	41	42	35	39	41
Spent refund on[c]					
Bills or other debt	79	78	82	82	77
Buy appliances	20	16	32	23	18
Buy car	12	10	17	19	9
Pay for education[d]	14	14	13	14	14
Other	39	42	31	41	38
Sample size	938	668	270	159	313

Source: Detroit Area Household Financial Services study.

a. Respondents are banked if they responded yes to having a checking account, a savings account, an account with a debit card but no checks, or any other account held at a bank, savings and loan, or credit union. Unbanked respondents responded no to having any of these types of accounts.

b. Conditional on receiving a refund.

c. Conditional on "spending all" or "spending some and saving some" of the tax refund.

d. Either the respondent's education or the household's children's education.

Individuals without a bank account are somewhat more likely to want the money faster than those with bank accounts. Moreover, unbanked households are 21 percentage points more likely than banked households to state that they used a RAL because they wanted to pay bills or debt faster. This differential potentially reflects the differences in timing of receipt of refund by direct deposit as compared with paper check, as well as other differences other than banked status, including income and asset holdings, factors that require further investigation. Unbanked households are also 12 percentage points more likely than banked households to take out a RAL in order to pay the tax preparer.

For policy purposes, it is important to assess whether there is a propensity among LMI households to save some or all of their refunds. Tax refunds, given the size of the lump sum relative to annual income, play an important role in most low- and moderate-income households' lives. About 84 percent of tax filers, and 60 percent of our sample of low- and moderate-income households, received a tax refund, and the average refund of those receiving one was $2,078. Table 9-3 presents results on how low- and moderate-income households use their refunds. More than 50 percent of low- and moderate-income individuals who received a tax refund indicate that they saved all or a part (10 and 41 percent, respectively) of their tax refunds. Almost half of those receiving tax refunds, however, spent the entirety of their refunds. Yet among those who spent some or all of their refund (90 percent), nearly 80 percent used their refund to pay down bills or other debt. That is, even among the group that spent some or all of their refund, most households indicated that they used the spending to increase net savings by reducing indebtedness (for related work, see Shapiro and Slemrod 1995).

In addition to its use for saving, the lump-sum nature of the tax refund may also make it useful for large-asset purchases in the face of liquidity constraints, or difficulties otherwise constraining consumption to save up for such purchases. About 20 percent of respondents used their refunds to buy appliances, and another 12 percent used their refunds to buy automobiles. Another 14 percent of respondents used their refunds to pay for their own education or their children's education, an important investment in human capital.

The propensity to save some or all of their tax refunds is high among both banked and unbanked individuals. While unbanked households are only half as likely to save all of their tax refunds, 40 percent of unbanked households saved at least some (or all) of their refunds, lower but not dramatically far behind the 53 percent rate for banked households. For both groups, the patterns of spending refunds are roughly similar. That is, among those households who spent some or all of their refunds, nearly 80 percent of both banked and unbanked households state that they used their refunds to pay down bills or other debt. Unbanked households are nearly twice as likely as banked households to have spent their refund to buy appliances (32 compared with 16 percent). For that purpose, saving plans tied to tax refunds may be a way for both of these types of households to save, especially given the difficulty these families have saving during the course of the year.

Table 9-3 also shows how households who do and do not receive RALs spend or save their tax refunds. Filers who took RALs are less than half as likely to save the entirety of their refunds as those who did not use RALs, but 5 percent of them still save all of it, and 44 percent of RAL users save some (or all) of their refund, not dramatically far behind the 53 percent of nonusers who save some (or all) of their refund. Filers who use RALs are 9 percentage points more likely than nonusers to spend all of their refunds (56 compared with 47 percent). Among those who spent some or all of their refund, RAL users and nonusers have similar spending patterns. About 80 percent of both groups spend some of their refund to pay down bills or other debt. Filers who receive RALs are 15 percentage points more likely to purchase a durable good, such as an appliance or a car. Given few differences in the use of the refund between RAL takers and nontakers, however, it appears that the receipt of a RAL is not well correlated with how individuals spend the money. That is, households who wait for their tax refunds and those who do not wait spend in similar ways. A comparison of the interest rates on most forms of consumer credit and the average cost of a RAL, measured as an annual percentage rate, suggests that the use of a RAL to pay down other debt is not economically justified for households holding traditional forms of credit.

Table 9-4. *Tax Receipt and Withholding Preferences of LMI Households,*
by Banked Status[a]

Respondent preference	All	Banked	Unbanked
More withheld and bigger refund	35	35	35
Same withheld and same refund	46	48	42
Less withheld and smaller refund	19	17	24
Less withheld and more taxes	6	5	10
Overwithhold	69	71	61
Sample size	938	668	270

Source: Detroit Area Household Financial Services study.

a. Respondents are banked if they responded yes to having a checking account, a savings account, an account with a debit card but no checks, or any other account held at a bank, savings and loan, or credit union. Unbanked respondents responded no to having any of these types of accounts. See text for description and wording of the withholding question administered to tax filers. Respondents "want to overwithhold" if they state they want more overwithholding or want the same amount of withholding while receiving a refund.

There are undoubtedly other costs associated with nonpayment of some debt not fully captured by this view.

Table 9-4 shows that nearly half of LMI taxpayers prefer their current withholding pattern, under which they mostly receive refunds. Holding total tax liability constant, another third would like to have more withheld, further reducing current income in exchange for receiving a larger refund. A much smaller group, about 19 percent, would like less withheld in order to have higher current income. Consistent with behavioral insights about framing, this percentage drops to 6 percent if the respondents are asked whether they would like less withheld in order to have a higher current income, if it means they would owe more in taxes at the end of the year, again, holding total tax liability constant.

Low- and moderate-income households prefer overwithholding, despite having no slack in their daily finances. Overall, 69 percent of households want to overwithhold their income. The preferences of LMI households for overwithholding in order to obtain a lump-sum refund, however, are somewhat at odds with the finding that the sample is, on average, socioeconomically disadvantaged, incurs debt during the year that is paid down with the tax refund, and feels financially insecure during the year (result not shown).[7] Also, households who want less withholding are more likely to experience food insufficiency (19 versus 11 percent) and material hardship (37 versus 28 percent) relative to those households who want the same or more withholding (results not shown). Even

7. More specifically, roughly 72 percent of the sample find it somewhat or very difficult to live on their total household income. During the year preceding the survey, over half of respondents in the sample did not have sufficient income to meet their expenses every month.

among households who prefer the current withholding system, tax refunds are often applied to past debt. It may be the case that such households incur debt knowing that they will be able to pay it back with their tax refund. It may also be possible that such households are aware that they lack self-control and would incur debt even if their incomes were smoother with less withholding; for these households, overwithholding, combined with credit constraints, may keep overall consumption lower. While the withholding system may make it difficult for some LMI households to smooth their consumption, other households may use the withholding system for their financial planning. The withholding system may provide a way to save and build assets without high out-of-pocket expense.[8] Some evidence in the DAHFS study suggests that households may use the withholding system as a precommitment device against overconsumption.[9] In the next chapter we test these propositions further.

Conclusions and Policy Implications

The key findings of this chapter are threefold. First, many low- and moderate-income households are connected to the tax system. Around 73 percent of the individuals in the sample filed tax returns, and 82 percent of those filing received tax refunds. This finding suggests that the tax system is critical to the financial lives of low-income households and may serve as a vehicle to integrate low- and moderate-income households into the financial mainstream.

Second, many LMI households use a paid preparer and take out RALs, often paying high fees. Given the societal goal of rewarding work and redistributing income to lower-income households, optimal income redistribution policy suggests that policymakers should focus on reducing the transaction costs associated with tax filing for low- and moderate-income households. Such steps could include measures to reduce tax complexity for low- and moderate-income filers (see, for example, Holtzblatt and McCubbin 2004; Barr 2004; President's Advisory Panel on Federal Tax Reform 2005). In addition, a series of measures could be undertaken to bring low-income households into the banking system (Barr 2004). Banked households may face less compelling incentives to take out RALs because their refunds can be direct deposited. As a result, they would most likely face fewer liquidity constraints and lower costs for converting the income into

8. Relative to those who want less withholding, individuals who want more withholding are more likely to use their refunds to purchase a car (13 versus 7 percent) or an appliance (24 versus 15 percent). They are also less likely to hold a credit card (42 versus 53 percent), and they have fewer assets.

9. In particular, individuals who want more withholding are more likely to spend some or all of their refunds. They are also more likely to report they would like an option permitting them to receive part of their refund immediately and put part in a savings or investment fund (split refund).

usable form because they would not need to cash the government refund checks. Thus policy initiatives to bring low-income households into the banking system could contribute to optimal income redistribution policy (Barr 2004). In addition, the IRS should work to develop methods to direct deposit tax refunds into accounts or prepaid debit cards for the unbanked (Barr 2007).

Third, the tax-filing process may provide an opportunity to encourage savings. Households in our study prefer to overwithhold. The findings of the study suggest that low- and moderate-income households may find savings plans that are tied to tax refunds (Duflo and others 2005) attractive, particularly those plans that are not focused solely on retirement. Despite the fact that most households in the study have difficulty saving regularly during the course of the year and hold few assets, many respondents save all or part of their refunds, and those who spend them often use the refunds to pay bills or other debt, thereby increasing net savings. A sizable group of respondents also use their tax refunds for lump-sum purchases, such as appliances and automobiles. This evidence suggests that individuals may view the withholding system as a means of short-term saving and as a precommitment device against overconsumption, although alternative explanations based on uncertainty regarding tax liability are highly plausible. We test the precommitment theory further in the next chapter.

References

Barr, Michael S. 2004. "Banking the Poor." *Yale Journal on Regulation* 21:121–238.
———. 2007. "An Inclusive, Progressive National Savings and Financial Services Policy." *Harvard Law & Policy Review* 1:161–84.
Bertrand, Marianne, Sendhil Mullainathan, and Eldar Shafir. 2004. "A Behavioral-Economics View of Poverty." Special issue, *American Economic Review* 94 (May): 419–23 (www.jstor.org/stable/3592921).
Duflo, Esther, and others. 2005. "Saving Incentives for Low- and Middle-Income Families: Evidence from a Field Experiment with H&R Block." Working Paper 11680. Cambridge, Mass.: National Bureau of Economic Research (www.nber.org/papers/w11680).
Finkelstein, Amy. 2007. "EZ-Tax: Tax Salience and Tax Rates." Working Paper 12924. Cambridge, Mass.: National Bureau of Economic Research (www.nber.org/papers/w12924).
Frank, Robert H., and Robert M. Hutchens. 1993. "Wages, Seniority, and the Demand for Rising Consumption Profiles." *Journal of Economic Behavior and Organization* 21:251–76 (doi:10.1016/0167-2681(93)90052-Q).
Friedman, Milton, and Rose Friedman. 1998. *Two Lucky People: Memoirs.* University of Chicago Press.
Holtzblatt, Janet, and Janet McCubbin. 2004. "Issues Affecting Low-Income Filers." In *The Crisis in Tax Administration,* edited by Henry J. Aaron and Joel Slemrod, 148–200. Brookings.
Kopczuk, Woijczek, and Christian Pop-Eleches. 2005. "Electronic Filing, Tax Preparers, and Participation in the Earned Income Tax Credit." Working Paper 11768. Cambridge, Mass.: National Bureau of Economic Research (www.nber.org/papers/w11768).
Loewenstein, George, and Nachum Sicherman. 1991. "Do Workers Prefer Increasing Wage Profiles?" *Journal of Labor Economics* 9:67–84 (www.jstor.org/stable/2535114).

Loewenstein, George, and Richard H. Thaler. 1989. "Anomalies: Intertemporal Choice." *Journal of Economic Perspectives* 3 (Autumn): 181–93 (www.jstor.org/stable/1942918).

Neumark, David. 1995. "Are Rising Earnings Profiles a Forced-Saving Mechanism?" *Economic Journal* 105, no. 428: 95–106 (www.jstor.org/stable/2235321).

President's Advisory Panel on Federal Tax Reform. 2005. *Simple, Fair, and Pro-Growth: Proposals to Fix America's Tax System* (http://govinfo.library.unt.edu/taxreformpanel/final-report/index.html).

Rhine, Sherrie L. W., and others. 2005. *Householder Response to the Earned Income Tax Credit: Path of Sustenance or Road to Asset Building.* Federal Reserve Bank of New York (www.newyorkfed.org/regional/Income_Tax.pdf).

Shapiro, Matthew, and Joel Slemrod. 1995. "Consumer Response to the Timing of Income: Evidence from a Change in Tax Withholding." *American Economic Review* 85:274–83 (www.jstor.org/stable/2118010).

Souleles, Nicholas. 1999. "The Response of Household Consumption to Income Tax Refunds." *American Economic Review* 89:947–58 (www.jstor.org/stable/117166).

Thaler, Richard H. 1990. "Anomalies: Saving, Fungibility, and Mental Accounts." *Journal of Economic Perspectives* 4 (Winter): 193–205 (www.jstor.org/stable/1942841).

Tufano, Peter, Daniel Schneider, and Sondra Beverly. 2005. "Leveraging Tax Refunds to Encourage Savings." Policy Brief 2005-8. Washington: Retirement Security Project (www.brookings.edu/~/media/Files/Projects/retirementsecurity/08_leveraging_tax_refunds.pdf).

10

Paying to Save

MICHAEL S. BARR AND JANE K. DOKKO

I n the United States, the Internal Revenue Service (IRS) collects taxes on earned income by requiring employers to remit a portion of the employees' paychecks as a prepayment of the taxes owed at the end of the year. If the amount prepaid is greater than the taxes owed, then the employee has overwithheld and is entitled to a tax refund in the amount of the difference. Overwithholding occurs at many income levels and is a common phenomenon among low- and moderate-income (LMI) taxpayers. In 2004 over 20 million LMI taxpayers filed for approximately $35 billion in federal tax refunds and reduced tax liability (Internal Revenue Service 2005). Given an average refund of over $1,700 among LMI households, the economic implications of overwithholding are potentially quite large.

Economists typically view overwithholding as welfare reducing and, therefore, undesirable as an individual decision as well as a policy. The withholding system changes the timing of income from what it would be if individuals paid their taxes in a lump-sum fashion at the end of the year. From the perspective of the permanent-income hypothesis, changes in the timing of income alone have no effect on individuals' ability to smooth consumption under an assumption about perfect capital markets. Because the U.S. Treasury does not pay interest on the amount overwithheld, however, overwithholding lowers the present value of lifetime income and makes individuals worse off. It is through this margin that the withholding system is welfare reducing if the permanent-income hypothesis provides an appropriate model of behavior. If, in addition, individuals cannot borrow or are credit constrained, overwithholding exacerbates the liquidity constraints they experience during times of low income on both the extensive and intensive margins, and crowds out precautionary saving. In most economic models, the payment of interest on the amount overwithheld is welfare enhancing, all else being equal.[1]

Whether LMI taxpayers share the canonical view of overwithholding is unclear. On the one hand, many LMI individuals would benefit from having their refund distributed evenly throughout the year, particularly in light of the credit constraints and high-cost borrowing opportunities available to this group. Indeed, many LMI tax filers take out refund anticipation loans (RALs), and pay a nontrivial fee to a tax preparer, in order to expedite the receipt of a tax refund (Barr and Dokko 2006). On the other hand, in experimental and nonexperimental settings, individuals state a preference for increasing consumption profiles to flat or decreasing levels, even when the former correspond to lower present values than the latter (Loewenstein and Thaler 1989; Loewenstein and Sicherman 1991; Frank and Hutchens 1993; Neumark 1995). The explanation for this finding, particularly in the context of tax overwithholding, remains an open question.

One methodological challenge to identifying whether individuals want to overwithhold, and why, has been the lack of appropriate data. Default rules, individuals' inertia, and existing tax administration rules, among other things, militate against interpreting the actual occurrence of overwithholding, given by tax-return data, as evidence that individuals want to overwithhold (Gale 1998). In this chapter, however, we present a measure of taxpayers' "preference for overwithholding" using a unique question administered in the Detroit Area Household Financial Services (DAHFS) study, a data set that we designed and collected through the Survey Research Center at the University of Michigan. This question asks individuals to express whether they want to overwithhold their income in a hypothetical scenario in which they must choose the time profile of how to receive their income and pay their taxes. In a sample of LMI tax filers, 69 percent report that they want to overwithhold their income.

This unique question, combined with a rich set of covariates, allows alternative explanations for individuals' preference for nonsmooth consumption profiles to be systematically addressed. These alternatives include individuals' loss aversion and mental accounting (Kahneman and Tversky 1979; Thaler and Shefrin 1981; Thaler 1990), risk aversion, the possibility of negative personal discount rates (Mishkin 1981; Courant, Gramlich, and Laitner 1984; Loewenstein and Sicherman 1991), status quo bias, and self-control problems related to dynamic

---

1. Technically speaking, if the U.S. Treasury were to pay interest on the amount overwithheld, individuals might not be better off, since higher taxes would finance this endeavor.

inconsistency and the divergence between short- and long-term discount rates (β and δ in Laibson's [1997] notation). We are particularly interested in examining whether individuals overwithhold as a precommitment device against overconsumption. To explore this question, we examine the correlation between individuals' preference for overwithholding and their portfolio allocation across different types of liquid and illiquid financial instruments. The sample of LMI tax filers is separated into five portfolio allocation groups: those with no assets, one liquid asset, one illiquid asset, several but mainly liquid assets, and several but mainly illiquid assets. This portfolio allocation measure proxies for individuals' desire to limit their access to their savings as well as their inability to save. The rich data on tax-filing behaviors and attitudes in the DAHFS data set permit an analysis of whether individuals' loss aversion, mental accounting, status quo bias, risk aversion, and negative personal discount rates are also related to their preference for overwithholding.

We find a correlation between a preference for overwithholding and portfolio allocation choices that is consistent with present-biased preferences and self-control problems. That a large majority of individuals express a preference for overwithholding is not consistent with the permanent-income hypothesis or precautionary behavior. Instead, the DAHFS study indicates that dynamic inconsistency motivates certain types of individuals to use the commitment device of overwithholding to constrain their consumption. Mental accounting and loss aversion explanations are less likely to explain the patterns in our data. Dynamic inconsistency among LMI tax filers has important implications for savings policies and for tax administration at large.

Theoretical Background, Related Literature, and Empirical Strategy

With sufficiently rich data, the myriad explanations for individuals' preference for rising or nonsmooth consumption profiles may be empirically distinguished. Models with present-biased preferences suggest that those seeking to precommit, either to limit overconsumption or to overcome procrastination, will also want to overwithhold. The approach of this chapter is based on existing models that predict a relationship between portfolio allocation and the desire to overwithhold (Laibson 1997; Laibson, Repetto, and Tobacman 1998, 2000; O'Donoghue and Rabin 1999; Angeletos and others 2001). In these studies, individuals have present-biased preferences of the form

$$U_t = E_t\left[u(c_t) + \beta\sum_{\tau=1}^{T-1}[\delta^{\tau} u(c_{t+\tau})]\right],   (10\text{-}1)$$

where $u(\cdot)$ is a twice-differentiable, concave utility function, c_t denotes consumption in period t, $\beta > 0$, and $0 \leq \delta \leq 1$. The parameter β reflects the individual's present-biasedness, and δ is the time-consistent discount factor.[2] Models with present-biased preferences suggest that those seeking to precommit, either to limit overconsumption or to overcome procrastination, will also want to overwithhold (Laibson 1997; Laibson, Repetto, and Tobacman 1998, 2000; O'Donoghue and Rabin 1999; Angeletos and others 2001).

To identify the savers who are seeking to precommit, the study categorizes tax filers into five asset allocation groups: nonsavers, savers with only one liquid asset, savers with only one illiquid asset, savers with multiple but mainly liquid assets, and savers with multiple but mostly illiquid assets. The study shows that this categorization permits an identification of the savers who seemingly limit their access to their savings and those who have difficulty saving (perhaps owing to procrastination). The theoretical prediction of existing models with present-biased preferences is testable by estimating the following relationship:

$$ o_i = \alpha + \sum_g \gamma_g P_{gi} + \varphi f(\mathbf{X}_i) + \varepsilon_i, \tag{10-2} $$

where o_i is an indicator for whether tax filer i expresses a preference for overwithholding, P_{gi} is an indicator for the tax filer's asset allocation group, $\mathbf{X}_i$ is a vector of demographic and socioeconomic controls, $f(\cdot)$ is an arbitrary and flexible function of the control variables, and ε_i represents unobservable characteristics of tax filers that are potentially related to whether they express a preference for overwithholding or to their asset allocation group. The unobservables may include things like financial-planning ability or a bias toward the status quo, to the extent that these are not captured by the proxy measures. The study applies ordinary least squares to uncover the γ_g coefficients, which are simply the regression-adjusted average likelihoods of wanting to overwithhold for the g asset allocation groups. For convenience, the study estimates equation 10-2 with a constant so the γ_g values represent the mean differences with respect to the group with no assets, and the estimate of α yields the percentage who want to overwithhold among those with no assets.

In models of present-biased preferences, the study predicts different magnitudes for the α and γ_g values.[3] In principle, the distribution of individuals across these asset allocation groups represents, among other things, their revealed preference for liquid and illiquid saving, which in turn depends on individuals' time

---

2. As these studies discuss, an attractive feature of formulating the lifetime utility function using the β–δ discount factors is that the dynamically consistent individual is one for whom β is equal to 1. The basis for this type of utility function is that individuals' short-term discount factors are, in laboratory settings, much smaller than their long-term ones.

3. Without making strong assumptions about the magnitudes of short- and long-term discount rates (β and δ in equation 10-1), as well as the nature of the income process, it is difficult to predict an exact magnitude for α or γ_g for the asset allocation groups under the present-biased model.

preference, risk tolerance, and income volatility. In addition, these asset allocation groups may reflect other motivations for saving in one or multiple liquid and
illiquid assets, such as dynamic inconsistency, mental accounts, or loss aversion.

Among the five groups identified, the study predicts different preferences for
overwithholding. Those with mostly liquid assets are expected not to want to
overwithhold if their revealed preferences given by their asset allocation favor
liquidity and they do not reveal difficulty with saving. Nonsavers are expected to
be less likely to precommit to saving. If illiquid savers are more likely to restrain
access to their savings, then the study predicts γ_g to be larger for this group. At
the same time, another group is also likely to want to overwithhold: procrastinators. Procrastinators, by definition, delay saving and thus have difficulty accumulating assets. If procrastinators are more highly concentrated among those with
only one asset, then this group is expected to be more likely to express a preference for overwithholding to counteract their procrastination. In sum, the study
predicts that two groups should express a larger preference for overwithholding:
those with illiquid assets and those with only one asset.

There are numerous challenges in exploiting the relationship between withholding preferences and asset allocation to detect dynamic inconsistency.
There are many other factors related to both asset allocation and wanting to
overwithhold. With the many variables in the DAHFS study's rich data set, we
argue, the independent relationship between asset allocation and the preference
to overwithhold is isolated. These control variables include measures such as
race, education, and other demographic variables as well as employment status,
income, income volatility, having a credit card, and whether the sample member participates "often" in his or her household's financial decisionmaking.
To be explicit, using these control variables does not isolate a causal effect
of portfolio allocation for two reasons. First, the many unobservable (to the
econometrician) determinants of portfolio allocation across liquid and illiquid assets makes specifying $f(\cdot)$, and thus isolating the exogenous variation in
portfolio allocation, particularly difficult. Second, the independent variation in
portfolio allocation, which proxies for a preference for liquidity, is not a well-
identified cause in that it cannot be manipulated in an experimental or quasi-
experimental sense (Holland 1986; Rubin 1986). However for our purposes,
we are not interested in estimating a causal relationship between portfolio allocation and wanting to overwithhold. Rather, ascertaining whether LMI tax
filers' behavior is consistent with models with present-biased preferences rests
on observing a particular correlation between asset allocation and a preference
for overwithholding.

Another important set of control variables includes measures of risk tolerance
and time preference. Previous research emphasizes that these preference parameters may contribute to individuals' choosing rising or nonsmooth consumption
profiles when faced with future uncertainty (Mishkin 1981; Courant, Gramlich,

and Laitner 1984; Loewenstein and Sicherman 1991; Frank and Hutchens 1993; Neumark 1995). If individuals are risk averse and tax liabilities are uncertain, overwithholding provides insurance against owing penalties to the IRS for the underpayment of taxes. Individuals who exhibit behavior consistent with negative discount rates may also want to overwithhold. To the extent that these preference parameters are omitted and are correlated with both portfolio allocation and withholding preferences, estimating equation 10-2 will result in biased estimates of γ_g across the portfolio allocation groups. Hence, finding heterogeneity in γ_g will not be informative of whether tax filers' behavior is consistent with models with present-biased preferences. To avoid this particular problem of inference owing to these omitted variables, the study attempts to control for both risk tolerance and time preference with survey measures also used by Robert Barsky and his colleagues (1997).

The study also explores whether mental accounting explains individuals' desire to overwithhold. An attractive feature of the dynamically inconsistent model with present-biased preferences is that it allows for a mental-accounting framework (Thaler and Shefrin 1981; Thaler 1990). As David Laibson (1997, 1998) shows, windfalls to liquid wealth result in different changes to consumption than do windfalls to illiquid wealth: present-biased individuals splurge more, given changes to liquid wealth. In this "mental-accounting" framework, having a preference for overwithholding may represent a preference for receiving a liquid windfall upon receiving one's refund rather than for using overwithholding as a precommitment device. This distinction is a subtle one, and it is important to recognize that both motives are driven by a self-control problem and the inability to commit to a consumption plan.[4] For this to affect an interpretation of the heterogeneity in the γ_g values as according with dynamically inconsistent behavior, the use of mental accounts must be correlated with the portfolio allocation groups, and the groups that want to overwithhold the most must also be the ones most likely to apply mental-accounting rules. To distinguish these two stories, this chapter presents data on whether tax filers view their refunds as windfall gains and use them to purchase durable goods. If there are similarities in these outcomes across the portfolio allocation groups, then it is less likely that the heterogeneity in overwithholding preferences across the portfolio allocation groups proxies for differences in mental accounting.

---

4. More generally, the mental-accounting framework holds the view that not all sources of income are the same and that different types of windfall gains result in different changes in consumption (Thaler 1990). That is, the mental-accounting framework need not be completely nested within models of dynamic inconsistency. Tax refunds may finance different types of consumption, such as durable goods purchases, if mental accounting plays a role in individuals' decisionmaking. In addition, individuals may be loss averse to the point that they will overwithhold their taxes to avoid having to write a check to the IRS. We defer a detailed discussion of these competing explanations to the next two sections.

Similarly, for loss aversion to color the interpretation of the relationship between portfolio allocation and wanting to overwithhold, the groups that are most likely to want overwithholding must also be the most loss averse. While the study provides no direct measure of loss aversion, the tax filers who are more likely to owe tax liability are identifiable by the size of their refunds. If loss aversion influences tax filers to want to overwithhold, then loss aversion may be manifested more strongly among those with a higher probability of writing a check to the IRS. This group may then express a stronger preference for overwithholding. By studying the behavior of this subsample of tax filers, the importance of loss aversion may be inferred. If, in addition, the relationship between portfolio allocation and wanting to overwithhold remains the same among the tax filers most likely to owe tax liability (as among all filers), then heterogeneity in loss aversion most likely does not explain tax filers' preference for overwithholding.

To examine whether dynamic inconsistency manifests in other contexts, other tax-filing behaviors are related to the portfolio allocation group. Upon filing their taxes, individuals choose how quickly they want to receive their refunds by choosing check, direct deposit, or a refund anticipation loan. They must also confront how to allocate their refunds between consumption and saving (including paying down debt). When choosing how quickly to receive their refunds, present-biased individuals trade off the cost of having cash in hand today (with a RAL) against the value of accessing their money at a future date, which includes both a larger net refund amount and the commitment value of illiquidity. Receiving a RAL provides an opportunity to unravel the commitment of overwithholding; however, present-biased individuals who value commitment may not take a RAL if the costs, which typically are associated with an annual percentage rate ranging from 150 to 500 percent, are too high.[5] Thus the variation in RAL take-up can help us explore whether those who want to overwithhold more are more likely to purchase a RAL. Moreover, once the commitment is undone, present-biased individuals who take out RALs may be more likely to spend their tax refunds than those who do not want to overwithhold.

Data and Sample

All tax filers were asked a question whether they would like $100 more, $100 less, or the same amount withheld each month relative to their current withholding pattern. The study defines the individuals who want to overwithhold their paycheck to be those who want more withholding or those who want to withhold at

5. There may be institutional reasons why present-biased individuals may not take out RALs. For instance, the unbanked are more than twice as likely as the banked to take out a RAL (see chapter 9).

the same level and received a refund in 2003 or 2004.[6] Individuals are assumed to report that they want to overwithhold if and only if they believe it to be welfare enhancing relative to the alternative of not overwithholding (that is, perfectly withholding or underwithholding).

To determine financial (that is, nonhousing, nonauto) portfolio allocation, this chapter examines responses to a series of questions about the types of savings a respondent has. Each sample member was asked whether he or she holds a range of formal (for example, money market) and informal (for example, money orders) assets. Respondents with more than one type of asset were asked a follow-up question to identify their main asset. Based on these responses, including the number and liquidity of their assets, tax filers were classified into nonsavers, savers with only one liquid asset, savers with only one illiquid asset, savers with multiple but mostly liquid assets, and savers with multiple but mostly illiquid assets.[7] Liquid savings instruments include money not in a retirement plan (money market funds, government savings bonds, treasury bonds, certificates of deposit, mutual funds, stocks, bonds), money in a bank account, cash, money orders, checks, jewelry, gold, appliances, electronics, and the contents of a bank safe deposit box.[8] Illiquid instruments are an individual retirement accounts (IRAs), a private retirement annuity account, pension, retirement plan, other tax-advantaged plans, real estate other than a primary residence, a business or farm, cash value in a life insurance policy, or withheld payroll taxes.

The study uses other unique variables from the survey to control for individual-specific characteristics that are correlated with portfolio allocation. Standard theoretical models of portfolio choice and saving behavior point toward income risk, risk aversion, time preference, and the relevance or importance of credit constraints. Income risk or volatility is given by a self-assessment of how much a

6. While it is possible for someone to want to withhold $100 less each month than their current pattern, but still want to overwithhold, the question allows this possibility to be partly ruled out. About half of the respondents who want less withheld receive refunds under $1,200, which means that their hypothetical refund (current refund less $1,200) would be less than or equal to zero. Thus one can infer that they do not want to overwithhold. Among those receiving refunds greater than $1,200, it may be the case that some who would prefer to withhold $100 less each month still want to overwithhold, so to this extent the study has an underestimate of those who would like to overwithhold.

7. Housing and automobiles are excluded when classifying the respondents' assets for three main reasons. First, practically speaking, given the relative value of these physical (versus financial) assets, almost everyone would be an illiquid saver (and there would thus be no variation to exploit). Second, houses and automobiles are different from other financial assets in that they have a substantial consumption value associated with them. Finally, in interpreting the heterogeneity in asset allocation as a revealed preference for liquidity, including housing and automobiles would result in a noisier interpretation.

8. While jewelry, gold, appliances, electronics, and the contents of a bank safe deposit box may not be equally liquid in the sense that there are different transaction costs associated with converting them to cash, the wording of these questions does not permit further refinement.

respondent's month-to-month income fluctuated during the year preceding the survey.[9] The risk tolerance and time preference questions are similar to those in the Health and Retirement Survey and discussed by Robert Barsky and his colleagues (1997). Risk tolerance measures the probabilities at which a respondent is willing to choose a gamble with lifetime income over the certainty of his or her lifetime income. The time preference variables measure whether a respondent would rather pay for a $300 appliance today or a series of higher amounts one year in the future. Barsky and others (1997) provide evidence that the survey measure of risk tolerance identifies individuals in the Health and Retirement Survey who are more likely to engage in risky behaviors.

Results

The results suggest that dynamic inconsistency may best explain the heterogeneity in wanting to overwithhold across portfolio allocation groups. Broadly speaking, individuals express a preference for overwithholding and forced saving through the tax system. The bases for this finding are threefold: First, the types of assets held by those with a greater preference for overwithholding are consistent with the predictions of models with a present-biased individual. Second, this finding is independent of other factors in the standard model that might explain how individuals save and whether they want to overwithhold their income, such as risk tolerance and time preference. Third, other tax-filing behaviors are consistent with dynamic inconsistency, but not as consistent with models of loss aversion or mental accounting.

Asset Allocation Groups

The five asset allocation groups we analyze map to underlying differences in saving behavior and attitudes. As seen in table 10-1, there is substantial variation in the portfolio allocation decisions of LMI tax filers. While some have no financial assets, most have at least one financial asset. In other words, an overwhelming majority of LMI tax filers are able to accumulate at least one type of financial asset. The group with only one illiquid asset is the smallest.[10] Tax filers with more than one but mostly illiquid financial assets make up the largest group.

In table 10-2, LMI tax filers' asset allocation across liquid and illiquid instruments reveals their behavior-constraining motives. Illiquid savers are 11 percentage points more likely than liquid savers to express that they use an illiquid asset to save because they find "it is not so easy to get to" their money. Further-

---

9. While the ideal measure of income risk would be of anticipated future income risk, the best available measure in the DAHFS study pertains to past income volatility.

10. The modal asset is an IRA or other retirement account for this group. It is intriguing that this group has an illiquid asset but not a bank account.

Table 10-1. *Ability to Save*[a]

Percent

	Mostly illiquid assets	Mostly liquid assets	One illiquid asset	One liquid asset	No assets
Expects to face major expense in the next 5–10 years for which currently unable to save	37.5 (3.7)	37.2 (4.6)	34.7 (10.4)	44.5 (6.5)	n.a. n.a.
Income does not cover expenses most or all months	16.1 (2.4)	14.2 (4.3)	14.9 (6.0)	24.3 (4.7)	25.3 (3.7)
In previous year, contributed to savings only "once or twice" or "never"	32.8 (3.8)	29.6 (4.1)	46.5 (11.2)	64.0 (4.4)	n.a. n.a.
Agrees that "it is hard to resist the temptation to spend money"	33.0 (3.8)	35.6 (4.2)	31.7 (7.8)	44.6 (5.0)	n.a. n.a.
Experienced hardships in previous year[b]	40.2 (3.3)	42.6 (4.1)	52.4 (8.2)	44.4 (4.6)	57.2 (4.7)
Sample size	185	180	38	117	130

Source: Detroit Area Household Financial Services study.

a. Standard errors in parentheses. Standard errors are clustered at the segment level. Asset amounts include the value of physical assets but do not include housing or vehicles. Sample includes respondents living in low- and moderate-income census tracts who filed a tax return in 2003 or 2004.

b. Measures of hardship include experiencing a major illness, food insufficiency, eviction, bankruptcy, and having the phone or utilities shut off in the year preceding the survey.

more, illiquid savers are 32 percentage points less likely to express that they use an illiquid asset because they find it "easy to get to" their money. The table illustrates that LMI tax filers use illiquid savings instruments for their constraining, or "lock-box," features.

There is suggestive evidence that portfolio allocation among LMI tax filers uncovers their ability to save. The ability-to-save measures reported in table 10-1

Table 10-2. *"Lock-Box" Saving*[a]

Percent

	Illiquid savers	Liquid savers
"Do you keep your savings in [this place] because you find it helpful that it is not so easy to get your money?"[b]	58.5 (2.6)	47.8 (2.7)
"Do you keep your savings in [this place] because you find it easy to get to your money, if you need to?"[b]	34.9 (3.5)	66.7 (2.7)
Sample size	223	297

Source: Detroit Area Household Financial Services study.

a. Standard errors in parentheses. Sample includes respondents living in low- and moderate-income census tracts who filed a tax return in 2003 or 2004.

b. Asked in reference to the sample member's main (or only) savings instrument. Percentages denote a "yes" response.

potentially reflect individuals' awareness of their tendencies to procrastinate or delay their saving, among other things. Those with mainly illiquid assets or one liquid asset are most unable to save based on their self-assessments. They are most likely to report that they feel unable to save for an anticipated major expense occurring five to ten years in the future. Both of these groups are also most likely to be unable to earn enough income to meet their expenses during most or all months in the year prior to the survey interview. Among those with one asset, the choice of the asset's liquidity need not necessarily reflect a preference for precommitment. That is because within this group, the ability to save overrides a preference for illiquid assets and precommitment. Tax filers with one liquid asset are nearly 20 percentage points more likely not to contribute to their savings than the group with one illiquid asset. Also, the former is over 10 percentage points more likely to agree that it is difficult to resist the temptation to spend money (see table 10-1). For these reasons, in a model with a present-biased individual, this group will be more likely than those with one illiquid asset to want to overwithhold. Furthermore, tax filers with one illiquid asset are almost 10 percentage points more likely to have experienced a hardship in the year preceding the survey interview, which in turn is likely to lower their demand for illiquid savings.[11]

Overwithholding Preferences and Asset Allocation

The top row in table 10-3 displays striking results on LMI individuals' withholding preferences. A large majority, or 69 percent, of LMI individuals would prefer to overwithhold their paychecks and receive a refund rather than underwithhold or withhold the "perfect" amount. In other words, many LMI individuals would like to use the federal withholding system in effect to save in a temporarily illiquid manner. This finding is particularly striking and, at first glance, seemingly inconsistent with the literature characterizing LMI individuals' high discount rates, binding liquidity constraints, and general need and preference for cash on hand (Lewis 1966, 1968; Lawrance 1991; Bertrand, Mullainathan, and Shafir 2004). Given that, on average, LMI tax filers receive a federal refund of around $1,700, they are willing to forgo roughly $45 in interest in order to force themselves to save.[12]

In addition, this finding presents a puzzle for the permanent-income hypothesis, according to which overwithholding is necessarily welfare reducing. If LMI

11. The study also examines behaviors related to self-control, such as gambling, buying lottery tickets, or having a drug- or alcohol-related problem. Unfortunately, there is not enough precision in the data to identify which of the portfolio allocation groups is most or least likely to have these self-control problems. However noisy, the data consistently point to tax filers with mainly illiquid assets or one liquid asset as those most likely to exhibit self-control problems.

12. For the calculations, see the calibration exercise later in this chapter.

Table 10-3. *Withholding Preference, by Portfolio Allocation Group*[a]
Percent

	All	Mostly illiquid assets	Mostly liquid assets	One illiquid asset	One liquid asset	No assets
Prefers to overwithhold paycheck rather than underwith- hold or exactly withhold	0.685 (0.027)	0.761 (0.037)	0.623 (0.048)	0.599 (0.073)	0.713 (0.047)	0.618 (0.045)
Summary statistic			*F* statistic = 3.43, *p* value = 0.013			
Sample size	650	220	145	38	117	130

Source: Detroit Area Household Financial Services study.

a. Standard errors are in parentheses. Sample includes respondents living in low- and moderate-income census tracts who filed a tax return in 2003 or 2004. The *F* statistic and *p* value correspond to a test of equality of the percentages. The *F* statistic is distributed with 4 numerator and 70 denominator degrees of freedom. Standard errors are clustered at the segment level.

tax filers were utility maximizing and making their saving decisions in line with the permanent-income hypothesis, few, if any, would express that they want to save through the tax system. This finding is also inconsistent with precaution- ary motives since individuals are better off accumulating precautionary saving through interest-yielding means, rather than by overwithholding their income. In other words, there are better financial instruments to exploit than overwith- holding one's income in building precautionary savings.

Consistent with models with present-biased preferences, there is heteroge- neity in withholding preferences across different types of portfolio allocation in table 10-3.[13] Notably, 76 percent of tax filers with mainly illiquid assets want to overwithhold, and 71 percent of those with one liquid asset want to do so. Tax filers with mainly illiquid assets are 14 percentage points more likely than those with mainly liquid assets to express a preference for over- withholding. The relationship between the liquidity of the asset portfolio and wanting "lock-box" saving (see table 10-2) supports a finding that, among those with more than one asset, those with a revealed preference for restricting their access to savings are more likely to express a preference for overwithhold- ing. Among those with only one asset, however, we find that the liquidity of assets does not correlate well with wanting to overwithhold. Based on the dis- tribution of responses in table 10-1, individuals with one liquid asset are more

13. The results of an *F* test suggest rejecting the null hypothesis that the percentages are the same across portfolio allocation groups at the 5 percent significance level.

likely to feel they are unable to save, and are more likely to value the forced saving aspect of overwithholding. Among those with one asset, concerns about ability to save outweigh wanting an illiquid asset in explaining preferences for overwithholding.

Standard Theories Explaining Wanting to Overwithhold

The rich data in the DAHFS study permit empirically distinguishing among many competing theories explaining why LMI tax filers want to overwithhold and why, more generally, they prefer rising or nonsmooth consumption and income profiles. We subjected the first-order correlation between portfolio allocation and withholding preferences shown in table 10-3 to alternative explanations for the patterns observed. These results are presented in table 10-4. Generally, the results suggest that rejecting the permanent-income hypothesis, precautionary, and other standard explanations is appropriate.

Under the permanent-income hypothesis and the standard portfolio-choice paradigm, neither illiquid nor liquid savers want to overwithhold, and there is no heterogeneity in this preference across portfolio allocation groups. In each of the specifications in table 10-4, an F test rejects the null hypothesis that the propensity to want to overwithhold is the same across the portfolio allocation groups. Furthermore, columns 2 and 3 support the conclusion that the pattern of withholding preferences is independent of the variation in demographic, economic, and financial characteristics across the portfolio allocation groups. In these columns, demographic, economic, and financial characteristics that may differ across the portfolio allocation groups are controlled for.[14] A cubic in age is included to acknowledge life-cycle heterogeneity in portfolio allocation, along with other demographic variables. Education dummies are used as a proxy for financial savviness. A control is also included for whether the tax filer is employed at the time of the survey interview, which proxies for whether someone has filled out a W-4 form. The inclusion of demographic, economic, and financial characteristics does not change the pattern of withholding preferences across the portfolio allocation groups, and the two groups that are most likely to want overwithholding include those with mainly illiquid assets or with one liquid asset.

Like the permanent-income hypothesis and the standard portfolio-choice model, overwithholding is welfare reducing in models of precautionary saving,

14. Specifically, the demographic controls include a cubic in age, education, number of children, race, sex, and marital status. Employment and financial variables include employment status, an indicator for whether respondent participates "a lot" in the household's financial decisionmaking, an indicator for whether the respondent sees himself or herself as financially secure, an indicator for whether the respondent has a great deal of confidence in the people running banks and financial institutions, an indicator for having a credit card, and an indicator for using a paid tax preparer. The control for income includes a cubic in the household's annual income in 2004.

Table 10-4. Relationship between Withholding Preference and Asset Allocation[a]

				Dependent variable is "wants to overwithhold"				
	(1)	(2)	(3)	(4)	(5)	(6)	(7)	(8)
Mostly illiquid assets	.126***	.136***	.158***	.148***	.129**	.149***	.130**	.131**
	(.044)	(.048)	(.051)	(.055)	(.057)	(.055)	(.056)	(.058)
Mostly liquid assets	.019	.024	.044	.033	.020	.031	.019	.021
	(.055)	(.059)	(.058)	(.060)	(.061)	(.061)	(.061)	(.060)
One illiquid asset	−.051	−.037	−.038	−.053	−.054	−.045	−.047	−.048
	(.083)	(.081)	(.080)	(.078)	(.078)	(.078)	(.077)	(.077)
One liquid asset	.106*	.139**	.140**	.113*	.115*	.096	.099	.100
	(.055)	(.057)	(.056)	(.060)	(.060)	(.063)	(.062)	(.063)
Summary statistic								
F statistic	2.957	3.059	3.187	2.805	2.579	2.641	2.340	2.303
p value	(0.026)	(0.022)	(0.018)	(0.032)	(0.045)	(0.041)	(0.063)	(0.067)
Controls								
Demographics	No	Yes	Yes	Yes	Yes	Yes	Yes	Yes
Employment and financial variables	No	No	Yes	Yes	Yes	Yes	Yes	Yes
Income volatility	No	No	No	Yes	Yes	Yes	Yes	Yes
Household income	No	No	No	No	No	No	Yes	Yes
Risk tolerance	No	No	No	No	No	Yes	Yes	Yes
Time preference	No	No	No	No	No	Yes	Yes	Yes
Ease of borrowing $500	No	No	No	No	No	No	No	Yes
Gets refund	Yes	Yes	Yes	Yes	Yes	Yes	Yes	Yes

Source: Detroit Area Household Financial Services study.

a. Allocation of nonhousing, nonauto assets. Standard errors are in parentheses. Sample includes respondents living in low- and moderate-income census tracts who filed a tax return in 2003 or 2004. The reference group consists of respondents who report they have no assets. Demographic controls include a cubic in age, education, number of children, race sex, and marital status. Employment and financial variables include employment status, an indicator for whether respondent participates "a lot" in the household's financial decisionmaking, an indicator for whether respondents see themselves as financially secure, an indicator for whether the respondent has a great deal of confidence in the people running banks and financial institutions, an indicator for having a credit card, and an indicator for using a paid tax preparer. The control for income includes a cubic in the household's annual income in 2004. All estimates are weighted and obtained from a linear probability model. Standard errors are clustered at the segment level. See text for further descriptions of the variables.

*Statistically significance at the 10 percent level, two-tailed test.
**Statistically significance at the 5 percent level, two-tailed test.
***Statistically significance at the 1 percent level, two-tailed test.

and it is more so for those facing greater income volatility. The results in columns 4 and 5 support the rejection of precautionary explanations for the heterogeneity in wanting to overwithhold across the portfolio allocation groups. Column 4 includes controls for past income volatility. If those with mostly liquid assets face more volatility in income and have a stronger distaste for overwithholding, the differences in withholding preferences should equalize after controlling for income volatility. However, the differences persist and remain statistically significant. A cubic in annual household income distinguishes column 5 from column 4. Income is highly correlated with the number and type of assets a tax filer holds; however, a statistically significant relationship between asset allocation and wanting to overwithhold remains.

Beginning in column 6, measures of risk tolerance and time preference are included as controls. The inclusion of these control variables sheds light on whether the heterogeneity in wanting to overwithhold across the portfolio allocation groups proxies for their differences in risk tolerance and time preference. If, for instance, those with mainly illiquid assets are more risk averse, then they may have a stronger preference for overwithholding to avoid owing taxes and penalties. Alternatively, if those with one liquid asset are more likely to have negative discount rates, then they may want to overwithhold more than the other portfolio allocation groups.[15] Columns 6 to 8 allow these alternative scenarios to be rejected.

Individuals may want to overwithhold if they fear being unable to anticipate the correct amount of their tax liability to perfectly withhold during the year; they may be concerned that they would be unable to pay their tax liability and any penalties for underwithholding at the time of filing their taxes. To address the possibility that this concern drives behavior and attitudes, column 8 includes an indicator for whether it is easy for the tax filer to borrow $500 as a measure of the extent to which liquidity constraints bind, in addition to whether someone has a credit card. In this most saturated model, individuals with mostly illiquid assets remain about 13 percentage points more likely to want to overwithhold, and this difference is significant at the 5 percent level. Individuals with one liquid asset are also 10 percentage points more likely to want to overwithhold, but this difference is barely insignificant at the 10 percent level. This point estimate, however, is similar in magnitude to the one in column 1.

---

15. In addition, controlling for risk tolerance and time preference suggests that portfolio allocation is correlated with wanting to overwithhold above and beyond what is implied by the permanent-income hypothesis. If, for instance, illiquid assets are riskier, then the standard portfolio-choice paradigm suggests that the relationship between asset allocation and withholding preference is driven by risk tolerance, with more-risk-tolerant (that is, less-risk-averse) individuals holding more illiquid assets and wanting to hold more illiquid assets.

We argue that the relationship between an individual's portfolio allocation and withholding preference is consistent with models with present-biased preferences but not with standard explanations. The basis for this claim is threefold. First, a large fraction of the DAHFS survey's low- and moderate-income sample wants to overwithhold, and it is assumed that they would not respond in this manner unless they believed overwithholding to be welfare enhancing (relative to underwithholding or exactly withholding). In models of dynamic inconsistency, overwithholding and restraining one's choice set can be welfare enhancing. Second, the study estimates a cross-sectional relationship between portfolio allocation and withholding preferences that is consistent with models with present-biased preferences. Finally, this estimated relationship is robust to the inclusion of control variables that, under alternative theories, ought to wipe away the relationship between portfolio allocation and withholding preference (see table 10-4).

Other Behavioral-Economics Explanations for Wanting to Overwithhold

Status quo bias, mental accounting, and loss aversion among individuals, rather than their dynamic inconsistency, may potentially explain the observed correlation between their portfolio decisions and their preference for overwithholding. If these alternative explanations are responsible for the greater propensity to want overwithholding among those with mainly illiquid assets and those with one liquid asset, then we should not interpret our findings as based on behavior-constraining motives. However, these alternatives do not appear to explain the patterns observed in the relationship between portfolio allocation and wanting to overwithhold.

Columns 1 to 8 of table 10-4 control for whether the tax filer received a refund in order to address the view that the heterogeneity in receiving a refund explains the variation in wanting to overwithhold. Put differently, using whether the tax filer received a refund as a control variable addresses the view that the status quo shapes individuals' preferences. If individuals who receive refunds do so because they like to overwithhold, and this phenomenon is correlated with portfolio allocation, then the explanation for individuals' preference for overwithholding is likely a result of status quo bias. In each column, it is shown that receiving a refund correlates well with wanting to overwithhold, and on average, those who get a refund are more likely to want to overwithhold than those who do not. However, the differences in withholding preferences and portfolio allocation persist after controlling for whether the respondent receives a refund and are therefore unlikely to be related to differences in the likelihood of refund receipt across the portfolio allocation groups. As individuals with mostly illiquid assets and those with one liquid asset are more likely than those with no assets to express a preference for overwithholding, it follows that dynamically

inconsistent behavior occurs independently of individuals' preference for the
behavioral default.

Table 10-5 addresses whether "mental accounting" and loss aversion are
better explanations than the study's interpretation of the relationship between
wanting excess withholding and portfolio allocation. The results in the first and
second columns support the conclusion that differences in mental accounting are
unlikely to explain the heterogeneity in wanting excess withholding across the
portfolio allocation groups. The first column shows that, conditional on receiving a refund, 28 percent of tax filers report they view their refund as a windfall,
which the study defines as survey respondents' agreeing with the statement, "I

Table 10-5. *Mental-Accounting and Loss-Aversion Explanations for Wanting to*
Overwithhold[a]

Percent unless otherwise noted

	Dependent variable		
	Refund is "windfall"	*Buys durable goods*	*Wants to overwithhold*
All filers	28[b]	33[b]	55
No assets	43[b]	27[b]	62
Mostly illiquid assets	−0.076	0.118*	0.183*
	(0.062)	(0.065)	(0.098)
Mostly liquid assets	−0.003	0.094	0.001
	(0.064)	(0.058)	(0.106)
One illiquid asset	−0.139*	0.113	0.124
	(0.076)	(0.092)	(0.151)
One liquid asset	−0.037	0.097*	0.127
	(0.053)	(0.055)	(0.104)
All controls	Yes	Yes	Yes
Sample	All	All	Refund ≤ $1,200
Sample size	650	650	312

Source: Detroit Area Household Financial Services study.

a. Standard errors in parentheses. Asset amounts do not include housing or vehicles. Sample includes
respondents living in low- and moderate-income census tracts who filed a tax return in 2003 or 2004. The
reference group consists of respondents who report they have no assets. Demographic controls include
a cubic in age, education, number of children, race, sex, and marital status. Employment and financial
variables include employment status, an indicator for whether respondent participates "a lot" in the household's financial decisionmaking, an indicator for whether respondents see themselves as financially secure,
an indicator for whether the respondent has a great deal of confidence in the people running banks and
financial institutions, an indicator for having a credit card, and an indicator for using a paid tax preparer.
The control for income includes a cubic in the household's annual income in 2004. All estimates are
weighted and obtained from a linear probability model. Standard errors are clustered at the segment level.
See text for further descriptions of the variables.

b. This percent is computed among those receiving a refund.

*Statistically significant at the 10 percent level, two-tailed test.

**Statistically significant at the 5 percent level, two-tailed test.

***Statistically significant at the 1 percent level, two-tailed test.

feel like I won the lottery."[16] Overall, relatively few tax filers categorize their tax refunds as lottery earnings.[17] The first column also shows the regression-adjusted differences in viewing a refund as a windfall across the portfolio allocation groups. While those with assets are generally less likely to think of their refund as windfall income than those without assets, there is no statistical difference in this mental-accounting measure across the portfolio allocation groups. Similarly, the likelihood of purchasing a durable good, such as an appliance or car, with a tax refund is not statistically different across the portfolio allocation groups. With both of these mental-accounting measures, the correlations in the data suggest that mental accounting is unlikely to explain the relationship between portfolio allocation and overwithholding preferences.

Given that the average refund size in this sample is large, at roughly $1,700, the loss-aversion explanation for tax filers' preference for overwithholding is not particularly compelling. Individuals need only overwithhold by $1 to avoid having to write a check to the IRS. Table 10-5 provides additional evidence against the loss-aversion explanation. The table's third column reports the relationship between wanting to overwithhold and portfolio allocation among the subsample of tax filers who receive a refund of less than $1,200. Applying this cutoff identifies the tax filers who, by one measure, have the highest probabilities of incurring a tax liability if they were to withhold $100 less each month. Among this subsample of tax filers, 55 percent want to overwithhold; contrary to the loss-aversion prediction, they are less likely to want excess withholding than those receiving larger refunds. That is, this finding suggests an inverse relationship between the likelihood of owing taxes at the time of filing and a preference for overwithholding, which is the opposite of what a model of loss aversion predicts. Furthermore, those with mainly illiquid assets and those with one liquid asset are shown to be the groups most likely to want excess withholding. They are 18 and 13 percentage points, respectively, more likely to want to overwithhold than the group with no assets. These point estimates are well within a standard error of what table 10-4 shows, so the likelihood of owing taxes at the time of filing, and thus loss aversion, does not affect the interpretation of tax filers' preference for overwithholding.[18]

Loss aversion can be an important motivation for some households to prefer overwithholding. Given the importance of framing in influencing individuals'

16. This mental-accounting measure is not exhaustive of the ways individuals may classify income. It may not entirely rule out the possibility that tax refunds are viewed differently from a regular paycheck; however, it does provide evidence whether tax refunds fall in the same mental account as lottery winnings.

17. In addition, few tax filers feel that they are able to buy something frivolous upon receiving their tax refunds (results not shown).

18. The estimated difference in their preference for overwithholding is much larger among the tax filers with one illiquid asset. The standard error on this estimate is so large, however, that it cannot be distinguished from the estimate in table 10-5.

expressed preferences (see Kahneman and Tversky 1979), the survey was designed to include a reframing of the withholding question so as to introduce the concept of loss. In particular, holding total tax liability constant, survey respondents who indicated that they wanted to withhold $100 less each month and have a $1,200 smaller refund at the end of the year were asked whether they would still want to withhold $100 less if they were to owe $1,200 more in taxes at the end of the year. Reframing the question in this way results in a 13 percentage point drop in the portion of tax filers who report that they want to withhold less than they currently do (from 19 to 6 percent). This finding suggests that loss aversion may be an important motivator among those who would otherwise want less withholding. Among those who prefer overwithholding, however, for reasons discussed in the previous paragraph, loss aversion does not appear to explain the relationship between portfolio allocation and their preferences for overwithholding.

Other Tax-Filing Behaviors

Table 10-6 estimates the relationship between portfolio allocation and whether a tax filer spends all of his or her refund. Overall, about half of the tax filers who receive their refunds report they spent all of it (see chapter 9). The table shows the heterogeneity in this estimate by portfolio allocation. Tax filers with mostly liquid assets, who are the least likely to want to overwithhold, are 16 percentage points less likely to spend all of their refund than are the other tax filers. Conversely, the tax filers who are most likely to want to overwithhold are just as likely to spend the entirety of their refund as those with one illiquid asset and those with no assets. Thus when their commitment is undone at the time that they receive their tax refund, the tax filers wanting to constrain their behavior are more likely or equally likely to spend all of their refunds. This finding is robust to a variety of controls.

For most tax filers, "spending" their refund means increasing their net saving by paying down their debt or paying other bills. When these tax filers spend their refunds, on average, 80 percent of them use the money to pay down debt or other bills (see chapter 9). Table 10-7 shows that the mostly liquid tax filers are least likely both to spend the entirety of their refund and to pay debt or other bills. The mostly illiquid tax filers are nearly 10 percentage points more likely to spend all of their refund in order to pay their bills and other debt than the mainly liquid group. Among the tax filers with only one asset, liquid and illiquid groups are equally likely to spend all of their refund to pay their bills and other debt. Overall, those who are more likely to want overwithholding are more or equally likely to spend all of their refunds to pay their bills or debt, despite their desire to precommit.

With this evidence, it is difficult to know whether respondents' consumption would have been different had they not overwithheld. That is, the study does not show whether the forced commitment constrained consumption or led to more

Table 10-6. *Relationship between Spending All of Tax Refund and Asset Allocation*[a]

| | Dependent variable is "spends all" | | | | | | | |
	(1)	(2)	(3)	(4)	(5)	(6)	(7)	(8)
Mostly illiquid assets	-0.118**	-0.078	-0.060	-0.057	-0.059	-0.061	-0.065	-0.070
	(0.057)	(0.072)	(0.070)	(0.071)	(0.071)	(0.069)	(0.070)	(0.070)
Mostly liquid assets	-0.185***	-0.156**	-0.141**	-0.136**	-0.138**	-0.149**	-0.153**	-0.159**
	(0.058)	(0.065)	(0.063)	(0.063)	(0.065)	(0.062)	(0.064)	(0.064)
Has one illiquid asset	0.057	0.066	0.073	0.087	0.087	0.082	0.083	0.084
	(0.092)	(0.095)	(0.092)	(0.091)	(0.092)	(0.092)	(0.094)	(0.094)
Has one liquid asset	-0.039	-0.028	-0.024	-0.018	-0.017	-0.005	-0.004	-0.006
	(0.059)	(0.064)	(0.062)	(0.062)	(0.062)	(0.060)	(0.060)	(0.061)
Summary statistic								
F statistic	3.758	2.743	2.284	2.305	2.163	2.629	2.510	2.686
p value	(0.008)	(0.035)	(0.069)	(0.067)	(0.082)	(0.042)	(0.049)	(0.038)
Controls								
Demographics	No	Yes	Yes	Yes	Yes	Yes	Yes	Yes
Employment and financial variables	No	No	Yes	Yes	Yes	Yes	Yes	Yes
Income volatility	No	No	No	Yes	Yes	Yes	Yes	Yes
Household income	No	No	No	No	No	No	No	Yes
Risk tolerance	No	No	No	No	No	Yes	Yes	Yes
Time preference	No	No	No	No	No	Yes	Yes	Yes
Ease of borrowing $500	No	No	No	No	No	No	No	Yes
Gets refund	Yes	Yes	Yes	Yes	Yes	Yes	Yes	Yes

Source: Detroit Area Household Financial Services study.

a. Allocation of nonhousing, nonauto assets. Standard errors in parentheses. Sample includes respondents living in low- and moderate-income census tracts who filed a tax return in 2003 or 2004. The reference group consists of respondents who report they have no assets. Demographic controls include a cubic in age, education, number of children, race sex, and marital status. Employment and financial variables include employment status, an indicator for whether respondent participates "a lot" in the household's financial decisionmaking, an indicator for whether respondents see themselves as financially secure, an indicator for whether the respondent has a great deal of confidence in the people running banks and financial institutions, an indicator for having a credit card, and an indicator for using a paid tax preparer. The control for income includes a cubic in the household's annual income in 2004. All estimates are weighted and obtained from a linear probability model. Standard errors are clustered at the segment level. See text for further descriptions of the variables.

*Statistically significant at the 10 percent level, two-tailed test.
**Statistically significant at the 5 percent level, two-tailed test.
***Statistically significant at the 1 percent level, two-tailed test.

Table 10-7. *Relationship between Paying Debt (and Spending All of Refund) and Asset Allocation*[a]

	(1)	(2)	(3)	(4)	(5)	(6)	(7)	(8)
					Dependent variable is *"pays debt"*			
Mostly illiquid assets	−0.144***	−0.108	−0.100	−0.096	−0.107*	−0.094	−0.107	−0.108
	(0.055)	(0.066)	(0.065)	(0.065)	(0.065)	(0.065)	(0.066)	(0.066)
Mostly liquid assets	−0.216***	−0.192***	−0.182***	−0.177***	−0.186***	−0.185***	−0.196***	−0.198***
	(0.052)	(0.060)	(0.057)	(0.055)	(0.057)	(0.055)	(0.057)	(0.057)
Has one illiquid asset	0.026	0.029	0.026	0.039	0.041	0.048	0.050	0.050
	(0.093)	(0.096)	(0.097)	(0.095)	(0.096)	(0.095)	(0.096)	(0.096)
Has one liquid asset	−0.033	−0.021	−0.021	−0.016	−0.014	−0.004	0	−0.001
	(0.058)	(0.060)	(0.058)	(0.056)	(0.057)	(0.054)	(0.055)	(0.055)
Summary statistic								
F statistic	6.274	4.637	4.067	3.948	3.935	4.704	4.799	4.836
p value	(0)	(0.002)	(0.005)	(0.006)	(0.006)	(0.002)	(0.002)	(0.002)
Controls								
Demographics	No	Yes	Yes	Yes	Yes	Yes	Yes	Yes
Employment and financial variables	No	No	Yes	Yes	Yes	Yes	Yes	Yes
Income volatility	No	No	No	Yes	Yes	No	No	Yes
Household income	No	No	No	No	No	No	Yes	Yes
Risk tolerance	No	No	No	No	No	Yes	Yes	Yes
Time preference	No	No	No	No	No	Yes	Yes	Yes
Ease of borrowing $500	No	No	No	No	No	No	No	Yes
Gets refund	Yes	Yes	Yes	Yes	Yes	Yes	Yes	Yes

Source: Detroit Area Household Financial Services study.

a. Allocation of nonhousing, nonauto assets. Standard errors in parentheses. Sample includes respondents living in low- and moderate-income census tracts who filed a tax return in 2003 or 2004. The reference group consists of respondents who report they have no assets. Demographic controls include a cubic in age, education, number of children, race sex, and marital status. Employment and financial variables include employment status, an indicator for whether respondent participates "a lot" in the household's financial decisionmaking, an indicator for whether respondents see themselves as financially secure, an indicator for whether the respondent has a great deal of confidence in the people running banks and financial institutions, an indicator for having a credit card, and an indicator for using a paid tax preparer. The control for income includes a cubic in the household's annual income in 2004. All estimates are weighted and obtained from a linear probability model. Standard errors are clustered at the segment level. See text for further descriptions of the variables.

*Statistically significant at the 10 percent level, two-tailed test.

**Statistically significant at the 5 percent level, two-tailed test.

***Statistically significant at the 1 percent level, two-tailed test.

borrowing. It is clear, however, that they spent enough to undo their forced saving, which is consistent with dynamically inconsistent behavior. Furthermore, this behavior is more prevalent among those who are more likely to want overwithholding.

Finally, table 10-8 illustrates the differences in the use of refund anticipation loans by portfolio allocation type. Overall, 38 percent of tax filers took out a RAL, which is correlated with using a paid tax preparer.[19] Interestingly, the two groups least likely to take out a RAL are the ones most likely to want overwithholding: mostly illiquid tax filers are 5 percentage points less likely to take out a RAL than mostly liquid tax filers. Those with one liquid asset are 15 percentage points less likely to take out a RAL than those with one illiquid asset. If the RAL take-up decision were simply one regarding whether to obtain the refund immediately rather than later, this finding would be inconsistent with models with present-biased preferences. Instead, the RAL decision is also about whether to unravel the commitment of overwithholding, at a nontrivial cost.

The tax filers who are most likely to want the commitment to save through overwithholding are, in fact, less likely to pay to undo it. In effect, they choose to wait for the refund rather than paying for a RAL to unravel the commitment. This behavior is consistent with present-biased individuals' valuing a commitment mechanism. Further work is needed to understand whether the RAL decision is driven by additional factors that differ across groups. For example, individuals without bank accounts must wait longer for their refund checks, and those with one illiquid asset may have a more pressing need for liquidity. Thus the institutional and economic benefits of taking out a RAL may be higher for these groups than for those with mainly illiquid assets or with one liquid asset.

Calibration Results

In the DAHFS study, the average refund is nearly $1,700, which corresponds to about $45 in forgone interest if the refund were evenly distributed each month rather than dispersed as a lump sum upon filing one's taxes.[20] To assess whether this trade-off is a plausible one given present-biased preferences, the study calibrates a simple model with quasi-hyperbolic discounting. The goals of the calibration exercise are threefold: first, to estimate the optimal level of overwithholding using values of β and δ found in the experimental literature (Ainslie 1992; Laibson, Repetto, and Tobacman 1998; Angeletos and others 2001; Frederick, Loewenstein, and O'Donoghue 2002; Shapiro 2005); second, for the optimal level of overwithholding, to find the associated willingness to pay

---

19. One of the control variables in table 10-8 is the likelihood of using a paid preparer, so the heterogeneity is probably not driven by differences in the use of a paid tax preparer.

20. This forgone interest is 2.8 percent of the amount overwithheld at a 5 percent interest rate, plausibly available at the relevant time period, and that is compounded monthly.

Table 10-8. Relationship between Taking a Refund Anticipation Loan and Asset Allocation[a]

				Dependent variable is "takes RAL"				
	(1)	(2)	(3)	(4)	(5)	(6)	(7)	(8)
Mostly illiquid assets	-0.182***	-0.187***	-0.118**	-0.122**	-0.116**	-0.124**	-0.117**	-0.113**
	(0.046)	(0.053)	(0.053)	(0.055)	(0.055)	(0.051)	(0.052)	(0.053)
Mostly liquid assets	-0.132**	-0.124**	-0.052	-0.055	-0.044	-0.067	-0.055	-0.049
	(0.055)	(0.055)	(0.052)	(0.055)	(0.056)	(0.052)	(0.052)	(0.055)
One illiquid asset	0.044	0.017	-0.015	-0.017	-0.017	-0.012	-0.011	-0.012
	(0.090)	(0.085)	(0.083)	(0.088)	(0.090)	(0.086)	(0.088)	(0.087)
One liquid asset	-0.211***	-0.187***	-0.162***	-0.162***	-0.165***	-0.168***	-0.171***	-0.169***
	(0.050)	(0.047)	(0.045)	(0.048)	(0.048)	(0.048)	(0.049)	(0.049)
Summary statistic								
F statistic	8.538	8.032	4.874	4.656	4.827	5.018	4.955	4.964
p value	(0)	(0)	(0.002)	(0.002)	(0.002)	(0.001)	(0.001)	(0.001)
Controls								
Demographics	No	Yes	Yes	Yes	Yes	Yes	Yes	Yes
Employment and financial variables	No	No	Yes	Yes	Yes	Yes	Yes	Yes
Income volatility	No	No	No	Yes	Yes	Yes	Yes	Yes
Household income	No	No	No	No	Yes	No	Yes	Yes
Risk tolerance	No	No	No	No	No	Yes	Yes	Yes
Time preference	No	No	No	No	No	Yes	Yes	Yes
Ease of borrowing $500	No	No	No	No	No	No	No	Yes
Gets refund	Yes	Yes	Yes	Yes	Yes	Yes	Yes	Yes

Source: Detroit Area Household Financial Services study.

a. Allocation of nonhousing, nonauto assets. Standard errors in parentheses. Sample includes respondents living in low- and moderate-income census tracts who filed a tax return in 2003 or 2004. The reference group consists of respondents who report they have no assets. Demographic controls include a cubic in age, education, number of children, race sex, and marital status. Employment and financial variables include employment status, an indicator for whether respondent participates "a lot" in the household's financial decisionmaking, an indicator for whether respondents see themselves as financially secure, an indicator for whether the respondent has a great deal of confidence in the people running banks and financial institutions, an indicator for having a credit card, and an indicator for using a paid tax preparer. The control for income includes a cubic in the household's annual income in 2004. All estimates are weighted and obtained from a linear probability model. Standard errors are clustered at the segment level. See text for further descriptions of the variables.

*Statistically significant at the 10 percent level, two-tailed test.

**Statistically significant at the 5 percent level, two-tailed test.

***Statistically significant at the 1 percent level, two-tailed test.

for the commitment mechanism; third, to find values of β and δ such that over-withholding $1,700 leaves a dynamically inconsistent individual at least weakly better off than if the individual were to perfectly withhold his or her taxes.[21]

The results of the calibration derive from a utility-maximization problem with the preferences in equation 10-1 and with perfect capital markets. An individual chooses consumption in each month subject to an annual budget constraint. For a given level of annual income, overwithholding reduces the amount of cash on hand available in months one to eleven and shifts the cash on hand to month twelve. With an isoelastic, intraperiod utility function,

$$u(c_t) = \frac{c_t^{1-\rho}}{1-\rho},$$

log-utility arises when $\rho = 1$. We use 0.996 as the value for δ and 0.958 as the value for β (Laibson, Repetto, and Tobacman 1998; Laibson 1997, 1998).[22] During the year, an individual has access to all of his or her annual income (cash on hand), except the amount overwithheld, which becomes available in the last period. In this highly stylized environment, with these parameter values for β and δ, this income process, and ρ equal to 1, an individual with an annual after-tax income of $24,000 finds $183 as the optimal level of overwithholding.[23] This individual is willing to pay $8, which is 4.4 percent of the optimal amount of overwithholding or 0.03 percent of his or her annual income, to have a commitment mechanism, relative to the outcome without overwithholding.

For an overwithholding amount of $1,700 to leave a quasi-hyperbolic dis-counter better off, the individual would need to be extremely present biased, with β equal to 0.81 and δ equal to 0.996. This monthly value for β corresponds to an annualized short-term discount factor of 0.08, which is outside the range usually accepted in the literature (Ainslie 1992; Frederick, Loewenstein, and O'Donoghue 2002). Furthermore, for more reasonable values of β, an individual's annual income must be quite high if $1,700 of overwithholding were to leave him or her (weakly) better off.

The calibration results suggest that the optimal level of overwithholding is low and that overwithholding by $1,700 is excessive. That is, this amount is unlikely to be the result of a utility-maximizing decision in a highly stylized environment in which there are no costs (pecuniary or otherwise) to changing

21. The precise details of the calibration exercise are available upon request. Generally, the study adapts the solution method in Shapiro (2005).

22. The calibration takes the month as the unit of time, and these parameter values correspond to annualized values of δ and β of approximately 0.95 and 0.60, respectively, which correspond to commonly used values in the literature.

23. Indeed, with isoelastic utility, the optimal amount of overwithholding is a constant fraction of an individual's annual income.

one's withholding pattern. In practice, there are significant costs to changing one's withholding pattern to match one's preference for the timing of income, such as tax administration rules and employer costs. In addition, the calibration exercise assumes that quasi-hyperbolic discounting is the sole reason for wanting a commitment mechanism against overconsumption, when in fact multiple motives are most likely behind this preference. For example, while our results suggest that status quo bias, mental accounting, and loss aversion do not drive the correlation between overwithholding and portfolio allocation, these factors may contribute to our understanding of overwithholding. The results of the calibration exercise suggest that while present-biasedness can explain the heterogeneity in wanting to overwithhold in the DAHFS study, it cannot explain the level of withholding.

Conclusion and Policy Implications

Looking at a unique measure of individuals' preference for overwithholding, the DAHFS study uncovers a manifestation of the self-control problems low- and moderate-income individuals confront when making their consumption and saving decisions. A large majority of LMI tax filers want excess withholding, in spite of the canonical view that it is welfare reducing. And wanting to overwithhold correlates with portfolio allocation across liquid and illiquid assets. Tax filers with one liquid asset or mainly illiquid assets are between 10 and 13 percentage points, respectively, more likely than other groups to want to overwithhold. This finding suggests that tax filers seek a precommitment device against the tendency to overconsume, as well as that the withholding system enables procrastinators to save. These results are consistent with the behavior of present-biased individuals who are dynamically inconsistent and seek commitment devices.

Low- and moderate-income individuals' preferences for overwithholding relate to dynamic inconsistency independent of the mental accounts that individuals form or to their loss aversion and distaste for owing tax liability. When individuals' behavior is dynamically inconsistent, they value precommitment mechanisms, which suggests that illiquid savings plans tied to tax refunds may provide an opportunity for LMI individuals to build assets (Barr 2004; Duflo and others 2005). In addition, other types of illiquid savings plans that are not focused solely on retirement may elicit higher take-up among LMI individuals. Individuals' behavior in the presence of mental-accounting rules and loss aversion also suggests tying savings plans to tax refunds, but knowing that individuals are dynamically inconsistent highlights the importance of making these accounts illiquid (Thaler 1994). Because the calibration results suggest that the optimal level of overwithholding is quite low relative to the size of the average refund, it remains an open question as to whether excessive overwithholding ought to be a desirable policy goal.

Researchers have argued that increasing withholding without altering tax liabilities may provide a way to encourage saving (Thaler 1994). Dynamic inconsistency combined with a plethora of high-cost borrowing opportunities somewhat qualify this view. Although forced saving in an illiquid asset is valued by dynamically inconsistent individuals, this welfare improvement should be weighed against the temptation of high-cost borrowing opportunities such as payday loans, credit cards with high interest and fees, and refund anticipation loans.[24] Indeed, excessively large amounts of overwithholding may exacerbate dynamically inconsistent individuals' tendencies to incur high-cost debt. Additional research incorporating a dynamic structural model and simulations is necessary to better understand these trade-offs.

In addition to leading individuals to value precommitment devices, dynamic inconsistency also results in procrastination. We argue that tax filers with one liquid asset want to overwithhold more than other tax filers because of their relative inability to save. To the extent that procrastination contributes to an inability to save, providing LMI individuals with a simple menu of savings opportunities to lower the cognitive cost of saving may encourage this behavior. This simplicity necessarily entails demystifying the fee structure and minimum-balance requirements, among other features, of savings and transaction accounts (Barr 2004).

That tax filers want to overwithhold means they are willing to pay in order to save. Given an average refund of $1,700, a LMI tax filer is willing to forgo $45 in interest in order to save in a temporarily illiquid asset and to restrict the availability of consumption opportunities. Aside from valuing present consumption more than consumption in the near future, there may be unobservable reasons why LMI individuals face pressures to consume more today. For example, LMI individuals often have others around them asking for financial help. In the Detroit study, 56 percent of respondents report lending money to family or friends in the previous 12 months (results not shown). Given the study's finding that LMI individuals are willing to put away their money where neither they nor those around them can access it, it would be useful to quantitatively distinguish this basis for present-biased preferences from the more traditional view.

References

Ainslie, George. 1992. *Picoeconomics: The Strategic Interaction of Successive Motivational States within the Person.* Cambridge University Press.
Angeletos, George-Marios, and others. 2001. "The Hyperbolic Consumption Model: Calibration, Simulation, and Empirical Evaluation." *Journal of Economic Perspectives* 15 (Summer): 47–68 (www.jstor.org/stable/2696556).

24. The refund anticipation loan delivers an amount based on an estimate of one's tax refund.

Barr, Michael S. 2004. "Banking the Poor." *Yale Journal on Regulation* 21:121–237.

Barr, Michael S., and Jane K. Dokko. 2006. "Tax Filing Experiences and Withholding Preferences among Low- and Moderate-Income Households: Preliminary Evidence from a New Survey." In *Recent Research on Tax Administration and Compliance: Selected Papers Given at the 2006 IRS Research Conference,* 195–213. Internal Revenue Service.

Barsky, Robert B., and others. 1997. "Preference Parameters and Behavioral Heterogeneity: An Experimental Approach in the Health and Retirement Study." *Quarterly Journal of Economics* 112:537–79 (www.jstor.org/stable/2951245).

Bertrand, Marianne, Sendhil Mullainathan, and Eldar Shafir. 2004. "A Behavioral-Economics View of Poverty." Special issue, *American Economic Review* 94 (May): 419–23 (www.jstor.org/stable/3592921).

Courant, Paul N., Edward M. Gramlich, and John P. Laitner. 1984. "A Dynamic Micro Estimate of the Life-Cycle Model." In *Retirement and Economic Behavior,* edited by Henry J. Aaron and Gary T. Burtless, 279–314. Brookings.

Duflo, Esther, and others. 2005. "Saving Incentives for Low- and Middle-Income Families: Evidence from a Field Experiment with H&R Block." Working Paper 11680. Cambridge, Mass.: National Bureau of Economic Research (www.nber.org/papers/w11680).

Frank, Robert H., and Robert M. Hutchens. 1993. "Wages, Seniority, and the Demand for Rising Consumption Profiles." *Journal of Economic Behavior and Organization* 21:251–76 (doi:10.1016/0167-2681(93)90052-Q).

Frederick, Shane, George Loewenstein, and Ted O'Donoghue. 2002. "Time Discounting and Time Preference: A Critical Review." *Journal of Economic Literature* 40:351–401 (www.jstor.org/stable/2698382).

Gale, William G. 1998. Comment on "Self-Control and Saving for Retirement," by David I. Laibson, Andrea Repetto, and Jeremy Tobacman. *BPEA,* no. 1: 177–85 (www.jstor.org/stable/2534671).

Holland, Paul W. 1986. "Statistics and Causal Inference." *Journal of the American Statistical Association* 81, no. 396: 945–60 (www.jstor.org/stable/2289064).

Internal Revenue Service. 2005. "Statistics of Income" (www.irs.gov/taxstats/index.html).

Kahneman, Daniel, and Amos Tversky. 1979. "Prospect Theory: An Analysis of Decision under Risk." *Econometrica* 47:263–291 (www.jstor.org/stable/1914185).

Laibson, David. 1997. "Golden Eggs and Hyperbolic Discounting." *Quarterly Journal of Economics* 112:443–77 (www.jstor.org/stable/2951242).

———. 1998. "Life-Cycle Consumption and Hyperbolic Discount Functions." *European Economic Review* 42:861–71 (doi:10.1016/S0014-2921(97)00132-3).

Laibson, David I., Andrea Repetto, and Jeremy Tobacman. 1998. "Self-Control and Saving for Retirement." *BPEA,* no. 1: 91–196 (www.jstor.org/stable/2534671).

———. 2000. "A Debt Puzzle." Working Paper 7879. Cambridge, Mass.: National Bureau of Economic Research (www.nber.org/papers/w7879).

Lawrance, Emily C. 1991. "Poverty and the Rate of Time Preference: Evidence from Panel Data." *Journal of Political Economy* 99:54–77 (www.jstor.org/stable/2937712).

Lewis, Oscar. 1966. *La Vida: A Puerto Rican Family in the Culture of Poverty; San Juan and New York.* Random House.

———. 1968. "The Culture of Poverty." In *On Understanding Poverty: Perspectives from the Social Sciences,* edited by Daniel P. Moynihan, 187–220. New York: Basic Books.

Loewenstein, George, and Nachum Sicherman. 1991. "Do Workers Prefer Increasing Wage Profiles?" *Journal of Labor Economics* 9:67–84 (www.jstor.org/stable/2535114).

Loewenstein, George, and Richard H. Thaler. 1989. "Anomalies: Intertemporal Choice." *Journal of Economic Perspectives* 3 (Autumn): 181–93 (www.jstor.org/stable/1942918).

Mishkin, Frederick S. 1981. "The Real Interest Rate: An Empirical Investigation." *Carnegie-Rochester Conference Series on Public Policy* 15:151–200 (doi:10.1016/0167-2231(81)90022-1).

Neumark, David. 1995. "Are Rising Earnings Profiles a Forced-Saving Mechanism?" *Economic Journal* 105, no. 428: 95–106 (www.jstor.org/stable/2235321).

O'Donoghue, Ted, and Matthew Rabin. 1999. "Doing It Now or Later." *American Economic Review* 89:103–24 (www.jstor.org/stable/116981).

Rubin, Donald B. 1986. "Which Ifs Have Causal Answers." Comment on "Statistics and Causal Inference," by Paul W. Holland. *Journal of the American Statistical Association* 81:961–62 (www.jstor.org/stable/2289065).

Shapiro, Jesse M. 2005. "Is There a Daily Discount Rate? Evidence from the Food Stamp Nutrition Cycle." *Journal of Public Economics* 89:303–25 (doi:10.1016/j.jpubeco.2004.05.003).

Thaler, Richard H. 1990. "Anomalies: Saving, Fungibility, and Mental Accounts." *Journal of Economic Perspectives* 4 (Winter): 193–205 (www.jstor.org/stable/1942841).

———. 1994. "Psychology and Savings Policies." *American Economic Review* 84, no. 2: 186–92 (www.jstor.org/stable/2117826).

Thaler, Richard H., and H. M. Shefrin. 1981. "An Economic Theory of Self-Control." *Journal of Political Economy* 89:392–406 (www.jstor.org/stable/1833317).

11

Behaviorally Informed Regulation

MICHAEL S. BARR, SENDHIL MULLAINATHAN,
AND ELDAR SHAFIR

Policymakers typically approach human behavior through the perspective
of the "rational-agent" model, which relies on normative, a priori analyses.
The model assumes that people make insightful, well-planned, highly controlled,
and perfectly calculating decisions guided by considerations of personal utility.
This perspective is promoted in the social sciences and in professional schools
and has come to dominate much of the formulation and conduct of policy. An
alternative view, developed mostly through empirical behavioral research, and
the one we articulate here, provides a substantially different perspective on individual behavior and its policy implications. According to this empirical perspective, behavior is an amalgam of human perceptions, impulses, judgments, and
decision processes. Actual human behavior, it is argued, is often unforeseen
and misunderstood by classical policy thinking. A more nuanced behavioral
perspective, it is suggested, can yield deeper understanding and improved regulatory insight.

For a motivating example, consider the recent mortgage crisis in the United
States. While the potential causes are myriad, a central problem was that many
people were offered and took out loans that they did not understand and could
not afford, with disastrous results for borrowers, financial firms, and the national
economy. Aspects of borrowing behavior are not captured in important ways
by the rational-agent model. At the same time, we argue, a behavioral policy
perspective that focuses only on the individual is incomplete. In some contexts,
firms have strong incentives to exploit, or to overcome, consumer biases. Thus

policy also needs to account for market context and the incentive and behaviors of firms. Moreover, firms will shape their conduct in response not only to the behavior of consumers and markets but also to the actions of regulators.

On Behavior

In contrast with the classical theory, which posits rational agents who make well-informed, carefully considered, and fully controlled choices, behavioral research has shown that individuals depart from this decisionmaking model in important ways. The availability and dissemination of data do not always lead to effective communication and knowledge; understanding and intention do not necessarily lead to the desired action; and purportedly inconsequential contextual nuances, whether intentional or not, can shape behavior and alter choices, often in ways that people themselves agree diminish their well-being in unintended ways. Individuals often exhibit temporal biases and misforecast their own behavior. By way of illustration only, we highlight how context, decisional conflict, mental accounting, knowledge and attention constraints, and institutions shape individual decisionmaking and behavior.

Context

Human behavior turns out to be heavily context dependent, a function of both the person and the situation. One of the major lessons of modern psychological research is the impressive power that the situation exerts, along with a persistent tendency to underestimate that power relative to the presumed influence of intention, education, or personality traits. In his now-classic obedience studies, for example, Stanley Milgram (1974) shows how decidedly mild situational pressures suffice to generate persistent willingness, against their own wishes, on the part of individuals to administer what they believe to be grave levels of electric shock to innocent subjects. Context is made all the more important because individuals' predictions about their behavior in the future are often made in contexts different from those in which they later find themselves. Derek Koehler and Connie Poon (2005; see also Lewin 1951) argue that people's predictions of their future behavior overweigh the strength of their current intentions and underweigh contextual factors that influence the likelihood that those intentions will translate into action. This can generate systematically misguided plans among consumers, who, reassured by their good intentions, proceed to put themselves in ill-conceived situations that are powerful enough to make them act and choose otherwise. The powerful impact of context on behavior, we argue, increases the importance of effective regulation and regulators' responsibility to assess effectiveness in particular contexts.

Decisional Conflict

Three decades of behavioral research have led to the realization that people's preferences are typically constructed, not merely revealed, during the decision-making process (Lichtenstein and Slovic 2006). The construction of preferences is heavily influenced by the nature and the context of decision. For example, the classical view of decisionmaking does not anticipate the implications of the conflict that people experience when making decisions. Each option, according to the classical view, is assigned a subjective value, or "utility," and the person then proceeds to choose the option assigned the highest utility. A direct consequence of this account is that offering more alternatives is always a good thing, since the more options there are, the more likely is the consumer to find one that proves most attractive.

In contrast to this model, behavioral research suggests that, since preferences tend to be constructed in the context of decision, choices often prove difficult to make. People often search for a compelling rationale for choosing one option over another. Whereas sometimes a compelling reason can be articulated, at other times no easy rationale presents itself, rendering the conflict between options hard to resolve. Such conflict can lead to the postponing of decisions or to the passive selection of a "default" option and can generate preference patterns that are fundamentally different from those predicted by accounts based on value maximization. In particular, the addition of options can excessively complicate (and thus "worsen") the offered set, while the normative assumption of rational choice is that added options only make things better (Iyengar and Lepper 2000; Shafir, Simonson, and Tversky 1993; Tversky and Shafir 1992).

Marianne Bertrand and colleagues (2010) conducted a field experiment with a local lender in South Africa to assess the relative importance of various subtle psychological manipulations in the decision to take up a loan offer. Clients were sent letters offering large, short-term loans at randomly assigned interest rates. In addition, several psychological features on the offer letter were also independently randomized, one of which was the number of sample loans shown: the offer letters displayed either one example of a loan size and term, along with monthly repayments, or four such examples. In contrast with standard economic prediction and in line with conflict-based predictions, higher take-up was observed under the one-option description than under the multiple-options version. The magnitude of this effect was large: relative to the multiple-options version, the single-option description had the same positive effect on take-up as dropping the monthly interest on these loans by more than 2 percentage points.

Mental Accounting

In their intuitive mental-accounting schemes, people compartmentalize wealth and spending into distinct budget categories, such as savings, rent, and entertainment, and into separate mental accounts, such as current income, assets, and future income (Thaler 1985, 1992). Contrary to standard fungibility assumptions, people exhibit different degrees of willingness to spend from their diverse accounts. Compartmentalization can serve useful functions in managing one's behavior, but it also can yield consumption patterns that are overly dependent on current income and sensitive to labels, which can lead to saving (at low interest rates) and borrowing (at higher rates) at the same time (Ausubel 1991).

An understanding of such proclivities may help firms design instruments that bring about more desirable outcomes. For instance, with respect to retirement saving, the tendency to spend one's savings is lower when monies are not in transaction accounts. Faulty planning, distraction, and procrastination all account for the persistent findings that saving works best as a default. Participation in 401(k) plans is significantly higher when employers offer automatic enrollment (Madrian and Shea 2001), and because participants tend to retain the default contribution rates, and have an easier time committing now to a costly step in the future, savings can be increased as a result of agreeing to increased deductions from future raises (Thaler and Benartzi 2004).

Knowledge and Attention

Standard theory assumes that consumers are attentive and knowledgeable and typically able to gauge and avail themselves of important information. In contrast, research suggests that many individuals lack knowledge of relevant options, program rules, benefits, and opportunities, and not only among the poor or the uneducated. Surveys show that less than one-fifth of investors (in stocks, bonds, funds, or other securities) can be considered financially literate (Alexander, Jones, and Nigro 1998), and similar findings describe the understanding shown by pension-plan participants (Schultz 1995). Indeed, even older beneficiaries often do not know what kind of pension they are set to receive or what mix of stocks and bonds are held in their retirement accounts (Lusardi, Mitchell, and Curto 2009).

The amount of information people can and do attend to is limited. Moreover, cognitive load has been shown to affect performance in everyday tasks. To the extent that consumers find themselves in challenging situations that are unfamiliar, distracting, or tense, all of which consume cognitive resources, less focused attention will be available to process the information that is relevant to the decision at hand. This, in turn, can render decisionmaking even more dependent on situational cues and peripheral considerations. These factors are likely to prove even more so for "low-literate" participants, who tend to experience even greater difficulties with the trade-offs between effort and accuracy, show overdependence on peripheral cues, and tend toward a systematic withdrawal from many market interactions (Adkins and Ozanne 2005).

Information cannot be equated with knowledge, and knowledge cannot be equated with behavior. People often do not fully process data that are imminently available because of limitations in attention, understanding, or perceived relevance, misremembering, or misforecasting one's own behavior. This is often underappreciated by program designers, who tend to believe that people will know what is important and knowable. In summary, for participants with limited cognitive resources, whose decisions are heavily dependent on insufficient knowledge, perceived norms, automatic defaults, and other minor contextual nuances, regulation merits even greater attention to these factors.

The Power of Institutions

The substantial influence of context on behavior implies, among other things, that institutions will come to play a central role in shaping how people think and what they do. By institutions, we mean formal laws and rules, firms and other organizations, structures and governments, and widespread market practices (see, for example, Sherraden and Barr 2005). Among other things, institutions shape defaults, the "favored" starting point. It is now well established that defaults can have a profound influence on the outcomes of individual choices. Data available on decisions ranging from retirement savings to organ donation illustrate the substantial increase in market share when a particular choice is made the default option (Johnson and Goldstein 2003; Johnson and others 1993). Contrary to a view that default is just one of a number of alternatives, in reality defaults persist. This persistence stems not only from confusion about available options, procrastination, forgetting, inertia, and other sources of inaction but may also be fostered by the perception that default is the most popular option (often a self-fulfilling prophesy), implicitly recommended by experts, or endorsed by the government.

Institutions also shape behavior. For example, many low-income families are, in fact, savers, whether or not they resort to banks, but the availability of institutions to help foster saving matters (Barr 2004; Berry 2004). Moreover, without the help of a financial institution, their savings are at risk (including from theft, impulse spending, and the needs of other household members), will grow more slowly, and may not be readily available as an emergency cushion or to support access to reasonably priced credit in times of need. Institutions provide safety and control. In circumstances of momentary need, temptation, distraction, or limited self-control, those savers who are unbanked are likely to find it all the more difficult to succeed on the path to long-term financial stability.

Consider, for example, two individuals with no access to credit cards: one person has a bank account and has his or her paycheck directly deposited into a savings account; the other person is unbanked and receives a paper check and cashes it. Whereas cash is not readily available to the first person, who needs to take active steps to withdraw it, cash is immediately available to the second, who must take active measures to save it. The greater tendency to spend cash in the wallet compared with funds deposited in the bank (Thaler 1999) suggests that the banked person will spend less on impulse and save more easily than the person who is unbanked. Holding risk- and saving-related propensities constant, the first person is likely to end up a more active and efficient saver than the second.

Direct deposit is an institution that can have a profound effect on saving and is increasing in usage (American Payroll Association 2002). The employers of the poor, in contrast, often do not require nor propose electronic salary payments. Instead, they prefer not to offer direct deposit to hourly employees, temporary or seasonal employees, part-timers, union employees, and employees in remote locations, all categories that correlate with low-paying jobs. The most frequently stated reasons for not offering direct deposit to these employees include lack of processing time to meet standard industry (Automated Clearing House) requirements, high turnover, and union contract restrictions. All this constitutes a missed opportunity to offer access to direct deposit to needy individuals, whose default often consists of going after hours to cash their modest checks for a hefty fee.

Furthermore, institutions provide implicit planning. Credit-card companies send customers timely reminders of due payments, and clients can elect to have their utility bills automatically charged, allowing them to avoid late fees if occasionally they do not get around to paying in time. The low-income buyer, on the other hand, without the credit card, the automatic billing, or the web-based reminders, risks missed payments, late fees, and disconnected utilities (followed by high reconnection charges). A behavioral analysis yields new appreciation for the impact of institutions, which affect people's lives, for example, by easing their planning, helping them transform their intentions into actions, or enabling their resistance to temptation.

Low-income households have little or no slack (Mullainathan and Shafir 2009). They cannot readily cut back consumption in the face of an unanticipated need or shock. When they do cut back, it is often on essentials. In many instances, cutting back means paying late, and paying late means incurring costly late fees, utility or phone reconnection fees (Edin and Lein 1997), and serious disruptions to work, education, and family life. In other cases it means costly short-term borrowing to avoid those consequences. In principle, the lack of slack should provide a strong incentive to low-income households to increase their buffer-stock savings to cope with their more volatile environment. Yet such households tend to have negligible liquid savings, in part because the financial system makes it difficult for them to get access to savings vehicles (Barr 2004).

Financial services may provide an important pathway out of poverty by mitigating income or expense shocks and facilitating saving and borrowing. Access to financial institutions allows people to improve their planning by keeping money out of temptation's way. Direct deposit and automatic deductions can remove the immediate availability of cash and put in place automatic planning. Financial institutions can make it easy for individuals to make infrequent, carefully considered financial-accounting decisions that can prove resistant to later intuitive error or to momentary mental-accounting impulses. In this sense, improving financial institutions can have a disproportionate impact on the lives of the poor. Moving from a payday lender and a check casher to a bank with direct deposit and payroll deduction can have benefits in improved planning, saving, and other outcomes far more important than the transaction cost saved.

Behavior, Markets, and Policy: A Conceptual Framework

A behavioral perspective allows one to account better for how individuals make decisions and is thus a useful corrective to the rational-agent model. Yet a model focused on individuals is, on its own, incomplete as a basis for policy. The perspective outlined above needs to be embedded in the logic of markets. A framework is required that takes into account firms' incentives with respect to individual behavior, as well as to regulation. This perspective produces two dimensions to consider: firm interactions with consumers and firm interactions with regulators.

First, the psychological biases of individuals can be either aligned with or opposed to the interest of firms that market products or services to them. Consider a consumer who does not fully understand the profound effects of the compounding of interest. Such a bias would lead the individual both to undersave and to overborrow. The individual would prefer not to have such a bias in both contexts. Firms would prefer that the individual not have the bias to undersave, so that funds intended for investment and fee generation would not diminish (abstracting from fee structures), but, at least over the short term, firms would be perfectly content to see the same individual overborrow (abstracting from collection costs).

Second, the market response to individual failure can profoundly affect regulation. In attempting to boost participation in 401(k) retirement plans, for example, the regulator faces at worst indifferent and at best positively inclined employers and financial firms.[1] With respect to credit, by contrast, firms often have strong incentives to exacerbate psychological biases by hiding borrowing costs. Regulation in this case faces a much more difficult challenge than in the savings situation. In forcing disclosure of hidden prices of credit, the regulator

---

1. In addition to encouraging savings, employers seek to boost employee retention and must comply with federal pension rules designed to ensure that plans are not "top heavy." We acknowledge that there are significant compliance issues regarding pensions and retirement plans, disclosure failures, fee churning and complicated and costly fee structures, and conflicts of interest in plan management as well as problems with encouraging employers to sign up low-wage workers for retirement plans. Yet as a comparative matter, market incentives to overcome psychological biases in order to encourage saving are more aligned with optimal social policy than are market incentives to exacerbate psychological biases to encourage borrowing.

often faces noncooperative firms, whose interests are to find ways to work around or undo interventions.

The mode of regulation chosen should take account of this interaction between firms and individuals and between firms and regulators. One might think of the regulator as holding two different levers, which we describe as changing the rules and changing the scoring.[2] When forcing disclosure of the annual percentage rate, for example, the regulator effectively changes the "rules" of the game—what a firm must say. A stronger form of rule change is product regulation: changing what a firm must do. Behavioral rule changes, such as creating a favored starting position or default, falls between these two types of rules. Rule changes are offered accompanied by scoring changes, but they are conceptually distinct. When imposing liability, the regulator changes the way the game is "scored." Liability levels can be set, in theory, to match (or exceed) the gains to the firm from engaging in the disfavored activity. Scoring can also be changed, for example, by providing tax incentives to engage in the favored activity or by imposing negative tax consequences for engaging in the disfavored activity. Typically, changing the rules of the game (without changing the scoring) maintains the firms' original incentives to help or hurt consumer bias, channeling the incentive into different behaviors by firms or individuals, while changing the scoring of the game can alter those incentives.

Understanding the interaction between individuals, firms, and regulators in particular markets highlights the care that must be taken when transferring insights in behavioral economics from one domain to another. For example, the insights of the most prominent example of behavioral regulation—setting defaults in 401(k) participation—ought not to be mindlessly applied to other markets. Changing the rules on retirement saving (by introducing defaults) works well because employers' incentives align with regulatory efforts to guide individual choice. Employers are either unaffected or may even be hurt by individuals' propensity to undersave in 401(k) plans.[3] They thus will not lean against an attempt to fix that problem. In other applications, where firms' incentives misalign with regulatory intent, changing the rules alone through defaults may not work since firms have strong incentives to work creatively around those rule changes. Interestingly, such circumstances may lead to regulations, such as "changing the scoring" with liability, that, though motivated by behavioral considerations, are not themselves particularly

2. We use this bimodal framework of regulatory choice to simplify the exploration of how our model of individual psychology and firm incentives affects regulation. We acknowledge that the regulatory choice matrix is more complex (see Barr 2005).

3. This is largely because of the existing regulatory framework: pension regulation gives employers incentives to enroll lower-income individuals in 401(k) programs. Absent this, it is likely that firms would be happy to discourage enrollment since they often must pay the match for these individuals. This suggests that defaults in savings work because some other regulation "changed the scoring" of the game.

Table 11-1. *Consumer Bias and Market Response*

Bias	Market is neutral toward or wants to overcome consumer fallibility	Market exploits consumer fallibility
Consumers misunderstand compounding	Consumers misunderstand compounding in savings →Banks would like to reduce misunderstanding to increase savings base	Consumers misunderstand compounding in borrowing →Banks would like to exploit misunderstanding to increase borrowing
Consumers procrastinate	Consumers procrastinate in signing up for earned-income tax credit →Tax filing companies would like to reduce procrastination to increase number of customers	Consumers procrastinate in returning rebates →Retailers would like to exploit procrastination to increase revenues

psychological in nature. That is, given market responses, rules based on trying to influence individual psychology through defaults may be too weak, and changes in liability rules or other measures may prove necessary.

This distinction in market responses to individual psychology is central to our framework and is illustrated in table 11-1. In some cases, the market is either neutral toward or wants to overcome consumer fallibility. In other cases, the market would like to exploit or exaggerate consumer fallibility. Thus when consumers misunderstand compounding of interest in the context of saving, banks have incentives to reduce this misunderstanding so that they can increase their deposits. When consumers misunderstand compounding in the context of borrowing, lenders may not have a strong incentive to remove this misunderstanding because they may be able to induce consumers to overborrow in ways that maintain or enhance profitability, at least over market-relevant time horizons.[4] When consumers procrastinate in signing up for the earned-income tax credit (and hence in filing for taxes), private tax preparation firms have incentives to help remove this procrastination so as to increase their customer base. When consumers procrastinate in returning rebates (but make retail purchases as if they are going to get a rebate), retailers benefit. Note the parallelism in these examples: firm incentives to alleviate or exploit a bias are not an intrinsic feature of the bias itself. Instead, they are a function of how the bias plays itself out in the particular market structure.

In our conceptual approach to the issue of regulatory choice, the regulator can either change the rules of the game or change the scoring of the game (see table 11-2). Setting a default in a 401(k) savings plan whose enrollment is top heavy with high-paid executives is an example of changing the rules of

4. This example abstracts from collection costs (which would reduce firm incentives to hide borrowing costs) and instead focuses on the short-term behavior generally exhibited by firms, as in the recent home-mortgage crisis.

Table 11-2. *Changing the Game*

Rules	Set the defaults in 401(k) savings Opt-out rule for organ donation
Scoring	Penalties for 401(k) enrollment top heavy with high-salary employees Grants to states that enroll organ donors

the game, as would be disclosure regulation and opt-out rules for organ donation. Specifically, the rules of the game are changed when there is an attempt
to change the nature of interactions between firms and individuals, as when the
regulation attempts to affect what can be said, offered, or done. Changing the
scoring of the game, by contrast, changes the payoffs a firm will receive for
particular outcomes. This may be done without a particular rule about how
the outcome is to be achieved. Pension regulation that penalizes firms whose
high-income employees are overrepresented in plan enrollments is an example
of how scoring gives firms incentives to enroll low-income individuals without
setting particular rules on how this is done. Changing rules and changing scoring
often accompany each other, but they are conceptually distinct.

Table 11-3 weaves these approaches together, illustrating our conceptual
framework for behaviorally informed regulation. The table shows how regulatory
choice may be analyzed according to the market's stance toward human fallibility.
On the left side of the table, market incentives align reasonably well with the goal
of overcoming consumer fallibility, and society's goal is to overcome that bias
as well. Rules in that context may have a relatively lighter touch: for example,
using automatic savings plans as a default in retirement saving or providing for
licensing and registration to ensure that standard practices are followed. Similarly,
scoring on the left side of the chart might involve tax incentives to reduce the
costs to firms of engaging in behaviors that align well with their marketing interests, and the public interest, but are too costly. On the right side of the table,
by contrast, market incentives are largely misaligned with the public interest in

Table 11-3. *Behaviorally Informed Regulation*

Regulation	Market neutral or wants to overcome consumer fallibility	Market exploits consumer fallibility
Changing rules	Public education on saving Direct deposit, auto-save Licensing	Sticky defaults (opt-out mortgage or credit card) Information de-biasing (payoff time and cost for credit cards)
Changing scoring	Tax incentives for savings vehicles Direct-deposit tax refund accounts	Ex post liability standard for truth in lending Broker duty of care and changing compensation practices (yield spread premiums)

overcoming consumer fallibility. In that context, rule changes will most likely need to be more substantial to be effective and may need to be combined with changing the scoring.

The discussion that follows illustrates the challenge to policies in the top right-hand corner of table 11-3. Changing the rules of the game alone will often be insufficient when firms are highly motivated to find ways to work around those rules. As such, setting a default alone—by contrast to defaults deployed in markets on the left side of the table—will most likely not work. Thus when we suggest opt-out policies in mortgages below, the challenge will be to find ways to make these starting positions "sticky" so that firms do not simply undo their default nature. In our judgment, achieving an effective default requires separating low-road from high-road firms and making it profitable for high-road firms to offer the default product (for a related concept, see Kennedy 2005). For that to work, the default must be sufficiently attractive to consumers and sufficiently profitable for high-road firms to succeed in offering it, and penalties associated with deviations from the default must be sufficiently costly so as to make the default "stick" even in the face of market pressures from low-road firms. It may be that in some credit markets, low-road firms have become so dominant that sticky defaults will be ineffectual. Moreover, achieving such a default is likely to be more costly than making defaults work when market incentives align, not least because the costs associated with the stickiness of the default involve greater deadweight losses, given that there will be higher costs to opt out for those for whom deviating from the default is optimal. These losses would need to be weighed against the losses from the current system, as well as against losses from alternative approaches, such as disclosure or product regulation. Nonetheless, given the considerations noted above, it seems worth exploring whether such sticky defaults can help to transform consumer financial markets.

Sticky defaults are just one of a set of examples we discuss as potential regulatory interventions based on the proposed conceptual framework. As noted above, given market responses to relevant psychological factors in different contexts, regulation may need to take a variety of forms, including some that, while perhaps informed by psychology, are designed not to effect behavioral change but rather to alter the market structure in which relevant choices are made. Given the complexities involved, this chapter's purpose is not to champion specific policies but rather to illustrate how a behaviorally informed regulatory analysis might generate a deeper understanding of the costs and benefits of particular policies.

Behaviorally Informed Financial Regulation

We review a set of ideas to illustrate our conceptual framework in three main areas of consumer finance: home mortgages, credit cards, and bank accounts. We use these three substantive areas to explore how changing the rules and changing the scoring can affect firm behavior in market contexts where firms have incentives to exploit consumer bias (as in credit) and in those where firms have incentives to overcome such biases (as in saving). Our proposals map into different quadrants of table 11-3. In the three years since we first published our work (Barr, Mullainathan, and Shafir 2008), there has been significant progress in implementing a number of these ideas.[5] We therefore also discuss how some of these ideas have been recently implemented in the Credit Card Accountability, Responsibility, and Disclosure (CARD) Act of 2009, the Dodd-Frank Wall Street Reform and Consumer Protection Act, and other policy initiatives. In addition, with the creation of the new Consumer Financial Protection Bureau (CFPB) under the Dodd-Frank Act, there is an opportunity to further learn from behavioral research and to experiment with new approaches.

Behaviorally Informed Home Mortgage Regulation

The financial crisis in the fall of 2008 devastated the U.S. economy and plunged the United States into a recession that shuttered American businesses, led to widespread job losses, and wiped out home values and household savings. The failure of our system of home mortgage regulation was in many ways at the center of these problems, as poorly originated home mortgages fed the financial system during the boom and helped it bust. Behaviorally informed home mortgage regulation could, as part of the broad set of reforms being implemented in our financial system, help to reduce the risk of catastrophic financial failure from going forward. Moreover, such regulation holds out the prospect of improving outcomes for individuals. For example, regulators could help to de-bias consumers by providing them with better information about the likely consequences of taking out a particular mortgage loan. Disclosure enforcement could be improved by increasing the potential liability for providing unreasonable disclosures. A "sticky" default could be implemented to focus mortgage borrowing on straightforward products. And the incentive structure facing brokers and lenders could be reformed.

De-biasing Borrowers

With the advent of nationwide credit-reporting systems and refinement of credit scoring, creditors and brokers know information about borrowers that borrowers do not necessarily know about themselves, including not just their credit scores but also their likely performance regarding a particular set of loan products. Creditors will know whether a borrower could qualify for a better, cheaper loan,

---

5. In the interests of full disclosure, one of us (Barr) was the assistant secretary of the treasury for financial institutions in 2009–10 and led the effort to put in place a number of these reforms in the CARD Act, the Dodd-Frank Act, and other Treasury initiatives.

as well as the likelihood that the borrower will meet his or her obligations under the existing mortgage or become delinquent, refinance, default, or go into foreclosure. Yet lenders are not required to reveal this information to borrowers. At the same time, the lack of disclosure of such information is most likely exacerbated by consumer beliefs. A consumer might believe the following: "Creditors reveal all information about me and the loan products I am qualified to receive. Brokers work for me in finding me the best loan for my purposes, and lenders offer me the best loans for which I qualify. I must be qualified for the loan I have been offered, or the lender would not have validated the choice by offering me the loan. Because I am qualified for the loan that must mean that the lender thinks that I can repay the loan. Why else would the lender loan me the money? Moreover, the government tightly regulates home mortgages; they make the lender give me all these legal forms. Surely the government must regulate all aspects of this transaction."

In reality, the government does not regulate as the borrower believes, and the lender does not necessarily behave as the borrower hopes. Instead, information is hidden from the borrower, information that, if available, would improve market competition and the borrower's outcomes. Given the consumer's probably false background assumptions and the reality of asymmetric information favoring the lender and broker, we suggest that creditors be required to reveal useful information to the borrower at the time of the mortgage loan offer, including disclosure of the borrower's credit score and the borrower's qualifications for the lender's mortgage products and rates. Creditors could be required to offer information regarding the typical repayment histories for borrowers of this type with this mortgage product. Such an approach corresponds to the disclosure of de-biasing information, in the top right of table 11-3.

The goal of these disclosures would be to put pressure on creditors and brokers to be honest in their dealings with applicants. The information might improve comparison shopping. Of course, revealing such information would also reduce broker and creditor profit margins. But as the classic market competition model relies on full information and assumes rational behavior based on understanding, this proposal attempts to remove market frictions from information failures and to move market competition more toward its ideal. De-biasing consumers would reduce information asymmetry and lead to better competitive outcomes.

Improving Truth in Lending

Optimal disclosure will not occur in all markets through competition alone because in some contexts firms have incentives to hide information about products or prices and consumers may not insist on competition based on transparency because they misforecast their own behavior. Competition under a range of plausible scenarios will not necessarily generate psychologically informative and actionable disclosure. Moreover, even if all firms have an incentive to disclose in meaningful ways, they may not disclose in the same way, undermining the goal of comparison shopping by consumers. If competition does not produce informative disclosure, disclosure regulation might be necessary. That is the basis for the Truth in Lending Act. But simply because disclosure regulation is needed does not mean it will work.

A behavioral perspective could focus in part on improving disclosures themselves. The goal of disclosure should be to improve the quality of information about contract terms in meaningful ways. Simply adding information, for example, is unlikely to work. Disclosure policies are effective to the extent that they present a frame—a way of perceiving the disclosure—that is well understood and conveys salient information that helps the decisionmaker act optimally. It is possible, for example, that information about the failure frequency of particular products might help ("two out of ten borrowers who take this kind of loan default"), but proper framing can be difficult to achieve and to maintain consistently, given that it may vary across situations. Moreover, the attempt to improve decision quality through an improvement in consumer understanding, which is presumed to change the consumer's intentions to act, and finally the consumer's actual actions, is fraught with difficulty. There is often a gap between understanding and intention and between intention and action.

Furthermore, even if meaningful disclosure rules can be created, sellers can generally undermine whatever ex ante disclosure rule is established, in some contexts simply by "complying" with it: "Here's the disclosure form I'm supposed to give you, just sign here." With rules-based ex ante disclosure requirements, the rule is set up first, and the firm (the discloser) moves last. While an ex ante rule provides certainty to creditors and facilitates comparison shopping, whatever gave the discloser incentives to confuse consumers remains in the face of the regulation. While officially complying with the rule, there is market pressure to find other means to avoid the salutary effects on consumer decisions that the disclosure was intended to achieve.

In light of the difficulties of addressing such issues ex ante, we propose that policymakers consider integration of an ex post, standards-based disclosure requirement. In essence, the new Consumer Financial Protection Bureau would determine whether the disclosure would have, under common understanding, effectively communicated the key terms of the mortgage to the typical borrower. This approach could be similar to ex post determinations of reasonableness of disclaimers of warranties in sales contracts under section 2-316 of the Uniform Commercial Code (see White and Summers 2006). This type of policy intervention would correspond to a change in scoring, in the lower right of table 11-3.

In our judgment, an ex post version of truth in lending based on a reasonable-person standard to complement the fixed disclosure rule under TILA might permit innovation—both in products themselves and in disclosure—while minimizing rule evasion. An ex post standard with sufficient teeth could change the incentives of firms to confuse and would be more difficult to evade. Under the current approach, creditors can circumvent TILA by simultaneously complying with its actual terms and at the same time making the required disclosures regarding the terms effectively useless in the context of the borrowing decisions of consumers with limited attention and understanding. The Truth in Lending Act, for example, does not block a creditor from introducing a more salient term ("lower monthly cost!") to compete with the annual percentage rate for borrowers' attention. Under an ex post standards approach, by contrast, lenders could not plead compliance with a TILA rule as a defense. Rather, the question would be one of objective reasonableness: whether the lender meaningfully conveyed the information required for a typical consumer to make a reasonable judgment about the loan. Standards would also lower the cost of specification ex ante. Clarity of contract is hard to specify ex ante but easier to verify ex post. Over time, through agency action, guidance, model disclosures, no-action letters, and court decisions, the parameters of the reasonableness standard would become known and predictable.

There would be significant costs to such an approach, especially at first. Enforcement would impose direct costs, and the uncertainty surrounding enforcement might deter innovation in the development of mortgage products. The additional costs of compliance might reduce lenders' willingness to develop new mortgage products designed to reach lower-income or minority borrowers who might not be served by the firms' plain-vanilla products.[6] The lack of clear rules might also increase consumer confusion regarding how to compare innovative mortgage products with one another, even while it increases consumer understanding of the particular mortgage products being offered. Even if the advantages of TILA for mortgage comparisons are coupled with the advantages of an ex post standard in promoting clarity, the net result may be greater confusion with respect to cross-loan comparisons. That is, if consumer confusion results mostly from firm obfuscation, then our proposal will quite likely help a good deal. But if consumer confusion in this context results mostly from market complexity in product innovation, then the proposal is unlikely to make a major difference, and other approaches focused on loan comparisons might be warranted (see, for example, Thaler and Sunstein 2008).

Despite the shortcomings of an ex post standard for truth in lending, we believe that such an approach is worth pursuing. To limit the costs associated with our approach, the ex post determination of reasonableness could be significantly confined. For example, the ex post standard might be applied solely by the Consumer Financial Protection Bureau, through supervision, rather than by courts. The ex post exposure might be significantly reduced through ex ante

---

6. Although industry often calls for "principles-based" approaches to regulation, in the course of the Dodd-Frank Act legislative debate, the financial sector strongly resisted this approach.

steps. For example, the bureau might develop safe harbors for reasonable disclosures, issue model disclosures, or use no-action letters to provide certainty to lenders. Moreover, firms might be tasked with conducting regular surveys of borrowers or conducting experimental design research to validate their disclosures; results from the research demonstrating a certain level of consumer understanding might provide a rebuttable presumption of reasonableness or even a safe harbor from challenge.[7] The key is to give the standard sufficient teeth without deterring innovation. The precise contours of liability are not essential to the concept, and weighing the costs and benefits will be required to detail the design for implementation.

Building "Sticky" Opt-Out Mortgages

While the causes of the mortgage crisis are myriad, a central problem was that many borrowers took out loans that they did not understand and could not afford. Brokers and lenders offered loans that looked much less expensive than they really were, because of low initial monthly payments and hidden, costly features. Families commonly make mistakes in taking out home mortgages because they are misled by broker sales tactics, misunderstand the complicated terms and financial trade-offs in mortgages, wrongly forecast their own behavior, and misperceive their risks of borrowing. How many home owners really understand the way the teaser rate, introductory rate, and reset rate relate to the London interbank–offered rate plus some specified margin, or can judge whether the prepayment penalty will offset the gains from the teaser rate?

Improved disclosures might help; however, if market pressures and consumer confusion are sufficiently strong, product regulation might prove more appropriate. For example, by barring prepayment penalties, one could reduce lock-in to bad mortgages; by barring very short-term adjustable-rate mortgages and balloon payments, one could reduce refinance pressure; in both cases, more of the cost of the loan would be pushed into interest rates, and competition could focus on a consistently stated price in the form of the annual percentage rate. Price competition would benefit consumers, who would be more likely to understand the terms on which lenders were competing. Product regulation would also reduce cognitive and emotional pressures related to potentially bad decisionmaking by reducing the number of choices and eliminating loan features that put pressure on borrowers to refinance on bad terms. However, product regulation may stifle beneficial innovation, and there is always the possibility that government may simply get it wrong, prohibiting good products and permitting bad ones.

---

7. Ian Ayres recently suggested to us that the burden might be placed on the plaintiff to use consumer survey data to show that the disclosure was unreasonable, similar to the process used under the Lanham Act for false advertising claims. In individual cases, this might be infeasible, but such an approach might work for claims brought by the Consumer Financial Protection Bureau.

For that reason, we proposed instead a new form of regulation.[8] We proposed that a default be established with increased liability exposure for deviations that harm consumers. For lack of a better term, we call this a "sticky" opt-out mortgage system. A sticky opt-out system would fall, in terms of stringency, between product regulation and disclosure. For reasons we explain below, market forces would likely swamp a pure opt-out regime; that is where the need for stickiness comes in. This approach corresponds to a combination of changing the rules of the game, in the top right of table 11-2, and changing liability rules, at the bottom right of that table.

The proposal is grounded in our equilibrium model of firm incentives and individual psychology. Many borrowers may be unable to compare complex loan products and act optimally for themselves based on such an understanding (see, for example, Ausubel 1991). We thus deploy an opt-out strategy to make it easier for borrowers to choose a standard product and harder for borrowers to choose a product that they are less likely to understand. At the same time, lenders may seek to extract surplus from borrowers because of asymmetric information about future income or default probabilities (see Bond, Musto, and Yilmaz 2005), and, in the short term, lenders and brokers may benefit from selling borrowers loans they cannot afford. Thus a pure default would be undermined by firms, and regulation needs to take account of this market pressure by pushing back.

Lenders would be required to offer eligible borrowers a standard mortgage (or set of mortgages), such as a fixed-rate, self-amortizing thirty-year mortgage loan or a standard adjustable-rate mortgage product, according to reasonable underwriting standards. The precise contours of the standard set of mortgages would be set by regulation. Lenders would be free to charge whatever interest rate they wanted on the loan and, subject to the constraints outlined below, could offer whatever other loan products they wanted outside of the standard package. Borrowers, however, would get the standard mortgage offered, unless they chose to opt out in favor of a nonstandard option offered by the lender, after honest and comprehensible disclosures about the terms and risks of the alternative mortgages. An opt-out mortgage system would mean borrowers would be more likely to get straightforward loans they could understand.

But a plain-vanilla opt-out policy is likely to be inadequate. Unlike the savings context, where market incentives align well with policies to overcome behavioral biases, in the context of credit markets, firms often have an incentive to hide the true costs of borrowing. Given the strong market pressures to deviate from the default offer, we would need to require more than a simple opt-out to make the default sticky enough to make a difference in outcomes. Deviation from the offer would require heightened disclosures and additional legal

8. This proposal was included in the Treasury Department's legislation for the new consumer financial protection bureau but was not included in the final legislation as enacted.

exposure for lenders in order to make the default sticky. Under our plan, lenders would have stronger incentives to provide meaningful disclosures to those whom they convince to opt out, because they would face increased regulatory scrutiny, or increased costs if the loans did not work out.

Future work will need to explore in greater detail the enforcement mechanism. For example, under one potential approach to making the opt-out sticky, if an early default occurs when a borrower opts out, the borrower could raise the lack of reasonable disclosure as a defense to bankruptcy or foreclosure. Using an objective reasonableness standard akin to that used for warranty analysis under the Uniform Commercial Code,[9] if the court determined that the disclosure would not effectively communicate the key terms and risks of the mortgage to the typical borrower, the court could modify the loan contract. Alternatively, the new Consumer Financial Protection Bureau could be authorized to enforce the requirement on a supervisory basis, rather than relying on the courts. The agency would be responsible for supervising the disclosures according to a reasonableness standard and would impose a fine on the lender and order corrective actions if the disclosures were found to be unreasonable. The precise nature of the "stickiness" required and the trade-offs involved in imposing these costs on lenders would need to be explored in greater detail, but in principle, a sticky opt-out policy could effectively leverage the behavioral insight that defaults matter with the industrial organizational insight that certain market incentives work against a pure opt-out policy in many credit markets.

An opt-out mortgage system with stickiness might provide several benefits over current market outcomes. Under the plan, a plain-vanilla set of mortgages would be easier to compare across mortgage offers. Information would be more efficiently transmitted across the market. Consumers would be likely to understand the key terms and features of such standard products better than they would alternative mortgage products. Price competition would more likely be salient once features were standardized. Behaviorally, when alternative products are introduced, the consumer would be made aware that such alternatives represent deviations from the default, helping to anchor consumers in the terms of the default product and providing some basic expectations for what ought to enter into consumer choice. Framing the mortgage choice as one between accepting standard mortgage offers and needing affirmatively to choose a nonstandard product should improve consumer decisionmaking. Creditors will be required to make heightened disclosures about the risks of alternative loan products for the borrower, subject to legal sanction in the event of failure reasonably to disclose such risks; the legal sanctions should deter creditors from making highly unreasonable alternative offers, with hidden and complicated terms. Consumers may be less likely to make significant mistakes. In contrast to a pure product-regulation approach, the

---

9. See discussion above relating to the reasonableness standard for disclosure.

sticky-default approach would allow lenders to continue to develop new kinds of mortgages, but only when they can adequately explain key terms and risks to borrowers.

Moreover, requiring that a default be offered, accompanied by required heightened disclosures and increased legal exposure for deviations, may help to make high-road lending more profitable in relation to low-road lending—at least if deviations resulting in harm are appropriately penalized. If offering an opt-out mortgage product helps to reward high-road firms, the market may shift (back) toward firms that offer home mortgage products that better serve borrowers. For this to work effectively, the default—and the efforts to make the default sticky—would need to enable the consumer easily to distinguish the "good" loan, benefiting both lender and borrower, and which would be offered as the default, from a wide range of "bad" loans.

There will be costs associated with requiring an opt-out home mortgage. For example, the sticky defaults may not be sticky enough to alter outcomes, given market pressures. The default could be undermined, as well, through the firm's incentive structures for loan officers and brokers, which could provide greater rewards for nonstandard loans. Implementation of the measure may be costly, and the disclosure requirement and uncertainty regarding enforcement of the standard might reduce overall access to home mortgage lending. There may be too many cases in which alternative products are optimal, so that the default product is in essence "incorrect" and comes to be seen as such. The default would then matter less over time, and forcing firms and consumers to go through the process of deviating from it would become increasingly just another burden (like existing disclosure paperwork) along the road to getting a home mortgage loan. Low-income, minority, or first-time home owners who have benefited from more flexible underwriting and more innovative mortgage developments might see their access reduced if the standard set of mortgages does not include products suitable to their needs.

One could improve these outcomes in a variety of ways. For example, the opt-out regulation could require that the standard set of mortgages include a thirty-year fixed mortgage, a five-year adjustable rate mortgage, and straightforward mortgages designed to meet the particular needs of first-time, minority, or low-income home owners. One might develop "smart defaults," based on key borrower characteristics, such as income and age. With a handful of key facts, an optimal default might be offered to an individual borrower. The optimal default would consist of a mortgage or set of mortgages that most closely align with the set of mortgages that the typical borrower with that income, age, and education would prefer. For example, a borrower with rising income prospects might appropriately be offered a five-year adjustable rate mortgage. Smart defaults might reduce error costs associated with the proposal and increase the range of mortgages that can be developed to meet the needs of a broad range of borrowers, including lower-income or first-time home owners. At the same time, however, smart defaults may add to consumer confusion. Even if the consumer (with the particular characteristics encompassed by the smart default) only faces one default product, spillover from too many options across the market may make decisionmaking more difficult. Moreover, it may be difficult to design smart defaults consistent with fair lending rules.

Consumer Financial Protection Bureau supervision would help to improve the standard mortgage choice set and to reduce enforcement costs over time. The bureau could be required periodically to review the defaults and to conduct consumer experimental design or survey research to test both the products and the disclosures, so that the disclosures and the default products stay current with updated knowledge of outcomes in the home mortgage market. Indeed, lenders might be required to conduct such research and to disclose the results to the CFPB and the public upon developing a new product and its related disclosures. In addition, the bureau might use the results of the research to provide safe harbors and issue no-action letters for disclosures that are shown to be reasonable. It could conduct ongoing testing of compliance with the opt-out regulations and disclosure requirements. Through these no-action letters, safe harbors, supervision, and other regulatory guidance, the CFPB could develop a body of law that would increase compliance across the diverse financial sectors involved in mortgage lending, while reducing the uncertainty facing lenders from the new opt-out requirement and providing greater freedom for financial innovation.

Restructuring Broker Incentives

One can reduce market incentives to exploit behavioral biases by restructuring brokers' duties to borrowers and reforming broker compensation schemes. Mortgage brokers have dominated the subprime market. Brokers generally have been compensated with yield spread premiums (YSP) for getting borrowers to pay higher rates than those for which the borrower would qualify (Jackson and Burlingame 2007; Guttentag 2000). As shown in the results of the Detroit study presented in chapter 7, borrowers who use mortgage brokers often pay higher points and fees than other borrowers and do not generally get lower interest rates in return. Moreover, African American borrowers pay higher interest rates and are more likely to have prepayment penalties and balloon payments than similar nonblack borrowers.

Brokers cannot be monitored sufficiently by borrowers (see Jackson and Burlingame 2007), and it is doubtful that additional disclosures would help borrowers be better monitors (see, for example, FTC 2007), in part because brokers' disclosures of potential conflicts of interest may paradoxically increase consumer trust (Cain, Lowenstein, and Moore 2005). Thus if brokers are required to tell a borrower that they work in their own interest, not in the interest of the borrower, the borrower's trust in the broker may increase: after all, the broker is being honest! Moreover, evidence from the subprime-mortgage crisis suggests that while in theory creditors and investors have some incentives to monitor brokers, they do not do so effectively.

It is possible to undertake an array of structural changes regarding the broker-borrower relationship. For example, one could directly regulate mortgage brokers through licensing and registration requirements. Recent U.S. legislation, the Secure and Fair Enforcement for Mortgage Licensing (SAFE) Act, now mandates licensing and reporting requirements for brokers. We have also argued that the duties of care that mortgage brokers owe to borrowers should be raised. A higher duty of care would more closely conform to borrower expectations about the role of mortgage brokers in the market. In addition, we have argued for banning yield spread premiums (as has now been enacted in the Dodd-Frank Act). Banning YSPs will likely reduce some broker abuses by eliminating a strong incentive for brokers to seek out higher-cost loans for customers. Even before Dodd-Frank, a number of lenders moved away from YSPs to fixed fees, with some funds held back until the loan has performed well for a period of time, precisely because of broker conflicts of interest in seeking higher YSPs rather than sound loans. Banning yield spread premiums reinforces these high-road practices and protects against a renewed and profitable low-road push for using YSPs to increase market share once stability is restored to mortgage markets. Banning YSPs constitutes a form of scoring change, corresponding to regulation in the bottom right of table 11-3 because it affects the payoff brokers receive for pursuing different mortgage outcomes.

Making Progress under the Dodd-Frank Act

The Dodd-Frank Act fundamentally reforms consumer financial protection policy in the United States. In the mortgage market, the Dodd-Frank Act undertakes a number of steps to regulate the relationship between borrowers and mortgage brokers. For example, the act requires registration and imposes a duty of care on mortgage brokers; bans steering borrowers to higher-cost products; and bans yield spread premiums. It requires that mortgage brokers and lenders assess a borrower's ability to repay based on documented income, taking into account the fully indexed, fully amortizing rate on a mortgage. It prohibits mandatory pre-dispute arbitration clauses. It enhances disclosure requirements. It requires the use of escrow of taxes and insurance for higher-cost loans and improves escrow disclosure for all loans. It provides for consumer protections when creditors use force-placed insurance and makes a number of changes to the Home Ownership and Equity Protection Act to make it more effective.

The Dodd-Frank Act also puts in place two provisions that foster standardization in the products offered to consumers, while permitting innovation beyond such standard products, similar to the approach for "sticky" defaults we suggested. First, it requires risk retention for securitization of mortgage loans but exempts certain qualified residential mortgages. These mortgages are designed to be standard, high-quality mortgage products with straightforward terms and solid underwriting. For loans falling outside this category that are securitized, the securitizer (or the originator) would need to retain capital to back a portion of the risk of the securitization. There would thus be a strong incentive to make qualified residential mortgages. Second, it sets out provisions for "qualified mortgages." These are mortgages as to which the ability-to-pay requirement is deemed to be met. Again, the act sets out an approach to standardization of the terms and underwriting of such mortgages. Lenders making nonqualified mortgages face a larger potential risk of liability in the event that such loans fail.

More fundamentally, the act puts in place a new Consumer Financial Protection Bureau to supervise major financial institutions and to set rules and enforce consumer protections across the market. In addition to its authorities to set rules for and enforce existing consumer financial protection laws, the CFPB has the authority to ban unfair, deceptive, or abusive acts or practices. The bureau can also prescribe rules for disclosures of any consumer financial product. In doing so, it will rely on consumer testing, can issue model disclosures that provide a safe harbor for compliance, and may permit financial institutions to use trial disclosure programs to test out the effectiveness of alternative disclosures to those provided for in the CFPB model form. The bureau is mandated to merge conflicting Real Estate Settlement Procedures Act and TILA mortgage disclosures into a simple form. Consumers are provided with rights to access information about their own product usage in standard, machine-readable formats. Over time, the CFPB may generate research and experimentation that will improve our understanding of consumer financial decisionmaking and in turn will support the bureau's supervision, rule writing, and enforcement.

Behaviorally Informed Credit-Card Regulation

Credit-card companies have fine-tuned product offerings and disclosures in a manner that appears to be systematically designed to prey on common psychological biases—biases that limit consumer ability to make rational choices regarding credit-card borrowing (Bar-Gill 2004). Credit-card companies provided complex disclosures regarding teaser rates, introductory terms, variable-rate cards, penalties, and a host of other matters. Both the terms themselves and the disclosures were confusing to consumers (GAO 2006). Behavioral economics suggests that consumers underestimate how much they will borrow and overestimate their ability to pay their bills in a timely manner; credit-card companies can then price their credit cards and compete on the basis of these fundamental human failings (Bar-Gill 2004). Just over 60 percent of credit-card holders do not pay their bills in full every month (Bucks and others 2009). Moreover, excessive credit-card debt can end in bankruptcy (Mann 2006). Ronald Mann (2007) has argued that credit-card companies seek to keep consumers in a "sweat box" of distressed credit-card debt, paying high fees for as long as possible before finally succumbing to bankruptcy. Behaviorally informed credit-card regulation might improve outcomes for consumers and reduce the negative externalities that result from bankruptcy.

Using Framing and Salience in Disclosures to Encourage Good Credit-Card Behavior

In earlier work, we proposed that Congress require that minimum payment terms be accompanied by clear statements regarding how long it would take, and how much interest would be paid, if the customer's actual balance were paid off only in minimum payments and that card companies state the monthly payment amount that would be required to pay the customer's actual balance in full over some reasonable period of time, as determined by regulation. These tailored disclosures use framing and salience to help consumers, whose intuitions regarding compounding and timing are weak, to make better informed payment choices based on their specific circumstances. Such an approach would correspond to changing the rules in order to de-bias consumers with behaviorally informed information disclosure, in the top right of table 11-2. Although credit-card companies have opposed such ideas in the past, the concept was included in the CARD Act of 2009, and disclosures based on the customer's actual balances have proved not to be overly burdensome.

Disclosures regarding the expected time to pay off actual credit-card balances are designed to provide a salient frame intended to facilitate more optimal behavior. But such disclosures may not be strong enough to matter. The disclosures are geared toward influencing borrowers' intentions to alter their behavior; however, even if the disclosure succeeds in shaping intention, we know that there is often a large gap between intention and action (Buehler, Griffin, and Ross 2002; Koehler and Poon 2005). In fact, borrowers would need to change behavior in the face of strong inertia and marketing by credit-card companies propelling them to make no more than minimum payments—at least during the upswing in an economic cycle. More generally, once enacted, market players opposed to such disclosures would promptly attempt to undermine them with countervailing marketing and other policies. Another cost may occur in the opposite direction: consumers who previously made payments more than the amount required to pay off their bills in the specified time frame may be drawn to pay off their bills more slowly than they did previously. Although it is too early to tell, recent preliminary research by Peter Tufano suggests that the CARD Act may have had a mixed effect—improving outcomes for borrowers who paid more slowly, while perhaps worsening outcomes for those who previously caught up more quickly than suggested by the statement's anchoring on a payoff plan of three years.

Providing a Payment Path

A related approach, geared directly toward shaping behavior rather than influencing intentions, would be to develop an "opt-out payment plan" for credit cards, under which consumers would automatically make the payment necessary to pay off their existing balance over a relatively short period of time unless the customer affirmatively opted out of such a payment plan and chose an alternative payment plan with a longer (or shorter) payment term (Barr 2007).[10] Consumers could opt out and set an alternative payment plan in advance, or could, with some modest friction costs introduced, opt out and change the plan at the time they receive their bill. Such an approach corresponds to changing the rules through opt-out policies, in the top right of table 11-2. The default rules and framing in the payment plan would create expectations about consumer conduct and in any event inertia would cause many households to follow the plan. Increasing such behavior would mean lower rates of interest and fees paid and lower incidence of financial failure. In any event, confronting an optimal payment plan may force card holders to confront the reality of their borrowing, and this may help to alter their borrowing behavior, or their payoff plans.

An opt-out payment plan will impose costs. Most important, as noted above, some consumers who, in the absence of the opt-out payment plan, would have paid off their credit cards much faster than the plan provides, might now follow the slower payment plan offered as the default, thus incurring higher costs from interest and fees, possibly even facing a higher chance of financial failure. Alternatively, some consumers may follow the opt-out payment plan when it is unaffordable for them, consequently reducing necessary current consumption such as medical care or sufficient food, or incurring other costly forms of debt.

Regulating Late Fees and Other Penalties

One problem with the pricing of credit cards is that credit-card firms can charge late and overlimit fees with relative impunity because consumers misforecast their behavior. They typically do not believe ex ante that they will pay such fees. Instead, consumers shop based on other factors, such as annual fees, interest rates, or various reward programs. In principle, firms need to charge late and overlimit fees to the extent that they wish to provide incentives to customers not to pay late or go over their credit-card limits. In practice, given the high fees they charge, credit-card firms are perfectly content to let consumers pay late and go over their card limits, in order to obtain fee revenue from such occurrences.

In earlier work, we proposed changing the scoring of the game (corresponding to a regulatory choice in the bottom right of table 11-2). Under our proposal, firms could deter consumers from paying late or going over their credit-card

---

10. For a related proposal, see Gordon and Douglas (2005) (arguing for opt-out direct debit for credit-card payments).

limits with whatever fees they deemed appropriate, but the bulk of such fees would be placed in a public trust to be used for financial education and assistance to troubled borrowers. Firms would retain a fixed percentage of the fees to pay for their actual costs incurred from late payments or overlimit charges, and for any increased risks of default that such behavior presages. The benefit of such an approach is that it permits firms to deter "bad conduct" by consumers who pay late or go over credit limits but prevents firms from taking advantage of the psychological insight that consumers predictably misforecast their own behavior with respect to paying late and borrowing over their limit. Firm incentives to encourage or charge more than deterrent value and costs for late payments and overlimit borrowing would be removed, while firms would retain incentives appropriately to deter these consumer failures and to cover the firm's costs when they occur.

Despite the benefits, there would of course be costs as well: in particular, the reduced revenue stream to lenders from these fees would mean that other rates and fees would be adjusted to compensate, and there is little reason to believe that the adjustments would be in consumers' favor. Indeed, the new fees might be constructed to be even more difficult for consumers to anticipate and avoid, exploiting the same or different consumer biases. Moreover, it might be difficult for regulators to determine the appropriate level for late and overlimit fees that would be retained by creditors and the portion that would be used for financial education.

Advances in the CARD Act of 2009

The CARD Act of 2009 enacts a number of key changes to the credit-card market that seriously consider behavioral insights and the incentives of firms to exploit consumer failings. For example, it provides for improvements in plain-language disclosures on credit-card agreements. It requires credit-card companies to notify consumers forty-five days in advance of certain major changes to card terms, such as changes in interest rates and fees. The act provides for consumer de-biasing: credit-card disclosures now include information on the time and cost of making only the minimum payment, as well as the time and cost of paying off the balance within three years. Moreover, consumers are provided with monthly and year-to-date figures on interest costs and fees incurred, so that they can more readily compare their anticipated costs with their actual usage patterns. The act requires firms to obtain consumers' consent—an opt-in—for overlimit transactions. It bans practices such as certain retroactive rate hikes on existing balances, late-fee traps (including midday due times, due dates less than twenty-one days after the time of mailing statements, and moving due dates around each month), and double-cycle billing. These practices have in common that consumers cannot readily shape their behavior to avoid the charges; the fees or practices in question are not readily shopped for in making a choice among credit cards; and disclosures are of little help. Given that consumers generally do not understand how payments are allocated across different account balances even after improved disclosures (Federal Reserve Board 2007, 2008), the act requires a consumer's payments above the minimum required to be applied first toward higher-cost balances. In addition, the act takes up our concern with late fees but goes beyond our proposals. Based on the same understanding that consumers do not shop for penalty fees and that they often misforecast their own behavior, it requires that late fees or other penalty fees must be "reasonable and proportionate," as determined by implementing rules; that in any event the fees not be larger than the amount charged that is over the limit or late; and that a late fee or other penalty fee cannot be assessed more than once for the same transaction or event. Furthermore, the act takes steps to make it easier for the market to develop mechanisms for consumer comparison shopping by requiring the public posting to the Federal Reserve of credit-card contracts in machine-readable formats; private firms or nonprofits can develop tools for experts and consumers to use to evaluate these various contracts. The Consumer Financial Protection Bureau will undoubtedly have occasion to review these and other requirements for credit cards in the future.

Increasing Saving by Low- and Moderate-Income Households

We have focused thus far in this chapter on improving outcomes in the credit markets using insights from behavioral economics and industrial organization. Our focus derives from the relative lack of attention to this area in the behavioral literature thus far and to the fact that credit markets most starkly pose a challenge to behavioral approaches that do not pay sufficient heed to the incentives facing firms to exploit consumer biases. Savings is also an area ripe for further attention, since much of the behaviorally informed policy work has thus far focused on using defaults to improve retirement saving. For many low- and moderate-income (LMI) households, however, there is a much greater need to focus on short-term savings options. The government responses required to serve the saving needs of this population are likely to be quite different from those aimed at retirement savings for middle- and upper-income households.

As described in earlier chapters, many low- and moderate-income individuals lack access to the sort of financial services that middle-income families take for granted, such as checking accounts or easily used savings opportunities. High-cost financial services, barriers to savings, lack of insurance, and credit constraints increase the economic challenges faced by LMI families. In the short run, it is often hard for these families to deal with fluctuations in income that occur because of job changes, instability in hours worked, medical illnesses or emergencies, changes in family composition, or myriad other factors that can cause abrupt changes in economic inflows and outflows. At low income levels, small income fluctuations can create serious problems in paying rent, utilities, or other bills. Moreover, the high costs and low utility of the financial transaction services used by many low-income households extract a daily toll on take-home pay. Limited access to mainstream financial services reduces ready opportunities to save and thus limits families' ability to build assets and to save for the future.

In theory, opt-out policies ought to work well here, as in the retirement saving world, in encouraging saving. However, while in general the market pulls in the same direction as policy in encouraging saving, market forces weaken with respect to encouraging saving for low-income households. This is because the administrative costs of collecting small-value deposits are high in relation to banks' potential earnings on the small amounts saved, unless the bank can charge high fees; with sufficiently high fees, however, it is not clear that using a bank account makes economic sense for LMI households. Indeed, the current structure of bank accounts is one of the primary reasons why LMI households do not have them. With respect to transaction accounts, high minimum-balance requirements, high fees for overdraft protection or bounced checks, and delays in check clearance dissuade LMI households from opening or retaining bank accounts. Moreover, banks use the private ChexSystems to screen out households who have had difficulty with accounts in the past. Behaviorally insightful tweaks, while helpful, are unlikely to suffice; rather, we need to devise methods to change the nature of the products being offered and, with them, the behavior of the consumers who open and maintain the accounts.

Proposals in this area pertain to changing the rules and the scoring on the left hand side of table 11-2, where markets may prove neutral to, or even positively inclined toward, the potential overcoming of consumer fallibility. We propose increasing scale and offsetting costs for the private sector, in order to increase saving by low- and moderate-income families, through three options: a new "gold seal" for financial institutions for offering safe and affordable bank accounts; various forms of tax credit, subsidy, or innovation prizes; and a proposal under which Treasury would deposit tax refunds directly into opt-out bank accounts automatically set up at tax time. The proposals are designed to induce firms in the private sector to change their account offerings by offering government inducement to reach scale, as well as to alter consumer behavior through the structure of the accounts offered. In particular, the government seal of approval, tax credit, or subsidy or bundling through direct deposit of tax refunds changes the scoring to firms for offering such products, while the opt-out nature of the proposal and other behavioral tweaks change the starting rules.

One relatively light-touch approach to improving outcomes in this area would be to offer a government "gold seal" for financial institutions that offer safe and affordable bank accounts. While the "gold seal" would not change the costs of the accounts themselves, it might increase the potency of the bank's marketing and thus reduce acquisition costs, or the goodwill generated might improve the bank's image overall and thus contribute to its profitability. Similarly, small prizes for innovation in serving low- and moderate-income customers might heighten attention to the issue and increase investment in research and development in using technology to serve the poor. Grants to local communities and nonprofits may increase outreach and improve the provision of financial education, which in turn would help banks and credit unions reach out to LMI customers.

To overcome the problem of the high fixed costs of offering sensible transaction accounts to low-income individuals with low savings levels, Congress could enact a tax credit for financial institutions for offering safe and affordable bank accounts to LMI households (see Barr 2004, 2007). The tax credit would be on a pay-for-performance basis, with financial institutions able to claim tax credits for a fixed amount per account opened by LMI households. The bank accounts eligible for the tax credit could be structured and priced by the private sector but according to essential terms required by regulation. For example, costly checking accounts with overdraft would be eschewed in favor of low-cost, low-risk accounts. In particular, these accounts would be debit-card based, with no check-writing capability, no overdrafts permitted, and no rejections for a past account failure, in the absence of fraud or other meaningful abuse.

Direct-deposit tax-refund accounts could be used to encourage savings and expanded access to banking services while reducing reliance on costly refund anticipation loans and check-cashing services (see Barr 2004, 2007; Koide 2007). Under the plan, unbanked low-income households who file their tax returns would have their tax refunds deposited directly into a new account. Direct deposit is significantly cheaper and faster than paper checks, both for the government and for taxpayers. Taxpayers could choose to opt out of the system if they did not want to directly deposit their refund, but the expectation is that the accounts would be widely accepted since they would significantly reduce the costs of receiving one's tax refund. By using an opt-out strategy and reaching households at tax time, this approach could help overcome consumer biases to procrastinate in setting up accounts. By reducing the time it takes to receive a refund and permitting a portion of the funds to be used to pay for tax preparation, setting up such accounts could help to reduce the incentives to take out costly refund loans, incentives that are magnified by temporal myopia and misunderstanding regarding the costs of credit. Such accounts would also eliminate the need to use costly check-cashing services for one's tax-refund check. Moreover, the account could continue to be used long past tax time. Households could also use the account just like any other bank account—to receive their income, to save, to pay bills, and the like. And, of course, they could use the accounts to receive their refunds in following years. The private sector account providers would benefit from the government's effectively reducing their acquisition costs for new customers. Such an approach could efficiently bring millions of households into the banking system.

The power of these initiatives could be significantly increased if they were coupled with a series of behaviorally informed efforts to improve take-up of the accounts and savings outcomes for account holders. For example, banks could reach out to employers to encourage direct deposit and automatic savings plans to set up default rules that would increase savings outcomes. With an automatic savings plan, accounts could be structured so that account holders could designate a portion of their paycheck to be deposited into a savings "pocket"; the savings feature would rely on the precommitment device of automatic savings, and funds would be somewhat more difficult to access than those in a regular bank account, in order to make the commitment more likely to stick. To provide necessary access to emergency funds in a more cost-effective manner than usually available to LMI households, the bank account could also include a six-month consumer loan with direct deposit and direct debit, using relationship banking and automated payment systems to provide an alternative to costly payday loans. With direct deposit of income and direct debit of interest and principal due, the loan should be relatively costless to service and relatively low-risk for the bank. With a longer payment period than usual for payday lending, the loan should be more manageable for consumers living paycheck to paycheck and would quite likely lead to less repeated borrowing undertaken to stay current on past payday loans.

The federal government made some progress toward these objectives over the past couple of years. The Treasury Department launched a pilot program in January 2011 to test different product attributes (including a savings feature) and prices for tax-refund accounts. In this initial pilot, Treasury could not test how a product would perform if it were set up automatically as a default for unbanked households to receive their tax refunds, with opt-out. Instead, the department worked with a prepaid-card vendor to mail offers for various debit cards to likely unbanked low- and moderate-income taxpayers and with a payroll-card provider to encourage employees with payroll cards to use those cards to receive their tax refunds. The pilot will be used to decide whether and how to structure a broader pilot or national initiative. The Federal Deposit Insurance Corporation also launched a pilot with a group of banks to test consumer demand and sustainability of a safe and affordable account, using an FDIC template or "gold seal" for such accounts. Finally, Treasury obtained authorization in the Dodd-Frank Act, and funding for the 2011 fiscal year, to experiment with a variety of methods to increase access to bank accounts for low-income households, including by supporting local Bank On efforts around the country, launching innovation prizes, and providing seed money for research and development into innovative technology and services.

Conclusion

We propose a conceptual framework for behaviorally informed regulation. The framework relies on a more nuanced understanding of human behavior than is contained in the classical rational-actor model. Whereas the classical perspective assumes people generally know what is important and knowable, plan with insight and patience, and carry out their plans with wisdom and self-control, behavioral research shows that people often fail to know and understand things that matter; that they misperceive and fail to carry out their intended plans; that the context in which people function has great impact on their behavior; and that institutions shape defaults, planning, and behavior itself. Behaviorally informed regulation would take account of the importance of framing and defaults, of the gap between information and understanding, and intention and action, as well as decisional conflict and other psychological factors affecting how people behave. At the same time, we argue, behaviorally informed regulation should take into account not only behavioral insights about individuals but also economic insights about markets.

In our framework, regulation requires integrating this nuanced view of human behavior with our understanding of markets. Markets can be shown to systematically favor overcoming behavioral biases in some contexts and to systematically favor exploiting those biases in other contexts. A central illustration of this distinction is the contrast between the market for saving and the market for borrowing—in which the same human failing in understanding and acting on the concept of compound interest leads to opposite market reactions. In the savings context, firms seek to overcome the bias; in the credit context, they seek to exploit it. At the same time, our framework retains the classical perspective of consumers interacting with firms in competitive markets. The difference is that consumers are now understood to be fallible in systematic ways and that firms have incentives to overcome or to exploit these shortcomings.

More generally, firms not only will operate on the contour defined by human psychology but also will respond strategically to regulations. And firms get to act last. Because the firm has a great deal of latitude in framing, product design, and sales practices, they have the capacity to affect consumer behavior and in so doing to circumvent regulatory constraints. Ironically, firms' capacity to do so is enhanced by their interaction with "behavioral" consumers (as opposed to the hypothetically rational consumers of neoclassical economic theory), since so many of the things a regulator would find hard or undesirable to control (for example, frames, design, complexity) can greatly influence consumers' behavior. The challenge of behaviorally informed regulation, therefore, is to have a deeper understanding of human behavior and of the ways in which firms are likely to respond to both consumer behavior and the structure of regulation.

We have developed a model in which outcomes are an equilibrium interaction between individuals with specific psychologies and firms that respond to those psychologies within specific markets. These outcomes may not be socially optimal. To the extent that the interaction produces real harms, regulation could potentially be usefully addressed to the social-welfare failures, if any, in this equilibrium. Taking both individuals and industrial organizations seriously suggests the need for policymakers to consider a range of market-context-specific policy options, including changing both the rules of the game and its scoring. We have explored some specific applications of this conceptual framework for financial services.

References

Adkins, Natalie Ross, and Julie L. Ozanne. 2005. "The Low Literate Consumer." *Journal of Consumer Research* 32:93–105 (doi:10.1086/429603).
Alexander, Gordon J., Jonathan D. Jones, and Peter J. Nigro. 1998. "Mutual Fund Shareholders: Characteristics, Investor Knowledge, and Sources of Information." *Financial Services Review* 7:301–16 (doi:10.1016/S1057-0810(99)00023-2).
American Payroll Association. 2002. "Survey Results: American Payroll Association 2003 Direct Deposit Survey." Last modified December 18 (http://legacy.americanpayroll.org/pdfs/paycard/DDsurv_results0212.pdf).
Ausubel, Laurence M. 1991. "The Failure of Competition in the Credit Card Market." *American Economic Review* 81 (March): 50–81 (www.jstor.org/stable/2006788).
Bar-Gill, Oren. 2004. "Seduction by Plastic." *Northwestern University Law Review* 98:1373–1434.
Barr, Michael S. 2004. "Banking the Poor." *Yale Journal on Regulation* 21:121–237.
———. 2005. "Modes of Credit Market Regulation." In *Building Assets, Building Credit: Creating Wealth in Low-Income Communities,* edited by Nicolas P. Retsinas and Eric S. Belsky, 206–36. Brookings.
———. 2007. "An Inclusive, Progressive National Savings and Financial Services Policy." *Harvard Law and Policy Review* 1:161–84.
Barr, Michael S., Sendhil Mullainathan, and Eldar Shafir. 2008. "Behaviorally Informed Financial Services Regulation." White paper. Washington: New America Foundation (http://newamerica.net/publications/policy/behaviorally_informed_financial_services_regulation).
Berry, Christopher. 2004. "To Bank or Not to Bank? A Survey of Low-Income Households." Working Paper BABC 04-3. Cambridge, Mass.: Harvard University, Joint Center for Housing Studies (www.jchs.harvard.edu/publications/finance/babc/babc_04-3.pdf).
Bertrand, Marianne, and others. 2010. "What's Advertising Content Worth? Evidence from a Consumer Credit Marketing Field Experiment." *Quarterly Journal of Economics* 125: 263–306 (doi:10.1162/qjec.2010.125.1.263).
Bond, Philip, David K. Musto, and Bilge Yilmaz. 2005. "Predatory Lending in a Rational World." Working Paper 06-2. Philadelphia: Federal Reserve Bank of Philadelphia (http://ssrn.com/abstract=875621).
Bucks, Brian K., and others. 2009. "Changes in U.S. Family Finances from 2004 to 2007: Evidence from the Survey of Consumer Finances." *Federal Reserve Bulletin* 95 (February): A1–A56.
Buehler, Roger, Dale Griffin, and Michael Ross. 2002. "Inside the Planning Fallacy: The Causes and Consequences of Optimistic Time Predictions." In *Heuristics and Biases: The Psychology of Intuitive Judgment,* edited by Thomas Gilovich, Dale W. Griffin, and Daniel Kahneman, 250–70. Cambridge University Press.
Cain, Daylian M., George Lowenstein, and Don A. Moore. 2005. "The Dirt on Coming Clean: Perverse Effects of Disclosing Conflicts of Interest." *Journal of Legal Studies* 34:1–25 (doi:10.1086/426699).
Edin, Kathryn, and Laura Lein. 1997. *Making Ends Meet: How Single Mothers Survive Welfare and Low-Wage Work.* New York: Russell Sage Foundation.

Engel, Kathleen C., and Patricia A. McCoy. 2007. "Turning a Blind Eye: Wall Street Finance of Predatory Lending." *Fordham Law Review* 75:2039–104.

Federal Reserve Board. 2007. *Design and Testing of Effective Truth in Lending Disclosures.* Washington (www.federalreserve.gov/dcca/regulationz/20070523/execsummary.pdf).

———. 2008. *Consumer Testing of Mortgage Broker Disclosures: Summary of Findings* (www.federalreserve.gov/newsevents/press/bcreg/20080714regzconstest.pdf).

FTC (Federal Trade Commission). 2007. "Improving Consumer Mortgage Disclosures: An Empirical Assessment of Current and Prototype Disclosure Forms." Staff report. Federal Trade Commission, Bureau of Economics (www.ftc.gov/os/007/06/PO25505mortgage disclosurereport.pdf).

GAO (U.S. Government Accountability Office). 2006. *Credit Cards: Increased Complexity in Rates and Fees Heightens the Need for More Effective Disclosures to Consumers.* Report 06-929 (www.gao.gov/new.items/d06929.pdf).

Gordon, Robert, and Derek Douglas. 2005. "Taking Charge." *Washington Monthly* 37, no. 12: 27–29.

Guttentag, Jack. 2000. "Another View of Predatory Lending." Working Paper 01-23-B. Philadelphia: University of Pennsylvania, Wharton School, Financial Institutions Center (http://fic.wharton.upenn.edu/fic/papers/01/0123.pdf).

Iyengar, Sheena S., and Mark R. Lepper. 2000. "When Choice Is Demotivating: Can One Desire Too Much of a Good Thing?" *Journal of Personality and Social Psychology* 79:995–1006 (doi:10.1037/0022-3514.79.6.995).

Jackson, Howell E., and Laurie Burlingame. 2007. "Kickbacks or Compensation: The Case of Yield Spread Premiums." *Stanford Journal of Law, Business, and Finance* 12:289–361.

Johnson, Eric J., and Daniel Goldstein. 2003. "Do Defaults Save Lives?" Policy Forum, *Science* 302 (5649): 1338–39 (www.jstor.org/stable/3835592).

Johnson, Eric J., and others. 1993. "Framing, Probability Distortions, and Insurance Decisions." *Journal of Risk and Uncertainty* 7:35–51 (doi:10.1007/BF01065313).

Kennedy, Duncan. 2005. "Cost-Benefit Analysis of Debtor Protection Rules in Subprime Market Default Situations." In *Building Assets, Building Credit: Creating Wealth in Low-Income Communities,* edited by Nicolas P. Retsinas and Eric S. Belsky, 266–82. Brookings.

Koehler, Derek J., and Connie S. K. Poon. 2005. "Self-Predictions Overweight Strength of Current Intentions." *Journal of Experimental Social Psychology* 42, no. 4: 517–24 (doi:10.1016/j.jesp.2005.08.003).

Koide, Melissa. 2007. "The Assets and Transaction Account: A Proposal to Deliver a Low Cost, High Value Transaction and Savings Account at Tax Time." Discussion paper. New America Foundation (November) (www.newamerica.net/files/nafmigration/ATA_Discussion_Paper.pdf).

Lewin, Kurt. 1951. *Field Theory in Social Science.* Edited by Dorwin Cartwright. New York: Harper & Brothers.

Lichtenstein, Sarah, and Paul Slovic, eds. 2006. *The Construction of Preference.* Cambridge University Press.

Lusardi, Annamaria, Olivia S. Mitchell, and Vilsa Curto. 2009. "Financial Literacy and Financial Sophistication among Older Americans." Working Paper 15469. Cambridge, Mass: National Bureau of Economic Research (www.nber.org/papers/w15469).

Madrian, Brigitte C., and Dennis F. Shea. 2001. "The Power of Suggestion: Inertia in 401(k) Participation and Savings Behavior." *Quarterly Journal of Economics* 116:1149–87 (www.jstor.org/stable/2696456).

Mann, Ronald J. 2006. *Charging Ahead: The Growth and Regulation of Payment Card Markets.* Cambridge University Press.

————. 2007. "Bankruptcy Reform and the 'Sweat Box' of Credit Card Debt." *University of Illinois Law Review* 2007:375–404.

Milgram, Stanley. 1974. *Obedience to Authority*. New York: Harper & Row.

Mullainathan, Sendhil, and Eldar Shafir. 2009. "Savings Policy and Decisionmaking in Low-Income Households." In *Insufficient Funds: Savings, Assets, Credit, and Banking among Low-Income Households*, edited by Rebecca M. Blank and Michael S. Barr, 121–45. New York: Russell Sage Foundation.

Schultz, Ellen. 1995. "Helpful or Confusing? Fund Choices Multiply for Many Retirement Plans." *Wall Street Journal*, December 22.

Shafir, Eldar, Itamar Simonson, and Amos Tversky. 1993. "Reason-Based Choice." *Cognition* 49:11–36 (doi:10.1016/0010-0277(93)90034-S).

Sherraden, Michael, and Michael S. Barr. 2005. "Institutions and Inclusion in Savings Policy." In *Building Assets, Building Credit: Creating Wealth in Low-Income Communities*, edited by Nicolas P. Retsinas and Eric S. Belsky, 286–315. Brookings.

Thaler, Richard. 1985. "Mental Accounting and Consumer Choice." *Marketing Science* 4:199–214 (www.jstor.org/stable/183904).

————. 1992. *The Winner's Curse: Paradoxes and Anomalies of Economic Life*. New York: Free Press.

————. 1999. "Mental Accounting Matters." *Journal of Behavioral Decision Making* 12, no. 3: 183–206 (doi:10.1002/(SICI)1099-0771(199909)12:3<183::AID-BDM318>3.0.CO;2-F).

Thaler, Richard H., and Shlomo Benartzi. 2004. "Save More Tomorrow: Using Behavioral Economics to Increase Employee Saving." In "Papers in Honor of Sherwin Rosen," supplement, *Journal of Political Economy* 112, no. S1: S164–S187 (doi:10.1086/380085).

Thaler, Richard H., and Cass R. Sunstein. 2008. *Nudge: Improving Decisions about Health, Wealth, and Happiness*. Yale University Press.

Tversky, Amos, and Eldar Shafir. 1992. "Choice under Conflict: The Dynamics of Deferred Decision." *Psychological Science* 3:358–61 (www.jstor.org/stable/40062808).

White, James J., and Robert S. Summers. 2006. *Uniform Commercial Code*, vol. 1. 5th ed. Practitioner Treatise Series. St. Paul, Minn.: West Publishing.

12

Epilogue: Crisis and Reform

MICHAEL S. BARR

W hen President Obama came into office three years ago, our financial markets were frozen, our economy was shrinking, and we were facing the worst economic crisis our country has endured since Franklin Roosevelt came into office facing the Great Depression. At the end of 2008 and beginning of 2009, our nation was losing nearly 800,000 jobs a month. Small businesses were closing their doors. And home prices were in free fall. The president acted boldly to save the economy and restart growth. Although the economy has been stabilized and businesses are hiring again, the country is not growing rapidly enough, millions of Americans remain out of work, and we face considerable economic risks, both domestically and globally.

When I was in government in 2009–10, we were focused not only on repairing the economy but also on the urgent obligation to fix the failures in our financial system that helped trigger the economic crisis that has cost American families and small businesses so dearly. The failures that led to the 2008 crisis had many causes. Regulators did not protect consumers or investors— and households and firms took on risks they did not fully understand. Legal loopholes and regulatory gaps allowed large parts of the financial industry and large parts of financial markets to operate without oversight, transparency, or restraint. And capital was increasingly inadequate to deal with the growing risks in the financial system. The passage of the Dodd-Frank Act provides a strong foundation on which we must now carefully build a more stable and resilient financial system—a system that protects consumers and investors, rewards innovation, and is able to adapt to and evolve with changes in the financial markets.[1]

The Dodd-Frank Act provides for supervision of major firms based on what they do rather than their corporate form. Shadow banking is brought into the regulatory daylight. The largest financial firms will be required to build up their capital and liquidity buffers, constrain their relative size, and place restrictions on the riskiest financial activities. The act comprehensively regulates derivatives markets with new rules for exchange trading, central clearing, transparency, and capital and margin requirements. It provides for data collection and transparency so that in no corner of the financial markets can risk build unnoticed. It creates an essential mechanism for the government to orderly liquidate failing financial firms without putting taxpayers at risk. And it creates a new Consumer Financial Protection Bureau to look out for the interests of American households.

Meanwhile, for the one in seven Americans who lives in poverty, or the millions of Americans who live in fear of falling out of the middle class, these times have been particularly devastating. As we have seen through the lens of the Detroit Area Household Financial Services study, conducted at the height of the financial boom, these families were the least prepared to handle the shock of the deep recession. They had little or no savings to fall back on and stood one medical emergency, or one major unexpected car malfunction, away from a personal economic crisis. They had no financial slack. When the crisis hit in 2008, families found themselves overleveraged and underresourced. Federal government policies helped to cushion the impact, but these households still faced huge setbacks. What these families were and are now seeking is some measure of financial stability.

Going forward, American families will undoubtedly need to try to save a larger share of income and to borrow more responsibly. Today, many Americans are rediscovering the importance of living within their means. They are saving more and reducing debt. And they are growing more careful about how they borrow and invest. These changes are necessary and healthy. Ultimately, they will build economic security for American families and make our economy stronger and more resilient. But households should not be left on their own to navigate a financial system that has become increasingly detached from their everyday needs.

A Three-Legged Stool

One of the critical ways we can help promote economic security is by making consumer financial markets work better for American families. As we have seen

1. Dodd–Frank Wall Street Reform and Consumer Protection Act, Pub. L. No. 111-203, 124 Stat. 1376 (2010).

in the Detroit study, low- and moderate-income individuals often lack access to basic financial services that could help them cope better with the lack of financial slack in their lives. Facing serious economic and structural constraints, these households turn to a variety of formal and informal institutions to meet their financial services needs—to receive their income and pay bills, to borrow, and to save. But the way our financial system is structured often makes transacting, saving, and borrowing more expensive (in monetary and nonmonetary ways) and less useful for the families who need it the most.

To improve the financial lives of low- and moderate-income households, we need to rely on a "three-legged stool" of financial education, access, and consumer protection. In each area, we could make significant strides by using behavioral insights. The evidence on consumer fallibility and on how firms behave in light of this fallibility suggests a framework, developed in the previous chapter, for understanding which types of mechanisms will work best in particular markets. It is helpful to divide consumer financial markets into two categories: those in which firms are neutral toward or have incentives for overcoming consumer fallibility; and those in which firms have incentives to exacerbate consumer biases. For example, providers of bank accounts have incentives to help individuals overcome the behavioral barriers to savings. Lenders, on the other hand, may have incentives to exploit biases that lead consumers to overborrow. And providers of all kinds have incentives to charge fees that are less salient for consumers or that take advantage of consumers' errors in predicting their own future product usage—such as late fees, overlimit fees, and overdraft fees.

The implications for policymaking in these two cases are different. Where firms are neutral to or have incentives to overcome consumer biases, changing the starting point or default may be highly effective on its own. The success in promoting retirement savings through the use of defaults is a well-known example. In this case, employers were at worst indifferent to and at best inclined to increase employee participation in defined-contribution plans. Where firms have incentives to exacerbate biases, changing the rules may not be enough. In these cases, firms will have incentives to work around the rules and render them less effective. For example, firms may comply with the letter of disclosure laws but act to undermine them by discouraging consumers from focusing on and understanding the content. In such cases, it may be necessary to change the way the game is scored to make a real difference for consumers.

This behavioral framework has profound implications as we think about how best to promote financial access. Defaults in the defined-contribution plan would serve as a prominent example of how behaviorally informed innovation can have a significant impact on the lives of everyday Americans. But there is a need for a lot more innovation that is informed by the interplay of consumer psychologies and firm incentives in market-specific contexts. We can help families seeking financial stability in three primary ways: enhancing individuals' core competencies in financial capability; promoting access to innovative financial products and services that meet consumer needs; and establishing and enforcing strong protections for consumers. Basic financial literacy is the necessary foundation for informed consumer decisionmaking. But to be effective, financial literacy must be combined with improved access to suitable financial products and strong consumer protections. Efforts in all three areas must be driven by evidence on how consumers and firms behave in the real world.

Financial Education

Financial education needs to be more firmly rooted in the ways in which individuals actually make financial decisions in particular contexts in the real world. There are three promising approaches in this regard. First, financial education providers can set core financial competencies and rigorously evaluate different approaches to conveying these competencies. The Treasury Department recently took the first step in putting forward a set of core competencies for the sector.[2] Second, rather than attempting to "teach" these competencies divorced from institutional context, financial education providers, financial institutions, and the public sector can seek ways to improve customer understanding in the context of particular financial choices the individual is faced with at particular moments in time—the choice to save for retirement at the moment of hiring, for example, or the decision to save at the time of filing for (or receiving) a tax refund. Third, policymakers and financial providers could view disclosures as a useful moment to increase financial understanding rather than as a moment to increase the amount of financial information provided. For example, under the Credit Card Accountability, Responsibility, and Disclosure (CARD) Act of 2009,[3] credit-card monthly disclosures must now inform consumers of the financial consequences of the decision to make only the minimum payment and to indicate the amounts needed to pay off the balance in a shorter time.

Financial Access

One area where more innovation is sorely needed is in expanding access to financial services that meet the needs of low- and moderate-income Americans. One challenge—and opportunity—we face in expanding financial access for low- and moderate-income Americans is harnessing low-cost electronic payment mechanisms, such as debit cards. The private sector has been innovating in this area, and the evidence from the Detroit study suggests a strong interest among low- and

2. Financial Education Core Competencies; Comment Request, 75 *Federal Register* 52596 (August 26, 2010).
3. Credit Card Accountability Responsibility and Disclosure (CARD) Act of 2009, Pub. L. No. 111-24, 123 Stat. 1734.

moderate-income households in a payment card. While cost was an important determinant of preference among survey respondents, so too were nonpecuniary factors; for example, households were especially concerned with whether the card had strong federal consumer protections and whether it had national branding.

As to the government's role, there may be ways that the government could help to accelerate changes in the payments system that benefit low- and moderate-income households and the market as a whole. Default arrangements—changing the rules—may help in this context because the providers of savings and trans-action accounts have incentives to alleviate consumer biases, for example, with respect to procrastination, to gather deposits. However, defaults on their own may be less effective in banking than they are in the retirement context. The reason is that the cost to serve individuals with small balances can discourage firms from serving low- and moderate-income populations. In this context, a combination approach is needed. It may be necessary to change the scoring as well as the rules, such as by designing creative solutions that help firms serve these populations with sustainable product economics.

The Treasury Department is taking an innovative approach to direct federal benefits payments that relates to these insights. The department is responsible for making ongoing payments to 70 million individuals for direct federal benefits, including Social Security, Supplemental Security Income, and Veterans, Railroad Retirement, and Office of Personnel Management benefits. Fifteen percent of these individuals still receive their benefits by paper check. Individuals who have accounts can use direct deposit. Individuals who are unbanked, or who prefer not to use direct deposit, receive payments on the Direct Express card. Direct Express is a debit-card account platform offered by a bank according to requirements established by Treasury. More than 1.4 million federal benefits recipients have opted into receiving benefits on Direct Express, which was launched in 2008. Customers report 95 percent satisfaction with the card's features. Direct Express is an example of how government can help make serving low- and moderate-income customers more sustainable for providers. In this case the government is bundling many customers' accounts together, allowing for a more favorable scale of operations for the provider. The states have key programs, too. Treasury established rules that better protect federal benefits payments from bank-account garnishment and enhanced requirements on the types of payment cards that are eligible to receive benefits payments, including prohibiting benefits from being deposited into accounts set up for payday-loan-type arrangements.

The Treasury Department is simultaneously undertaking other efforts to improve the electronic delivery of federal benefits payments. For example, for the 2011 tax season Treasury piloted an initiative to improve tax administration by offering selected low- and moderate-income households an opportunity to receive their tax refund on a debit card. There is an enormous opportunity to improve financial outcomes for low-income households by setting up an automatic way for these households to receive their tax refunds through direct deposit to a bank account or prepaid card. In the coming years, Treasury should focus on bringing these tax-refund accounts to scale at the national level. Another major element of these efforts is an initiative called Bank on USA, for which President Obama sought funding in the fiscal year 2011 budget. These funds will build on the local Bank On movement, made up of local coalitions dedicated to promoting access to mainstream financial products.

Consumer Financial Protection

While education and access are critical, so too is consumer protection. In an environment of weak and ineffective regulations, the tendency of some consumer financial markets to end up in "races to the bottom"—as we saw in the housing market—is not likely to be overcome solely by consumer education and access.

The CARD Act, which President Obama championed and signed into law in May 2009, is an example of regulation written for a market and product in which the provider has a strong incentive to usher consumers to suboptimal choices— to rack up lots of late fees and to make only the minimum payment each month. Nearly 80 percent of American families have a credit card, and over 40 percent of families carry a balance on their cards. Before passage of the act, Americans were paying $15 billion, annually, in penalty fees.

The CARD Act combines common sense disclosures with protections from practices designed to make use of consumer fallibility for the benefit of the credit-card issuer and the detriment of the consumer. For example, the act bans unfair rate increases, including rate increases on existing balances owing to universal-default clauses and severely restricted retroactive rate increases owing to late payment. It bans unfair fee traps, including weekend due dates, due dates that change each month, and payment deadlines in the middle of the day. And it ends the confusing and unfair practice of so called double-cycle billing.

The CARD Act also used a de-biasing approach by requiring minimum-balance warnings that help to inform consumers of the consequences of their actions by displaying how long it would take to pay off an existing balance, if the consumer paid only the minimum payment each period; and the amount the consumer would need to pay each period to pay off the balance in thirty-six months. Credit-card companies know that the impact of compound interest on credit balances is not necessarily intuitive to most consumers. The consumer may even, incorrectly, assume that the credit-card issuer has a primary interest in the consumer paying down the balance sooner rather than later and therefore has set the minimum payment to an amount in line with that objective.

So imagine the shock that a consumer has when he or she learns that paying a minimum payment of $150 each month on a $7,000 credit-card balance would take twenty-two years to pay off in full. Or the relief of learning—on that same page—that an extra $60 payment each month would reduce the time it took to pay off that balance from twenty-two years to three years and save more than $5,000 in interest payments along the way. That's meaningful disclosure. That's disclosure that empowers families to make choices that are right for them. Now undoubtedly we will learn from this process. Many consumers will be helped by the minimum payment disclosures, but some may end up paying off more slowly. These disclosures will, of course, have to be improved and changed over time. That is what we need: evidence-based openness to change.

The CARD Act changes to the credit-card market were followed the next year by the Dodd-Frank Act changes to the mortgage market. Consumer-protection failings in the mortgage markets quite likely contributed significantly to the abusive practices that fed the housing boom and bust. The act directly takes on these past failings. For example, it bans yield spread premiums to brokers for getting borrowers to take on higher-cost loans and the broker steering practices that often accompanied high-cost lending; it requires creditors to assess and document the borrower's ability to pay, rather than making no-doc loans to those who cannot afford them; it makes reforms to escrow practices so that it is harder for creditors to hide the all-in monthly costs of a loan, including taxes and insurance; and it requires key changes to make disclosures simpler—reducing the paperwork burden on creditors while giving households a fighting chance to understand the terms of their home mortgage loans.

Before Dodd-Frank, our system was largely incapable of supporting a successful regulatory structure for consumer protection. Fragmentation of rule writing, supervision, and enforcement made it impossible to create a comprehensive and well-calibrated consumer regulatory regime. Jurisdiction and authority for consumer protection was spread over many federal regulators, which had higher priorities than protecting consumers. Banks could choose the least restrictive supervisor among several different banking agencies. And a large number of non-bank providers, from home mortgage originators to payday lenders, escaped any meaningful federal supervision completely.

Now, with the Dodd-Frank Act's creation of the Consumer Financial Protection Bureau we have a chance to do more than play catch-up in regulating consumer financial markets. The bureau provides a historic opportunity to build a successfully regulatory structure for consumer protection, one that is designed to promote financial inclusion, preserve consumer choice, and provide for more efficient and innovative markets for consumer financial products—markets that operate on the competitive basis of price and quality rather than hidden fees. The Consumer Financial Protection Bureau will provide, for the first time, a consumer agency with necessary mission focus, marketwide coverage, and consolidated authority. It will be an agency that focuses not simply on more regulation but on smarter, more coherent, and more effective regulation. Regulation that is designed and implemented with an understanding—and respect—of classical models but is not blind to the compelling insights into consumer decisions derived from behavioral economics. Regulation that seeks to empower consumers to find the most suitable financial products from among many seemingly indistinguishable choices and provides a level playing field for the financial sector.

What I find most curious about the voices of opposition to the Consumer Financial Protection Bureau—an agency whose primary principles are accountability, transparency, fairness, and access—is that their logic rests on the premise that empowering consumers is somehow antithetical to free markets. Opponents appear to be stuck in a debate that presumes that regulation and efficient and innovative markets are at odds. In fact, the opposite is true. Markets rely on good faith and on trust and fair dealing. Markets require transparency that reflects economic reality rather than distortions caused by misleading sales pitches and hidden traps. And the discipline of the market requires clear rules.

The financial crisis led to fundamental reforms of our financial system, but the process of reform is not over. The Consumer Financial Protection Bureau is just getting started on its work, and the other regulators responsible for implementing the Dodd-Frank Act still must finish the job. Meanwhile, some in Congress have been trying to hamstring reform by starving the agencies of necessary funding, blocking nominees required to enforce the law, or seeking to repeal key parts of the act. For the low- and moderate-income households we interviewed for this book, these reforms are no abstraction. These families can ill afford a financial system that imposes unnecessary costs, confusion, and complications on their daily lives. Our nation must take the steps necessary to ensure that the financial system works better for everyone.

About the Authors

Michael S. Barr is Professor of Law at the University of Michigan Law School. Barr served as Assistant Secretary of the Treasury for Financial Institutions and was a principal architect of the Dodd-Frank Wall Street Reform and Consumer Protection Act.

Ron Borzekowski is a Research Section Chief at the Consumer Financial Protection Bureau. He served as Senior Economist at the Board of Governors of the Federal Reserve System and as Deputy Research Director for the Financial Crisis Inquiry Commission.

Jane K. Dokko is an economist in the household and real estate finance section of the Board of Governors of the Federal Reserve System.

Eleanor McDonnell Feit is Research Director of the Customer Analytics Initiative at the Wharton School of the University of Pennsylvania.

Benjamin J. Keys is Assistant Professor at the Harris School of Public Policy at the University of Chicago. Keys previously worked as an economist at the Board of Governors of the Federal Reserve System in the division of research and statistics.

Elizabeth K. Kiser is an Assistant Director in the division of research and statistics at the Board of Governors of the Federal Reserve System.

Sendhil Mullainathan is Professor of Economics at Harvard University and Assistant Director for Research at the Consumer Financial Protection Bureau. He founded Ideas42, a behavioral economics research institute.

Eldar Shafir is the William Stewart Tod Professor of Psychology and Public Affairs in the Department of Psychology and the Woodrow Wilson School of Public and International Affairs at Princeton University. He serves on President Obama's Advisory Council on Financial Capability. He is a codirector of Ideas42.

Index